THERE WAS ONCE
A NATION....

The Nez Perce Indians loved the land they settled and roamed. Their food was plentiful, their horses could outride the wind, their lives and their people were good. They were peace loving and they welcomed the white man. But they were Indians — and the white man stole their land.

Treaty by treaty the Nez Perce were raped, wrung dry of everything but their dignity and courage — and the great chieftain who would lead them in valor to their last tragic battle....

"Epic."

Los Angeles Times

"Outstanding!"

American Historical Association

"I WILL FIGHT NO MORE FOREVER"

*Chief Joseph
and the Nez Perce War*

Merrill D. Beal

BALLANTINE BOOKS · NEW YORK

ISBN 0-345-32131-6

This edition published by arrangement with the University of Washington Press. Prepared under the terms of a cooperative agreement between the National Park Service and Idaho State College.

Manufactured in the United States of America

First Ballantine Books Edition: October 1971
Eleventh Printing: March 1989

Cover photograph courtesy of the Historical Society of Montana, Helena.

CONTENTS

Flight toward Canada

Seventh Cavalry Success

Exile Decreed, Applied, and Abandoned

FOREWORD

Although much has been written about the Nez Perce Indian tribe and their famous leader, the young Joseph, the flow of publications will and should continue. Joseph and his band remain an example and inspiration to those who today are seeking recognition as human beings, equal in the sight of God and therefore entitled to like status among men. Those who recognize that such aspirations must not for long remain unfulfilled can derive from Nez Perce history examples of the consequence of policies conceived in ignorance and colored with disdain of the culture and way of life of minority peoples who are reluctant to renounce their heritage and values in order to become submerged in the society of the predominant majority.

Besides illuminating generally the ideology of freedom and dignity, the experiences of the Nez Perces with the United States government and with their white neighbors can serve a most useful purpose. The Indian problem remains to plague the American people and their government. It should be noted that during the last quarter-century federal legislation has reflected a recognition of past gross injustices and errors in the treatment of our first natives. In the Wheeler-Howard Act of 1934, there was a belated acknowledgment that the

Indian culture had attributes worth preserving both for the Indians and for the rest of the world. Sins of omission and commission on the part of our government against the original owners of our soil were openly admitted in the Indian Claims Act of 1946, and provision was made for compensation.

The policy of integration ushered in by Public Law 280, enacted in 1953, is regarded by some as the Magna Charta for the red man, and by others as an entering wedge toward the final and complete spoliation of Indian resources. There can be little dispute, however, over the fact that the complete absorption of all minority groups into the American body politic is indispensable to the integrity of our democracy. Nevertheless, political assimilation does not require that all be cast into one cultural mold. Better understanding of Indian faiths, such as the Dreamer cult to which many of the Nez Perces subscribed, will promote a more sympathetic appreciation of other so-called primitive religions.

Merrill D. Beal has joined Francis Haines, Sr., and Lucullus Virgil McWhorter as a leading authority on Nez Perce history. Haines contributed the first scholarly historical work, *The Red Eagles of the North* (1939). In 1955 he published a revision taking cognizance of newly available data. McWhorter's monumental harvest of Indian sources was in the process of being threshed and winnowed when he died in 1944. Progress on his manuscript had proceeded sufficiently so that Ruth Borden was able to complete the book as the original author would have wished, and it was published in 1952. Beal acknowledges fully his debt to these and to other scholars in kindred fields, particularly anthropology. He provides, however, a fresh interpretation and an impressive amount of new data, particularly on the reaction of whites and white communities to the crisis of 1877, and on the experiences of the military in fighting and pursuing the Indians. The end product is definitive, but Beal's work is not final. Like every other good book on Pacific Northwest history, it opens as many new issues as it affords answers. The author's own awareness of this seems to be reflected in his restraint in judging controversial historic figures.

As indicated above, there is no foreseeable end to the literature on the Nez Perces. A new book of fiction has just appeared, and there is word of another popular history. The pursuit of the Nez Perce theme will go on, for a world surfeited with deceptive success stories can ill afford to forget a people and their leader who attained their true moral stature as they were facing their doom.

HERMAN J. DEUTSCH

Washington State University

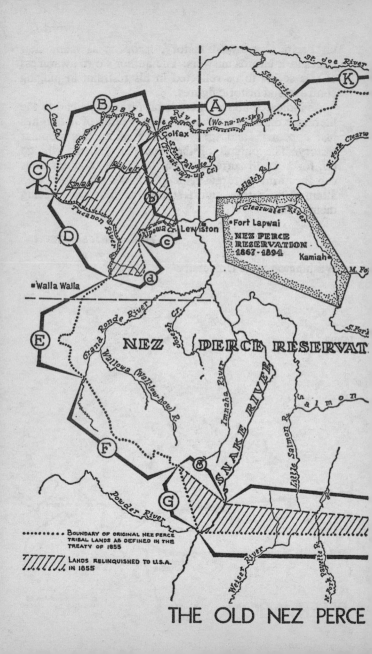

THE OLD NEZ PERCE

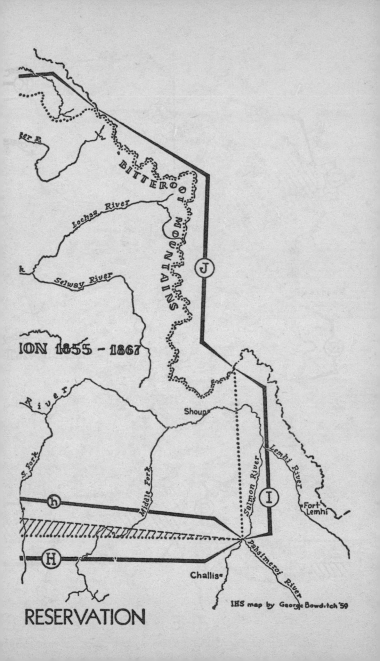

ION 1855 - 1867

RESERVATION

IHS map by George Bowditch '59

PREFACE

In June, 1958, an arrangement was made by officers of the National Park Service and Idaho State College, according to which I was to prepare an accurate, documented historical account of the Nez Perce campaign of 1877, with special reference to the Battle of the Big Hole. When the Idaho State Board of Education had approved the proposal, I began to follow my instructions to secure "first hand knowledge from . . . survivors or descendants of those who participated in the action, and make a search of the Library of Congress and National Archives, and contact all historical sources in general."

It was a large order, and six of the eighteen months specified for the completion of the history were spent in gathering the bulk of data. My wife and I visited much of the retreat route and many of the battle-grounds that I would be describing, and we also worked in many libraries and historical societies in Idaho and Montana. Contemporary accounts of the campaign were carefully checked in the hope that some new interpretations would be disclosed, and artless comments by soldiers or volunteers, recorded at the time they were made, have been avidly sought and heavily weighted.

I have carefully examined the reports of the Nez Perces, as recorded during and after the campaign. These sources, however biased, have been of great value, and the accounts by the Indians have been included along with the official reports and the newspaper accounts. Otherwise, the history would be not only unbalanced, but untrue. There are many sweeping and passionate denunciations of the nontreaty Nez Perces. For example, Scout J. W. Redington claimed that "Chief Joseph and his outfit were murderous marauders." Conversely, historian Jacob P. Dunn held Joseph in high prestige and flatly stated, "The meanest, most contemptible, least justifiable thing the United States was ever guilty of was its treatment of the Lower Nez Perces." Thus, both sides have set forth extreme declarations regarding their motives, purposes, and actions.

L. V. McWhorter's editorial work in *Yellow Wolf* and his valedictory *Hear Me, My Chiefs* disclose the salient elements from the Nez Perce viewpoint. General Oliver O. Howard's *Reports* to the War Department and his *Nez Perce Joseph* present the white man's case and describe the pattern of military activity. Neither prudence nor integrity would allow me to accept McWhorter's characterization of the Nez Perces as patriots, or to agree with Howard's description of them as barbarian hostiles.

I have found no startlingly fresh interpretations of the causes, prosecution, and consequences of the campaign. However, some evidence and evaluations included in this study will no doubt weaken certain accepted views and strengthen some points less clearly understood.

The roles of Indian and white leadership have been placed in perspective. The tribal contribution has been stressed without minimizing the important guardianship of the chiefs. Joseph conforms better to the symbol of protector and diplomat than to that of superlative War Chief. The evidence does not support the legend of his military genius. In fact, Joseph did not outrank his colleagues in either the formulation or execution of strategy.

On October 15, 1877, the *New York Times* stated that the Nez Perce War, "on our part, was in its origin and motive nothing short of a gigantic blunder and a crime." I regard that appraisal as an oversimplification of a complicated problem. Furthermore, I did not find the United States military officers deficient in either imagination or energy. The conflict involved two skillful forces, both effectively utilizing the arts of wilderness warfare for a protracted period in a baffling environment.

Although I am under no obligation to express my personal opinion concerning the justice of the Nez Perce War, here it is.

I believe that the chiefs, the responsible men of the tribes, and a very large percentage of the nontreaty Nez Perces were opposed to a war in 1877. When General Howard sent troops against them at White Bird Canyon they stood their ground and won an impressive battle. Thereafter, they gravitated toward a course of retreat and made a pathetic effort to avoid further conflict with the United States. In attempting to escape, or bypass, the military they demonstrated outstanding resourcefulness, and in the end they resisted capture so desperately that they lost their tribal status. Although their great exertions and heavy casualties won universal admiration, a decent consideration for justice compels concurrence with the judgment expressed by Secretary Carl Schurz: "This bloody conflict might have been avoided by a more careful regard for the rights of an Indian tribe whose former conduct had been uniformly peaceable and friendly."

The valiantly conducted and nobly lost Nez Perce campaign has had a tremendous appeal for Indians and white men. A Nez Perce named William M. Stevens remembered that in his youth the old warriors were called upon to relate their experiences in tribal gatherings. These narrations were characterized by dignity and restraint. Boasting was wholly absent, but sadness was all-pervading. The pathos of these accounts of flight and exile is still cherished among many Nez Perces.

That a similar influence affected the general public is evidenced by the manner in which the nontreaty Nez Perces have been honored in the bestowal of names upon geographical features and human constructions. "Nez Perce," "Joseph," and "White Bird" are applied to creeks, trails, mountains, passes, towns, roads, a county, and a great dam. Monuments have been erected and heroic memorials proposed, and a considerable amount of literature has evolved. I hope that this account of the Nez Perce campaign will enlarge understanding and enhance appreciation for our dynamic western border history.

M. D. B.

ACKNOWLEDGMENTS

In the preparation of this work I have received help from numerous sources. Many of these have been recorded in the notes and bibliography. National Park Service officials responsible for the conception and implementation of the project are as follows: Ronald F. Lee, Chief, Division of Interpretation; Howard W. Baker, Director, Region 2; Merrill J. Mattes, Historian, Region 2; and Lemuel A. Garrison, Superintendent, Yellowstone National Park. David Condon, Frank Sylvester, Aubrey L. Haines, and Robert N. McIntyre were very helpful in outlining contractual procedures and National Park Service objectives. My son, Merrill David Beal, Jack Williams, and Robert Burns assisted materially in the preparation of a base map of the Big Hole Battlefield, and in making suggestions pertaining to prospective museum requirements for the Big Hole Battlefield National Monument. Seasonal Park Naturalists Herbert T. Lystrup and Ted C. Parkinson of Yellowstone National Park cooperated by arranging tours of duty for me during the summer of 1959 so that early morning hours could be devoted to this project.

The following Idaho State College officials have advised and assisted with the project in various ways: Dean Robert C. Stevenson, Dean Junius Larsen, William J. Bartz, Ray J. Davis, Albert E. Taylor, and Lloyd Furniss.

The following librarians and archivists have provided information and material service: Mrs. Clare Smith and Mrs. Joseph Tocnnis, Miles City, Montana; Natalie Sliepievich and Mrs. T. G. Fulmer, Anaconda, Montana; Eli Oboler and Alice McClain, Idaho State College, Pocatello; Donald E. Smith and Mary Avery, Washington State University, Pullman; Carling Malouf and Kathleen Campbell, University of Montana, Missoula; James T. Babb, Yale University; and Lucille Wagner, Yellowstone National Park Library, Mammoth, Wyoming.

The following historical society directors, historians, and archivists have provided data and documents concerning many subjects: Earl H. Swanson and Mary Strawn, Idaho State College Historical Museum, Pocatello; Holman J. Swinney, Merle W. Wells, and Edith B. Mathews, Idaho State Historical Society, Boise; Virginia Walton, Historical Society of Montana, Helena; Dorothy Williams and Rella Looney, Oklahoma Historical Society, Oklahoma City; Stetson Conn, Chief Historian, Military History, Washington, D.C.; Victor Gondos, National Archives, Washington, D.C.; and Herman J. Deutsch, Professor of History, Washington State University, Pullman.

Documents, letters, and miscellaneous data were also received from Colonel Virgil F. Field, Fort Lewis, Washington; Senator Henry Dworshak, Washington, D.C.; Ned M. Reilly, Mobile, Alabama; Francis Haines, Monmouth, Oregon; W. D. Ackerson, Wichita, Kansas; Elvin Henninger, Dubois, Idaho; Mabel Ovitt and Mrs. Robert Gregg, Dillon, Montana.

Sven Liljeblad, Joseph A. Hearst, and Forester A. Blake, three colleagues, read the entire manuscript and offered much encouragement. My wife, Bessy, rendered valued assistance in assembling and sifting data and typing and proofreading the manuscript.

FROM PEACE TO WAR

1. THE NEZ PERCES AT HOME

Many and extensive speculations have been made concerning the origin of the Indian race. Scientists, theologians, and philosophers have offered plausible explanations, but none is considered wholly satisfactory. Physical traits and cultural patterns of the Indians tell much, and their legends and traditions tell more, but we still know too little to establish more than a theory or a faith. As Europeans explored America they discovered natives in all areas. Indeed, their pattern of distribution seemed quite proportionate to the resources available by the processes of direct appropriation. Whether the earlier migrants originally came from Asia or Asia Minor, all evidence supports the theory that the American aborigines had been on this continent from time immemorial.

Apparently the antiquity of the Nez Perces parallels the ages of other peoples with whom they were identified. They constituted the principal branch of the Shahaptian linguistic family inhabiting the Columbia Plateau. Nez Perce legends imply that tribal claims upon their areas of occupation are ancient.

The Nez Perces speak a Shahaptian tongue closely related to such languages as the Umatilla, Wallawalla, and

3

Yakima of Oregon and Washington. They have referred to themselves variously as Nimipu, Kamuinu, and Tsutpeli, each name signifying "the people."[1] In 1805 Lewis and Clark, en route to the Pacific Ocean, applied the name Chopunnish to them. Sometime between that date and 1835, French-Canadian traders probably bestowed the name Nez Perce (pierced nose) upon a branch of them. According to their own tradition, the name was first applied to the delegates who reached St. Louis in 1831 in search of the white man's light, truth, or power ("big medicine"). The misnomer has clung to them ever since.[2] The tribesmen accepted the name and pronounced it něz pûrs or něz pûrses (sometimes něz pûrsî) rather than using the French pronunciation. The acute accent often written over the final *e* may therefore be omitted.[3]

Nez Perce Characteristics

Biologists and geographers have explained the reciprocal relationships between heredity and environment. Hence it is expedient to describe the principal characteristics of these people and their homeland. General agreement exists concerning their salient traits. In body they were tall, stately, well formed, and energetic. General O. O. Howard reported that the men were five feet eight inches on an average, compactly built and graceful of movement. The women were several inches shorter; their faces were bright and comely. Nez Perce intelligence was of high order, manifested by personal and group self-reliance, prosperity, and responsibility. Self-respect and personal dignity were fostered by belief in a guardian spirit, or *Wyakin* power. This influence gave the Nez Perces personal direction and a common feeling of destiny.

Meriwether Lewis described them thus: "The Chopunnish [meaning Nez Perces] are in general, stout, well-formed, active men. They have high noses and many of them on the aquiline order, with cheerful and agreeable countenance."⁴ In temperament they were friendly, pleasant, and inclined toward peace. As hunters and warriors they were unexcelled, being skillful, loyal, and brave. Their standards of honor and truthfulness were exceptional. L. V. McWhorter characterized them as "the wilderness gentry of the Pacific Northwest."⁵ In 1877, General Nelson A. Miles expressed the consensus in saying, "They were a very bright and energetic body of Indians; indeed, the most intelligent that I had ever seen. Exceedingly self-reliant, each man seemed to be able to do his own thinking, and to be purely democratic and independent in his ideas and purposes."⁶ This was surely a strong recommendation for a band of prisoners of war.

The Nez Perce Homeland

Tradition places the Nez Perce nesting place in the Kamiah Valley by the forks of the Clearwater River. From there they spread north and south along the base of the Bitterroot Range and also westward toward the Columbia River. The most extensive description of their homeland bounds them on the west by the Cascades, on the east by the Bitterroots, and on the south and the north by the forty-fourth and forty-sixth parallels. Of course the Nez Perces, like other nomads, visited more far-flung areas, directed by their needs and feelings of relative security.

Notable trails were developed by their hunters. One led south up the Little Salmon River to the upland meadows, thence down the Weiser River to the Lower Snake River country. The Nez Perce Trail followed the ridges that separate the Clearwater and Salmon rivers, into the lush Selway country. From there it struck eastward across the Bitterroot Range and followed the Nez

Perce Fork of the Bitterroot River to its valley. The Lolo Trail, most famous of the three major trails, strikes east from the forks of the Clearwater River. It will be described in detail later on. Several trails gave the people access to the valleys nestled in the northern reaches of the Blue Mountains. To the northwest lay the Palouse prairies open to approach along numerous trails. Although this vast area is quite amorphous in character, it does possess a focal point, namely, the confluence of the Snake and Clearwater rivers. These streams bore the names Kimenem and Kooskooskia, respectively, and their point of union (elevation 740 feet) was called Tsceminicum, meaning "meeting place of the Nimipu."

The climate in the Nez Perce land varies with the elevation. In general, Pacific Ocean influences are dominant. However, the ten-thousand-foot-high Bitterroots, with from forty to fifty inches of precipitation, divert the cooler continental weather influences along the eastern periphery. The balancing of these forces yields a climate favorable for all forms of life to be found between the latitudes and elevations mentioned.

The flora of the region was lush, beautiful, and valuable. Evergreens, cottonwoods, aspens, maples, and birches grew rank. Serviceberries, hawthornes, and huckleberries flowered and ripened upon the slopes. Grasses and sedges flourished everywhere, but fairly carpeted the lowlands. Camas fields abounded, and those at Weippe and Camas were so vast as to be called prairies. The rich earth yielded a great plenty and fair variety of good substantial food.

In general, the Nez Perce land is a well-watered province, and the waters teemed with fish. The salmon was so plentiful that a river system bears its name. This country of alternating valley, prairie, and mountain, interlaced with streams, provided an ideal habitat for many kinds of animals, in great numbers. Elk, deer, sheep, goats, antelope, rabbits, fowl (upland and water), and their respective predators, bears, wolves, foxes, and coyotes, were all available to the hunters. Besides being productive, the Nez Perce country is a region of sheer beauty. Francis Haines has captured something of its grace in this paragraph:

> From the first breath of spring until midsummer, the Nez Perce country is a blaze of color. Blue windflowers, purple shooting stars, yellow bells, blue bells, blue and purple penstemon, blue and yellow lupine, yellow sunflowers, and Indian paintbrush in various hues follow one another in wild profusion. Mingled with the flowers are many important food plants, the feathery leaved cowish (cous or kouse), the pink bitterroot, and, above all, the camas, covering the open meadows with blue carpets until at a distance they resemble little lakes.[7]

Another sensitive observer has said, "I am thinking of a scene I would describe, but cannot do it justice—Summer time in Tsceminicum; the dust, the purple haze hanging in the canyons, the blue-green background of Craig Mountains, and red Indian summer sun just dropping over the horizon, reflected in Snake River."[8] The Nez Perces were fully cognizant of the value of their homeland and felt a deep affection for it.

The Nez Perce land, although so abundant, does not seem to have been too heavily populated. Isaac I. Stevens estimated the population at 3,300 in 1855, in a homeland of two hundred square miles. The Nez Perce Jonathan "Billy" Williams made a large map of the area, in which he placed and named seventy-five villages. These calculations suggest that the ratio of people to resources was very favorable for an abundant life. There was room enough for all, and the various clans found specific regions to suit their tastes and lived amicably together. The districts occupied by the bands of five chiefs, who went on the warpath in 1877, were as follows: Chief Joseph, the Wallowa and Imnaha valleys, Oregon; White Bird, along the Salmon River and its tributaries; Toohoolhoolzote, astride the highlands lying between the Salmon and Snake rivers; Hush-hush-cute, in the big bend country west and south of the Snake River; and Looking Glass, upon the Middle Fork of the Clearwater River.

The Nez Perce Way of Life

The following description of attitudes and customs is subject to the limitations that always arise in connection with the appraisal of another culture. In this case the monumental labors of H. J. Spinden and L. V. Mc-Whorter have been carefully assessed.

The individual had high status in life. He was never dominated; freedom of action was understood and observed. He was expected to discover a sense of destiny and pursue it for the good of all. Family ties were close; relatives lived together, teaching and counseling one another. The principal men often established polygamous family relationships, although usually there were not more than two wives.[9] The family, whether large or small, was basic and cohesive.

The typical family hut was conical in shape, covered with rush mats. For winter use huts were erected over excavations several feet deep. There were also large, gabled lodges built with much care, which functioned as meeting halls or as dwellings for several families under one roof. These communal buildings or "long houses" had A-shaped roofs of cattail or tule mats, reaching to the ground. Such a house might be 150 feet in length, contain twenty fireplaces, accommodate a hundred people or more, and, if so, constitute the entire village.[10] These domiciles were well furnished by the craftsmen. Bison robes and other skins provided warmth and decoration. Tule and rush mats were plentiful, and utensils of all sorts were woven and shaped from the same materials. Basketry was the most important craft and was used in trade. The permanent settlements were situated on the rivers, where each group formed a single village community. Some villages were permanently occupied, but there were also outlying camps for seasonal occupancy. The size of a village population could fluctuate from winter to winter, since adherence to a given group by individual families was rather loose. The largest camps were credited with a population of up to three hundred individuals, but mostly the villages were much smaller, and all members were more or less related. A village site was always in close proximity to a good fishing place, which together with the surrounding land was considered property of the village. There were probably some seventy such little communities among the Nez Perces at one time; the names and exact locations of about forty of them are known.[11]

Tribal Organization and Procedures

Chieftainship was neither hereditary nor permanent for an entire tribe. Each village group might have several chiefs, one of whom was temporarily recognized as leader. Lack of compulsion upon tribesmen put the leaders on their mettle. The prestige of leadership came as a result of many coups. Chieftainship was achieved by merit and held by accomplishment. The time may have been when ten scalps made a chief, but certainly ten successful horse-stealing raids won distinction for a warrior.

Nez Perce apparel and foods were derived from resources at hand. They were fully dressed at all times, except in war. The men wore a breechcloth, a shirt, leggings, moccasins, and a blanket. Women dressed in skins, too, wearing long, loose gowns. They also made inner garments of bark fibers; their millinery consisted of fez-shaped basketry caps.

Food-gathering was essentially a family responsibility, with a rough division of labor. Men hunted for the large animals, and women and children trapped small ones, fished, and gathered the fruits of earth. Communal rabbit drives were conducted, and roots and berries were often secured in similar fashion.

The most important root food was the bulbous camas. When not eaten at once, these nutritious bulbs were roasted in pits, then pounded into a mash, made into loaves, cooked again, and stored for future consumption. Other edible roots included cowish, bitterroot, carum, wild carrot, and cow parsnip. The country was rich in berries, which when sun dried formed an important food reserve. In times of shortage, sunflower seeds, lichens, pine nuts, and the inner bark of trees were also eaten.

The Nez Perce Stockmen

The failure of American Indians to domesticate any of the native mammals, with the exception of dogs, is difficult to understand, in view of their outstanding success as horsemen. Indians acquired horses from Mexico early in the seventeenth century. By 1690 the Idaho Shoshonis had acquired substantial herds, and shortly thereafter their northern neighbors were "forking" horses. Herds flourished upon the ample Nez Perce grazing lands. The tribesmen were more than enthusiastic about horses; they were actually scientific in the management of their herds. Lewis and Clark observed that they were skillful at gelding animals. Their selective practices were conducted with an eye for both type and beauty; indeed, a flair for the exotic is evidenced by the marvelous Appaloosa horses they developed. Early traders spoke of this spotted type as "A Palouse horse," and in time, through slurred pronunciation, this became "Appaloosa."

Perhaps the Nez Perces were the only Indians to practice selective horse-breeding without lessons from white men. Lewis and Clark found them in possession of thousands of horses. One man is said to have owned fifteen hundred.[12] Eighty years later the Indian agent in Oklahoma Indian Territory confirmed their continuing interest and skill by observing, "The Nez Perces appear to be natural herders, and show more judgment in the management of their stock than any Indians I ever saw."[13]

Horses thrilled the Nez Perces. Upon them they hunted, fought, raced, and traveled with great zest. Racing courses were found throughout the land, and the tribesmen gathered to test and bet upon their favorites. Mounts were trained to appear elegant for parading purposes, and the joy of equestrian ownership was widespread. The Indians mounted their steeds from the right and preferred to ride bareback in hunting and fighting; otherwise, they used a buckskin pad for a saddle.

This wealth of prime horses made the Nez Perces exceptionally mobile. They could journey to the Snake River country, trade horses with the Shoshonis, and return with bison robes and other items. Furthermore, they were equipped to make long hunts into the upper Missouri country in quest of bison. The bison, having moved westward beyond the Continental Divide about 1600, were beginning to dwindle there about 1830. The hunting excursions involved great distances and much time, lasting from two to five years. Only the most rugged tribesmen undertook the journeys, however well planned and led they were to be.

There were many desirable way stations, such as valleys of the Bitterroot, Sun, Deer Lodge, Milk, Big Hole, Beaverhead, Salmon, and Yellowstone rivers, where living conditions were pleasant in season. The expeditions required able leadership and large numbers, because access to the hunting areas involved intertribal contention, and the hunters were subject to attack by the Blackfeet and the Crow. However, this prospect did not intimidate the Nez Perces; indeed, the danger inherent in the situation was an impelling factor. They outfought or outran the enemy according to the dictates of prudence. They made enemies and allies depending upon the circumstances. In any case, the experiences of the long hunts had a mighty impact upon the tribe. Young men made big medicine; great reputations were acquired for skill and bravery. Renowned hunters and warriors evolved in every band, and the tribe as a whole achieved tremendous *esprit de corps*. Surely these hunts reinforced the concept that the Nez Perces were the bravest of the brave. These experiences weakened Nez Perce ties with village chiefs and strengthened allegiance to the hunter-warrior leadership. Still, each tribe had two natures: one consisted of the moderate nomadic element intent upon the profits of husbandry, while the other was far-ranging and adventurous. This duality sometimes created a problem at tribal councils.

These Indians were quite as successful in raising cattle as they were in horse culture. Most of the Nez Perces realized that fresh meat was better than dried bison meat dragged a thousand miles on "the crotch," or travois. Hence they acquired cattle from the immigrants. The historian Yellow Wolf suggests the extent of this interest and the concomitant well-being in a few words: "We were raising horses and cattle—fast horses and many cattle. We had fine lodges, good clothes, plenty to eat, enough of everything. We were living well. Then General Howard and Indian Agent Monteith came to bother us."[14]

Yellow Wolf failed to mention the fact that crop-raising was also a factor in the Nez Perce economy. Indeed, by 1877, it was a basic interest among the mission Indians. Even the nontreaty groups practiced farming, although only on an ancillary basis.

The Nez Perce Religion

Having described the sanguine character of Nez Perce temporal affairs, it is natural to observe that they did not live by bread alone. Their high barbarian status was due to the possession of disciplined spirits. Plateau Indian spiritual concepts and practices have been painstakingly investigated by many scholars. The following interpretation is based upon the research of L. V. McWhorter, Kate C. McBeth, and Sven Liljeblad. A quotation from Liljeblad's "Indian Peoples of Idaho" presents a salient concept:

The leading motive in the religion of the Plateau Indians was the desire in every individual to receive help and power from the spiritual world. Success and security depended, in their way of thinking, on personal contact with the one spirit fated to become one's guardian through life. This contact was reached through dreams and visions. Training and search for these revelations began early in a person's life. At the age of ten or twelve, every child, whether boy or girl, was sent alone to some desolate place to fast and keep vigil day and night until the desired vision occurred. In this vision or in his troubled dreams, the child met for the first time the supernatural being who would from then on become his guardian spirit, and whose advice and aid he would constantly seek. Whether the apparition was that of an animal, a natural phenomenon, or something else, it taught its protégé a sacred song that was made public at the Guardian Spirit dance.[15]

Special dances were held when the occasion warranted; otherwise dancing ceremonials were roughly calendarial, related to the first salmon catch, the first root digging, or the first berrypicking of the year. These occasions resemble Christian celebrations quite closely, and Nez Perce dances welcoming the return of a victorious war party bear a close resemblance to white men's practices.

L. V. McWhorter, in summarizing their religion, states flatly that the Nez Perces believed in immortality of all life. The individual's relationship to the spirits (powers and principalities) might be intimate indeed. He could invoke them to serve in the role of guide and protector. The key to this relationship was known as *Wyakin. Wyakin* might be a single force or a combination of mystic forces acting in unison. The missionary Kate C. McBeth observed the use of some flexibility in regard to truthtelling:

> According to their ideas, there was no sin in telling a lie the first time. There was a little sin if told the second time, but the third time, it was unpardonable. Anyone understanding this, and putting the question three times, would be sure to get the truth the third time. This is some of the old teaching of their heathenism.[16]

From what has been written, it is apparent that the Nez Perces were a considerable people. They were well endowed with natural resources, and the same may be said of their homeland.[17] They found joy and inspiration in the environment, and it was reflected in their bearing and spirit. One might expect that, as a prosperous and self-possessed people, aware of their dignity and power, they would cherish the status quo and regard any prospects of modification with a shudder. Their history demonstrates that they welcomed outsiders and were intrigued by new ideas.

2. A GOLDEN AGE OF INDIAN RELATIONS

As a general rule, good relations between white and Indian peoples were of short duration. Favorable conditions prevailed between the Nez Perces and their white neighbors, however, for nearly sixty years, from 1805 to 1863. A longer and better record would be anomalous.[1]

The arrival of the Lewis and Clark expedition in the Nez Perce country was a notable event in the history of both peoples. The explorers emerged from the Bitterroots on September 20, 1805, weary and in desperate need of friends. Friendship was generously provided, and Chief Twisted Hair and his associates, Black Eagle, Halvats, Ilp-ilp, Red Bear, Cut Nose, Broken Arm, and Speaking Eagle, held councils from time to time with the captains as they traveled in the territory between the principal forks of the Clearwater and the Columbia rivers. The language barrier was formidable, but it was partly overcome by a complicated combination of English, French, Shoshoni, Minnetaree, and Nez Perce. The concept of American sovereignty was somehow conveyed by the captains, and the chiefs imparted information concerning the route of travel and the nature of the hinterland. The expedition horses were left in the care of Chief Twisted Hair and repossessed the next year in fair condition. William Clark described this chief as a cheerful, sincere man, and other entries suggest that other chiefs conformed to the same general pattern. The explorers described these Indians as a whole as a quiet, civil people, tractable in disposition, willing to be instructed, but also proud and haughty. Although the captains did not precisely say so, several entries leave the impression that the Nez Perce Indians were their favorites.

The Religious Influence

Mountain men formed a similar estimate of these people. They noticed that the Nez Perces were strongly religious. In fact, the trappers thought that what they learned about the Nez Perce beliefs, legends, and practices bore a close relationship to Christianity. The Indians in turn discovered that the white man's religion was interesting, and, since trappers were such masterful men, it seems logical that the Nez Perces would seek more philosophical knowledge than they could get from that source.

In quest of such knowledge, a delegation set out for Saint Louis in 1831. Their friends the Flatheads joined them in this visionary enterprise, and three of the delegates actually reached their objective. They presented their request for the white man's secret power to William Clark. The visit attracted considerable interest, and by 1833 it was being described in such church organs as the *Christian Advocate* and the *Zion City Herald*. Indeed, several other Nez Perce and Flathead delegations journeyed to Saint Louis during the same decade with similar objectives, and these successive expeditions functioned as catalytic agents to mission societies.

Students of Northwest history know the story of Jason Lee's immediate response to the first call for

Indian missionaries in the Pacific Northwest. Although the Lee party bypassed the Nez Perces, the American Board Mission sent Rev. Samuel Parker to make a reconnaissance of that mission field in 1835. Nez Perces served as his guides during much of his six-month tour, and he felt secure all the while. On July 6, 1836, when Marcus Whitman and Henry Harmon Spalding and their wives arrived at the Rocky Mountain Company rendezvous on a branch of the Green River, a strong delegation of Nez Perces was there to meet them. Whitman and Spalding established their missions at Waiilatpu and Lapwai. The latter station was in the middle of the Nez Perce country, and it played a significant role in the subsequent history of this tribe.

Spalding recognized that the Christian purpose would be achieved best if settled community life could be developed. He also realized that white expansion would raise havoc with the old bison-hunting and salmon-fishing economy. If the Nez Perces were to become Christian farmers their chance of survival was good. To that end he served as both pastor and foreman, and in both roles his bearing was austere. He and his wife Elisa labored with great zeal, and the fact that the Nez Perce Christians became the most advanced Indians in the arts of civilized life is due to the Spaldings. Mrs. Spalding was a superb missionary. She taught reading and writing in an effortless manner. It is said that her memory still lingers among the Nez Perces. One reason the Indians loved her was that "she had a quiet heart, was not excitable, and readily picked up the language."[2]

Many Indians responded to Spalding's temporal endeavors. They hoed the soil, planted crops, tended stock, and helped erect a blacksmith shop and sawmills and gristmills. By 1839 a hundred families were engaged in farming, and a second mission station was opened at Kamiah.

However well conceived and salutary, both facets of Spalding's mission program divided the Nez Perces.

Some resented his attacks upon liquor, gambling, and polygamy; others, or perhaps mainly the same ones, objected to farming. In this manner the Nez Perces were divided into Christian and heathen categories. The treaty and Christian Indians, and the nontreaty and heathen Indians, were partially, but not entirely, mutually exclusive. Between the two groups there was little difference in the fundamental concepts of truth and morality.

Rivalry between Presbyterian and Roman Catholic missionaries was disconcerting to the natives.[3] Each religion was graphically described by elaborate drawings and diagrams, such as the Catholic Ladder and its Protestant counterpart. Nez Perce mastery of theological tenets was impressive, and little trouble developed until about 1846, when Indians from eastern areas brought accounts of happenings on other frontiers. Joe Lewis and Tom Hill, a Delaware, advised the Indians to abandon Christianity and return to their tribal gods. This influence played a part in the Whitman Massacre, on November 29, 1847. Although the Spaldings were not driven out, Nez Perce restlessness made their position seem untenable. As a result, the Nez Perce missions were suspended for fourteen years, but many of the converts retained both their faith and farms. Spalding and his second wife reopened the missions in 1862. An act of Congress, passed in 1869, parceled out the Indian reservations to different Christian denominations. Under that law the Nez Perce Reservation was awarded to the Presbyterians.[4]

Spalding's return to Lapwai was the occasion of a Nez Perce revival. Hundreds were baptized as a result of his teaching and preaching. The converts were often given Christian names. One convert, by name Tu-ela-kas, was named Joseph; his son, given the same name, became a renowned chief. Several of the men were appointed to offices as deacons and elders. In fact, a few assisted Spalding with the preaching. Among these were

Timothy, Archie, Lawyer, Enoch Pond, Peter Lindsley, Silas Whitman, Solomon Whitman, Felix Corbett, William Wheeler, and Jonathan "Billy" Williams.[5] The great missionary died on August 3, 1874. He was buried at Spalding, a site properly marked as a state park in honor of the principal instruments in bringing civilization to the Nez Perces and to all of Idaho.

An accurate measurement of the total impact of the mission upon the Nez Perce nation is impossible. Mission partisans have pointed to the freedom of the Nez Perces from the usual Indian superstitions concerning natural phenomena. For instance, those in flight through Yellowstone National Park in 1877 paid no heed to the geysers and paint pots. Superintendent P. W. Norris said they had "acquired sufficient civilization and Christianity to at least overpower their pagan superstitious fear of earthly fire-hole basins and brimstone pits."[6]

Lieutenant C. A. Woodruff believed their Christian teaching prevented them from engaging in the awful barbarities that usually characterize Indian hostilities. The nontreaty, heathen warriors did not subscribe to this view; they attributed their conduct to the traditions and mores of the tribe. One historian suggests that in the Nez Perces (as in most humans) there was an odd mixture of this world and the next—a love for both adventure and devotion.[7]

The Miners Meet the Nez Perces

The mining frontier advanced rapidly upon the Pacific Northwest during the late 1850's. Supported by the military force strongly established at Walla Walla, the advance upon the Nez Perce land was delayed but not to be denied.

A former California prospector named Elias Davidson Pierce was the discoverer of gold in the Clearwater district on February 20, 1860. Pierce had been trading with the Nez Perces for three years, and he had learned from them that evidence pointed to gold deposits. Upon making the discovery Pierce and his associates proposed to exploit the mineral. However, the Indian agent, A. J. Cain, objected on the grounds that such a course was illegal and inexpedient. He foresaw the outcome of a gold rush on the Nez Perces. Cain induced Indian scouts to blockade all trails, but the Pierce party stealthily re-entered the reservation, and the rush was soon under way. Fortunately, the Nez Perces were peaceful; they believed that miners were evanescent like trappers, that they would soon pan the gold from the sand bars and be on their way. This was a serious error in judgment, because mining was not an individual venture; rather, it involved a considerable economy.[8] There would be transportation, trading, farming, and gambling interests to consider.

Agent Cain's arguments were well received in Walla Walla; many citizens questioned the propriety of en-croaching upon the Nez Perce reservation. It could be dangerous; it would be better to arrange a new treaty and proceed legally. However, enterprising Nez Perces quickly adjusted to the gold rush. For example, Chief Reuben joined forces with William Craig (a squaw-man) in building a ferry and warehouse at Lewiston. Other Nez Perces built bridges and charged tolls. Chief Lawyer and Chief Eagle-from-the-Light fumed and threatened as the town of Lewiston sprang up, and as the miners encompassed the entire Nez Perce domain. But once the reservation had been opened (to miners only) north of the Clearwater, by an agreement on April 11, 1861, it was inevitable that demands would be made for admission to the interior Salmon River district. An agreement to this effect was reached at the Council of Slate Creek on the last day of December.

It has been estimated that approximately fifty million dollars was taken by the miners from the Nez Perce reservation during the 1860's. Thousands of white men swarmed over their domain, and their offenses sorely tried the endurance of the Nez Perces. Although they frequently petitioned the agent to protect them against outrages, the Nez Perces avoided hostile retaliation. This performance is unprecedented in the annals of Indian relations, and it is a tribute to the self-confidence and good will of the natives.

The Settlers Remain

As the Indians expected, most of the miners did leave the reservation in due course, but conditions were never the same. A few remained, by native sufferance, as ranchers and farmers. Others operated stage stations with the accompanying appurtenances. These people raised hay and livestock and cut timber. In 1874, when a group of Nez Perces gathered upon the Camas Meadows to dig the bulbs, they found the crop ruined by the farmers' pigs. In their wrath the Indians destroyed some fences, whereupon the settlers demanded military protection during the next root-digging season. Obviously the tensions were mounting between the seminomads and the white people of steady habits who resided within the bounds or close upon the peripheries of the Nez Perce reservations. By 1876 the dynamic frontier civilization began pressing upon the Nez Perces. Their turn to conform had arrived. It is strange that they had not read the signs more clearly.

Nez Perce Military Service

The Nez Perces had observed the subjugation of several tribes. The Whitman Massacre produced a series of wars: the Cayuse War, 1847–50; the Rogue River War, 1850–56; and the Yakima War, 1855–59. Although these wars did not involve the Nez Perces directly, they were affected by some of them. Nez Perce scouts assisted the military force in the Yakima War. Colonel George Wright mentioned them in dispatches as having rendered effective service as spies, guides, guards, and fighters. When the colonel asked Lawyer what the chiefs would like as rewards for their people, he replied: "Peace, plows, and schools."[9]

In conclusion, it is evident that the Nez Perce Indians were worthy of being fostered and protected in their attempt to improve side by side with the white man. Although against war, they were brave and spirited. They were well disposed, industrious, and tolerant. The following statement by Senator J. W. Nesmith, of Oregon, is representative of many written endorsements of the tribe: "I have known the Nez Perce tribe since 1843. They were under my charge as Superintendent of Indian Affairs from June 1857 until July 1859. They are the finest specimens of the aboriginal race upon this continent, and have been friendly to the whites from the time of Lewis and Clark."[10] It took years of close contact with the white man to bring forth the darker elements in Nez Perce nature. Even then, the negative reaction was not a general one, nor was it as fierce and barbaric as those exhibited by many warriors of all races.

3. Will Fight for These Forests

reads: "They were efficient members of them. Nez Perce scouts assisted the military forces in the Yakima War..."

3. INDIAN TREATIES AND CONTROVERSIES

A proper understanding of the Indian problem encountered at mid-nineteenth century in the Pacific Northwest requires a review of American Indian policies after the colonial era. Every student is aware of the oft-repeated cycle governing white and Indian relations: A council was held and a treaty made; Indians ceded lands in return for presents and for promised annuities; boundary lines were marked and declared inviolable. Peace lasted a few years but was destroyed by the encroachment of settlers who crossed the line to hunt, prospect, graze stock, and farm. These invasions brought protests, massacres, battles, and ultimately victory to the troops. Then a new treaty was made, and the cycle inevitably operated upon the next frontier.

The white man's procedures have been called cynical, dishonorable, and wicked, but these terms may not be absolutely justified. For one thing, the settlers at any given time and place were quite sincere in respect to the terms. But the influence of "Manifest Destiny" was driving thousands upon the frontiers. The Canadian boundary was threatened in 1812–14; and the Spanish boundary in Florida gave way under the pressure of military invasion and diplomacy in 1818 and 1819. The

Mexican War, in turn, compelled Mexico to yield a great domain in 1848. A great nation was evolving, and Indian claims to vast regions as tribal hunting grounds were naturally taken with a grain of salt by the frontiersmen. As tensions developed, leading statesmen analyzed the basic issue.

In 1802 John Quincy Adams posed the question arising in these circumstances:

> The Indian right of possession itself stands, with regard to the greatest part of the country, upon a questionable foundation. Their cultivated fields; their constructed habitations; a space of ample sufficiency for their subsistence, and whatever they had annexed to themselves by personal labor, was undoubtedly by the law of nature theirs. But what is the right of a huntsman to the forest of a thousand miles over which he accidently ranged in quest of prey? Shall the liberal bounties of Providence to the race of man be monopolized by one of ten thousand for whom they were created? Shall the exuberant bosom of the common mother, amply adequate to the nourishment of millions, be claimed exclusively by a few hundreds of her offspring?[1]

Answering his own questions, the learned statesman explained that heaven had not designed natural economy upon such untenable moral grounds as those postulated by the natives or the bleeding-heart romanticists who championed their cause. The basic morality of the Adams attitude is defensible, but the administration of the policy has been full of errors.

In retrospect, it appears that a major mistake was made at the very outset, when white negotiators recognized Indian tribes as sovereign nations. Thus, agreements were called treaties, a name that implied some degree of equality between signatories. In most cases this was a complete fiction, because tribes were so decentralized that one or more clans invariably rejected the action. Dignity there was, but stability and unity were not characteristics of Indian "nations." The lesson of independence came easily to the Indians, and they learned it well. When something would happen concerning interpretation or application of the treaty, the parties would be found in disagreement. Finally, the government would be obliged to assume United States jurisdiction and enforce it unilaterally. Of course this was war, and the tribe was subdued. Hence, the constitutional *modus operandi* was improperly conceived and it led to everlasting trouble.

Besides, the American Indian policy was changeable, fluctuating between two extremes. One viewpoint regarded Indians as predatory wild animals, entirely lacking any sense of moral responsibility. In 1865, Granville Stuart recorded an old timer's opinion of depravity in the Indian nature: "They are the most on sartainest varmints in all creation, and I reckon thar not mor'n half human, for I never seed a human arter you'd fed and treated him to the best fixin's in your lodge, just turn round and steal all your horses, or any other thing he could lay his hands on. . . ."[2]

Then there was the romantic conception that visualized the Indian as an unspoiled child of nature, simple, magnanimous, and brave—a Noble Redman.

Others took a middle ground, admitting that Indians were barbarians, creatures of reckless habits and uncertain responses, but that it was incumbent upon civilized Christians to exercise great patience toward them. The "Quakers' Policy" abhorred the frontier practice of taking life for life, horse for horse, and treachery for treachery. These different viewpoints not only produced confusion among the whites, but they also baffled the Indians.

No doubt Indian behavior seemed equally strange and provocative to frontiersmen. In general they regarded all Indians as an encumbrance upon the landscape and a barrier to progress. From every frontier came incessant resolutions, petitions, and recitations relating to the Indian menace. Different programs were administered by changing administrations.

Sometimes the policy of pressing the Indian into the white man's mold was in the ascendancy. Inducements were made to disengage the individual from the tribe, divide lands in severalty, grant citizenship, and coax the Indian to adopt the white man's ways. Confronted by great inertia, if not stubborn reluctance, the policy would then revert to the concept of reconstructing the Indian community system upon the old pattern of tribal ownership. Tribal reaction to any given plan was never uniform, and ultimate dissatisfaction with its application was inevitable.

The typical Indian agent was not always an estimable person and the licensed Indian trader was often still worse. Both generally followed typical carpetbag practices. The idea of fleecing the Indian could be justified by high authority. In 1803 President Thomas Jefferson wrote the following to William Henry Harrison:

> To promote this disposition to exchange lands which they (Indians) have to spare and we want, for necessaries which we have to spare and they want, we shall be glad to see the good and influential among them in debt, because we observe that when these debts get beyond what the individuals can pay, they become willing to lop them off by a cession of lands.[3]

After studying America's four-hundred-and-fifty-year-old record of Indian history, a careful scholar of the subject reached this conclusion: "We still have the problem which faced our first settlers, namely, what shall be done with the Indians?"[4]

The foregoing account of the Indian problem was designed to prepare the reader for what happened in the Pacific Northwest. Reference has been made to the restlessness caused by the Whitman Massacre and the wars that trailed in its wake. During the course of these hostilities, Joel Palmer, Oregon Superintendent of Indian Affairs, inaugurated a series of conferences for the purpose of settling the Indians upon reservations. In 1853 Isaac I. Stevens became Governor of Washington Territory and Superintendent of Indian Affairs. Stevens was a man of large views, with energy and a desire for action. He devoted nearly all of his time during 1855 to arranging councils among the tribes occupying the Washington Territory. The conference for the Columbia Plateau tribes, to be at Walla Walla, was scheduled for May, 1855.

The Walla Walla Council of 1855

The council ground was situated on the right bank of Mill Creek, a tributary of the Walla Walla River. It was a beautiful plain, deeply carpeted with grass and flowers. On May 23, Governor Stevens and an entourage of about one hundred aides and military guards established a camp and prepared for the reception of the Indian delegations. The Nez Perces, some twenty-five hundred strong, arrived the next day. They posted an American flag in the middle of their campground. Hal-hal-tlossot, or Lawyer, was head chief and negotiator. He perceived the trends of the time, trusted the government, and definitely oriented his followers toward peace and civilization.

Then came the Cayuses, Yakimas, Umatillas, and Walla Wallas, led by We-ah-te-na-tee-ma-ny, Young Chief, Pu-pu-mox-mox, Yellow Serpent, and Kam-i-ah-kan. Each tribe had a hierarchy of subchiefs; among the Nez Perce subchiefs were Looking Glass (the elder), Spotted Eagle, Joseph (the elder), James, Red Wolf, Timothy, and Eagle-from-the-Light.

When the tribes were all settled, more than five thousand Indians constituted the host. The Stevens party was actually in jeopardy, and a Cayuse-inspired plot was designed to exploit the precarious situation. At this juncture, Chief Lawyer moved his lodge into the midst of the government camp, thereby disclosing to his compatriots the Nez Perce posture in case of trouble. This and other Nez Perce actions, including their conventional observance of the Sabbath, were responsible for an entry in Stevens' diary, May 27: "The Nez Perces have evidently profited much from the labor of Mr. Spalding. . . . their whole deportment throughout the service was devout."[5]

Ample time was taken in preliminary deliberations, and the council was not formally opened until May 29. For the next two weeks the government's case for reservations was carefully unfolded by Joel Palmer, Governor Stevens, and others. Each tribe received interpretations, and their spokesmen responded in a generally favorable manner. There were to be three reservations—one on the upper drainage of the Yakima River for the Yakimas, Klikitats, Palouses, and kindred bands; another, for the Nez Perces, a tract of three million acres embracing land on the north side of the Snake River, both the Clearwater and the Salmon river valleys on the east of the Snake, and the lower Grande Ronde, Wallowa, and Imnaha valleys on the west of the Snake; and a third at the headwaters of the Umatilla River in the Blue Mountains, for the Umatillas, Cayuses, and Walla Wallas. These reservations were to belong to the Indians, and no white man could come upon them without Indian consent. An agent, with schoolteachers, mechanics, and farmers, would take charge of each reservation. Instructions would be given, gristmills and sawmills built, and annuities in clothing and tools would be vouchsafed for twenty years. At first the resources were to be used in common, but later lands would be granted in severalty, enough for each family. In addition, the Indians could fish, hunt, pasture, and gather roots in vacant lands outside their reservations. Trade could be developed with the white people in surrounding areas, and civilization would be acquired by such means.

Each day the Indians listened in silence or debated energetically for a few hours; then they would fare forth to the Nez Perce camp and indulge in horse and foot races. The evenings were devoted to discussions in the different camps.

Debates in general session were presented with dignity and power by men of different tempers. Yellow Serpent exhibited distrust and sarcasm, and yet he was perceptive: "I think you intend to win our country. . . . In one day the Americans become as numerous as the grass. . . . Suppose you show me goods, shall I run up and take them? That is the way with all of us Indians as you know. Goods and the earth are not equal. Goods are for using on the earth."[6] A more friendly chief named Steachus understood what was at stake: "My friends, I wish to show you my heart. If your mother were in this country, gave you birth and suckled you, and while you were suckling, some person came and took away your mother and left you alone and sold your mother, how would you then feel? This is our mother—this country—as if we drew our living from her. . . ."[7]

Nez Perce massive unity and quiet confidence was a large factor in bringing all the tribes into line. Then an upset was threatened as Chief Looking Glass arrived with a hunting expedition from the buffalo country. Rushing into camp, he shouted, "My people, what have you done? While I am gone, you have sold my country. I have come home, and there is not left me a place to pitch my lodge. Go home to your lodges. I will talk with you."[8]

The council was adjourned until the following day, when Looking Glass made many objections and demanded much more land, whereupon Lawyer abruptly left the council. This act caused the various chiefs to reaffirm their willingness to sign the treaties. The Nez Perces repudiated the extreme position taken by Looking Glass and agreed to sustain Lawyer as their head chief. This course brought Looking Glass into agreement, and his signature followed Lawyer's and preceded Joseph's on the final treaty, which bore the signatures of fifty-six chiefs. Eagle-from-the-Light and other Nez Perce chiefs were satisfied with their reservation of five thousand square miles, plus promises to spend $60,000 for initial improvements and $200,000 in the usual annuities. It was a good treaty, and the prospect of peace and prosperity for some thirty-six hundred people was bright if its provisions could be held inviolate.

Governor Stevens had conducted the negotiations in a democratic way, and as he prepared to journey across the mountains to make similar treaties with the Plains Indians, he discharged his military escort and enlisted a Nez Perce guard. Among the warriors chosen for this duty were Looking Glass and White Bird.

Meanwhile, Old Joseph returned to the Wallowa country and planted poles around that portion of the reservation in order that white men would not inadvertently trespass. He also drew a remarkable parchment map, sixteen by eighteen inches, upon which the natural features were delineated. These actions disclosed his suspicion that the preservation of Indian rights required vigilance.

Old Joseph had been baptized by Spalding on November 17, 1839, and he remained faithful to the interests of the mission until it was abandoned eight years later. At that time he had an altercation with a rival chief at Lapwai and returned to the Wallowa Valley. One of the missionaries characterized this move as apostasy. His sons, Joseph and Ollokot, were seven and four, and they had been affected by the mission influence up to that time. Thenceforth, traditional tribal ways probably gained ascendancy. In any case, Old Joseph was somewhat on the defensive in regard to the mission and reservation system. He taught his sons to raise horses and cattle, and eat the native things of the earth. Their freedom to live the old ways might be preserved if they never trusted the white man or his red allies.

The love of the Wallowa Valley ran deep in their feelings. They called the place Kahmuenem, after a trailing vine that grew along the banks of the Wallowa River. Popularly, the name Wallowa means the valley of winding waters. It is a handsome, alpine-type valley, nestling at the base of the well-watered Blue Mountains. Guarded by these mountains on the south and west and by the deep canyons of the Snake and Grande Ronde rivers on the east and north, the Wallowa is a sequestered region. The Imnaha Valley, angling away to the southeast toward the Snake, was lower in elevation. Hence, it was an ancient wintering area. Here Joseph's band of Nez Perces hoped to live their lives and seek happiness in their own way.

The Pressures Mount

The impact of miners upon the Nez Perce Reservation in the Clearwater area has been described in the preceding chapter. With this impact, the foundation for specific grievances was laid, for in spite of the treaties the Indians were not effectively protected from marauders. The United States Senate did not ratify the 1855 treaty until 1859. As a result, payments and annuities were not received until 1860. By then gold had been discovered, and within a year more than ten thousand miners were roaming at large on the reservation. Under pressure from the chiefs, Superintendent of Indian Affairs E. R. Geary secured an agreement from the miners not to go south of the Clearwater River. The agreement was violated, however, and miners stole livestock or blamed Indians for loss of their own.

Such behavior was bound to occur once the miners

were allowed on the reservation. Their aggressive tendencies could not be controlled by anything less than a firm, efficient, impartial system of government, and that was seldom available in the gold fields. Besides, the Indians were tolerant, since a profitable commerce had developed. Many were becoming wealthy by exchanging horses, cattle, and foodstuffs for gold. Still, tension existed from the outset, and on April 28, 1862, the *Oregon Statesman* printed a penetrating estimate of the situation as reported by William Purvine:

> If open hostilities have not commenced with the Nez Perces, it is not because they have not been outraged to that degree when "forebearance ceases to be a virtue." In return for the continued friendship in time of want, and generous acts of hospitality always so readily extended towards the whites by these Indians, they now reap an abundant harvest of every species of villainy and insult.

The June 21, 1862, issue of the *Washington Statesman* contains an account of the death of three Indians at the hands of drunken miners. When the Nez Perce chiefs demanded justice their pleas were ignored. One reaction from the white majority was wholly unjust. A Lewiston paper, the *Golden Age,* advised the settlers to help themselves to land regardless of treaty obligations; while a Boise paper made the sinister suggestion that blankets might be infected with smallpox and distributed where they would do the most good.[9] The level-headed citizens rejected such approaches to the problem; instead, these citizens joined the Nez Perce agitation for a council to iron out the difficulties.

The Treaties of 1863 and 1868

The tension increased with the passing of time. Several restless chiefs demanded a council in 1861, but

Lawyer was opposed and it was not held. The next year a permanent military garrison was established at Lapwai. This show of strength brought the various chiefs and their escorts to Lapwai for a council in November, 1862. The reservation officials were not ready to negotiate, however, so the meeting was postponed until mid-May of 1863. The chiefs left Lapwai in a surly mood in spite of the exertions of William Craig and Robert Newell to pacify them.[10]

After a winter of nervousness the chiefs and their delegations assembled at the appointed time and place. Superintendent Calvin H. Hale was in charge of the council. He was flanked by Commissioners Charles Hutchings and S. D. Howe. Attendants and supporters included Robert Newell and William Craig, as well as the military officers on the post. When the council opened, the Nez Perces insisted upon having Perrin B. Whitman as interpreter. This demand delayed the proceedings for two weeks, as he was living some distance away.

The commissioners started the negotiations with a proposition to reduce the size of the 1855 reservation from five thousand square miles to five or six hundred square miles along the south side of the South Fork of the Clearwater. At the Indians' protest, the commissioners agreed to double the proposed area and pay an indemnity of $75,000 in the form of material utilities.

At this juncture, Lawyer, backed by the more sedentary Lower Christian Nez Perce headmen, proposed that the Upper Nez Perce chiefs should surrender their homelands and that the government should pay the Nez Perce nation $262,500 to facilitate the establishment of all Nez Perces upon the Lapwai reservation. All prior commitments under the Treaty of 1855 regarding benefits and annuities were to prevail. The Upper Nez Perces denounced this proposition as a swindle—"the thief treaty." Under such terms they would lose four and one-half million acres in return for certain costs of moving and preparations for a confined life. They stressed the fact that there were too many people and too much livestock to be so restrained. But that was part of the plan; they would be forced to reduce their herds and become farmers.

Among the fifty-two signatures, all Christians except one, was Henry H. Spalding's. The proposal was in accord with the educational policy he was then administering. The missionaries were all in favor of the plan, and on June 9, 1863, the treaty was signed. Old Joseph, White Bird, Looking Glass, Eagle-from-the-Light, Toohoolhoolzote, and all their associates rejected the decision. Years later, Yellow Wolf voiced their point of view: "Chief Lawyer, Chief Timothy, Chief Jason, Chief Levi and other headmen of the Upper Nez Perces had sold our homes. Sold our country which they did not own. . . ."[11] Then and there the traditional unity of all Nez Perce people was shattered. Each chief reverted to the much earlier status of an independent leader in his own village. Thus the Treaty of 1863, and its amendments of 1868, did more than reduce the limits of a reservation; it disrupted the Nez Perce tribe. Hereafter they would be much more vulnerable to white domination. Although sensing that separatism would render each band helpless before its enemies, Old Joseph tore a copy of the treaty to shreds, destroyed his long-treasured New Testament, and departed for the Wallowa. These acts marked his first deviation from the path of loyalty to the government and devotion to the principles of Christianity. He regarded the treaty proceedings as unjust and hypocritical. This time he returned to Wallowa in an intractable mood.

Naturally the commissioners justified their course. It was in keeping with the interests of the government and the church. Besides, it was also the handiwork of Chief Lawyer, who was head chief for the Nez Perces. The commissioners held that the Indians were bound by majorities, hence Old Joseph and the others should be required to come within the confines of the reduced reservation. In reference to Old Joseph, the case was conclusive. The fact that he signed the Treaty of 1855 implied a surrender of any specific rights to any particular portion of the whole reserve, such as the Wallowa Valley. He retained only an undivided interest in the reservation. No further attempt to appease the dissenters was made until tensions had increased still more.

The chiefs did what they could to consolidate their positions. Old Joseph was determined to hold the Wallowa country, and made this point clear to his sons Joseph and Ollokot. The land was sacred; it contained the bones of ancestors and provided life and strength to the living. Disillusioned in regard to Christianity because the Nez Perce Christians and their white allies had repudiated him, Old Joseph and his people found solace in the teachings of the Dreamer cult. This was a cosmic faith that affirmed immortality for all life. The earth was created perfect and complete; therefore it should not be disturbed by man. A Shahaptian medicine man named Smohalla was the high apostle of this belief. He spoke as follows:

> My young men shall never work. Men who work can not dream, and wisdom comes to us in dreams. . . . You ask me to plough the ground. Shall I take a knife and tear my mother's bosom? You ask me to dig for stone. Shall I dig under skin for her bones? You ask me to cut the grass and make hay and sell it and be rich like white men. But dare I cut off my mother's hair?[12]

Given to trances, Smohalla would awaken and utter pronouncements in accord with Nez Perce traditions and dispositions. Bereft of their Christian moorings, the isolated nontreaty Indians responded to this doctrine. As might be expected, the distressed Nez Perces believed that a faithful adherence to this doctrine would open a way for deliverance from their oppressors. For this partial apostasy they were roundly condemned by the Lapwai Nez Perces and their white associates.

When Old Joseph died in 1871 he could be sure that his sons would be faithful to the promise given him— never to sell the Wallowa Valley. The old chief's stern injunction would forever ring in Joseph's ear:

> My son . . . you are the chief. . . . Always remember that your father never sold his country. You must stop your ears whenever you are asked to sign a treaty selling your home. A few years more, and white men will be all around you. They have their eyes on this land. My son, never forget my dying words. This country holds your father's body. Never sell the bones of your father and your mother.[13]

Joseph disclosed the impact of his father's teachings in two sentences: "I buried him in that beautiful valley of the winding waters. I love that land more than all the rest of the world."[14] This intense, all-pervading, never-to-be-lessened affection for an ancestral homeland is not easily condemned. Thenceforth, Joseph was a dedicated man; he had sworn to preserve the Wallowa country for his father's people, and he was to face fearful odds in his attempt to do so.

Although only thirty-one, the young chief was not anxious for military action. By nature he was more diplomat than warrior; the predominant element in his character and destiny was that of guardian of his people. He would reason with his adversaries from a position of justice and strength. Concerning the Wallowa issue, he argued as follows:

> If we ever owned the land we own it still, for we never sold it. In the treaty councils the commissioners have claimed that our country had been sold to the Government. Suppose a white man should come to me and say, "Joseph, I like your horses, and I want

to buy them." I say to him, "No, my horses suit me, I will not sell them." Then he goes to my neighbor, and says to him: "Joseph has some good horses. I want to buy them, but he refuses to sell." My neighbor answers, "Pay me the money, and I will sell you Joseph's horses." The white man returns to me and says, "Joseph, I have bought your horses, and you must let me have them." If we sold our lands to the Government, this is the way they were bought.[15]

More Pressures against Nontreaty Clans

In the meantime racial tensions increased, because the settlers lost patience with the recalcitrant Indians. They wanted Indian lands, and in the circumstances trouble broke out over almost anything. One historian said most quarrels resulted from stock, women, and liquor, singly or in combination. Add to that, covetousness for land, and the prospect for friction was compounded.

Since gold was not found in the Wallowa Valley, Joseph's country was bypassed by the miners. Deep canyons and high mountains isolated the area from farmers. But by 1871, white stockmen were poised to grasp the Wallowa meadows. Responsive to this pressure, some newspapermen and certain Oregon officials, such as Governor Leonard A. Grover, began agitating for the removal of an Indian barrier to progress. Encouraged by this propaganda, bold cattlemen began driving their herds into the valley. Joseph lodged a protest with the Bureau of Indian Affairs, whereupon T. B. Odeneal, Indian Superintendent of Oregon, and Indian Agent John B. Monteith of Lapwai were appointed to investigate. They held a meeting with the stockmen and Indians in Wallowa in August, 1872.

Predisposed to recommend the removal of the Nez Perces, these men discovered that the land was not particularly arable, owing to high elevation. Late spring and early fall frosts precluded the evolution of a fruited plain under any auspices. Hence, the committee recommended that the upper Wallowa Valley, the lake, and the adjacent mountains be set aside permanently as a hunting reserve for the whole Nez Perce tribe. The report further advised that white settlers should be compensated for improvements and removed at government expense. This proposal was in the nature of a compromise. Still, it was reasonable in the circumstances. Therefore, the Indian Bureau approved the report and forwarded it to Washington, D.C.

An executive order was signed by President Ulysses S. Grant on June 16, 1873. It reserved a tract of 1,425 square miles, but unfortunately the boundaries of the reserve granted did not conform with those recommended by the committee or claimed by Joseph. All parties involved were dissatisfied with the new reservation. Even if allowances are made for the lack of accurate maps, the fact remains that the Indian Bureau was responsible for a serious blunder.

Agent Monteith did his best to salvage the reserve, but it was not enough. The new boundaries relegated the Nez Perces to a small and less productive part of their country, while confirming the settlers' right to occupy the bottom lands on the Wallowa River. Joseph requested the privilege of taking his case to Washington, but Monteith denied this request.

Meanwhile, in June, 1875, the Indian Bureau had the executive order rescinded, thereby restoring the issue to status quo; that is, the Wallowa country was again opened to homesteading in spite of the Nez Perce claims. Had Joseph been allowed to present the matter at national headquarters at that time, it is likely that the Nez Perces would be dwelling in part of the Wallowa Valley today. The rejection and the rescinding of the executive order of 1873 created an impasse, and the old homesteaders remained and new ones pressed in. Continuing tension in the Wallowa area required the presence of military troops to maintain a truce. This provided a market for the settlers' hay, but no advantages for the Indians were visible. After the commission rendered its verdict, the Nez Perces were on the defensive. Any awkward move would be reported to Monteith.

Thirteen years of controversy had produced a chronic Indian problem, but unlike many others, the Nez Perce situation was openly acknowledged. In rejecting the government offers, the chiefs did not become sullen and mute; instead, they were active, persistent, and articulate. Occasionally a sagacious white man would champion their cause. One such person was A. L. Lindsley, of Portland, Oregon, who wrote a letter to General O. O. Howard on January 9, 1876, that admirably assessed the legal and moral merits of the case. He wrote:

> The original owners of the Wallowa Valley and the region around it are the Nez Perces. Their title has never been rightfully extinguished. In fact, the fair construction of treaty stipulations confirms the Indian title. . . . The treaty of 1863 was not adopted by the Nez Perce Tribe, but by a part only. . . . Several bands continued to protest against it and would not accept its proffered benefits. . . . With keen logic and rude diplomacy they pleaded their cause in several interviews. . . . The Government is bound by its own engagement to fulfill the original Treaty, until it can procure an honorable discharge from its obligations.[16]

Lindsley urged the appointment of a high official commission composed of qualified men who would solve the problems by wise and patient management. He warned General Howard that an attempt to force the bands upon the existing reservation would fail and cause bloodshed as in the Modoc War.

On January 8, 1876, General Howard received a

comprehensive report from Major Henry Clay Wood, entitled *Joseph and His Land Claims* or *Status of Young Joseph and His Band of Nez Perce Indians*. Wood's account was full, clear, and nonpartisan in nature. His judgment regarding this principal issue was unequivocal:

> The nontreaty Nez Perces cannot in law be regarded as bound by the treaty of 1863; and in so far as it attempts to deprive them of a right to occupancy of any land its provisions are null and void. The extinguishment of their title of occupancy contemplated by this treaty is imperfect and incomplete. . . .[17]

Major Wood did not suggest that Joseph's band had exclusive ownership; they simply held their portion of a tenancy in common. This right could only be extinguished with their full and free consent, or by a just and necessary war. Thus, Major Wood went on record in favor of negotiations that recognized the Nez Perce land claims as valid. Subsequently, in a second report, Wood stated that Joseph should be placed on a reservation "if the settlement be amicably effected," but added, "Until Joseph commits some overt act of hostility, force should not be used to put him on any reservation."[18] Although Wood's appraisal of the situation was both fair and realistic, the Nez Perce position became increasingly untenable. In these circumstances, their status could be placed in jeopardy by any incident.

In April of 1876, two settlers named McNall and Findley entered a Nez Perce hunting camp and accused one Wilhautyah of stealing their horses. The Indian denied the charge and, when grabbed by McNall, effectively defended himself. For so doing he was shot by Findley. Later the men found their horses, but Monteith failed to redress the Nez Perce grievance.

In September, 1876, tension mounted to such a degree that Joseph mobilized his people, occupied a strategic position on a high bluff, and challenged the aggressors to settle the issue. A forced march of eighty-eight miles in twenty-five hours brought Lieutenant Albert Gallatin Forse and his company to the valley in time to prevent a clash. Lieutenant Forse was impressed by the sportsmanship, confidence, and disposition of the Nez Perces. He reported that "Joseph could have fallen upon the settlers in detail, killing them and destroying their property. . . . An enemy could not approach him without being under his fire for the distance of more than a half-mile."[19] The significance of Joseph's tribal guardianship was to be appreciated nine months later.

Although a conflict was averted, the impasse persisted, and because of the imminent danger of hostilities action was taken in Washington. On October 3, 1876, Zachary Chandler, Secretary of the Interior, appointed a commission to visit the Nez Perces and adjust the difficulties existing between them and the settlers. Three members of this committee were D. H. Jerome of Michigan, A. C. Barstow of Rhode Island, and William Stickney of Washington, D.C. The trio was characterized by Mrs. John B. Monteith as "excellent men . . . all kings of finance, but with not a speck of Indian sense, experience, or knowledge."[20] The other commissioners were General Oliver O. Howard and Major Wood, both well acquainted with the problem,[21] and both in favor of the Nez Perce claim to Wallowa. Major Wood's views had been documented and were well known. General Howard had made it clear that the rescinding of the presidential order of 1873 had been unfair to the Nez Perces. In his report of 1875 he wrote, "I think it is a great mistake to take from Joseph and his band of Nez Perces Indians that valley . . . and possibly Congress can be induced to let these really peaceable Indians have this poor valley for their own."[22]

By mid-November the nontreaty chiefs were at Lapwai to participate in the proceedings that had been arranged. It was soon apparent that the purpose of the council was to bring all nontreaty Indians upon the Lapwai reservation. Major Wood's judicious opinion was discarded in favor of the claim that Old Joseph's acceptance of the Treaty of 1855 "implied the surrender of any specific rights to any *particular* portion of the *whole* reserve which included the Wallowa Valley, only retaining an undivided interest."[23] Young Joseph's claim was still more uncertain in view of the principle of majority decision. Therefore, Joseph should be required to live within the limits of the present reservation. The commissioners' five recommendations were as follows:

1. Leaders of the Dreamer belief should be returned to their agencies forthwith, and suppressed or exiled to the Indian Territory (Oklahoma).

2. Military occupation of the Wallowa Valley should be ordered while the agent effected settlement of Joseph's band on vacant reservation lands.

3. Unless the Nez Perces were willing to settle quietly within a reasonable time, force should be employed to remove them to the reservation.

4. Any Indian depredations, disturbance, or overt acts of hostility would warrant the use of force.

5. Other nontreaty Indians should be similarly treated by the various Indian agencies in the area. The Lapwai Indian agent should be fully instructed to carry into execution these suggestions, relying on the department commander when necessary.[24]

On January 6, 1877, Agent J. B. Monteith received the necessary authority from Indian Commissioner J. Q. Smith to implement the commission's recommendations.[25]

Thus, the Nez Perces were asked to surrender a million acres of land for allotments upon vacant lands in the Lapwai reservations. These lots were the least desirable, and there were only sixty of them, of twenty acres each. The chiefs were courteous, dignified, and good-natured, but unyielding. There were too many Indians and too much livestock to be crowded along the Clearwater reserve. In their view, the commissioners came increasingly under the influence of Agent Monteith. He convinced them of the desirability of changing the nontreaty hunters, stockmen, and Dreamers into farmers, husbandmen and Christians. Eliminating their huge herds, their nomadic habits, and their general independence would be best for all. According to Monteith, the nontreaty Indians ridiculed the steady habits of reservation Nez Perces and extolled the merits of their own more carefree lives.

In such curt manner the commissioners arbitrarily vested the power to determine the destiny of several thousand souls in the hands of an Indian agent who had lost the confidence of the nontreaty people. Actually, by this time many Lapwai Nez Perces were dubious about receiving the nontreaty Indians. They agreed that the reservation would be too crowded.

The Year of Decision, 1877

Since the commission had specified a reasonable time, it was assumed that the moves would be made in 1877. Early in January the Department of Interior issued instructions to effect the removals. On January 13, General Howard was directed by General William Tecumseh Sherman to occupy the Wallowa country, which had been intermittently policed for three years.

On January 6, 1877, in pursuance of his instructions, Agent Monteith sent an embassy of four Nez Perce leaders, friends of Joseph, notifying the chiefs that it was the wish and purpose of the government for them to come to the reservation by April 1. During the second day of deliberation, Joseph spoke as follows: "I have been talking to the whites many years about the land in question, and it is strange they cannot understand me; the country they claim belonged to my father, and when he died, it was given to me and my people, and I will not leave it until I am compelled to."[26]

On March 17, 1877, Joseph's brother Ollokot called upon Monteith at Lapwai. The subchief affirmed that he was inclined toward a peaceful solution, saying, "I have eyes and a heart, and can see and understand for myself that if we fight we would have to leave all and go into the mountains. I love my wife and children and could not leave them."[27] Ollokot then persuaded Monteith to arrange a final council with General Howard at Lapwai. In the meantime, before Howard moved from Walla Walla he received a direct request from Joseph for an interview at Walla Walla. This was granted, and on April 21, Joseph's brother Ollokot and others met the general. Ollokot, speaking for Joseph, affirmed their peaceful intentions and requested another general meeting at Lapwai in May. Howard agreed to meet all of the nontreaty chiefs in twelve days, and the Nez Perce delegates went away satisfied.

The final council was convened at Lapwai on May 3, with General Howard in charge. Others present included Monteith, Whitman, Chiefs Joseph, Ollokot, White Bird, Toohoolhoolzote, Looking Glass, Hohtalekin, and Hush-hush-cute, and lesser leaders belonging to each band. The chiefs came in an attitude of leisure, answering every salutation in kind and exhibiting good will. They wanted a repetition of the November hearing, because they felt that their case had not been properly understood by the commissioners at that council.

It was soon obvious that Howard was there as a general. His commissioner mantle was only partly upon him. In a letter to Colonel J. C. Kelton, Howard described the duality of his role in this way: "If it was not for exercising great carefulness, I could make short work of the matter given me in charge."[28] Howard's inclination can be appreciated by anyone who reads the newspaper editorials that urged a display of strength.[29] Yet, in allowing the council to convene, he had obviously granted an opportunity for the presentation of grievances. Joseph seized every occasion to present his problem: there were too many people to live in one place; an Indian should not be confined upon a small spot of earth; his claim to the Wallowa country was incontestable. Joseph was a fair, friendly, and eloquent man, and everyone agreed that "the serious and feeling manner in which he uttered these sentiments was impressive."[30] However, Howard's demeanor disclosed that, in his view, the time for diplomatic consideration had passed. As Howard's restlessness became apparent, a chief of another temper tried a different approach. Toohoolhoolzote, a medicine man, challenged Howard's right to enforce the order of removal or interfere in any way with his clan's way of life. He asked provocative questions about the author of creation, the origin of human species, and the right of one to coerce another. Howard described him as a "cross-grained old growler" and blamed the chiefs for allowing him to speak. Howard's version of a part of the discussion follows:

> The agent says very pleasantly: "The law is, you must come to the reservation; the law is made in Washington. We don't make it."
> To other similar remarks the old Dreamer replied fiercely: "We never have made a trade. Part of the Indians gave up their land. I never did. The earth is part of my body, and I never gave up the earth."
> I replied: "You know very well that the government has set apart a reservation, and that the Indians must go upon it. If an Indian becomes a citizen, like old Timothy of Alpowa, he can have land like any other citizen outside, but he has to leave his tribe,

and take land precisely as a white man does. The government has set apart this large reservation for you and your children, that you may live in peace, and prosper."

The rough old fellow, in his most provoking tone, said something in a short sentence, looking fiercely at me.

The interpreter quickly says: He demands, "What person pretends to divide the land, and put me on it?"

In the most decided voice I said: "I am the man. I stand here for the President, and there is no spirit good or bad that will hinder me. My orders are plain, and will be executed. I hoped that the Indians had good sense enough to make me their friend, and not their enemy."[31]

The altercation continued, and Howard had the old chief placed in the guardhouse. In justification he stated, "My conduct was summary, it is true, but I knew that it was hopeless to get the Indians to agree to anything so long as they could keep this old Dreamer on the lead and defy the agents of the government. . . ."[32] The Nez Perce historians had their own interpretation of the incident. Yellow Wolf affirms that Toohoolhoolzote said, "You have brought a rifle to a peace council. If you mean but thirty suns for gathering our stock, yes. We will have to fight."

Still, he was only speaking for himself. None of the chiefs intended to fight. All were in agreement with Joseph's analogy, "We were like deer. They were like grizzly bears. . . . If I should fight the whites I would lose all. No man in the world would take all his property and burn it in a fire. So it is with me."[33] The chiefs were offended by Howard's haughty tone and the thirty-day ultimatum. From their viewpoint, several months were needed for the task Howard assigned to them. However, Monteith argued that "if he [Joseph] is allowed to have his own way at this time, it will only make him more stubborn in the future."[34] Howard was governed by this reasoning, and yet he must have realized that an arbitrary course in the circumstances was pregnant with danger.[35]

An Agreement Is Reached

The chiefs requested the release of Toohoolhoolzote, and it was granted. They also agreed to examine the vacant lands on the reservation. Howard led the delegation over the areas available, and a plan of distribution was evolved. Joseph would locate his band on the upper Clearwater; White Bird agreed to go on the Clearwater above Kamiah; Hush-hush-cute would settle on the Clearwater just above the agency; Looking Glass would return to his place between the forks of the Clearwater. Toohoolhoolzote missed the tour, and he was left to sulk awhile. However, his people were closely associated with White Bird's band.

After the excursion, the chiefs met for a final interview at the agency on May 14. In the meantime, Captain Trimble's company of First Cavalry had arrived at Lapwai, and reports of the approach of Whipple's and Winters' companies gave Nez Perce acceptance a sense of urgency. Accordingly, an agreement was reached. It was entered in good faith, but the element of haste made it quite unpalatable. However, their word had been given, and, since every chief except Toohoolhoolzote was opposed to war, they returned to their ancestral homelands to gather their stock and lodges.

4. ON THE WARPATH

In the foregoing chapters the general history and essential background of the Nez Perce people have been delineated. The stage has been set for a consideration of the specific causes that produced the imbroglio of 1877. Every war has its major and minor causes. As explained, the chief cause of the Nez Perce War arose from the friction inherent in the quite sudden mixing of two races possessing different cultures. Then, there was the inevitable violation of treaties by miners and others, usually with the support of government officials. This policy forced the nontreaty Nez Perces into a position that they felt was justified by neither law nor morals. They had been uniformly friendly and cooperative; indeed, it has been claimed that they had shed no Caucasian blood before June, 1877. While this claim may not be absolutely true, it is certain that no offense had been committed by a whole tribe, or even a clan.[1] Considering the tensions that resulted from the invasion of their domain, it is fair to say that their self-restraint and general peacefulness were commendable. Conversely, it should be remembered that miners were well-armed, resolute, desperate men. Indeed, many were veterans from other Indian frontiers and the Civil

War. In dealing with Indians, most frontiersmen were quite determined to have their own way.

The Nez Perce Round-up

Upon the adjournment of the Lapwai sessions in mid-May, the nontreaty Indians returned to their "reservations" to gather their livestock and move to the Lapwai reservation. One can only imagine their feelings as they moved over their domains in unaccustomed haste. Their search for livestock took them upon the higher parks of the Wallowas. Their more-than-half-wild animals, long accustomed to an open range, were extremely elusive, and hundreds escaped the round-up net. The dissatisfaction of the Nez Perces at leaving their land was intensified as they passed seasonal campgrounds and ancestral graves, in this search.

Limited to what pack animals and travois could carry, the Indians were forced to abandon much household and ranch equipment, along with all permanent improvements. How the chiefs induced their tribesmen to yield to these matters can only be surmised. It must be remembered that the right of each individual to pursue his own course was inviolable. The chiefs could not coerce a person, and yet the clansmen agreed to the moving. At the Snake River a watery ordeal confronted them. The mighty Snake was at flood tide, several rods deep and two hundred yards wide. The Salmon River was smaller, less treacherous, but still formidable. The crossings were difficult. Tight rafts were made from skins, and horsemen towed them across, ferrying over the helpless people and the duffle. Able-bodied men and women fended for themselves, and no lives were lost. The range horses were driven into the stream, but hundreds stampeded back to the old ranges and were never recovered by the Indians.[2]

A Fatal Pause

By early June the various clans had met at an ancient gathering place called Tepahlewam, at the head of Rocky Canyon near Tolo Lake. Here the people basked in the sun, curried and adorned their favorite horses, and gaily paraded about the encampment. At night there were spirited discussions by the elders, and dancing for the youths. Preparations for the final move were also being made. Joseph and Ollokot were on the opposite side of the Salmon River butchering cattle, while women were gathering and drying cowish roots. The wife of one Haymoon Moxmox (Yellow Grizzly Bear) had her supply on a canvas when a mishap occurred. A procession of parading horsemen came by, and the last horse, double-ridden by two young men, got out of hand and stepped on the bulbs. The husband rebuked the youths roughly. "See what you do! Playing brave, you ride over my woman's hard-worked food! If you so brave, why you not go kill the white man who killed your father, Eagle Robe?"[3] This barbed taunt struck Wahlitits to the core. Forgetting his promise to his dying father not to avenge his death, he answered, "You will be sorry for your words." Grizzly Bear had goaded a superb runner, swimmer, and horseman. Wahlitits possessed indomitable courage and skill. In fact, he was an idol to many Nez Perce youth.

After brooding over the insult and having drunk too much whisky, Wahlitits became impassioned. At dawn the next day, June 13, he and his cousins, Sarpsis Ilppilp and Swan Necklace, left the camp. Swan Necklace was practically kidnapped, since he did not know the purpose of the mission; it was intended that he should hold the horses. Wahlitits and Sarpsis went raiding upon their own responsibility, as by Nez Perce custom they had a right to do. Their destination was the scene of Eagle Robe's murder, on the Salmon River; their intended victim was Larry Ott, the murderer. "But that worthy, taking alarm, had fled to the Florence mines where he was later seen garbed as a Chinaman and panning gold with them. Balked thus of their prey, they rode up Slate Creek determined to pay their respects to Richard Devine."[4] This settler had always had an implacable hatred of Indians. He had wantonly killed a cripple named Da-Koopin, and this deed rankled in many Nez Perce spirits. The trio surprised him in his house and shot him. They appropriated his rifle, ammunition, and a fine horse. On the morning of June 14, they killed another Indian-hater named Henry Elfers. Their next victims were Robert Bland and Henry Beckroge. Samuel Benedict, who had slain a drunken Indian in 1875, was wounded. People in other Salmon River ranches and at Benedict's store were terrorized before the warriors returned to camp. Swan Necklace entered the camp and informed the people of the crimes, while the two others held aloof at a point called Round Willows to avoid casting guilt upon the tribe as a whole. They reasoned that if recruits joined them at a distance, that was another matter.

The elders had been holding informal councils since occupying the Tepahlewam campsite on June 3, and a session was in progress when Swan Necklace returned from the Wahlitits-Sarpsis raid on the night of June 14. The council lacked representation, since the best warriors were not there and Joseph and Ollokot were still absent. They were discussing the usual question: Should they fight or not fight? Old Rainbow advised against war: "A small bunch of Indians yourselves, you are hardly strong enough to put up a war against the whites. You cannot make any kind of fight with only rifles against so many whites with big guns. Wait until summer comes. . . . Then we shall have a big council of all the tribes. We shall then find out what to do."[5]

At this juncture someone shouted: "You poor people

are holding council for nothing. Three young men have come . . . bringing horses belonging to a white settler they killed yesterday sun! It will have to be war!"[6]

Mid-June Madness

Reactions were various. Chief White Bird kept his own counsel, but he was against any demonstration. However, it is said that Big Dawn and Two Moons were elated, and rode through the camp appealing for able-bodied supporters for the rebels. Their appeals were not in vain. On the morning of June 16, sixteen young men and Yellow Bull, the father of Sarpsis, joined the two avengers at Round Willows. These men were all ready for action, and a second foray was launched. Any restraints they may have had evaporated after they secured a barrel of whisky at Benedict's store-saloon on lower White Bird Creek. The details of another dozen atrocities committed during the next two days are horrible. Only the names of those murdered need to be mentioned here: Harry Mason, for blacksnake whipping two unarmed Indians; Samuel Benedict (wounded on the 14th), for killing an Indian, wounding two more, cheating, and selling whisky to Indians; August Bacon, for unknown reasons. J. J. Manuel was wounded and his wife probably died in their home, which was burned. Others known to have died as a result of this raid were James Baker, William Osborne, and French Frank.

Disagreement prevails concerning the number of victims who fell before the raiders. General Howard lists fourteen, while James W. Poe makes the count fifteen, and Arthur Chapman says there were twenty-two. McWhorter has stressed the point that the carnage wrought should be balanced against twenty-four years of murdering and thieving by gold seekers and cattlemen.

It was a bloody trail and no extenuation can be offered, except perhaps that of the special frenzy induced by whisky. The expeditions were primitive, punitive ones, and the angry men lost much discrimination because of the heavy drinking. Their minds befuddled by alcohol, the Indians sought primitive justice, a life for a life, remembering tribal records of thirty Nez Perces murdered by white men. Sober reflection would have persuaded them that they were taking a course that would array all men against them and might bring inevitable ruin to the entire tribe.

Surely the willful raiders deserve to be censured, but they should also be understood. They were disconsolate, homeless, and desperate. From the beginning of time, angry, distraught men have attempted to solve complex problems by recourse to summary acts. These Nez Perce youths were not degenerates; men of their fire are called patriots when their causes succeed. Inevitably, when a combination of pressures and influences brings the status of a liberty-loving people into jeopardy, an explosive situation evolves.

Chief Joseph's Dilemma

Neither of the White Bird Canyon raids stemmed from tribal action taken in the Tepahlewam camp. They were not inspired by tribal councils, but were rather the acts of hotheaded individuals. All but one of these were members of White Bird's band, and they sought revenge upon settlers who had injured them. After the second raid the avengers entered White Bird's camp and made announcements like this: "General Howard spoke of the rifle in a peace council. He made a prisoner of our speaker, Chief Toohoolhoolzote. We will stir up a fight for him."[7] General Howard states that horses and other trophies of the raids were displayed and an impression was created that there was plenty of booty for everyone if courage and effort were put forth.

When the avenging parties were at work, Joseph and

Ollokot were beyond the Salmon River butchering beef. Later, when the camp was in turmoil over the bad news, Joseph was preoccupied by the birth of a child in his family. Since his wife was separated from the main camp, the full impact of events bypassed him.

When he learned what had happened, the tribesmen were in motion. Some headed for the Clearwater, their original objective, but hasty consultations among the chiefs brought agreement to assemble at a camp called Sapacheap (also Lahmotta), situated at the bottom of White Bird Canyon. This place offered security from surprise attack. By this time, reports of the atrocities had spread over the countryside. Several well-meaning white friends were bold enough to enter the Tepahlewam camp. J. M. Crooks was one of them, and after assessing the temper of the Indians he felt fortunate in escaping, and his report added tempo to the alarm. On the evening of June 14, a Mount Idaho settler named Lew Day volunteered to ride to Lapwai for military aid. He warned all homesteaders en route to seek protection in the settlements. In so doing some of them encountered belligerent Indians. Four of them were killed, including Day, and several were wounded.

After June 14, the nontreaty Nez Perces were destined to have no rest for many months. Joseph's clan, slower to respond to the excitement, was fired upon by fleeting attackers that night. The next morning, Joseph decided to join the others.[8] Had he been like Chief Lawyer, he would have hastened to Lapwai and placed the blame on a score of heads and one tribe, and pleaded for a military escort to his assigned place on the reservation. Instead, he led his people to White Bird Creek and waited with the other clans. The initiative now rested in other hands. Would General Howard send delegates or troops? Not knowing, the chiefs were restless, although none wanted war.

In 1879, Joseph described his own dilemma:

I would have given my own life if I could have undone the killing of white men by my people. I blame my young men and I blame the white man. . . . My friends among the white men have blamed me for the war. I am not to blame. When my young men began the killing my heart was hurt. Although I did not justify them, I remembered all the insults I had endured, and my blood was on fire. Still I would have taken my people to the buffalo country without fighting, if possible.

I could see no other way to avoid war. We moved over to White Bird Creek, sixteen miles away, and there encamped, intending to collect our stock before leaving; but the soldiers attacked us and the first battle was fought.[9]

Only a peace party from Lapwai could have prevented war. In Howard's view, Joseph, by his posture and past attitude of independence, had become the principal antagonist. Still, if he had courted war, it would have taken place in the Wallowa Valley, not at White Bird Creek. This was the wrong place, the victims were not known to him, the aggressors upon his band were triumphant in Wallowa Valley. The whole project was in conflict with his agreement and judgment. The Indians' grievances were heavy indeed, and they had exhausted all means for an equitable settlement, but the chance of successful resistance against the United States was negligible. These things Joseph understood, but his band was now an integral part of the Nez Perce force. Hence, he and the other chiefs were caught in the coils of an Indian uprising.

There is one point of view that puts a different interpretation upon the behavior of the chiefs. A local historian affirms that all of the promises made at Lapwai were insincere and that every subsequent move was "marked by treason, treachery, and murder."[10] This interpretation rules out the fact that events transpire in the affairs of all societies that are not on schedule. It also casts the chiefs in the role of foolish men.

The camp at the base of White Bird Canyon was well chosen for defense. Backed by the Salmon River, it was flanked by ample ridges and ravines. Buttes served as outposts on higher elevations. The physical conformation made possible an admirable disposition of limited manpower. The environment mutely states, "If they mean to have a war, let it begin here." A trap had been set for invaders.

The Military Takes the Field

Arriving at Lapwai on June 14, General Howard awaited reports of the arrival of the nontreaty Indians at their respective stations on the reservation. Instead, at 4:30 P.M. he received news from reliable Nez Perce and white sources of the first outrages committed upon White Bird settlers. As reports multiplied and rumors spread, Howard dismissed all thought of peace. By 8:00 P.M. he had mounted two companies and started them toward White Bird Canyon. The forces consisted of Companies F and H, First Cavalry, comprising ninety-nine men, under command of Captain David Perry. Howard described him as a soldier elegant in appearance, competent and confident. Other officers included Captain Joel G. Trimble and Lieutenants Edward R. Theller and W. R. Parnell, "four resolute young (married) men."

When the ninety troopers wheeled into formation, General Howard saluted Captain Perry and said, "Good-bye, Colonel. You must not get whipped." "There is no danger of that, Sir."[11] And so it seemed.

After slushing through muddy trails all night, the command paused for breakfast at Cottonwood. By evening the command reached Grangeville, where they planned to rest, having traveled seventy miles in twenty-four hours. But the aroused citizenry, impatient to see the Indians punished, demanded immediate action. Perry unwisely succumbed to their pressure, expecting heavy volunteer support. When the march resumed at 9:00 P.M., only eleven volunteers were on hand.

Shortly after midnight, the command reached the plateau ridge that overlooked White Bird Creek.[12] The men rested here until the dawn of June 17 would facilitate their descent upon the hidden camp three thousand feet below. Perfect quiet prevailed, but the lighting of a pipe produced a "coyote cry" which echoed among the hills, and the Nez Perces were thus alerted. Thereafter, black piercing eyes, aided by a pair of field glasses, searched the ravines for a glimpse of the invaders.

Before 3:00 A.M. the troops were in motion, and within the hour, as they emerged from the draw that fanned out toward the bottom of the canyon, a group of six Indians was observed advancing under a white flag. The military record is ominously silent about this gesture, whereas all Nez Perce historians stress it, and Yellow Wolf wrote that Wettiwetti (known to the whites as John Boyd) was leader of the truce team. He also remembered that Wettiwetti shouted, "What do you people wanted?"[13]

THE CAMPAIGN IN IDAHO

5. THE BATTLE OF WHITE BIRD CANYON

When Captain Perry's column emerged from the ravine upon a benchland, he deployed his troops. Trimble directed the right flank while Theller's force constituted the skirmish line, and the citizens formed on the left. Captain Perry moved forward with an advance patrol, including Scout Arthur Chapman and Trumpeter John Jones. When this unit was hailed by the Indian truce party there was a moment of surprise. Then Chapman fired two shots. Wettiwetti and company backed away unhurt; waiting Nez Perce marksmen returned the fire and Trumpeter Jones was killed by a lucky shot in the first volley.

Nez Perce warriors, generally estimated at about seventy, were distributed along the ridges and buttes that protected the camp. Consequently, at the outset they fired from concealed positions. Their marksmanship proved deadly accurate. Within minutes a dozen soldiers were knocked out of their saddles. Frightened, riderless horses made it difficult for soldiers to control their own mounts. Meanwhile, the warriors advanced on foot and horseback as conditions warranted. Their advantages became increasingly apparent as pressure was applied to the confused troops. The death of the second trumpeter disrupted the communication of orders, and both of Perry's flanks were soon turned. General Howard has described the breakup:

> Two of the citizens at the butte were wounded; then their companions gave way and began to fly. Some of the cavalrymen, too, had already taken the trail to the rear, at a run. Companies were badly broken. Colonel (brevet) Perry endeavored to close all together for mutual protection. . . . Retreat was ordered, and was commenced in pretty good shape.[1]

Far up the ravine, Lieutenant Theller and eighteen men were slain in one place; Theller's watch stopped at 9:00 A.M. Captain Perry and Lieutenant Parnell lived to tell what happened. Perry's descriptions of the events are unequivocal: "The men on the left, seeing the citizens in full retreat and the Indians occupying their places, and the right falling back in obedience to orders, were seized with a panic that was uncontrollable, and then the whole right of the line, seeing the mad rush for horses on the left, also gave way and the panic became general."[2]

Perry made efforts to reform his troops as they scrambled up the ravines, but organized fighting was impossible. At times a given squad would halt and fight until they were flanked out of position. In such fashion the plateau was finally reached, but the Nez Perces persisted. At the end of the day, and of the retreat, Perry wrote this statement: "It was only by the most strenuous efforts of Colonel (brevet) Parnell and myself in organizing a party of twenty-two men that a single officer or man reached camp. The Indians fought us to within four miles of Mount Idaho, and only gave it up on seeing we would not be driven any farther, except at our own gait."[3]

Lieutenant Parnell's report corresponds quite closely with Perry's, and he mentioned an interesting tactic: "In the meantime, the Indians had driven a large herd of loose ponies through our line, and scattered among the ponies were some sixty or seventy warriors who immediately attacked us in the rear, demoralizing the troop, many of whom were recruits."[4]

Assessment of the Battle

Lieutenant Parnell, a veteran of some experience, implies that he expected Perry to resist the assault more effectively. Upon another point his criticism was wholly forthright: "It was bad judgment and certainly not tactical to put the entire command on the line, leaving no reserves whatever in either troop, and, to increase the danger of such a fatal error, the men were in the saddle in an exposed position, while the Indians were on foot, taking cover in the grass and rocks."[5]

Some students of the battle have stressed the mediocrity of military leadership and poor training of the troops. Perhaps this case has been overdrawn. As Parnell stated in another part of his report, "When the officers and enlisted men of our little regular army go out on a campaign, they go in obedience to orders. They go for business strictly, and not a picnic. They go to protect the lives and properties of our sturdy pioneers on our frontier against the most bloodthirsty and relentless foe of our race."[6]

The commanders of frontier posts gave their recruits rigorous training. Below is a description of the routine that appears in a report sent from Fort Ellis by Major James S. Brisbin on October 26, 1877, to the Assistant Adjutant General of the Department of Dakota, St. Paul, Minnesota:

On the 18th of October 1876 I returned to this Post, bringing with me one hundred and sixty three recruits and one hundred and sixty five horses for the Cavalry. The recruits and animals were at once assigned to

Companies, and the work of setting up the men and training the horses began, exercises were had almost daily, until late in the season, and by January the men were pretty well up in the school of the soldier, Company and Battalion drill. Target practice and drills were often held in extremely cold weather, because I believed the services of the Battalion would be required early in the spring, and because soldiers should be taught to ride and shoot at all seasons of the year.

This viewpoint was confirmed by Captain E. S. Farrow in his memorandum on the Battle of White Bird Canyon. He described the magnificent coolness of Perry and the quick cooperation of his good officers, but recognized that the troops had entered a trap that was sprung by skillful warriors.

As already noted, the troops entered White Bird Canyon at a disadvantage, and everything that happened kept them off balance. An artless statement from a soldier told the story: "The Indians were prepared for us and anticipated our arrival, for as we got into the canyon they had us flanked on all sides and we were completely routed. It seemed to be a race of 'God for us all and the devil take the hindmost.' "[7]

The warriors pursued the fleeing troops to a point within sight of Mount Idaho. Then they returned to the battlefield, where they added thirty-six rifles and a number of revolvers to their arsenal. The cavalry was equipped with U.S. Carbine (Springfield) Rifles, Model 1873, of .45 caliber, using center-fire metallic cartridges. The bodies of thirty-four dead soldiers were found. Two wounded soldiers and two wounded volunteers escaped with the command. Contrary to Indian custom, the dead were not stripped, scalped, or mutilated. In fact, no scalps were taken by the Nez Perces at any time during the war, although Howard's Indian scouts did not observe this code.[8]

Battle Casualties

Two Nez Perce warriors, named Chellooyeen and Espouyes, were wounded, and none was killed at White Bird. These few casualties support the conclusion that Indian maneuvering and marksmanship were excellent and that, conversely, the cavalrymen's performance in these respects was poor on this occasion. Perry's forces were not outnumbered, nor were the Indians any better armed. Indeed, some of the seventy warriors who participated in the battle acquired their only weapons from fallen soldiers.[9]

The Battle of White Bird Canyon has been classed with the Little Big Horn as an overwhelming defeat. Actually, the two battles are similar only in respect to an absence of military caution and accessible reserves. The manpower was equally balanced at White Bird.

The burial of the thirty-four soldiers was not attended to until June 27, ten days after the battle. Each was interred where he fell, and the burial ground is far-flung. In 1927, the remains of an unknown soldier were inadvertently uncovered by road builders. Early in September of that year a group of Idaho County citizens established near the site a monument, upon which appears this inscription:

Before you to the westward lies the historic White Bird battle ground of the Nez Perce Indian War in which 34 men gave their lives in service for their country June 17, 1877.
Beneath this shaft lies one of these men who rests where he fell.[10]

6. AFTERMATHS, SKIRMISHES, AND
REPERCUSSIONS

༄༄༄༄༄༄༄༄༄༄༄༄༄༄༄༄༄༄༄༄༄༄༄༄༄༄༄༄༄༄༄༄

The reports of the White Bird battle that stemmed
from Mount Idaho on the evening of June 17 dwarfed
the alarms arising from the raids of the three preceding
days. Accounts were sped by couriers, motivated by
both courage and fear, to Kamiah, Florence, Cottonwood, and Lapwai. From the latter station General
Howard telegraphed the facts and his estimate of the
troops needed to many cantonments. The response was
immediate, and scattered fragments of the army con-
verged upon the battle area as fast as possible. General
Howard cogently summarized the mobilization:

Troops were in motion from Walla Walla . . . Wal-
lula, Vancouver, Stevens, Canby, Townsend, Kla-
math. . . . Soon Lapwai, or Lewiston, draws like a
lodestone; not only these but the artillerymen, on the
wing from Alaska, hurried on to the field without
stopping to breathe; and further help from California
and Arizona; and Boise draws its accessions from all
the forts within the range of three hundred miles, yes,
even from the harbor of San Francisco. So, afterwards, Lewiston calls loud enough to be heard in
Georgia, and the companies of the Second Infantry
came flocking together.[1]

In addition to regular troops, companies of volunteers were organized in Oregon, Washington, and Idaho. Some of them quickly arrived in the field from each of these places. Meanwhile, the settlers on Camas Prairie and its environs were hastening toward Grangeville, Mount Idaho, and Lapwai, or Lewiston. An exceptional service was performed by a friendly Nez Perce woman named Tolo, who rode the twenty-six miles from Grangeville to Florence and returned with twenty-five volunteers. The impetus for a general territorial mobilization was supplied by Governor Mason Brayman.

Governor Brayman's Role in the War

On June 19, when Governor Mason Brayman received notice of the Battle of White Bird Canyon, he sent the following telegram to the War Department: "Disastrous Indian war began no territorial law creating militia only twenty regulars here I want authority to organize mount and provision volunteers at government charge Immediate action necessary."[2] Secretary G. W. McCrary denied Brayman's request for authority to organize militia upon the terms stated, but advised him to request arms and ammunition from General Howard.

Having served as a captain in the Civil War, the governor adopted a military posture. On June 19, he issued General Orders No. 1, designating himself as commander in chief and John Hailey as ordnance officer and quartermaster, and defining the terms governing the organization and operation of volunteer companies. Public response was enthusiastic, and companies were organized in Boise, Idaho City, Silver City, Rocky Bar, Salubria, Emmett, Salmon City, Mount Idaho, Grangeville, and Lewiston. Only the last three were ever to be in the war theater, but that fact was not perceived by the governor, and as a result his conduct became rather ludicrous. Idaho did not have a militia law, and this lack made the governor extremely cautious about assuming the responsibilities inherent in a war situation. Hence, arms were issued with much deliberation and only to the companies nearest Boise. Appeals from citizens in the north were referred to General Howard. As a result, Alonzo Leland, editor of the *Lewiston Teller,* expressed the hope that Howard would drive the hostiles toward Boise "so as to give Milton Kelly and Brayman opportunity to employ our territorial arms, and show their bravery."[3]

Notwithstanding the lack of arms and ammunition, the volunteers in the north accepted their responsibilities, armed themselves, and faithfully reported their activities to the governor. By July 7, the Mount Idaho, Grangeville, and Lewiston companies had formed a regimental organization officered by Colonel Edward McConville, Lieutenant Colonel George Hunter (Dayton, Washington), Major George Shearer, and Adjutant B. F. Morris.[4] L. F. Grover and E. P. Ferry, governors of Oregon and Washington, requested arms and ammunition for volunteers. Upon the recommendation of Colonel Alfred Sully on July 12, 1877, the Secretary of War authorized these governors to raise a combined force of from two to four hundred volunteers. Two hundred volunteers immediately assembled in Washington Territory and were inducted by Howard. After the Clearwater battle they joined Colonel Frank Wheaton's cavalry and marched north to Coeur d'Alene, where they were mustered out.

In late July, when it was apparent that there was no danger in the south, Governor Brayman sent Lieutenant Wilson and twenty Bannock scouts north with rifles and ammunition. Perhaps Brayman is the only governor who ever specifically armed one band of Indians to protect settlers against another tribe.[5] (The *Avant Courier* of Bozeman, Montana, on June 28, 1877, carried an interesting proposal along that line from Captain C. E. S. McDonald. His plan called for twenty thousand Indian troops from various tribes to be used in dealing with any Indian problem.) It should be noted that Governor Brayman secured pledges of neutrality from the Paiute, Bannock, and Shoshoni chiefs when the first word was received of the Nez Perce uprising. Although Brayman's course was criticized in the north, it was praised in the south. Actually, the citizens of these two sections seldom saw eye-to-eye on anything because of Idaho's geographic features, which divided the territory in two parts.

Affairs in the Nez Perce Camp

Although the Nez Perces had won a notable victory at White Bird Canyon, it did little toward settling their minds upon a course of action. A realistic conception of the forces the incident was bound to release upon them would have filled them with dismay. They supposed that their enemies would consist of only such troops as Howard had close at hand. If they could elude or defeat him, they could, if need be, leave his military department and find an asylum in the buffalo country on the Missouri. Even so, time was short, and wisdom would have decreed a quick departure. Instead, they stayed in camp for ten days. Although the rebelling Nez Perces were almost universally referred to as Chief Joseph's band, the White Bird battle did not effectuate a consolidated body, nor did any subsequent engagement produce unity. The group was a confederation governed by a council that might choose different leaders to act as war chiefs from time to time. The war chief was always controlled by the council, and a band might sever its connections at will. The warriors did not agree to any military discipline, although the war chief's wish was generally accepted as a command. The management of a sustained campaign in these circumstances was extremely democratic, and the procedures more bumbling than dictatorial. It seems clear, nevertheless, that Chief Joseph's role in the campaign can be most accurately described as guardian of the entire tribe. He became the symbol of unity, the man of character and prestige, the superlative representative of the cause.

Joseph was considered to be the dominant leader by every officer and civilian who reported the progress of the campaign. General Howard obviously believed that Joseph was war chief. In a telegram to General Irwin McDowell from Mount Idaho, dated June 27, 1877, Howard stated, "Joseph is the fighting chief."[6] All of his memoranda and reports thereafter carried that implication. Besides, it was much easier to mention one name than to list a half-dozen. Newspaper accounts perpetuated this representation, and the more difficult names of his compatriots were neglected. Then, too, the distance, difficulties, and duration of the campaign provided an aura for romance, heroism, and legend. Finally, the fortunes of war removed other chiefs from the surrender scene, and Chief Joseph stood forth at the surrender in solitary majesty.

Surely the decision of the chiefs to cross the Salmon River at Horseshoe Bend and await the arrival of General Howard was in line with Joseph's reluctance to leave the Nez Perce homeland. Yellow Wolf gave to the great warriors Five Wounds and Rainbow credit for the river-crossing plan. The chiefs gave orders: "We will give them the road. Do not bother them. Let them come across the Salmon. We do not have to cross to them. We are not after them. They are after us. If they come to our side, we can fight them if we want."[7] Once over the river, they established camps, rehearsed their retreat plans, and awaited Howard's arrival. The plan was to decoy Howard across the river and retreat into the baffling mountains to the south. This action could suggest at least three alternatives: a trap for Howard in the Seven Devils region, flight to the Weiser River and lower Snake River country, or a recrossing of the Snake into the Wallowa country. The last course would have strengthened Joseph's defensive case and position. The plan actually chosen was to elude Howard in the mountains, circle back and cross the Salmon at Craig's Ferry. Then, while his floundering forces were days behind, the tribe could dash across the Camas Prairie and perhaps leave Idaho and Howard's jurisdiction by way of the Lolo Trail.[8]

General Howard Enters the Campaign

Howard had been mobilizing forces by telegraph, and he decided to enter the field with the forces at hand on June 21. In addition to the Perry command of some sixty men, the general had assembled eight new companies of regular troops and a small company of volunteers from Walla Walla. His entire force consisted of four hundred soldiers and one hundred volunteers and packers.

On June 27, Howard's command reached the Salmon River and established a camp opposite that of the Indians, several miles upstream from White Bird Creek. Captain Tom Page and his Walla Walla volunteers were discharged at this point, but their place was taken by a veteran mountain man, Colonel George Hunter, and his company of volunteers from Dayton, Washington. Howard considered his forces equal to the challenge, but he was at a loss as to procedure.

Nez Perce braves could be seen across the river; indeed, they taunted the soldiers with remarks about coming over for a fight and by flourishing red blankets as an insult to the military emblems.[9] At least that was the interpretation the officers placed upon such gestures, and they were eager for action. But the roaring Salmon presented a formidable barrier, and while ropes, rafts, and boats were assembled Colonel Hunter and two companions swam the river to reconnoiter.

They discovered that since the Nez Perce host had moved into the mountains, a crossing could be made without danger of interference. In a letter to his wife on June 30, a Lapwai agency official named Francis M. Redfield recorded a significant judgment of the situation: "I do not think the Inds will stand a fight— think they will retreat and cross Snake River. There is a prospect that he [Joseph] will not be captured for the next three months."[10]

Howard's forces managed to cross the Salmon on July 1. Lieutenant H. L. Bailey described the hazard involved: "This morning a number of horses and mules were made to swim the river and a famous swim they made of it. Some of them were turned over and over, and others carried away down stream, but I think all got over."[11]

After spending a full day in the crossing, Howard was to discover that the Indians had broken camp, threaded a course among the hills, and reached Craig's Ferry twenty-five miles downstream. The following dawn found them recrossing the Salmon, and by evening they were camped at a place called Aipadass, en route to Camas Prairie. On July 5, Howard arrived at Craig's Ferry, where he learned that the Indians had gained two days in their hide-and-seek strategy. Howard's account of his attempt to cross the Salmon at this point is revealing: "The river here a perfect torrent, lost us our raft, which tumbled down the rapids at a swift rate with all on board, for three or four miles."[12] Despairing of a successful crossing at Craig's Ferry, the command returned to the mouth of White Bird Creek to make the crossing. This experience must have reminded the general that the chiefs had pleaded for an extension of time beyond the June 15 deadline because of flood conditions. On July 8, Howard's command reached Grangeville.

An objective appraisal of Howard's Salmon River

expedition would pronounce it as a complete failure. Meanwhile, the forces Howard had left upon the prairie were having trouble. Before leaving to pursue the Indians across the Salmon River, Howard had provided for the security of the settlers by posting small units of troops and volunteers at Cottonwood, Mount Idaho, and Grangeville. As a special precaution he had ordered Captain Whipple to conduct Chief Looking Glass and his band to Grangeville for safekeeping. A series of skirmishes followed thereafter.

The Attack on the Looking Glass Band

Since Looking Glass's ancestral home was on the Middle Fork of the Clearwater River, his band was not involved in the affair at White Bird Canyon. He had opposed the 1863 reduction of the original reservation and was classed as a malcontent, but after visiting with the migrating Nez Perces at Tepahlewam for several days he and his associates had returned to their homes on the Clearwater before the White Bird raids took place. Looking Glass and his tribesmen were driven into an alignment with the rebels because General Howard, distrusting the neutral posture of Looking Glass, ordered Captain Whipple to take two companies, with Gatling guns, and surprise and arrest the chief and control his Indians.

Whipple's command arrived at the edge of the Nez Perce village at dawn on July 1. A volunteer scout named Dutch Holmes, a squaw man, called for a parley in Nez Perce. Chief Looking Glass sent Peopeo Tholekt to see what was wanted. The soldiers demanded Looking Glass, whereupon Peopeo returned for instructions. The surprised chief directed Peopeo to return with an old man named Kalowet, and tell the white men to go away: "Leave us alone. We are living here peacefully and want no trouble. . . . Do not cross to our side. We ran away from the war."[13]

While the demand for Looking Glass was being renewed, Scout Holmes shot an Indian named Red Heart in the thigh. Other rifles were discharged from the hillside, killing a youth named Black Raven and wounding Peopeo Tholekt and Tahkoopen. The parley, whether with or without the presence of Looking Glass, had lasted long enough to put the suspicious Indians on the alert, and they mounted their horses and fled through the woods. The village, no longer defended, was burned and pillaged, and the garden plots were laid waste by trampling horses. A squaw and her papoose were killed or drowned when riding a swimming horse across the Clearwater River. The troops captured between six and seven hundred horses. In reporting this raid, Howard ruefully stated, "Of course we thus stirred up a new hornet's nest, and did not get Looking Glass and his treacherous companions into custody."[14]

Looking Glass and his band, having taken an honest stand for peace, were rewarded by an attack that left them homeless. Naturally, the members of this band, with few exceptions, hastened to join forces with the belligerents when they reached the Clearwater. Within a few days Captain Whipple was to feel the mounting wrath of Nez Perce warriors caused by the Looking Glass attack.

The Attack on the Rains Party

After raiding Looking Glass's village, Captain Whipple returned to the prairie and entrenched his troops near the Norton house, now Cottonwood. On July 3, he dispatched civilians William Foster and Charles Blewett to scout the Mahoney Creek area for roaming Indians. They encountered an advance guard of the main Indian band just emerging from Salmon River. Indian rifles cracked, and young Blewett was shot, his horse bolting. Foster escaped and returned to Cottonwood. Upon receiving this report, a high-spirited lieutenant named Sevier M. Rains set out with a select detail of ten soldiers and Billy Foster. Their objective was to rescue Blewett, if he were alive, and ascertain the number and disposition of the foe.

When the Rains reconnoitering party was observed by a band of Indians under the leadership of Five Wounds, the warriors gave chase, and the soldiers were subjected to rapid, accurate fire. Several men were struck down in flight, and the horses of the rest became winded. Dismounting, the soldiers sought protection behind rocks, but the outnumbering Nez Perces ended their resistance with a couple of volleys and finally annihilated them. The many shells found upon the defense site were spent ineffectually, as not an Indian was struck in this engagement.[15]

When news of the sad fate of the Rains party reached Whipple, he organized his command and prepared to leave Cottonwood, having learned that the main Nez Perce force had just returned from its decoy journey south of Salmon River. Since Whipple expected Perry to arrive from Lapwai with supplies and ammunition, he went out to meet him on the morning of July 4. By midafternoon, these two officers and their slender forces, including a score of scouts and volunteers, were all reassembled at Cottonwood. Scouts evidently informed them that, while there were still warriors in the area, the principal band had gone by.

Fearful of a sustained attack, Perry and Whipple deployed their forces along lines extending north and south of the house. Rifle pits were constructed at several points. Desultory firing and gestures of attack were made by the warriors while the end of the Indian column disappeared in the distance.

The Randall Party Imbroglio

A more serious foray took place near noon on July 5, when two horsemen were observed approaching Cottonwood from Mount Idaho. Some of the Indians who had been pinning the Cottonwood forces down attempted to intercept these two men. Outrunning their foes, the horsemen arrived at the Norton house and called attention to a party of seventeen volunteers, led by D. B. Randall, behind them. By this time Nez Perce fire was concentrating on this group, and the situation began to resemble the one in which Rains was caught on July 3. Citizen volunteers exhibited great apprehension and appealed to the captains to send out a rescue force. But, in the eyes of the volunteers, the officers, calculating the risks, were more cautious than brave.

The initiative of leadership fell to volunteer George M. Shearer, who, mounting his horse, shouted that "it was a shame and an outrage to allow those men to remain there and perish without an effort being made to save them."[16] After Shearer dashed away, Captain Whipple deployed a line of footmen as skirmishers and started for the group, which was one and one-half miles away. This move encouraged Lieutenant Shelton and a troop of cavalry to enter the action, and, as the combined forces, numbering nearly a hundred, approached, the Indians withdrew from the field. Randall's party was spared extermination by stopping to make a fight of it and by Shearer's valor in producing action. However, Randall and Ben F. Evans were killed, and A. B. Leland, D. H. Houser, and Charley Johnson were wounded. Shearer criticized the officers because of their tardy arrival. In support of Shearer's position, a soldier's voice chimed from the ranks: "Shearer, you need not come to the 7th Cavalry for assistance, as you will not get any."[17] The remark was intended as an additional rebuke to the officers. It is clear that although the prospect of fighting the Nez Perces had thrown many kinds of men together, it had not produced a strong *esprit de corps*.[18] Although the volunteers had given a good account of themselves in these skirmishes, it was a mournful and distraught cavalcade that entered Mount Idaho the next day. In 1931, a monument was erected near Cottonwood in honor of the "Valiant Seventeen."

In the skirmish with the Randall group, the Indians suffered their first fatality of the war in the death of Owyeen. The bold dashes and sorties made by the remarkable Nez Perce warriors kept the cavalry at bay while the Indian cavalcade crossed the prairie, moving toward the forks of the Clearwater River.[19]

The Affair on Misery Hill

While the Rains and Randall scouting parties were being harassed, General Howard emerged from his chase across the Salmon River. By then, the Nez Perce bands had crossed Camas Prairie over their old trails. Volunteers at Mount Idaho were eager to pursue them, and on July 10, a company of eighty, under Colonel McConville, set out for the Clearwater country. Scouts warned them against ambuscades, and McConville deemed it expedient to move along Doty Ridge. When some Indian sharpshooters disclosed themselves, the command hastened to an eminence, where a dark camp was established. Fearing an attack, the volunteers dug trenches and settled down without sufficient food, water, or fuel. During the night they were besieged by Ollokot and his warriors, and "Misery Hill" thus earned its name. The warriors crept close to attack, but no one was hurt. Several horses were killed and forty-eight fell into the Indians' hands. The volunteers answered the Indian fire, and one Sam Hardy fired incessantly. When asked why, he replied, "It's so dark I can't see, but I thought it was a good idea to keep the ark moving."[20]

Two of the volunteers, Luther P. Wilmot and Ben Penney, rode over to Howard's camp, at a place named Walls, to discuss a battle plan. It was proposed that Howard should circle and attack from east of the Clearwater and McConville move in from the west. However, Wilmot got into an altercation with Captain Perry over the latter's management of the White Bird battle and his reluctance to rescue the Randall party. Their tempers flared, the mission failed, and the volunteers left in anger.[21] Since the fire signal Wilmot and McConville had agreed upon was not observed, the volunteers withdrew from Misery Hill and returned to Mount Idaho.

They were frustrated and disgusted over the failure of the military forces to unite and defeat the Indians. The settlers shared their feelings, as an expression by E. B. Whitman attests: "Chief Joseph's magnanimity may save us, and that is all."[22] This and similar items appearing in the *Lewiston Teller* disclose the low morale of the citizens.

7. THE BATTLE OF THE CLEARWATER

Once the main body of Nez Perces struck for the Clearwater River on July 5, it seemed obvious that a union with Looking Glass would soon eventuate. The two groups did in fact join forces upon a campsite just above the junction of the south and middle forks. Estimates of the total number of people, and of the warriors separately, vary considerably. Howard placed the figures at 700 and 325, respectively. He attributed the unusual proportion of fighting men to women, old people, and children to the presence of numerous renegades from other tribes.[1] Historian Francis Haines estimated the warrior strength at 191, but Chief Joseph stated that there were 250 warriors in the Clearwater battle.

The warriors were aware of McConville's volunteers on Misery Hill and gave them as much attention as necessary. They evidently expected Howard also to approach from that quarter. Instead, he crossed the South Fork of the Clearwater well above the camp and came through the woods from the southeast. Critics affirm that the military forces stumbled on the Indians, but in any case, whether by accident or design, the Indians were surprised. The command could not rush the camp, however, because it was at a much lower elevation and there were several transverse ridges and ravines intervening.

Confidently accepting the challenge, the warriors fanned outward and upward to meet and flank the troops. Howard and his officers also had confidence, and his men were ready for action. The command consisted of four hundred regulars and over a hundred scouts, volunteers, and packers. Besides possessing a preponderance of power, Howard's forces were well balanced. Perry, Trimble, Wimple, and Winters were in charge of the cavalry units, and reinforcements of the same class were to be brought in later by Captain Jackson. The Twenty-first Infantry troops were commanded by Burton, Mason, Miles, and Miller. The Fourth Artillery, with Gatling guns and howitzers, was commanded by Bancroft, Fletcher, Morris, Otis, and Rodney. Howard referred to both infantry and artillery as battalions. Surely, here was a formidable force, and Major Keeler of General McDowell's San Francisco staff was on hand to observe the action.

Battle Events on July 11

Howard deployed his forces along an arc line in making the descent, and the Nez Perces countered with much the same pattern in Indian fashion. Mobile and stealthy, they darted between rocks and trees until coming within range of the invaders. This occurred as part of the troops reached a barren plateau. They entrenched, but the area was without water. Comparable action transpired along other ridges and ravines, so that mobility decreased and the battle became one of position. Sharpshooters on both sides fired from recumbent positions; caution characterized the battle during the afternoon, and no advantage was apparent. At the outset the jackass battery of artillery was too high, but, after considerable excavating, the muzzles were lowered and shot began reaching the village.

A diversion occurred when Lieutenant H. L. Bailey and Scout Frank Parker made a dash to the rear to obtain much-needed ammunition. Once the Indians threatened to intercept a pack train, but quick cavalry action saved the goods, if not the lives of two packers. At another time, an alpine spring became an objective for both sides, but neither was able to control it that day. Altogether, the battleground was hotly contested with occasional demonstrations on both sides in attempts to turn flanks and throw the enemy off balance. Such maneuvers were resisted all along the line. Night drew on, and with it renewed exertions were made on both sides toward better fortifying their respective positions.

Howard's presence and energy along the line, together with the spirited direction of veteran officers, kept the men ready. What kept the warriors under equal control? Instead of one supreme chief, each of five tribes had its own leader. In these circumstances, there was much improvising, less coordination, and more chance for dissension. Obviously warrior discipline was more closely related to the volunteer system than to the regular army. This situation, of course, gave flexibility of action to any brave who had the courage and sagacity to exercise it. Yellow Wolf related one of his experiences in this battle. He and others were fighting under Chief Toohoolhoolzote, when they discovered that they were being hemmed in on three sides by the cavalry:

Our chief looked around . . . and gave orders that we go. He was last to leave. We crawled a ways, then ran . . . bullets were singing like bees. . . . Nobody stopped for horses . . . then I came to myself. I missed my horse, and I grew hot with mad! I made myself brave! I turned and ran for my horse—many soldiers

shooting at me. Why, I did not care what I ran into!
I got my horse.

He remembered that his uncle had said, "If we die in
battle it is good. It is good dying for your rights, for
your country."[2]

All Nez Perce men were not so brave; indeed, a considerable number of Indian warriors defected from the
camp that very night, and the resulting discord had a
bearing upon the battle fortunes of the next day.

The Second Day, July 12

At daylight Howard had every available man on the
line. A cavalry charge, led by Miller and Perry and
supported by Otis' howitzer battery and Rodney's company on foot, won the contested spring. Increasing use
of artillery heightened military morale. Pressure of
numbers and general good management produced
gradual gains. The Indian forces could not match the
solidity of Howard's lines. The warriors attempted
to turn the extreme flank, but "going so far to the left
was the cause of their defeat."[3] Continuing thrusts and
sorties kept the Indians on the defensive, and then, in
midafternoon, Jackson's reserve cavalry entered the
fray. McConville's volunteers were also approaching
the battlefield, and this knowledge, together with
increasing disaffection in Nez Perce ranks, lowered
the Indians' morale. Howard described the tactics of
Miller and Rodney as striking across the terrain at an
angle and "rolling up the enemy's line." In the usual
attempt to double back upon their assailants, the
Indians encountered reserves. Howard states, "For a
few minutes there was stubborn resistance at Joseph's
barricades; then his whole line gave way. Immediately
the pursuit was taken up by the whole force, infantry
and artillery . . . and cavalry as soon as they could

saddle and mount. The movement was decisive. The Indians were completely routed."[4]

The battle demonstrated that Howard had mounted a considerable offensive. His command was staffed by two colonels, three majors, twenty-five captains and twenty-eight lieutenants.[5] Although the entire organization was not joined in battle, the impact of depth in strength was brought to bear upon the faltering Nez Perces.

The Indians Withdraw

Howard described how the warriors went tumbling through the woods, over rocks, across ridges and ravines, into the river. The river was no obstacle to the Nez Perces, but the soldiers found it "too deep and rapid . . . to ford, [and] they here waited for the cavalry under Perry. The cavalry worked its way as rapidly as it could . . . and crossed slowly into the Indian camp."[6]

Before the general Nez Perce withdrawal from the firing line, Chief Joseph had assessed the situation and hastened to assume his role as guardian of the village. Yellow Wolf described the menace: "The women, not knowing the warriors were disagreeing, quitting the fight, had no time to pack the camp. Chief Joseph did not reach them soon enough."[7]

Perry's action was decisive until he reached the stream, where he hesitated. For this he was later censured by Howard. Whether his delay was due to an interpretation of orders or to prudent consideration of the hostile sharpshooters beyond the river, the respite enabled Joseph to escape.[8] It was only 5:00 P.M., so the band moved away downstream to the left and established a safe camp on a bluff beyond the mouth of Cottonwood Creek, near present-day Kamiah. Appraising the new situation, Howard allowed his troops to bivouac near the deserted Indian village. It was a shambles from heavy artillery fire, but the tribal treasures of generations were left behind, a considerable reward to the looters.[9]

Although the Indians had not been captured, a battle had been won in that they were driven from the field. The final assault of the troops was described as impressive, and Major Keeler sent a wire to General McDowell, reporting the news of "a most important success. . . . Nothing can surpass the vigor of General Howard's movements and action."[10] The major knew how critical McDowell was becoming as a result of Howard's failure to fulfill his promise wired to San Francisco on June 15 ("Think we shall make short work of it"[11]). Actually, the general's failure to pursue the enemy with vigor and force after driving them from the field on July 12 constitutes his most serious mistake during the campaign.

Releases gave Howard's casualties as thirteen killed and twenty-two wounded. He calculated that Indian casualties included twenty-three killed, about forty wounded, and forty captured. Indian denials of these figures were emphatic. They claimed their casualties were four killed and six wounded.[12]

Discord among the warriors had begun on the night of July 11. Roaring Eagle and others testified later that some argued, "No use fighting when soldiers are not attacking our camp." These sentiments increased and were repeated in council. That there were issues to be settled, there can be no doubt. Should they fight the next day, surrender, return to Wallowa, or seek a new home among the Crows in Montana? The arguments started that night continued informally for three days, and the last course was finally agreed upon in the council on July 15, at Weippe Prairie. Meanwhile, the chiefs feinted and improvised their action and strategy.

Maneuvers around Kamiah

It seemed apparent that the Nez Perces were in no haste to forsake the country. They had waited for pursuers at White Bird, the Salmon, and the Clearwater. Now they marked time again, evidently reasoning, as Yellow Wolf so quaintly stated, "But we were not whipped! Had we been whipped, we could not have escaped from there [Clearwater] with our lives."[13] Surely they took their time in escaping. The rebels here developed an uncanny semaphore signal whereby they allowed Howard's movements to pace them. They called him "General Day after Tomorrow," because of his policy of giving them a two-day lead in the campaign.

On July 13, the Nez Perces crossed the Clearwater in their skin boats and established camp. Howard surveyed their position and failed to pounce upon them. Perhaps he expected an offer of surrender, but, as none came, he ordered McConville's volunteers and Jackson's cavalry to move down the Clearwater, cross at Greer's Ferry, and attempt to blockade the Lolo Trail.[14] This movement was launched at daylight, and it did not escape the chiefs' notice. The Indians produced a flag of truce, and, seeing this, Howard sent an order halting the column.

This gesture toward a parley proved to be a delaying tactic, but before this fact was perceived the camp was struck and the Indian caravan began climbing the mountain toward the Lolo Trail. As the rear guard left the river, it is said, a brave impudently slapped his hand upon his bare buttocks as a gesture of the disdain in which the commanders were held.

Because of the ruse it was midafternoon before Howard's detachment resumed the march to Greer's Ferry. In the meantime the ferryboat had been cut loose and was on a sandbar on the other side of the river.

When Howard was informed of this fact he ordered McConville and Jackson back to Kamiah.[15] On July 13, Howard settled down at Kamiah for a fortnight, attending to dispatches, making plans for the pursuit, and waiting for reinforcements. This exceptional delay was his second mistake, and its consequences were never quite overcome. As the general waited, he reflected upon the state of affairs confronting him. The newspapers had printed inventories of property damage and losses of cattle and horses. There were seventy fatalities and nearly as many wounded. It had already become a rough campaign, and the end was not in sight. Still, it was expedient to evaluate the situation, which Howard did in saying, "The Indians had been stopped in their murders, had been resolutely met everywhere, and driven into position and beaten [Clearwater]; and the vast country [Idaho] was freed from their terrible presence."[16]

Later, in a summary printed in the Portland *Daily Bee Supplement,* November 11, 1877, the general stated that his success at the Clearwater quieted the restlessness among the Cayuses, Spokanes, Coeur d'Alenes, Columbia renegades, and others. "Yet," he said, "the campaign needed to be prolonged, persistent pursuit and final capture to put to rest forever the vain hopes of these dreaming, superstitious nomads." Of course he could not know then that in 1878 he would be involved in the Bannock War, which also had considerable proportions.

Meanwhile, on July 14, the Indians had made a toilsome sixteen-mile journey over the mountain to the Weippe meadows, where they met Chief Red Heart and his band returning from a hunt in the bison country. This band did not join the fleeing Nez Perces. In fact, a number of the Nez Perces returned to Kamiah with Red Heart. Howard took the combined groups captive, and they constituted the forty he mentioned in his report concerning the Clearwater battle.

On July 20, E. C. Watkins, Indian Inspector, sent a significant communication to Indian Commissioner J. Q. Smith. Watkins stated that he had arrested four Nez Perce braves who disobeyed him. He also noted that sixteen Indians came in from Joseph's band and surrendered. Consequently, Howard was forced to deal with the problem of prisoners. He organized a field military commission, appointing Watkins as Judge Advocate. Not sure if he could accept the position, Watkins sought instructions from Smith. In his letter of July 20, Watkins urged that the commission be authorized to sentence Indians guilty of participating in the war to exile in the Indian Territory. He said, "I have threatened this from the start, and I think the fear of being sent so far away has kept some from joining the hostiles."[17]

Watkins' appointment as Judge Advocate was not confirmed, but his suggestion in regard to punishment was endorsed by the commissioner. However, Secretary of War McCrary advised postponing legal action and the ultimate disposition of prisoners until a later date.[18]

A chiefs' council was held at the Weippe camp, in which a definite long-range plan was reached. The combined tribes agreed to cross the Lolo Trail and continue east to the land of the Crow nation. Chiefs Looking Glass and Toohoolhoolzote and the great warriors Rainbow and Five Wounds argued most persuasively for this course. They considered the Crows their brothers, and they argued that their combined strength would be mutually beneficial. Looking Glass, in particular, spoke longingly of the "Old Woman's Country" (Yellowstone River basin) and extolled the loyalty of his former Crow allies who dwelt there. Howard's big guns could not be taken over the rough mountains. Possibly he would not follow at all. Looking Glass would lead the way and take command, if the chiefs assented; and they did. Joseph was definitely reluctant; he did not want to take his people among strangers. Besides, what

were they fighting for if not for their country? He was
in favor of crossing the Lolo Trail but eventually returning when things had settled down. One informant
reported that when Joseph was chided for his attitude
toward the campaign he replied: "This is your fight,
not mine. I will conduct the retreat of the women and
children. It is your task to keep the soldiers away."[19]
Whether this report is true or not, he had already assumed the role of guardian, and the end of the trail
was far away. On the morning of July 16, the nontreaty Nez Perces filed eastward upon one of the rough-
est adventures in military annals.

CROSSING THE BITTERROOT RANGES

8. CROSSING THE LOLO TRAIL

As the Nez Perces turned their faces away from the Clearwater country, they adjusted their minds to the problems before them. They would travel peaceably; no white man would be bothered. Their enemies were only in Idaho. "Montana people are not our enemies. The war we leave here in Idaho."[1] Yellow Wolf thus recorded their viewpoint, and much sorrow and expense might have been spared if this attitude had been understood and accepted by all concerned.

Before starting up the trail, the chiefs assigned five warriors to serve as a rear guard. The precaution proved to be wise, for Howard sent Major Edwin C. Mason and Colonel Edward McConville, with a strong force of cavalry, volunteers, and Indian scouts in hot pursuit. The scouting unit of their command was ambushed in midafternoon of July 17. Three of the friendly Nez Perce scouts were hit, one fatally, and one of the wounded died later. This assault stopped the military company, which returned to Kamiah.

Several of Joseph's braves secretly followed the command back to the Clearwater camp and managed to return with several hundred ponies. Many of these ponies belonged to the fleeing warriors and they followed the trail from instinct.

Once again Howard had been given a lesson in the futility of half measures in dealing with the Indians. Nothing short of a full effort was likely to bring the chiefs down. This must have been in his mind as he planned his moves during the next ten days.

Howard Plans the Campaign

The general had two problems to solve: The Camas Prairie settlements must be protected, and the rebels must be captured. His first plan was to leave a small garrison at Kamiah, take the rest of his force and pick up additional reinforcements assembling at Lewiston, then hasten north and head for Missoula along the Mullan Road. It was a sensible plan because wagons could be used in transporting the infantrymen and supplies. Objections were registered by the Camas Prairie settlers, because Colonel John Green, expected from Boise to protect the settlements, had not yet arrived. In the circumstances, the settlers were afraid that the chiefs might return and find them defenseless. Therefore, this plan was abandoned. Howard waited until Green arrived; then he added McConville's regiment of volunteers to Green's regulars. Next, he organized his infantry and cavalry into right and left columns. Colonel Frank Wheaton went northward to impress any of the "Columbia River renegades" who might be thinking of joining the rebels. There was also a chance that Wheaton might arrive in the Bitterroot Valley before Joseph and thereby block him from one direction. Meanwhile, Howard would follow the Indians along the Lolo Trail. Lolo Pass was the eastern border of the Department of Columbia, but General Sherman's order was to pursue the hostiles regardless of boundary lines.[2] On July 27, several days before he left Kamiah,

Howard telegraphed this message to General McDowell in San Francisco: "Can not troops at Missoula or vicinity detain Joseph till I can strike his rear? . . . My troops will push through rapidly."[3]

The formulation and preparation of these plans consumed ten days. As a result, as the general states, "A fearful newspaper clambor came from the rear, of 'Slow! Slow! No ability; will never catch the Indians!' "[4] These sentiments were taken up by the press of the nation. A faultfinding campaign was launched that was destined to last for three months. In effect, Howard was represented as "a friend of the Indian; a talker, not a fighter; lacking energy, who rested on Sunday— the 'Praying General.' . . ."[5] His character and attitudes were belittled and his excellent record, crowned by heroism at Gettysburg, was forgotten. Friends issued denials of false charges, and details of the records were offered in refutation, but nothing of this sort could stem the tide. The country was upset, the army and the administration were embarrassed, and the attitudes of generals McDowell, Sherman, and Sheridan were not unaffected. Howard explained the delay in this way: "I did attempt to force matters . . . but the disturbed condition in my Department absolutely prevented this. It was too much of a risk to run for either the return of Joseph's or the breaking out of other Indians in the next ten or twelve days. . . ."[6] It seems expedient to point out that Howard's force was partially constituted of infantry. That he was attempting to capture a particularly cunning foe has already been demonstrated. Actually, criticism was not limited to Howard; indeed, the army, the Indian agents, and missionaries were all charged with ignorance, incompetence, and dereliction. In the circumstances, Howard was probably glad to leave Kamiah behind and move into the wilderness of the Lolo Trail!

The column that finally stretched away from Kamiah on July 30 was several miles long. Two days before Howard entered the west end of the Lolo Trail, the Nez Perce band of comparable proportions emerged from the east. The character and history of the trail must next be described.

Description and History of Lolo Trail

The Lolo Trail crosses the Bitterroot Mountains, which separate the Clearwater and Bitterroot water systems. On the western end the trail conforms to the divide that separates the North and Middle (Lochsa) forks of the Clearwater River. Toward the eastern end, it crosses a north-south divide known as Lolo Pass, over seven thousand feet high. Strangely enough, the Continental Divide does not conform to the Bitterroot Range, although it is generally higher and more rugged than the Rocky Mountain cordillera. The length of the Lolo Trail is about 250 miles. It is a tortuous trail in all respects; it tends to follow ridges that are arranged in tandem fashion with intervening canyons. For generations before the arrival of Lewis and Clark, the Lolo had been a hunter's trail, and it was still unchanged in 1877.[7] No labor was expended upon it in Indian times. It threaded through handsome stands of fir, spruce, cedar, and dense undergrowth of brush. The passage was dim, narrow, and twisting. Even Indians were often puzzled in their efforts to follow it.[8]

The Trail was made known to Americans by Lewis and Clark. They toiled and suffered upon it for three weeks, both in going to and in returning from the Pacific Ocean. Their journal entries of September, 1805, and June, 1806, are similar. Clark made the following entries on September 2 and September 15: "This day we passed over emence hils and some of the worst roads that ever horses passed, our horses frequently fell . . . the one which carried my desk, &

small trunk TURNED OVER AND ROLLED DOWN A Mountain for 40 yards and lodged against a tree."[9]

A notation by Meriwether Lewis on June 14, 1806, was in the same vein: "It was with great difficulty that the loaded horses could assend the hills and mountains, the[y] frequently sliped down."[10]

A trail so difficult for horses would be more distressing for men, and Clark's account of their situation on September 19, 1805, near Hungry Creek, confirms this fact: "The men are growing weak and losing flesh very fast; several are afflicted with the dysentery, and eruptions of the skin are very common."[11]

The trail was not improved with the passing decades. Indeed, a Forest Service highway paralleling it was not completed during the nineteenth century, and an adequate highway for the general public was not completed until the early nineteen-sixties.

The Nez Perce Crossing

In crossing the trail in July, 1877, the only advantages the Indians had over Howard's forces lay in their knowledge of the country and their ability to live on the slender resources it afforded. The Nez Perces traveled efficiently, because each family constituted a self-sufficient unit within its respective tribe. Relatives always stayed together, and they blended easily with other clan-united families. A clear division of labor was made; hunters, herders, root- and berry-gatherers—all hands understood their business. The Indians' ability to find and eat roots and bark when game and fish were scarce was also a great advantage. The pursuing soldiers wondered why so many trees were scarred. They did not know that the inner bark and the juices between layers were nourishing to man. Indian lodges were raised and struck with precision that came from much practice. Ponies were packed with similar speed and skill. Nez Perce horses were tough and swift, and they were plentiful. These fleeing red men always managed to have several remounts per person. Their total herd probably exceeded three thousand. They crossed the Lolo Trail between July 16 and July 27 without any particular hardship.

Upon reaching Lolo Creek at a point within an easy day's travel of its confluence with the Bitterroot River, the Indians stopped to rest and hold council. There were hot springs at this place, which they called Nasook Nema (Salmon Creek). It was the place Lewis and Clark had named "Traveler's Rest." At these springs the Indians found two white boys vacationing from their homes in the Bitterroot Valley. Intending to prevent misrepresentation of their peaceful intentions, the Indians took young Pete Matt and William Silverthorn captive, but they escaped that night. Their report created a considerable stir among the citizens in the valley.[12]

Meanwhile, Nez Perce scouts had discovered the presence of soldiers and volunteers in a log barricade designed to block their exit from the canyon. They did not realize that their arrival had been anticipated and that plans and forces had been put in motion to capture them. Since this phase of the campaign is both significant and complicated, it will be treated in a separate chapter.

Howard Crosses the Lolo Trail

Howard's cavalcade left Kamiah on July 30, in a drenching rain. Although considerable preparation for the crossing had been made, it was not an easy one. In fact, Howard's pack train could not have made this journey if the trail had not been widened in many places. This hard work was efficiently performed by a corps of Idaho frontiersmen, under the command of

Captain W. P. Spurgin, Twenty-first Infantry. Before the campaign ended these skilled laborers were dubbed "Spurgin's Skillets" by the troops. Howard's pack train consisted of several strings of mules, each headed by a bell mare. Without this pack train of provisions, Howard's men would have been in no condition to ride, walk, or fight. Howard was satisfied to achieve a daily march of sixteen miles, because so much timber had to be cut away. A few notes from his journal describe the details: "Poor grazing, indeed, here. The only feed consists of dwarf lupine and wire grass. Several mules were exhausted, and some packs of bacon were abandoned by the way."[13]

The commanders were vigilant at all times.[14] At night a campsite was carefully chosen, occupied, and posted. A modicum of shelter for the officers, the cooks, and the packs was provided by tents. A common mess and bonfire helped preserve good relations among the men. The morning schedule started with reveille at three or four o'clock, breakfast at four or five, and march at five or six, according to circumstances. Howard described the reaction to the crossing in one sentence, "None of us will ever forget the now famous Lolo trail, with its sharp-edged, irregular mountains and its endless forests." Then, thinking of his critics, he wrote:

"Didn't the hostile Indians go here?" the reader inquires. Yes; they jammed their ponies through, up the rocks, over, and under, and around the logs, and among the fallen trees, without attempting to cut a limb, leaving blood to mark their path; and abandoned animals, with broken legs, or "played out," or stretched dead by the wayside.

Our guide, Chapman, says, in frontier parlance, "No man living can get so much out of a horse like an Indian can." Had we, for three days, along the Lolo trail, followed closely the hostiles' unmerciful example, we would not then have had ten mules left on their feet fit to carry our sugar, coffee, and hard-bread.[15]

Actually, the Indians appreciated Howard's predicament much better than did the public. They made great fun of the infantrymen, calling them "walk-a-heaps" and "squaw soldiers." Even the cavalryman was at a disadvantage, because his activity was limited to the speed and endurance of one horse. If his horse faltered and failed him, he found a place with the infantry.

In considering these factors, it appears that Howard did very well in crossing the Lolo Trail in nine days. Arriving on August 8 at the log barrier across the mouth of the canyon, Howard learned that the Nez Perces had bypassed the barrier on July 28. He was then briefed upon the events that had transpired there during the past fortnight.

9. AFFAIRS AT FORT FIZZLE AND IN MONTANA

Lolo Creek runs eastward until it unites with the Bitterroot River, which flows north a dozen miles to its point of confluence with the westward-flowing Hellgate River. The united stream, called Clark Fork, flows in a northwesterly direction to the Columbia. Missoula was situated at the junction of the Hellgate and the Bitterroot rivers. Several farming settlements were located up the narrow Bitterroot Valley. Stevensville, near the site of Fort Owen, was also the site of Saint Mary's Mission. Others towns, located upstream at fairly equidistant points of about twenty miles, were Corvallis and Hamilton. The valley pinches off a short distance above Ross Hole. At that point one trail led due south over the Lewis and Clark Trail of 1805, across a divide (Lost Trail or Gibbon Pass), on to the North Fork of the Salmon River; the other trail struck east over the Continental Divide, where it followed Trail Creek into the Big Hole Valley. William Clark and his party followed this course eastward in 1806. Captain Lewis and his larger group went to the Missouri via the shorter Hellgate route. The Hellgate, so named by the Flatheads because it came from the Blackfoot

Indian country to the east, was the portal to the principal trails.

Alternative Routes of Travel

The fleeing Indians were headed for the Buffalo Illahee, which was located in the massive plains region lying between the Upper Missouri and the Lower Yellowstone valleys. From the Bitterroot Valley the Nez Perces could reach their objective by any of several routes. In the interest of safety, considering Canada as their goal, the shortest route from Lolo Creek was down the Bitterroot River to its confluence with the Hellgate River. The trail crossed the river below Missoula and went directly north across the Flathead Reservation and the Tobacco plains toward Canada. Some of the more apprehensive warriors, like White Bird and Red Owl, were in favor of this course. But the chiefs were thinking more about hunting bison than fleeing to Canada from imaginary pursuers. The shortest eastern route to the bison country was north to Missoula, thence eastward upstream along the Hellgate to the mouth of the Big Blackfoot River. Then the trail followed the Blackfoot to Cadotte's Pass, crossed a divide leading to the headwaters of the Dearborn River, and then led to the Sun River, which flowed into the Missouri directly west of the Highwood and Little Belt Mountains. A variant from this trail consisted of following the Little Blackfoot River, crossing at Mullan's Pass, and then going down the Smith River to the Musselshell and Judith Basin country.

Still another route, instead of turning up either the Big or Little Blackfoot rivers, quartered southward to the Deer Lodge River and led to a valley of the same name. From that lush pasture land trails led away in various directions: northeastward toward Helena, southeastward toward Butte, Pipestone Pass, and the Three

Forks area. A disadvantage common to all of these routes except the one leading northward from Missoula was the location of towns and forts within striking distances.

An alternative to all of these was the circuitous Bitterroot–Big Hole route, which veered away to the south, especially when linked with the Snake and Madison rivers and the Clark Fork of the Yellowstone River. This trail looped around and came in at the southeastern end of the bison country. Although this was the longest and hardest route, it was chosen because the friendly Crows could be reached without the prospect of encountering hostile Indians or whites, once the Bitterroot villages were passed.

Indian and white relations in the Bitterroot Valley were similar to those in the Clearwater country. In both places there were reservation and nonreservation Indians and an agency and mission. There were also white settlements and a military post.

The Indian Situation in the Bitterroot Valley

The Bitterroot Valley was part of the ancestral home of the Flatheads. These Indians had a long history of friendly relations with the Nez Perces. The 1831 delegation to Saint Louis was, as was pointed out above, a joint undertaking. Nez Perce bison hunters had passed through this district for about forty years, and they had sometimes wintered here. In fact, one Nez Perce clan of six lodges, led by Lean Elk (Poker Joe) and temporarily residing in the Bitterroot Valley, had recently joined the fleeing Nez Perces.

The Flathead record in dealing with the white man was comparable to that of the Nez Perces up to the White Bird battle. In 1855, their great Chief Victor negotiated a treaty with I. I. Stevens that reserved the Bitterroot Valley above Lolo Creek for his tribe.

In 1872, Secretary of Interior James A. Garfield negotiated another treaty exchanging this reservation in
favor of one called Jocko, farther north and border-
ing upon Flathead Lake. Victor's son, Chief Charlot
(also Charlos and Carlo), refused to either sign the
treaty or move. On this account, the commissioner ignored him and his clan, and elevated Chief Arlee to
the position of head chief.

Chief Charlot and his band were not forced onto
the reservation; they were regarded as civilized, do-
mesticated Indians. They were not disturbed, being
simply allowed to carry on as residents of the valley,
subject to the laws of Montana only. This situation
prevailed until Charlot signed an agreement on November 3, 1889, and the following year his band moved
to Jocko. One wonders whether a similar policy of patience would not have succeeded equally well in the
case of the nontreaty Nez Perces.

Since the treaty Flathead Reservation was located
only forty miles north of Missoula, everyone was greatly concerned about the Flatheads' attitude toward the
runaway Idaho Indians.

The Military Situation in Western Montana

Montana settlers in this area had enjoyed peaceful
relations with the Flatheads. Their experiences with
the Nez Perces were equally satisfactory; as seasonal
visitors, the Nez Perces had been well behaved, and
their trade was welcome. Indeed, many settlers knew
various hunters personally and counted them as friends.
These sentiments were reciprocated by the Nez Perces,
who therefore approached the valley with a friendly
attitude. The issue at stake was whether the judgment
and justice of the understanding settlers would with-
stand the alarm and pressure of the poorly informed
and less well-disposed citizens in Missoula, Deer Lodge,
Butte, Helena, and Virginia City.

Extensive campaigns against the Dakota and Sioux tribes in eastern Montana had brought a half-dozen forts into being in that area. However, the placid character of Indian relations in the west had not required the development of comparable centers of protection. This fact was set forth in the *Helena Herald* on June 28, 1877, a short time after the news of White Bird battle arrived:

There is a large scope of country from Walla Walla to Fort Shaw that has been completely ignored by the military arm of the government. It contains as great numbers of Indians as any other part of Montana and in case of an uprising, such as has frequently occurred among normally peaceful Indians in this country, the inhabitants would be completely at the mercy of the rifle and scalping knife.

It is true, however, that two forts had been established west of the Missouri River. Fort Shaw was erected on the Sun River in 1867, and three years later Fort Baker was built eighteen miles north of White Sulphur Springs.

In December, 1875, plans were made for the establishment of a fort near Missoula; and on June 7, 1877, the erection of Fort Missoula was started. Captain Charles C. Rawn and a detachment of the Seventh Regiment United States Infantry from Fort Shaw were assigned to the new post. Construction was well started when Rawn received information that the Idaho hostiles had started toward Montana on the Lolo Trail. Accordingly he directed Lieutenant Francis Woodridge and four enlisted men to reconnoiter the eastern end of the trail and ascertain the Indians' position. Two days later, Rawn dispatched Lieutenant C. A. Coolidge, a soldier, and several civilian volunteers to follow and support Woodridge. The two details met on the twenty-second, and Woodridge had not seen the Nez Perces, although he thought he had penetrated the

Clearwater drainage. That very day, however, a half-breed Nez Perce named John Hill told them that the tribe was indeed moving eastward. This information was sent to Fort Missoula by a courier who arrived late that night.

Captain Rawn telegraphed the news to his superiors and was ordered to intercept the Indians and prevent them from entering the valley. He assembled a small force of thirty soldiers and left for Lolo Creek on July 25. The captain selected a narrow place in Lolo Canyon and erected a breastwork of logs across the canyon. Although few in number, Rawn's command was ready to do its duty.

In addition to the army unit, there was volunteer activity in Montana. However, since, as in Idaho, there was not a formal militia system, this important group will be described as it enters the action rather than as a formal element such as the Indians, settlers, and military factors. The role of Colonel John Gibbon's command will also be discussed later.

The Nez Perces, then, came to Montana with peaceful motives, but for five weeks the residents of Montana had been reading about terrible atrocities and bloodthirsty invincible warriors.

Responses to the Nez Perce Entrance

The Nez Perce entrance into Montana was viewed by many as an invasion. Montana newspapers had been publishing detailed accounts of the Nez Perce uprising from the outset. Indeed, the most complete reports of the war from beginning to end appeared in the *Helena Weekly Independent,* the *Helena Daily Herald,* the Bozeman *Times,* the Butte *Miner,* the *New Northwest,* and the *Avant Courier.*

When the news arrived that the Nez Perces had

started east upon the Lolo Trail, a high note of alarm was sounded. The shortage of federal forces in the west and the lack of any state militia were pointed out. The dangers of a war on the Idaho scale, or greater, were set forth in a vivid fashion. An appeal for action accompanied every report printed concerning the Nez Perce War. Inevitably, every official charged with responsibility for the public safety went into action, and measures were taken on several fronts simultaneously.

Peter Ronan was the Indian agent on the Flathead Reservation at Jocko, Montana. Newspaper editorials suggesting that his charges might join the Nez Perces caused him to take every precaution. He first secured pledges from the reservation chiefs, Arlee, Michelle, and Enos, to keep their young men under firm control. Then he hastened to the Bitterroot Valley and obtained a similar promise from Chief Charlot. Indeed, Ronan reports, "Upon the approach of the Nez Perces, Charlo sent out a band of his warriors to cooperate with the whites, his son commanding."[1] Ronan's measures, together with the peaceable disposition of the chiefs, prevented the Flatheads from giving any aid or comfort to the Nez Perces. The agent boasted that "not a single Indian of the above mentioned tribes is in the hostile camp."[2] Not only did the Flatheads keep their young men under control, they also kept their pony herd intact. A letter to Governor Potts from W. B. Harlan, Stevensville, explains how this was possible: "The Flatheads . . . are herding their horses close to the mountains, probably as a precaution against a raid of the Nez Perce."[3]

Of course this strict role of neutrality may not have satisfied anyone. Yellow Wolf expressed both disillusionment and unbelief: "They were helping the soldiers. Always friends before, we now got no help from them, the Flatheads. No help any time."[4]

Actually, Chief Charlot and a delegation of twenty

warriors did present themselves to Captain Rawn at Fort Fizzle. But it was understood they would not fight. They wore white turbans on their heads as a mark of identification, in case a mix-up occurred. The Nez Perces knew these white headcloths meant, "Don't hurt me!"

On July 13, the day after the Battle of the Clearwater, Governor B. F. Potts of Montana sent the following telegram to President R. B. Hayes: "The Idaho Indians appear to be heading for western Montana. I respectfully ask authority to raise five hundred volunteers to meet the Indians soon as they reach our border the situation is critical." Secretary McCrary sent Potts a reassuring reply to the effect that General Sheridan, with headquarters in Chicago, was watching the campaign and that there were sufficient regular army forces to protect the lives and property of the people. General Alfred Terry, who was in charge of the Department of Dakota, which embraced Montana, concurred with the secretary and Sheridan. However, their opinion was not held so firmly by generals Sherman and McDowell.

Indeed, McDowell sent Potts a message from San Francisco on July 23, which was printed in the *Helena Weekly Independent* on July 26. The governor was asked what he could do to help arrest or detain the hostiles. Potts wired McDowell to the effect that he would arm the people to protect their homes, but lacking authority to organize a militia he was unable to arrest and detain Joseph.

A man of action, the governor went to Missoula immediately, and in response to the excitement of the people and the urgency of the situation, he issued a call for volunteers on July 26. The proclamation declared that Montana was invaded by hostile Indians from Idaho, and that fewer than fifty United States soldiers were on hand to oppose them. The organized volunteer militia of Missoula and Deer Lodge were therefore to report forthwith at Missoula. Potts did not pledge either Montana or the United States to pay for supplies. A second appeal, General Order Number 4, issued from Deer Lodge on July 31, specifically called for three hundred volunteers, "each man to furnish his own horse and such arms and equipment as he can. . . . Subsistence will be furnished companies as they report to me until they are disbanded."[5]

The response to these appeals was enthusiastic, both before the Nez Perces entered the Bitterroot Valley and after they departed from there in peace. The citizens were stirred up and willing to serve. Several hundred were assembled at the mouth of Lolo Creek when the Nez Perces reached that place on July 28.

At that critical time, Governor Potts sent a telegram to William A. Clark at Deer Lodge, requesting him to go to Butte and organize a company of volunteers. Clark hurried there and succeeded in organizing a battalion, which elected him major. The Butte people expected the Nez Perces to come their way; hence, Clark's volunteers rode over to Deer Lodge to blockade them. There they learned that the Indians had gone up the Bitterroot Valley peaceably, and that Gibbon was pursuing them rapidly.

At this juncture the Butte volunteers considered riding the hundred miles south to the Big Hole Basin. In fact, they went as far as French Gulch, when a message from Governor Potts ordered them back to Butte. Consequently, they missed a fair chance to participate in the Big Hole battle.

Volunteer feelings were mixed concerning this matter. Probably those who were most disappointed were the ones who later joined Clark in going to the relief of Gibbon. However, the volunteers must have had some reservations about becoming an integral unit in the campaign, because, according to the *Montana Stan-*

dard of August 10, the volunteers took this oath: "We obey all orders of Governor Potts, and the officers chosen by ourselves, but not to be under command of any United States officer." This posture was contrary to General Sherman's advice and instruction to Potts. In a telegram from Bozeman, dated August 2, the general stated: "I approve of what you are doing and if your volunteers act under the regular officers I am sure Congress will pay for the necessary stores for their maintenance. . . . This is about all we can do. These Indians should not be allowed to traverse Montana for the Buffalo Country but should be captured or forced back on Howard."[6]

The organization of a volunteer force in Helena was effected at a public meeting in International Hall on July 30. The governor's call and the general necessity for the move were discussed by Martin Maginnis, Robert C. Walker, Wilbur F. Sanders, and W. F. Chadwick. The response was enthusiastic and the cadres for cavalry, artillery, and mounted infantry companies were formed. These volunteers held themselves in readiness pending the possible movement of the Nez Perces toward the Prickly Pear country.

James E. Callaway and Thomas J. Farrell, former officers in the Union and Confederate armies, respectively, took the lead in organizing the Virginia City volunteers. Although a hundred men joined up, only half the number were willing to leave home and enter the campaign. Most of them needed horses, and O. B. Varney and Farrell, joint owners of the VF Ranch in Madison Valley, agreed to provide about fifty. Thus, mounted and equipped, forty-two men elected Callaway and Deimling as colonels and the command left to join Howard in the Beaverhead Valley by August 17. This was a week after the Big Hole battle, but they were to be on hand for a brush with the Nez Perces at Camas Meadows on August 20.

The Fort Fizzle Affair

Meanwhile, Captain Rawn, assisted by five officers and thirty enlisted men, had on July 25 started the erection of what was later to be known as Fort Fizzle, a crude but sturdy barricade eight miles from the mouth of Lolo Canyon. Within a few hours nearly two hundred volunteers arrived, and finally a band of Flathead Indians, under Chief Charlot, came into the redoubt.

The Hot Springs Nez Perce camp was only a dozen miles upstream. Hence, the chiefs soon learned of "Captain Rawn's Corral." There is no evidence that this development either frightened or angered them. Instead, they sent word to Rawn that they desired to talk.

Many versions have been given of the parley that followed. This is Captain Rawn's official account:

My intentions were . . . to compel the Indians to surrender their guns and ammunition and to dispute their passage by force of arms into the Bitter Root Valley. On the 27th of July, I had a talk with Chiefs Joseph, White Bird, and Looking Glass, who proposed, if allowed to pass unmolested, to march peaceably through the Bitter Root Valley, but I refused to allow them to pass unless they complied with my stipulations as to the surrender of their arms.

For the purpose of gaining time for General Howard's forces to get up, and for General Gibbon to arrive from Shaw, I appointed a meeting for the 28th, with Looking Glass, accompanied by one Indian, and myself by Delaware Jim (interpreter)—the meeting to take place in open prairie and not within range of the rifles of their whole camp. The meeting was held accordingly, but I submitted to him the same conditions as before, towit: that if they wished to enter the valley they must disarm and dismount, surrendering all stock. Looking Glass said he would talk to his people and would tell me what they said at

9 A.M. the next day. Distrusting him I would not agree to that hour, but proposed 12 M. We separated without agreement. Nothing satisfactory having resulted from the conference I returned to the breast works expecting to be attacked. In the meantime that portion of the volunteers (some 100 or more) who represented Bitter Root Valley hearing that the Nez Perces promised to pass peaceably through it determined that no act of hostility on their part should provoke the Indians to a contrary measure, and without leave left in squads of from one to a dozen. On the 28th the Indians moved from the canon to the hills, ascending the sides one-half mile in my front, passed my flank, and went into the Bitter Root Valley. As soon as I found they were passing around me, and hearing that they had attacked a rear guard, I had established to prevent desertions, I abandoned the breastworks, formed skirmish line across the canon with my regulars, and such of the volunteers as I could control, and advanced in direction Indians had gone. They did not accept a fight but retreated again into Bitter Root. At the mouth of Lo Lo and before reaching it all the volunteers had left me, but a dozen or twenty Missoula men, and I was obliged to return to this post [Fort Missoula].[7]

Even this forthright account requires some explanation. Rawn gives very little of what must have been said in two parleys. Neither does he mention the fact that Governor Potts attended the meeting. Did White Bird demand that guarantees for the personal security of the Nez Perces and their property be given? And, was Rawn unable to give any assurance as to what the ultimate terms might be? Did Rawn finally agree to allow the Indians to bypass him without a fight? Finally, Nez Perce informants say there was only one parley.

Conclusive answers to these questions have never been given. It is apparent that the chiefs were sincere diplomats, seeking for solutions befitting their record and strength. They knew Rawn's force could not stop them, and they obviously discovered that he lacked authority to make a satisfactory peace. In these circumstances the chiefs were not disposed to give up anything. Surrender was out of the question. Rawn confirmed this in a letter on July 27: "They showed disposition to fight."[8] The evidence L. V. McWhorter obtained from Nez Perce informants upon this point seems irrefutable. Thus, while desperate enough to force their way through the canyon, the warriors considered prudence better than valor and exerted themselves to avoid a show of strength.

While the talking was going on, Nez Perce scouts had found a way of outflanking Rawn's stronghold by climbing up a northward-inclined ravine, then following eastward along a series of lateral gulches, and finally going down Sleeman Creek into the Bitterroot Valley. When a volunteer named W. B. Harlan informed Rawn that the Nez Perces were going around him, the captain rejected the information and remarked that there were too many "God Almightys" around camp. Of course, the report was correct, and while the move was being launched at daybreak on July 28, a few warriors conducted a demonstration in front of Rawn's breastworks. Accounts differ as to the matter of gun play. Some say a few high shots were fired, while others simply state that the fort was rendered impotent without the firing of a single shot. One author characterized this strategical move as "the boldest, most fearless, audacious, and confident tactical movement. It surpasses McClellan's flank movement from Chickahominy to James River, or Grant's from Rapidan to Richmond. They moved armies . . . moving by night. But Joseph moved his entire possessions of effects and families."[9]

The Indians were not pursued, but they might have been. A native of the valley, who made a study of its history, claims that Nez Perce scouts who preceded the move reassured the settlers behind the lines.[10] This view was confirmed by Duncan McDonald, who states that two volunteers named Henry McFarland and Jack Walsh fell into Nez Perce hands during the move. Looking Glass told them to go home and take care of their women and children and affairs generally. The message spread and the settlers accepted it at face value. Amos Buck, W. B. Harlan, and other volunteers who left records of this event, concur in this representation. In any case, the chiefs believed that they had done what they could to prevent trouble in Montana. Chief Joseph later described his understanding of the whole situation in this way:

> Here [Lolo Canyon] another body of soldiers came upon us and demanded our surrender. We refused. They said, "You can not get by us." We answered, "We are going by you without fighting if you will let us, but we are going by you anyhow." We then made a treaty with these soldiers. We agreed not to molest any one and they agreed that we might pass through the Bitter Root country in peace. We bought provisions and traded stock with white men there.
>
> We understood that there was to be no war. We intended to go peaceably to the buffalo country, and leave the question of returning to our country to be settled afterward.[11]

Yellow Wolf confirmed this view in saying, "We traveled through the Bitter Root Valley slowly. The white people were friendly. No more fighting! We had left General Howard and his war in Idaho."[12]

These Indian accounts conform with Captain Rawn's report that the volunteers deserted Fort Fizzle in great numbers; more than a hundred rode away. Another two hundred were assembled at Missoula and Stevensville. Still more were organized at Deer Lodge, and yet the unhurried Nez Perces were not attacked during their eight-day sojourn in the Bitterroot Valley.

Civilian Reactions and Opinions

The phenomenal Nez Perce stratagem caused much bewilderment in Butte and Helena. On July 30, the *Helena Daily Herald* explained the development as demonstrating "how easy any Indian force, whether seeking pillage or only escape, could pass around, through, and by our untrained troops. So far as infantry goes, except to defend the larger towns or some fortified position, they are as useless as boys with popguns. Even mounted and well-armed soldiers need skillful leadership to be of any account."

This interpretation of the event was too superficial. It minimized the good Nez Perce record, contacts, diplomacy, and armed might. It also ignored the fact that the settlers were actuated by much more good will than bad at this particular time. They were not anxious to fight, and the lack of military power at Fort Fizzle did not inspire reckless action.

A letter to Governor Potts, written on July 31 by Chauncy Barbour, editor of the *Weekly Missoulian,* disclosed a strange compound of good and poor judgment about the affair. He advised the governor to take command and strike the Nez Perces hip and thigh. In his opinion, they had really hoped to surrender to Rawn. Since that failed, he wrote,

> . . . they camped on an open place with their women and children, exposed themselves to slaughter, and they either thought we were cowards or else they wanted us to oppose them with force so that they might surrender. If you find them hiding away their women and children in some secure place and meeting you defiantly you will know that they are earnestly on the war path.

Then came his bellicose appeal to the governor: "Wipe out the disgrace that has been put upon us, and never let any regular officer again command Montana Militia."[13]

Three days later, on August 3, the governor received another letter from the same Chauncy Barbour, praising him for his failure to act as advised in the previous letter.

> If you had taken command of the militia and precipitated hostilities, you would have merited our unmixed condemnation. It is best as it was, and our people now with one accord congratulate themselves that our welfare was in the hands of discreet men. There were some restless spirits among us . . . who have nothing to lose, who would have precipitated a fight even at the expense of seeing this country ravaged.[14]

These contradictory letters illustrated the complex nature of a society under stress. Perhaps it was the weight of second sober thoughts about families and property, rather than pride, prestige, or humanity, that impelled the Bitterroot settlers to allow the Indians to pass.

The Military Position

The chiefs' assumption that the war was over was not shared by the army officers. Howard's persistence in pursuit has been described, and his command reached the Bitterroot Valley on August 8. Rawn returned to Fort Missoula, where he wrote a considerable report in justification of his conduct at Fort Fizzle. The name of his breastworks suggests the ridicule that was heaped upon him by armchair critics and the press. It should be stated that his superiors, including General Sheridan, found no fault with his actions. His force was small, the volunteers were hesitant, and the Nez Perces were strong and determined. However, the United States Army had other officers and soldiers within striking distance of the Nez Perces, and several elements of the Seventh Infantry were already en route to Fort Missoula to accomplish what Rawn had failed to do.

On July 25, Captain George L. Browning, two officers, and thirty-two enlisted men left Fort Ellis for Missoula. They reached their destination on July 30, after traveling a distance of two hundred and forty miles. On July 28, the day the Nez Perces went around Fort Fizzle, Colonel John Gibbon left Fort Shaw with officers and enlisted men assembled there from Fort Baker and Fort Benton. According to a letter the colonel sent to Governor Potts on July 27, he expected to encounter the Indians somewhere along the Blackfoot River.[15] But they had deliberately chosen the Bitterroot–Big Hole route to avoid such an encounter. By traveling through wilderness region they would be able to live on the country Indian-fashion without disturbing the white men. In taking the southern route they would also avoid Fort Ellis, which was situated on the Three Forks–Bozeman trail, and Fort Shaw, which blocked the Blackfoot River–Cadotte Pass–Sun River approach. Surely their choice of this route would definitely prove that their intentions were peaceful.

Gibbon's command reached Fort Missoula on August 3, having come 149 miles. There they were organized into a battalion of seventeen officers and nearly one hundred fifty enlisted men, representing parts of six companies of the Seventh Infantry. Their duffle, arms (including trowel bayonets issued at Fort Missoula), and supplies were placed in mule-drawn wagons. This command started up the Bitterroot Valley on the morning of August 4. General Howard's force would fall in upon the same road five days later. Surely the prosaic lives of the settlers were bound to be disrupted by these exceptional scenes. How many of the young men would be tempted to join Gibbon by the prospects of excitement and spoils that appertain to the fortunes of war?

10. FROM LOLO CREEK TO THE BIG HOLE BASIN

▧▧▧▧▧▧▧▧▧▧▧▧▧▧▧▧▧▧▧▧▧▧▧▧▧▧▧▧▧▧▧▧

After bypassing Fort Fizzle, the Nez Perces established camp near Stevensville. As in former times, they visited the town and transacted business. The chiefs and merchants agreed that no liquor should be sold to the Indians. One man violated the agreement, so his supply was locked up by the merchants.[1] An Indian who drank too much was seized by Chief Looking Glass and sent to camp under guard. W. B. Harlan stated that Looking Glass patrolled the main street for two days to see that none of the Indians started trouble. Obviously their triumph in avoiding trouble at Fort Fizzle had not made the chiefs arrogant.

The settlers in turn exercised wisdom in matters of accommodation. Many of them sent their families and certain goods to nearby Fort Owen, which they buttressed against the prospect of assault. Otherwise, they pursued their affairs in a nearly normal fashion. Amos Buck expressed their viewpoint in his commentary upon Colonel Gibbon's subsequent critical reaction to the Indian trading:

> We were utterly surprised and chagrined to note that
> he severely criticized the people of Bitter Root Valley

for giving aid to Joseph's band by selling them supplies. It is said that a man is not accountable for what he does not know, hence if General Gibbon had been correctly informed of the dire situation here his report would have read quite differently.[2]

It is probable that if Mr. Buck and the thirty-three of his compatriots who joined the colonel's command as volunteers, and the citizens generally, had been more consistent, Gibbon's spirit of vengeance might have been modified. As it was, the Nez Perce train moved up the valley at the easy pace of about twelve miles per day. The Indians' general demeanor remained the same as at Stevensville, and the pattern of settler reaction was also comparable. As an insurance against misunderstanding the Corvallis settlers constructed a log-sod type of fort a mile north of the village. Bastions were constructed at opposite corners, and J. L. Hubble served as captain of the guards. A similar fort was erected near Hamilton, where John B. Catlin had charge.

The warriors were no more than amused by these fortifications. Some of them rode up close, examined them, and conversed with the people inside. In like manner, a few settlers approached the Indian camps, and it is said that they were prevailed upon to leave their ammunition. They were not robbed; in fact, it was reported that cartridges were purchased at a dollar apiece.[3]

However, some of Toohoolhoolzote's most unruly young braves did enter the home of Myron Lockwood. They helped themselves to flour, coffee, several tools, and articles of clothing. In recompense for this pilfering, Looking Glass compelled them to put Lockwood's brand on seven of their horses and turn them into his pasture. White people found it difficult to understand that Indian ethics permitted a warrior to take food whenever it was needed. Actually, all Bitterroot records and traditions support the fact that these Indians, however unwelcome in the circumstances, behaved at least as well as regular troops are likely to do with equal leisure to ramble around an inhabited area.

Notes of Alarm for the Chiefs

A few miles below Ross Hole the Indians camped near the famous Medicine Tree. This tree was a symbol of peace and neutrality; but during the night a warrior named Lone Bird received strong impressions of imminent danger. He rode through the camp shouting, "My shaking heart tells me trouble and death will overtake us if we make no hurry through this land! I can not smother, I can not hide what I see. I must speak what is revealed to me. Let us be gone to the buffalo country!"[4]

Several days before, Wahlitits had received and announced a premonition of personal death and tribal doom. But neither of these forecasts, nor yet another to come three days later, aroused the chiefs. Looking Glass was in charge of the trek, and as Yellow Wolf said, "Looking Glass was against anything not first thought of by himself. White Bull always sided with him. They said, 'No more fighting! War is quit!' "[5] On the night of August 5, the Indians were camped above Ross Hole. Eight days had been consumed in leisurely traveling from Lolo Creek to that point—a distance of one hundred miles.

The next morning the Indians ascended an old buffalo trail that went up a hogback and over the Continental Divide north of Gibbon Pass. They probably camped midway on Trail Creek and reached the Big Hole Basin early on August 7. In spite of the warnings concerning dangers ahead, everything indicated that the chiefs intended to stop here for several days. They were proceeding as if conditions were normal, as in earlier pilgrimages through the country.

Colonel Gibbon's Pursuit

Colonel Gibbon left Fort Missoula on August 4, with a force of 17 officers and 146 enlisted men. His infantry and supplies were transported in a mule-drawn wagon train managed by Hugh Kirkendall and other settlers. At Fort Owen, a mountain howitzer was added to Gibbon's collection of weapons. The colonel did not receive any orders or hear any reports that inclined him toward thoughts of peace or diplomacy.

Gibbon was a fighting man and he had a single purpose, namely, to overtake, punish, and capture the Nez Perces. A graduate of West Point, he had achieved the rank of Brigadier General in the Army of the Potomac. In fact, his regiments were called the Iron Brigade, because of their commendable record. Gibbon had played an active role in the subjugation of several tribes in eastern Montana. During a tranquil period in 1872 he accepted an exploring assignment in newly created Yellowstone National Park. He led a company of men up a northern branch of the Madison River and, as a result, the stream was named in his honor.[6]

Bitterroot Civilian Volunteers

When Howard learned that Gibbon's command consisted of one hundred and sixty-three men, he remarked that a hundred more soldiers were needed. But Gibbon entertained no such dubiety. At least he gave the settlers that impression as his cavalcade moved up the valley. At Corvallis, a stockman named Joe Blodgett was employed as a scout and guide, because he had

ranged cattle in the Ross Hole and Big Hole country
for a decade.[7] Other Corvallis men decided to offer their
services to Gibbon, and they requested their fort captain, J. L. Hubble, to be their spokesman and leader.
He advised them against entering the campaign, in view
of the peaceful way the Nez Perces had conducted themselves. However, he agreed to present their request to
Colonel Gibbon, and, if it was accepted, lead them as
far as Ross Hole but no farther. Accordingly, he spoke
to Gibbon, who at first responded in a surly manner,
but later consented to accept the volunteers.[8] Another
group of citizens, from Skalkaho, took similar action,
with John B. Catlin acting as their captain. At the outset,
Catlin was definitely opposed to breaking the truce,
but Lynde C. Elliott and other settlers endeavored to
persuade him that the wrongs committed by the Indians in Idaho should be avenged. Although the argument did not appeal to Catlin, he finally agreed to be
their leader. It is fair to note that many citizens deplored this action, and only thirty-four volunteers actually left the valley. Captain Hubble turned back at
Ross Hole, and, at Sleeping Child, a volunteer named
Johnny Chaffin convinced himself that "these Indians
haven't done me any harm," whereupon he turned
back.[9]

After accepting them grudgingly, Gibbon proceeded
to make good use of these volunteers by adding them
to Lieutenant Bradley's company of cavalry. As border
settlers they were skillful horsemen, good trackers, and
fine riflemen.

Any assessment of motives other than patriotism
would be highly speculative. Some of the settlers claimed
that Nez Perce horses were uppermost in the minds of
several volunteers. A. J. Noyes, a historian of the
volunteers, quoted one of them to this effect: "Now
some have accused us of going out just to steal the
horses; that gives the wrong impression, we did not
think of that until the general made us the offer. He told

us that we could have all the horses except enough to mount the command, if we could whip the Indians."[10] Noyes also claimed that two rustlers, named Alex Matt and Jor Gird, became camp followers with nothing in mind but horse-stealing. Then, too, the gold pouches of the Indians also offered an inducement. The Corvallis Chaffins still tell about William Chaffin's visit to the Nez Perce camp and his admiration of a highly decorated shirt worn by a medicine man. Upon returning home he said, "If I go, I'll get that shirt."[11] It is probable that sheer adventure was the major motivation. Young Thomas Crittenden Sherrill explained his feelings this way: "I did not realize what General Gibbon's men were up against. But I wanted to go . . . no matter what the conditions."[12] He was accompanied by an older brother named Millard Fillmore Sherrill, but a younger one named Winfield Scott had to stay home to do the chores! Could anyone deny that the spirit of national pride ran high in the Sherrill family?

Gibbon's command moved twice as fast as the Nez Perces, making thirty miles a day. Hence, on August 7, his men were toiling up the hogback east of Ross Hole, only one day's travel behind the Nez Perces. That evening Lieutenant Bradley offered to make a night march with a mixed command of sixty cavalrymen and volunteers. His objective was to reconnoiter the Indian position and, if possible, stampede their horses. By morning Bradley's party reached the upper periphery of the Big Hole Basin. Bradley called a halt, hid his troops in an off-trail cove, and prepared breakfast. Afterwards, he, Lieutenant Jacobs, and Sergeant Wilson moved forward until they heard the sound of axes in the woods at the base of the mountain. Then, carefully searching for a vantage point, they climbed a tall pine tree and beheld the Indian village in a meadow a mile to the northeast. A messenger hastened back up the trail to inform Gibbon of the situation.

Having less than twenty miles to travel, the main

command arrived by evening of the eighth at the spot, within six miles of the Nez Perce camp, where Bradley's men were hidden. Gibbon ordered a rest at that point until 11:00 P.M., when he hoped to move closer to the village. Gibbon's plan called for a swift attack at dawn.

Howard's Progress toward the Big Hole Basin

Gibbon no doubt wished Howard was also within striking distance. He assumed this was impossible, however, for no reply had reached him from a messenger, named Pardee, whom he had dispatched to Howard on August 4. Howard received the message on August 6, two days before he reached the Bitterroot Valley, and he realized that Gibbon might soon overtake and engage the Indians. He selected a sergeant named Owen Sutherland and a Bannock scout to carry his reply to Gibbon: "General Howard is coming on, as fast as possible by forced marches, with two hundred cavalrymen, to give the needed reinforcement."[13] Sutherland was told to push on day and night until he reached Gibbon. Of course, this command implied the use of a horse-relay system, and the riders secured fresh mounts from ranchers, as they were needed. In one instance, Sutherland mounted a roan colt that twisted upward and sideways in a rotating motion, then landed so stifflegged that the cinch broke and Sutherland was catapulted against the corral fence. The jolt, combined with sheer fatigue, was enough to cause him intense suffering, but the sergeant rested awhile, then remounted and pressed on. The Bannock scout had by now deserted. Sutherland reached the edge of the Big Hole battlefield at noon on August 9; by that time, the most savage part of the battle was over, and Gibbon's command was in a precarious position. Sutherland wrote his appraisal of the desperate situation and sent it by messenger to Howard.

Howard's whole command reached the Bitterroot Valley on August 8. He sent his cavalry ahead in all haste and made arrangements for mule-wagon transportation of the infantry. Overtaking the cavalry, Howard formed "Camp Gibbon" well up the valley on August 9. That night, obsessed by forebodings, he decided to take twenty of the fastest mounts and their riders to overtake Gibbon. He later described the trip thus: "As dawn appeared, in a column of twos, we moved out of camp; took a steady, firm trot, and, except in a few instances where the roughness of the trail prevented speed, kept at that gait all day."[14] Gibbon's messenger to Howard chose an alternate route north of Ross Hole and missed Howard. Instead, he met Captain Mason with the main body of Howard's cavalry.

Although he lacked knowledge of the battle, the tireless Howard did not stop until he had traveled over fifty miles, including the six-mile climb up the hogback to the Continental Divide. While he was making camp upon the headwaters of Trail Creek on August 10, seven of the Bitterroot volunteers came in on foot and related their harrowing experiences in the battle of the preceding day.

Sutherland's personal messenger to Howard also unwittingly bypassed the general's camp, but he, too, met the main cavalry on the eleventh. At 10:00 A.M. on that day, Howard reached the besieged camp occupied by Gibbon and his men, and he learned the details of the Battle of the Big Hole.

11. THE BATTLE OF THE BIG HOLE

The Big Hole Basin is a crescent-shaped alpine valley, 6,800 feet in elevation, girdled by the Rocky Mountain cordillera on the west and the Pioneer Range on the east. The basin, sixty miles long and fifteen miles wide, is more oasis than prairie, with streams flowing in from every canyon and crossing the meadows. Flowing northeastward, these streams funnel into the north and south forks of the Big Hole River and unite before leaving the basin to merge eventually with the Beaverhead River and form the Jefferson River.

Sagebrush and flowers adorn the valley fringes, pine forests border the western side of the basin, and grasses and sedges carpet the valley floor. In 1877 the basin was unmodified by man, although cattlemen had grazed herds upon its borders since 1874. The meadow had served as a summer range for elk, deer, and bison. No one had built a homestead or thought of wintering in this "Land of Big Snows," and the Big Hole Basin presented a scene of the utmost tranquility.

The Nez Perce Village

Expecting to rest several days, the Indians had established camp with exceptional pains and some artistry. This basin constituted a traditionally neutral zone between the roving bands of the east and of the west. The Nez Perces regarded it as a way-station area, to which they had a hereditary right. Their village was situated in a meadow along the east bank of the Big Hole River. Eighty-nine lodges were so arranged as to conform rougly to a V with the apex upstream. There was a partly open court in the middle.

Lieutenant Bradley, scouting from a pine tree, noticed that the women were gathering firewood and cutting lodge and travois poles. These would need several days for drying. Men were fishing and hunting to provide food for the more than six hundred people. The Nez Perces called this basin Iskumlselalik Pah, meaning "Vale of the Squirrel," and surely the atmosphere on that August day suggested only a peaceful natural wilderness.

A Battle Plan Unfolds

Bradley and his two companions carefully observed this primeval setting from a military viewpoint. The village was situated in a meadow next to the river, which ran in a northeasterly direction, roughly parallel to the mountain on the west and about a quarter of a mile away from it. Upon the intervening space grew dense stands of willows interspersed by an irregular pattern of shallow sloughs (old river courses) and grassy plots. Two-fifths of a mile to the southwest, jutting out a hundred feet from the regular mountain base, was a little creek-built plateau covered with a thick stand of pines. A few of the pines were growing among the willows in the bottomland close to the stream.

The soldiers recognized that the Nez Perce village was vulnerable to a surprise attack, providing no guards were posted between the edge of the hill and the camp. Having memorized details of the terrain, the scouts rejoined their comrades up Trail Creek. Messengers were sent up the trail to Gibbon, apprising him of the situation. By sunset the colonel's command reached Bradley's cove. Food was prepared without fires, the plan of attack was formulated, pickets were posted, and the balance of the command lay down to rest until 11:00 P.M. After that hour Gibbon proposed to move within a few hundred yards of the village without detection, wait for daylight, and then attack.

Official records do not indicate that a no-quarter type of assault was deliberately adopted. However, Tom Sherrill states that as the volunteers were discussing the forthcoming attack it occurred to them that no mention had been made of prisoners. They asked Major Catlin about the matter, whereupon he spoke to Gibbon, who replied, "We don't want any prisoners." In reporting this terse and ominous remark to the volunteers, Catlin said, "Boys, you know what to do now."[1] Tradition reports that hours later, when the village was dimly perceived, an order was passed along the battle line to "aim low in firing at the lodges." This order, combined with the exceptionally ferocious assault that followed, tends to support Sherrill's statements.

The Slumbering Indians

Meantime, the Nez Perces were oblivious of danger. Warriors were slumbering in the midst of their families. No precautions of any kind had been taken. Indeed, some of the people had stayed up late on August 8, chanting and dancing, because there was nothing for them to fear. And yet, on that very morning, a discussion of their situation had taken place among the principal warriors. Several had expressed great uneasiness over the lack of any sentinels on the back trail. The refrain of previous warnings was rephrased: "What are we doing here? . . . While I slept, my medicine told me to move on; that death is approaching us . . . my advice is to speed through this country. If not, there will be tears in our eyes in a short time."[2] These forebodings impelled Sarpsis Ilppilp, and Seeyakoon Ilppilp, to offer their services as back-trail runners. But they made the mistake of conditioning the service upon the loan of some fast horses owned by a wealthy man named Semu (Coals of Fire, also Blacktail Eagle), who refused their request.[3] At this juncture, Five Wounds interceded with Chief Looking Glass and an argument ensued. The chief took the position that sending sentinels would be breaking faith with the Bitterroot settlers. Yielding to the arrogant chief's remonstrances, Five Wounds said, "All right, Looking Glass, you are one of the chiefs! I have no wife, no children to be placed fronting the danger that I feel coming to us. Whatever the gains, whatever the loss, it is yours."[4] Ironically enough, Five Wounds died fighting against the great odds this lack of caution imposed upon the warriors. Since no scout was sent, the chiefs did not know that an armed force was then moving toward them. Their code of ethics convinced them that no one would execute a surprise attack upon a sleeping and undefended camp.

Colonel Gibbon Flanks the Village

According to plan, at 11:00 P.M. Gibbon aroused his command. Seventeen officers, 132 enlisted men, and 34 volunteers were lined up on the trail. The rest, consisting of fourteen soldiers, were assigned to bring up the supply wagons and howitzer the next day. A march of five miles brought them to the basin rim, and they followed it along an old trail for a mile until they were directly west of the Indian camp. A band of ponies was grazing above them on the hillside, and the possibility of their neighing was a threat. However, the men passed by cautiously and in single file. The command deserves much credit for this wolflike entrance upon the enemy's flank. The movement was so stealthily executed that it failed to startle the horses, and the camp dogs did not get the foreign scent.

The command settled down along a twelve-hundred-yard segment of the trail and waited. Gibbon considered rounding up or stampeding the horses, but trusted guides, H. O. Bostwick from Fort Shaw, and Joe Blodgett from Bitterroot, advised him against this measure. They pointed out that he was about to do battle with the Nez Perces and not the Sioux. Therefore, it would be imperative to keep his command together. Then Bostwick, who was half Indian, briefed Gibbon upon precisely what sights and sounds to expect from the campground, assuming that their presence was unknown: "after a while you will see some fires built up if we are undiscovered."[5] As Bostwick had promised, an hour or so before daylight the squaws filed out, replenished their waning fires, chatted together for a few moments, and returned to their slumbering families.

The Deployment

Meanwhile, Gibbon's men meditated upon their position and orders to move forward in a three-pronged assault upon the V-shaped camp. The central sector was composed of the companies commanded by Combo and Sanno. The left wing, or downstream force, including Catlin and the volunteers, was under Bradley. The right, or upstream, force was commanded by Logan.

Two companies under Rawn and Williams were to be held in support, but developments required their prompt commitment to action with Logan's men. The other eleven officers were distributed along the line. The signal for attack was to be the first shot fired upon the instant of Indian discovery.

Assured of the advantages incident to complete surprise, the command was more than eager to launch an attack. Surely the time, place, plans, and circumstances seemed auspicious to the veteran officers and experienced soldiers. Everything seemed to be in their favor. Thus, at about 3:30 A.M. on August 9, as the first streaks of graying light flickered into the valley, the skirmishers moved off the trail on to the bottoms and began threading their way among the willows, laurel, and sloughs, toward the camp. They had worked their way to within about two hundred yards of the village, when a solitary Indian left his lodge, mounted a pony tethered nearby, and inadvertently rode squarely into the middle of the skirmish line. Lieutenant C. A. Woodruff later wrote, "He leans forward on his horse to try and make out, in the dim light, what is before him."[6] Yellow Wolf identified the rider as Natalekin, a man of dim vision, too old to fight. He was shot down by a volley from the rifles of four volunteers.

The Battle

The skirmishers dashed toward the village and plunged into the river and up the bank loudly cheering and shooting into the lodges. As dazed Indians appeared, the attackers fired at them without discrimination. In such a melee, women and children could not be distinguished from the men. Quick to apprehend the situation, the Indians ran in various directions, mostly toward the attackers, because the willow-lined river afforded protection denied by the meadow on the east. They jumped into the water and hid behind banks and clumps of bushes. Many, rushing from their lodges without weapons, had to hustle back again. Wives and children assisted in matters of supply. Pandemonium, if not panic, prevailed for a few moments; then strong voices of leadership were heard calling for steadiness and courage. Fear and panic gave way to a fierce desire for self-preservation, and the Nez Perces bravely began an attempt to resist destruction or abasement with every resource at hand—rifles, clubs, and hands. Recovering from the shock, experienced Indian sharpshooters made their way toward strategic positions. Then effective shots came from all directions—from the brush, the creek banks, the open prairie, and even the distant hill.

Perhaps this partial recovery was expedited by a miscalculation on the part of troops on the right wing. These soldiers quickly took over the upper end of the village and, having orders to burn it, attempted to do so. But the damp lodges did not ignite easily, and this diverting of the soldiers' attention, though short, was costly. If, as Yellow Wolf claims, only a score of warriors were armed at the outset, the few moments' lull helped many more to find their guns. For five hours the battle was touch and go. The action was desperately fierce and absolutely relentless. All accounts characterize the battle as sharp and furious.

As the troops moved into the camp, the Nez Perces moved out. Gibbon's description of this action is both candid and graphic:

The Indians being terribly punished in the first attack. Large numbers being killed in their lodges, etc. The Indians who escaped, however, soon rallied, and as our line was insufficient to cover the whole front of the camp, the Indians were abled to pass around our flanks and take position in the willows and wooded hills in our rear, from which points they kept up a destructive fire on our men, who were exposed in the field. Every possible effort was made to clear the willows along the river banks of Indians. But as fast as they were driven out in front, others would appear in the rear.[7]

Then cross fire developed and gradually the warriors began to fight effectively, not in units, but singly. In Indian fashion they sifted back toward the campsite and engaged the troops in close fighting. As Lieutenant Woodruff writes, "The village has become the hottest place in the vicinity. . . ."[8] Yellow Wolf described the fighting.

> We now mixed those soldiers badly. We could hit each other with our guns. . . . A tall soldier sprang behind those bushes. Hohots Eloloht was back of those willows. Both their guns were empty. They clubbed with their guns, then grabbed each other. . . . Both struggled for their lives. Eloloht called twice to his *Wyakin* [medicine power] for help. . . . Lokochets Kunnin came running. He shot the tall soldier and killed him. The bullet broke one bone in Eloloht's arm. . . . We could not well count how many dead soldiers, but we killed a good few. . . .[9]

Bradley and Logan, having secured the upper end of the village, proposed to move into the lower, but they were both killed before this movement was executed. Several of the greatest Nez Perce warriors were killed early in the struggle. When mighty Rainbow fell, a hush came upon his compatriots, and his old warmate, Pahkatos, took wild risks in seeking revenge. Fierce battle cries were shouted by White Bird and Looking Glass: "Fight for women and children! . . . Now is our time. Fight! It is better we should be killed fighting. . . ."[10]

Chief Joseph and Chief Ollokot, knowing their wives had been shot, fought in mute fury. When Wahlitits beheld his fighting wife die from a bullet in the breast,

A mountain Train. 5 miles

B Line of advance

C intrenched position

D Indian Herd

E Beaver creek

F Brush along m.

G Indian Camps

Indian look out

£F Inglish Killed

Looking Glass

Capt Logan Killed

Trees

The

Cotter look mountains

Homer Coon's sketch of

the Big Hole battlefield

he charged to his death into the midst of a group of soldiers, whereupon his battlemate, Sarpsis Ilppilp, sought revenge and was also killed. Angus McDonald states that a third of the warriors were slain in attempting to protect their families. The braves called on their *Wyakin* powers and blew their magic bone whistles, to little avail. Their freedom of action was hampered by the guardian role the surprise attack had imposed upon them.

Meanwhile, Gibbon was endeavoring to follow these shifting scenes as he moved along the fringe of battle on horseback. After several hours of fighting there was no semblance of a skirmish line or any other formation. Troop movements were kaleidoscopic and confused. Sensing that a fearful counteroffensive was forming, Gibbon plunged into the marsh, crossed the river, and emerged on the campsite, where his horse was shot and he was wounded in the left thigh. In fact, both Gibbon and Lieutenant Woodruff were wounded at this juncture in the battle. Gibbon soon observed that half of his officers were killed or wounded and that there was danger of panic. Therefore, at about 8:00 A.M., he reluctantly ordered a retreat toward the little tree-covered plateau less than a mile to the rear. Achievement of that position would remove the men from the line of fire coming from the sharpshooters on the hillside. It would also reduce the effectiveness of the marksmen hidden in the willows below the siege point.

Gibbon's Withdrawal

The colonel did not describe the method of retreat, but Tom Sherrill said he heard him shout, "Charge that point and rake the brush with your rifles!"[11] Historian Brady states that Gibbon gathered his men, formed them in two lines, back to back, and ordered them to charge in both directions.[12] Actually, this double sweeping effort occurred earlier in the battle. Gibbon undoubtedly ordered his men to return to the base of the side hill where they had been deployed before the battle.

This retrograde movement brought the troops and civilians in Bradley's company under the galling fire of a deadly marksman stationed on the hill behind one of the Twin Trees.[13] It was then that volunteer V. Birch became frightened and shouted, "It's another Custer Massacre, let's get out of here!" An officer called, "Don't you think of it, you'll all get killed."[14] The retreat was, in fact, orderly. All official reports affirm that discipline, courage, and cooperation prevailed. Lieutenant J. T. Van Orsdale's report to the Assistant Adjutant General is typical: "I cannot but express the highest praise of the bravery and coolness of the men. I did not see a single man hesitate or falter, the principal difficulty being to restrain their ardor and save ammunition."[15]

Gibbon recorded the accomplishment of the retreat in this way:

This movement was successfully accomplished, such of our wounded as we could find being carried with us, and the few Indians who occupied the timber being driven out. Here we took up our position, and sheltering ourselves behind the trees, fallen logs, etc., replied to the fire of the sharp-shooters who soon gathered around us, occupying the brush below and the timber above. For a time their fire was very close and deadly, and here Lieutenant English received a mortal wound. Captain Williams was struck a second time, and a large number of men killed and wounded. The Indians crawled up as closely as they dared to come, and with yells of encouragement, urged each other on; but our men met them with a bold front, and our fire, as we afterwards learned by the blood and dead Indians found, punished them severely.[16]

Gibbon's own account provides some justification for an act of near-insubordination by John B. Catlin. Just before the retreat he met Captain Rawn, and they agreed that a withdrawal from the thickets to a bench-land southeast of the camp would be expedient. That position would deny the sharpshooters forest cover at close quarters, and at the same time cut off their withdrawal to the south. Gibbon's choice of the wooded promontory prevailed, but when Catlin arrived at that place he saw the weakness of the situation and ejaculated, "Who in hell called a halt here?" When told that General Gibbon had ordered it, he replied, "I don't give a damn, it's a hell of a place to camp!" This so amused General Gibbon that he did not call Catlin to account for his disrespect.[17]

Catlin's criticism of the spot is understandable, but the place he and Rawn had selected also left much to be desired. Both were without water, but at least the site chosen by Gibbon afforded logs and shade. The men made the most of their limited resources. They used logs as barricades, and behind these slender defenses trenches were dug with the trowel bayonets issued at Fort Missoula.[18] The outlines of these trenches can still be seen.[19]

Unfortunately, the Indian warriors were not discouraged by the trenches. Still circling around at a distance, they found elevated positions from which an effective bombardment was possible. Some crept close, using trees and logs for cover. One sharpshooter, firing from a hidden position in a tree below "Gibbon's corral," killed several soldiers before he was brought down. Another "was so securely perched behind a dead log that he killed four men in one rifle pit before he himself was picked off, and then his naked yellow body fell so close to the fortification that his friends did not venture to recover it."[20]

The men were thus immobilized, and the position was subjected to a twelve-hour siege. There was no cooked food or water, although Lieutenant Woodruff's horse was conveniently killed within the lines and its flesh was eaten.

The Howitzer Episode

About noon the men were startled by two booms from the howitzer. That weapon and the supply train had not been brought down the trail during the night march. When the howitzer appeared on the hillside, it was spied by a group of Nez Perce horsemen. As they rushed forward, the cannon was fired twice, but before it could be loaded again the Indians seized it. In so doing, they killed Corporal Sale and wounded Sergeant Daly and Sergeant Frederics. The other six men in this detail escaped with the wounded men, and two privates kept on going back along the trail until they reached the Bitterroot settlements, where their exaggerated accounts of the situation created great alarm. The other men reached the supply wagons and prepared to defend them against an assault. But none came, either because of the formidable posture of the men, as Gibbon claimed, or because the warriors failed to find their hiding place, as Yellow Wolf reported. The warriors did come upon a pack mule carrying over two thousand rounds of ammunition for Springfield rifles, and, since a number of these rifles had been picked up on the battlefield, this proved to be a considerable windfall.

None of the Indians could fire the howitzer; it was therefore dismantled, rolled downhill, and buried by Peopeo Tholekt.[21]

In making such a successful recovery from the surprise attack the Indians would seem to have had the power to annihilate the besieged soldiers, as did the Sioux at the Custer Massacre. The conditions at the Big Hole were different from those on the Little Big

Horn, however, in that the Nez Perces were attempting to preserve their whole tribal existence, they had few warriors left, and a great many of their people had been killed. The white soldiers were well sheltered in the trenches, and it was now clear to the chiefs that reinforcements would soon arrive. About thirty warriors were therefore assigned to continue the siege, and the others turned back to the village.

A Mourning People

Perhaps thirty Indians were killed within the confines of the village. Some twenty bodies were found along the riverbanks and in the nearby thickets, and many more were scattered across the marsh and up the hillside. As the dead were gathered in, a great wailing arose. As the people mourned, they wept with such feeling that the battle-toughened men in the trenches listened and trembled. Years later, Gibbon wrote, "Few of us will soon forget the wail of mingled grief, rage, and horror which came from the camp four or five hundred yards from us when the Indians returned to it and recognized their slaughtered warriors, women, and children."[22]

The Indians buried their dead as well as they could. Having no tools for such a purpose, they placed the bodies in little ravines under cutbanks and shoved loose parts of overhanging banks upon them. Tom Sherrill counted fifty-seven, "strung out lengthwise under a bank, each wrapped in a buffalo robe, with a chunk of earth caved down on their bodies."[23]

Next, the Nez Perces prepared for flight. The wounded needed saddles and blankets, but much equipment was discarded. Many travois were rigged up and attached to ponies, and the wounded were strapped on. Yellow Wolf's description of this phase is full of pathos: "Wounded children, screaming with pain; women and children crying, wailing for their . . . dead! The air was heavy with sorrow. I would not want to hear, I would not want to see again."[24]

Grave Chief Joseph superintended the moving, and Hototo, also called Lean Elk and Poker Joe, served as war leader in the place of Looking Glass, who had been temporarily demoted because of his failure to act upon wise suggestions for more haste and vigilance.

Although the chiefs had the main caravan on its way south by midafternoon, the siege upon Gibbon's position persisted. A detail of about thirty mounted warriors took over that duty. They established a sort of rendezvous in a tree-circled space of several rods, located near the southwest ridge, a rifleshot beyond the trenches. From that vantage point they could observe the trail entering the basin and also the siege ground. The thirty braves circled back and forth through the woods and shot at Gibbon's men upon occasion. Gibbon's supply of ammunition was shrinking and greater caution in firing became necessary. The hostiles sensed this fact and their vigilance was never relaxed.

Toward evening the members of the command feared that Nez Perce pressure was being intensified. A volunteer and a soldier, sharing a trench, stood up and shouted, "Here they come boys! Look out! They are going to burn us and massacre all of us!"[25] Gibbon's report describes the development this way: "A strong wind was blowing from the west and, taking advantage of this, the Indians set fire to the grass intending, doubtless, to follow up the fire and make a dash upon us whilst we were blinded by dense smoke. But fortunately the grass was too green to burn rapidly, and before the fire reached any of the dead timber lying about us, it went out."[26] Lieutenant Woodruff confirmed Gibbon's report and added an ornamental touch:

And with a whispered fear each strong man sees
That smoke is curling toward us o'er the hills,

> And fire is wafted onward by a gentle breeze,
> And shouts of triumph the thick air fills.[27]

Both sides were on guard all afternoon and evening. Lack of water, food, blankets, and medicine produced suffering, and dismal forecasts and cries of anguish were uttered. Yellow Wolf described this phase of the siege:

> In low places hard to see, we crawled close to those trenches. We heard soldiers talking, swearing, crying. . . . The night grew old, and the firing faded away. Soldiers would not shoot. Would not lift head nor hand above the hiding. . . . We did not charge. If we killed one soldier, a thousand would take his place. If we lost one warrior, there was none to take his place.[28]

By that time the Indian patrol had been reduced to less than a dozen under the leadership of Ollokot.[29]

This reduction of guards, together with the darkness, gave Gibbon a chance to take some action. A detail of volunteers obtained water from the river, and several messengers were sent out with appeals for aid. When Gibbon asked for a volunteer to take a message to Deer Lodge, an Englishman named William Edwards was the first man to respond. Other citizens, not holding him in high esteem as a frontiersman, then offered to go, but Edwards was selected. Impressed by the gravity of his task, Edwards said, "I will risk my life to save you and your men." Gibbon offered him a horse and a few dollars, but there was no food.[30] Rifle in hand, Billy Edwards started out on foot and walked through the siege line. He eventually acquired a horse, reached his destination, and asked for a complete relief party. He also sent this telegram to Governor Potts: "Big Hole, August 9, 1877. Had a hard fight with the Nez Perces, killing a number and losing a number of officers and men. We need a doctor and everything.

Send us such relief as you can. John Gibbon, Colonel Commanding."[31]

A short time after Edwards left, Sergeant Wilson was sent up the trail to locate the wagons; they were too successfully hidden, and he missed them. Gibbon also authorized a Bitterroot volunteer named Billy Ryan to leave for the settlement on the North Fork of the Salmon River (later Gibbonsville) and warn the miners that the hostiles were headed up Ruby Creek. These official departures probably had a bearing upon the action of seven Bitterroot volunteers, who left for home without leave and met Howard on the trail near the Continental Divide early on the morning of August 11.

The Nez Perce warriors had decided that further fighting was futile. They assembled at their rendezvous above the trenches and waited for daylight. At dawn they heard a horseman approaching and shouting to the soldiers. It was Oliver Sutherland, Howard's messenger. No attempt was made to injure or intercept him, and he entered Gibbon's camp. The warriors correctly interpreted Sutherland's arrival as meaning that reinforcements were on the way. At daybreak on August 10, they fired a two-volley salvo and withdrew from the battle area to join the tribe. The Battle of the Big Hole had lasted exactly twenty-four hours.

Sutherland had not seen Gibbon's wagon train, so a detail of soldiers went in search of it, and they found it intact. The supply outfit reached Gibbon's camp toward evening. Food and blankets were now available, but the wounded were without medical care until Howard's command arrived.

Howard Reaches the Battlefield

General Howard and his advance guard reached the camp at 9:00 A.M. on August 11. Gibbon greeted him with a cheery hello and Howard replied, "Well, Gibbon, how do you do?"

"Oh, I'm not much hurt; a flesh wound in the thigh."[32]

Gibbon briefed Howard on the campaign, and afterward they rode around the battlefield and observed the fresh graves where the dead soldiers and volunteers had been buried by a detail under the direction of Captain Comba. They also noted the partially covered Indian remains with a shudder. A day later their feelings were much more revolted by the indignities that had been committed upon the bodies of Nez Perces by Howard's Bannock Indian scouts, and by the looting of the village. The latter act was the beginning of the most wanton, persistent, and insatiable vandalism upon a battlefield known in western America.

Gibbon concluded his narrative of the Big Hole battle, as related to Howard, in these words: "And here you find us, some killed, many wounded, but in no way discouraged. It was a gallant struggle. Who would have believed that those Indians would have rallied after such a surprise and made such a fight?"[33] An assessment of certain issues involved in the answer to Gibbon's question will be made in the following chapter.

12. CASUALTIES, EVALUATIONS, AND REACTIONS

An objective assessment of battle casualties by impartial observers would preclude partisan claims and minimize errors resulting from partial surveys and faulty memories. Such an assessment cannot always be made.

Estimates of Nez Perce Losses

Colonel Gibbon's report states, "Captain Comba, who had charge of our burial party, reports eighty-three (83) dead Indians found on the field, and six more dead warriors were found in a ravine some distance from the battlefield after the command left there."[1] This constitutes the most official estimate; however, its accuracy has been questioned by many.

Lieutenant Albert G. Forse stated, "I do not wish to criticize Gen. Gibbon's report, but it certainly gave the public the wrong impression."[2] Forse based his complaint upon knowledge he received from several officers who were in the fight. They agreed that about seventy women and children were killed; therefore, Gibbon's estimate would reduce the warriors slain to nineteen.

143

According to Forse, these officers believed that many more warriors were killed.

Information from Indian sources fails to bring the problem into clearer focus. Duncan McDonald, who talked with Chief White Bird within a year of the battle, stated that eighty-seven were killed, all told, of whom thirty-three were warriors. Chief Joseph said, "In the fight with General Gibbon, we lost fifty women and children and thirty fighting men."[3] Even that forthright statement leaves a question unanswered, namely, how many nonfighting men died? Yellow Wolf was careful to differentiate between the two in stating that "only twelve real fighting men were lost in that battle. But our best were left there."[4] Husis Owyeen tallied the number of dead on his buffalo-horn drinking cup, but his tally was considered incomplete. L. V. McWhorter summarized the results of his painstaking efforts to get an accurate count in this way: "It is impossible at this date to evaluate the figures accurately. Probably between sixty and ninety Indians were killed."[5] Reference has been made to the fact that many wounded were taken from the battlefield on travois. It is definitely known that Ollokot's wife, Fair Land, died at the first camp beyond the battlefield, and two warriors died at the second. How many more lives were ended by the rigors of forced travel remains a matter of speculation.

In any case, the battle losses were disastrous to the Nez Perces. Before the Battle of the Big Hole, their losses were insignificant; thereafter, nearly every family was disrupted. Besides, a dozen veteran warriors were struck down, and the tribal strength was therefore broken. Some, like Joseph and Ollokot, lost wives; more lost children. The warriors' cold bitterness and reproach of Gibbon was expressed by Joseph in these words: "The Nez Perce never make war on women and children; we could have killed a great many . . . while the war lasted, but we would feel ashamed to do so."[6] He thereby defined a standard toward non-combatants that warriors are still unable to uphold.

After the Big Hole battle, the war took on a grimmer aspect for the Nez Perces. The war had followed them into Montana, and, indeed, it had increased in ferocity and tempo. From now on all white men were bound to be their enemies, and yet their own fighting power had been greatly reduced. In spite of these facts the chiefs were determined to press along upon this circuitous route to safety if it took all summer.

Meanwhile, the mourning cavalcade reached Swamp Creek, after traveling a dozen miles. There they formed a camp called Takseen, meaning "The Willows." That night the care of the wounded was the first objective, although the people must have been extremely cold and hungry.

Early white visitors to this campsite reported seeing parts of splints and bandages involved in the dressing of wounds.[7] This aspect of Nez Perce suffering should not be ignored. Yellow Wolf's cogent summary is adequate: "Traveling was hard on the wounded. So bad that when we reached more safe places, several of them stopped. Remained scattered and hidden away. A few of them were never afterwards heard of."[8] Determined to prevent a surprise attack upon their distraught people at the Swamp Creek camp, the warriors prepared a number of stone rifle pits on the edge of a clearing, athwart the practical approach to the stopping place.[9]

On the morning of August 10, the siege detail rejoined the tribe as it was packing for the second day of travel. Although haste was now imperative, the wounded could not be forced beyond fifteen miles each day, and several people died along the way during the first few days.

J. W. Redington, one of Howard's scouts, found an aged woman in an abandoned camp. She requested death at his hands, and, though Redington refused, Bannock scouts obliged.[10] Howard records a similar instance wherein the same ruthless scouts dispatched an old, ill medicine man named Kapoochas.[11] These people were no doubt left behind at their own request—it was the Indian way.

Gibbon's Casualties

Colonel Gibbon listed his casualties before leaving the battlefield. The accuracy of his report has been verified. There were twenty-nine fatalities and forty wounded. Five civilian volunteers were killed, and four wounded. The Bitterroot volunteers thus sustained a 30 per cent casualty rate. H. O. Bostwick, the Fort Shaw guide, was also killed. There were, therefore, twenty-four soldiers killed and thirty-six wounded. Of these numbers, two officers were killed and five wounded. Lieutenant William L. English died of his wounds ten days after the battle. The rate of casualties among officers was nearly 50 per cent. Below is Gibbon's official report to the Assistant Adjutant General, Department of Dakota. This report, dated at Fort Shaw on September 2, 1877, is on file in the National Archives as Document 3595 DD 1877.

LIST OF KILLED AND WOUNDED AT BATTLE OF BIG HOLE,
AUGUST 9, 1877

KILLED

Company "A"
Captain William Logan
Private John B. Smith

Company "B"
1st Lieutenant James H. Bradley

Company "D"
Corporal William H. Payne
"   Jacob Eisenhut
Musician Francis Gallagher

Company "E"

Private Mathew Butterly

Company "F"

Private William D. Pomroy
" James McGuire

Company "G"

1st Sergeant Robert L. Edgeworth
Sergeant William H. Martin
Corporal Domminick O'Connor
" Robert E. Sale
Private John O'Brien
" Gottleib Manz

Company "H"

Private McKindra L. Drake (orderly for Colonel Gibbon)

Company "I"

Sergeant Michael Hogan
Corporal Daniel McCaffrey
Private Herman Broetz

Company "K"

1st Sergeant Frederick Stortz
Musician Thomas Stinebaker
Artificer John Kleis

Second Cavalry, Company "L"

Sergeant Edward Page

WOUNDED

Colonel John Gibbon, Seventh Infantry (left thigh, severe flesh wound)

Company "A"

1st Lieutenant C. A. Coolidge (both legs above knees, right hand, severe)
Private James C. Lehman (right leg, serious)
" Charles Alberts (under left breast, serious)
" Lorenzo D. Brown (right shoulder, severe)
" George Leher (scalp, slight)

Company "D"

Sergeant Patrick C. Daly (scalp, slight)
Corporal John Murphy (right hip, severe)

Musician Timothy Cronan (right shoulder and breast, serious)
Private James Keys (right foot, severe)

Company "E"

Sergeant William Wright (scalp, slight)
"   James Bell (right shoulder, severe)

Company "F"

Captain Constant Williams (right side, severe; and scalp, slight)
Sergeant William W. Watson (right hip, serious)
Died Aug. 29, 1877
Corporal Christian Luttman (both legs, severe)
Musician John Erickson (left arm, flesh)
Private Edwin D. Hunter (right hand, severe)
"   George Maurer (through both cheeks, serious)

Company "G"

Sergeant John W. H. Frederics (left shoulder, flesh)
"   Robert Benzinger (right breast, flesh)
Private John J. Connor (right eye, slight)
"   George Gaughart (right shoulder, thigh & wrist, severe)
"   James Burk (right breast, serious)
"   Chas. H. Robbecke (left hip, slight)

Company "I"

1st Lieutenant William L. English (through back, serious; and scalp slightly) Died Aug. 19
Corporal Richard M. Cunliffe (shoulder and arm, flesh)
Private Patrick Fallon (hip and leg, serious)
"   William Thompson (left shoulder, flesh)
"   Joseph Devoss (ankle and leg, serious)

Company "K"

2nd Lieutenant C. A. Woodruff (both legs above knee and left heel, severe)
Sergeant Howard Clarke (heel, severe)
Private David Heaton (right wrist, severe)
"   Mathew Devine (fore-arm, serious)
"   Philo O. Hurlburt (left shoulder, flesh)

Second Cavalry, Company "F"

Private Chas. B. Gould (left side, severe)

CITIZEN VOLUNTEERS

Killed	Wounded
L. C. Elliott	Myron Lockwood
John Armstrong	Otto Lyford
Davis Morrow	Jacob Baker
Alvin Lockwood	William Ryan
Campbell Mitchell	
H. O. Bostwick, Post Guide Fort Shaw, killed	

RECAPITULATION

	Killed	Wounded	
Officers Seventh Infantry	2	5	one officer since died
Enlisted men Seventh Infantry	20	30	one enlisted man since died
Enlisted men Second Cavalry	1	1	
Volunteers (citizens)	5	4	
Bostwick (citizen)	1		
Post guide at Fort Shaw	—	—	
Total	29	40	

September 2, 1877   (signed)   John Gibbon
                               Colonel, Seventh Infantry
                               Command District of
                               Montana

Surely this was a formidable list of casualties for a battle of such short duration. The toll was heavy because of the exceptional action and passion during every moment of the five-hour fray, after which, siege conditions prevailed for twenty hours. In Regimental Order No. 27, Gibbon took pains to mention the zeal, courage, and energy of both officers and men. His report says, "I found it out of the question to make any attempt at discrimination, and will simply mention the names of those who were present in the battle."[12]

Gibbon's appreciation of the valor displayed by officers and men was also disclosed by his recommendation that Congress should enact a law giving officers below the grade of field officer, and soldiers wounded in battle, the same increase of pay as they were then entitled to for every five years of service. For himself, he requested a brevet.

Although Gibbon listed the volunteers who were killed and wounded, he failed to give them special mention in his report. This slight was duly noted and resented by the participants, who felt that their contribution to the enterprise had been valuable. However, on September 5, 1877, Gibbon sent a memorandum to General E. D. Townsend, in which he suggested that provision be made by law to place the volunteers on the same footing as the soldiers in regard to pay, allowances, and pensions.

Relief for Gibbon's Wounded

When Howard reached Gibbon's camp at 10:00 A.M. on August 11, he was impressed with its resemblance to "a hospital guard. So many wounded; nearly half lying cheerful, though not able to move; many white bandages about the head and face; some arms in slings; there were roughly constructed shelters from the heat. . . ."[13]

Later in the day Howard's command arrived, and the men received medical care from Dr. Charles T. Alexander and Dr. Jenkins A. Fitzgerald. These services were enlarged on August 13, when William A. Clark arrived with thirty-five volunteers, two doctors, and four wagons. A relief party of twenty wagons and three doctors, accompanied by Thomas Stuart and sixty volunteers, also arrived from Helena. Equipment brought along included ambulances and tents. With five doctors and their assistants on the job the wounded were made as comfortable as possible.[14]

A number of Sisters of Charity from Helena were left at French Gulch to prepare overnight accommodations there. Similar service was accorded the wounded at Anaconda by Mr. and Mrs. Evans. Surely the response to Gibbon's call for aid was speedy and adequate.

Upon arriving at Deer Lodge the wounded were placed in St. Joseph's Hospital, where Lieutenant William L. English died. The other wounded soldiers and volunteers remained in Deer Lodge until they were able to return to their posts and homes.

Battle Evaluations

All who participated in the struggle at the Big Hole, or viewed the shambles wrought, described it as one of the most bitterly fought battles in the annals of warfare. Veterans of the Civil War compared the battle to the action on Little Round Top in Gettysburg. Other students declare that it was a bloodier battle than Waterloo. Will Cave describes it as "the hardest-fought, most stubbornly-contested, long-drawn withal fiercest conflict in the annals of warfare between settlers or soldiers and American Indians."[15]

The extreme intensity of the battle stemmed from the fact that Gibbon's command was smarting under the general criticism, from all directions, of the military action. Therefore, the colonel, although not Custer-like in boldness, was extremely anxious to redeem the honor and prestige of the army. On the other hand, the Nez Perce chiefs saw at once that the fate of their tribe was at stake. The result was a battle of great ferocity. One facet of this passion involved the killing of women and children. They were apparently fired upon both de-

liberately and by accident. Gibbon's report on this matter is indisputable:

> Logan's company being sent in on the run on the ex-
> treme right, a heavy fire was at once opened along
> the whole line of tepees. The startled Indians rushing
> from them in every direction, and for a few moments
> no shots were returned. Comba and Sanno first struck
> the camp at the apex of the V, crossed the main
> stream, and delivered their fire into the tepees and
> the Indians as they passed them.[16]

Sergeant C. N. Loynes confirmed this report in these
words: "We received orders to give three volleys, then
charge. We did so."[17] Of course, such a bombardment
was bound to kill indiscriminately. After that, much
depended upon the temperaments of the soldiers (or
volunteers) and the circumstances.

Colonel Gibbon states that he came upon several
women bearing children in their arms. Upon seeing
him, they held them forward saying, "Only women and
children here. . . ." He further states, "The poor, in-
offensive women and children . . . we no way disturbed."[18]

John B. Catlin was wholly forthright in his view of
this matter: "You may ask why did we kill the women
and children. We answer that when we came up on
the second charge, we found that the women were using the Winchesters with as much skill, and as bravely,
as did the bucks. As to the children, though many were
killed, we do not think that a citizen or soldier killed a
child on purpose. . . ."[19] G. O. Shields justified indiscriminate slaughter upon the ground that all Nez Perces
were bloodthirsty. He recorded the statement of a scout
who was with Bradley that they spared three squaws
huddled in the willows early in the fighting. After the
battle all three were found dead; one held a rifle and
a revolver was lying near the hand of another. These
circumstances were sufficient to convince Shields that

women generally took an active part in the battle. Tom Sherrill not only shared this opinion, but he recalled specific incidents: "An Indian and a squaw were near together when the Indian was shot. The woman dropped behind a small clump of brush, catching a revolver from the dying Indian, and as the soldiers approached she rose up from behind the brush and shot pointblank at the nearest, which happened to be Logan. She was immediately riddled with bullets."[20] Sherrill also observed the shooting of a lone woman in flight; and he mentioned hearing a fellow bragging about killing two women. There was the well-known case of an eighteen-year-old girl who was struck in the mouth with a rifle butt. The blow knocked her teeth out, but she recovered and was afterward called In-Koho-Lio (girl with broken teeth). After the campaign she married Andrew Garcia and bore him two sons.

McWhorter received slender confirmation from Indian informants that several women did participate in an early stage of the fighting. Red Wolf saw two women help drive soldiers from the camp. Yellow Wolf told how Wahlitits' wife grabbed his gun as he fell, and killed the soldier who had shot him. Then he added, "I heard she had been wounded before Wahlitits was killed. She was the only woman who did fighting in that battle that I knew about."[21]

The foregoing accounts of the battle in general, as well as other details not yet discussed, still leave the issue of victory or defeat unsettled.

Who Won the Big Hole Battle?

This question is difficult to answer. Colonel Gibbon was aware of that fact when he wired Governor Potts: "Had a hard fight with the Nez Perces, killing a number and losing a number of officers and men."[22] A victory message would have read differently. Colonel Nelson

A. Miles, who later achieved a decisive victory over the same tribe, sent a message that was exulting in character.

If Gibbon could not report victory, neither did he suffer a defeat. General Alfred H. Terry, commanding the Dakota Department, expressed the official viewpoint in this telegram to Gibbon: "Your dispatches of the 9th and 11th are received. I beg that you will accept for yourself, your officers, and your men my heartiest congratulations for your most gallant fight and brilliant success. . . ."[23] Terry went on to suggest that Gibbon's hands would be so full in taking care of the wounded that he could very well leave further pursuit of the Nez Perces up to Howard. Obviously Gibbon had failed to check the Nez Perce flight. On the other hand, his command had survived and couldn't be considered entirely beaten, although perhaps Howard's arrival alone saved it from extermination.

The foregoing view represents both the official and historical interpretation of the battle. The press and the public almost unanimously praised Gibbon and his men. They were all valiant fighters; if they fell short of full triumph, it was only because of disparity in numbers. To be sure, there were some who saw the battle in a different light. Angus McDonald called Big Hole a stunning defeat for the flag, and he denied that the Nez Perces had any advantages. Admittedly there were a few more men on the chief's side, but only a score or so were experienced warriors, whereas Gibbon had sixteen officers and a considerable body of battle-trained men. Besides, army men were more disciplined and responsive to orders. Then there was the matter of weapons; Indian arms were not uniformly efficacious. Perhaps a fourth of their guns were not adjusted to accessible munitions. Finally, Gibbon had the advantage of momentum, precision, time, and place.[24] In spite of all these factors, the Nez Perces had managed to throw the attackers back to the rifle pits.

Volunteer Captain John B. Catlin also regarded the battle as a defeat. He said, "We were whipped to a frazzle . . . but we broke the backbone of the Nez Perce nation. They never rallied again, so to speak."[25] Most students of the campaign might agree with Catlin's admission of defeat, but not in respect to Indian rallying power.

The Nez Perces were above all persistent. They had achieved a victory at White Bird Canyon, dominated the Camas Prairie situation, and demonstrated fighting power at the Clearwater and diplomatic skill at Fort Fizzle. The Battle of the Big Hole dealt them a serious blow, but they were able to recover. Now they resumed the flight that was destined to last fifty-five days and extend a thousand miles beyond Big Hole.

It was this over-all record that won the Nez Perce warriors so much renown. Standards for determining the fighting qualities of Indians cannot be absolutely agreed upon. Some students, however, would place the Nez Perces at the very top, claiming that their record in the campaign of 1877 entitled them to be rated among the first warriors of the world. This reputation would be difficult to reconcile with a simple verdict of defeat in the Battle of the Big Hole.

Renewal of Activity

Various arrangements were made with different parts of Gibbon's command. Captain Browning, with Lieutenant Wright and Lieutenant Van Orsdale and fifty soldiers, volunteered to accompany Howard for several marches before returning to their posts. Therefore, on the morning of August 13, Howard's full command, reinforced by this unit, started south in pursuit of the Nez Perces.

The rest of the command accompanied Gibbon to Deer Lodge. From there, companies A, D, G, and I returned to Missoula. Captain Richard Comba reported that his men in Company D, Seventh Infantry, had marched 549 miles since July 24, in going from Camp Baker to the Big Hole and back to Fort Missoula.

After the elimination of the dead, wounded, and absent-without-leave from the Bitterroot fighters, there were still eighteen volunteers on hand. There is nothing to indicate that any of these men wanted to join Howard in pressing the pursuit. However, Tom Sherrill states that several fresh citizens went on with Howard's scouts, "looking for more Indian trouble, but as General Howard dragged his army slowly behind the Indians, never trying to overtake them, our boys got tired and came back."[26] The veteran volunteers started up the mountain for home, and before reaching the summit they met some men from their home valley with "a wagon load of everything that was good to eat, which had been prepared by the settlers' wives, and with many articles for the wounded."

When William A. Clark and Thomas Stuart reached the battlefield with their volunteers, Howard had departed. These leaders and their men were eager for action, and their combined strength was sixty-two men. There were men from Butte, Deer Lodge, and Sheridan; all were well mounted, equipped, and ready. By making rapid marches they overtook Howard on the fifteenth.

Clark and Stuart offered their services as scouts to occupy passes and assist in holding actions. They at first understood that Howard was pleased with this proposition. But on the sixteenth they received word that he desired them to join his main column and protect his right flank in the regular routine. This prosaic assignment was unacceptable to the captains, and they decided to return home "for the simple reason that they did not believe General Howard, at his rate of progress at that time and previously, would overtake the Indians at all."[27] Howard recorded his annoyance over the manner in which some volunteers thronged his tent to offer criticism and advice concerning his management of the campaign.

There was one company of Montana volunteers that persisted in its purpose. It was the Callaway-Farrell company organized in Virginia City. They joined Howard near Bannock on August 15 and accepted service on his terms.

The people of Montana were no more satisfied with General Howard's record than Idaho people had been. Newspapers reflected the dissatisfaction of the volunteers. On August 23, the Bozeman *Avant Courier* praised the valor of the volunteers in the Battle of the Big Hole, and the eagerness of all Montana residents to avenge the blood of the innocent and repel a merciless and insolent foe. The article then denounced the federal government for failing to authorize Governor Potts to provide what was needed to sweep the Indians from the field. The *Helena Herald* decried the blunders, tardiness, and inability that characterized Howard's role in the campaign. In the same vein, the *Helena Weekly Independent* complained that "after laying over a day and two nights at Gibbon's battlefield, Howard only made 72 miles in the next three days."[28] The *New Northwest* printed an article by S. F. Dunlap that found fault with everyone but the volunteers. "Why were they not vigorously pursued by Gen. Howard? . . . We [the volunteers] are suffering in the loss of time, our hay crop is going to destruction. . . . We are spending money for scouts, fortifications, etc., and the rest of the country looks and mocks at our calamity. . . ."[29]

Of course the Big Hole battle, coming within fourteen months of the Custer Massacre, aroused the whole nation and attracted the attention of the world. There were rumors to the effect that a general uprising of Indians might result unless the Nez Perces were soon captured. Other newspapermen reflected the views of Montana editors and added considerable criticism of their own. The *Idaho Semi-Weekly World* of August 17 no doubt stated what nearly all of Howard's critics were thinking: "Of one thing we feel quite confident . . . General Howard ought to be relieved and someone else placed in command of the forces. . . . Rapid pursuit and rapid striking is the only way to fight Indians successfully. Following a hundred miles behind with an army and pack or wagon train six miles long is not forcible." Everyone seemed to forget that half of Howard's force consisted of infantry, and that the Nez Perces had several thousand tough ponies and were therefore able to change mounts frequently.

As if an unsympathetic press were not enough, Howard brought official displeasure upon himself by the contents of a letter he mailed to General Irvin McDowell on August 14, from Bannack City, Montana. After describing the status of the pursuit at the moment, he questioned the expediency of his orders of July 29 "to follow them up, no matter where they go . . . regardless of boundary lines."[30] He wrote: "Is it worthwhile for me to pursue them further from my department unless General Terry or General Crook will head them off and check their advance? . . . Without this cooperation the result will be, as it has been, doubtful."[31]

Howard committed a double error by asking for new orders when old ones were so clear, and implying that the Department of Dakota was not fully cooperating. In view of public clamor for more dynamic leadership, it is understandable that McDowell's answer chided Howard for looking to others for help instead of relying upon his own forces. Howard also sent a letter to Governor Potts, in which he admitted that the Nez Perces could "beat him running." This letter came to General Sherman's attention, and his stern reaction will be described in a later chapter.

Vandalism on the Battlefield

Both of the opposing forces at the Big Hole had ample opportunity to mutilate the remains of enemy dead during and after the battle. Although there was talk among the volunteers about taking scalps, there is no proof that any were taken by either side. Lieutenant Forse was able to make this commentary in reference to the entire campaign: "I did not see all the dead, but from inquiries made at the time I failed to find anyone who had seen a body that had been scalped or mutilated in any way."[32] Howard's Indian scouts did not conform to this code of ethics. Howard recorded their despicable behavior: "See these women's bodies disinterred by our own ferocious Bannock scouts! See how they pierce and dishonor their poor, harmless forms, and carry off their scalps! Our officers sadly look upon the scene and then, as by common impulse, deepen their beds and cover them with earth."[33]

The Bannocks not only performed such atrocities, but they celebrated in scalp dances at night.[34] Visitors to the battlefield recorded the gruesome details of continuing vandalism. Indians were disinterred and their burial robes carted away. Clothing was searched for gold and parts of apparel were removed. Amede Bassette visited the battlefield on August 30 and found "many Indian relics such as bead collars, bead-trimmed moccasins, rings . . . and many other little things, but nothing of any value whatever."[35] About the same time, a newspaper reporter named Parker visited the area and wrote, "The scene was fearful, yet satisfactory." He erroneously stated that Toohoolhoolzote's head was cut off and taken away for ethnological purposes.[36]

After several weeks, cold weather drove some bears down from higher elevations, and they began scavenging among the bodies. When this fact was reported to

Captain Rawn at Fort Missoula, he ordered Lieutenant J. T. Van Orsdale and six enlisted men to reinter the bodies of their comrades-in-arms. The detail left Missoula on September 20, found conditions as represented, and followed their instructions.[37] Years later, these remains were to be officially removed to other places. The original inadequacy and continuing neglect of the Indian graves left them exposed to vandals, wild beasts, and recurring floods. In 1938, McWhorter invited several Indian veterans of the campaign to visit the battlefield. Their expenses were to be paid and they would be feted by the residents of the Big Hole Basin. Still they declined. One said, "I might cry when I see where my friends and kindred were killed."[38]

13. INCIDENTS ON THE ROUTE TO CAMAS MEADOWS

⌐⌐⌐⌐⌐⌐⌐⌐⌐⌐⌐⌐⌐⌐⌐⌐⌐⌐⌐⌐⌐⌐⌐⌐⌐⌐⌐⌐⌐⌐⌐⌐⌐⌐⌐⌐⌐⌐

After leaving their camp on Swamp Creek the Nez Perces skirted the Big Hole Basin along the edge of the forested foothills. After ascending Pioneer Creek they crossed Skinner Meadows, then traveled over a pass and descended South Bloody Dick Creek to the mouth of Stevenson's Canyon.[1] There they crossed a ridge to the west and entered Horse Prairie, where they camped on August 12. Lean Elk (Poker Joe) was charged with the responsibility for tribal defense at this time, and he rearranged their marching order. The family unit was discarded, and the women, children, advanced guards, and horses were pushed forward, leaving a concentration of manpower to guard the rear.[2] This procedure was a defensive, rather than an aggressive, one, but the people of Bannack City, not knowing their intentions, took steps to defend themselves.

Bannack City Prepares for an Attack

Beating drums called all of the citizens together, and plans for the defense, even siege, of the village were presented. Women and children were quartered in Hotel

161

Meade, where extra food, water, clothing, and bedding were quickly assembled. Men hastened to throw up breastworks of dirt and logs on two knolls south of town. John Poindexter volunteered to ride north and urge Howard to send reinforcements, and Melvin Trask led a little expedition to Horse Prairie to warn settlers of the danger.[3] Mrs. Dunk Waddams set out on horseback for Medicine Lodge Creek in Sheep Basin on a similar mission. Some of her relatives were working there and she was concerned about their safety. Meanwhile, the Nez Perces adhered to the base of the western mountains.

Howard arrived at Bannack City on August 14, where he was joined by volunteer forces under the command of William A. Clark and others. Bannack was safe, but misfortune befell some of the settlers on the upper Horse Prairie. An advance guard of scouting Indians came upon the Montague-Winters ranch, where seven men were working. As the scouts approached the house a gun was discharged, and the Indians rushed the place. There they killed William Flynn. Then they killed two men in a hayfield. One was W. S. Montague, an early settler in the area; the other was James W. Smith. The ranch house was ransacked in a search for bandage material. Five miles above this place the Indians surprised Meyers and Cooper. The latter escaped but Meyers was slain. A settler named William Farnsworth was killed, but a man of retarded mentality was allowed to live. The Holahan home was entered but not damaged, possibly because two pictures of angels were hanging on the wall.[4] Several other men escaped from the scouting party by quickly appraising the situation and hiding.[5] A considerable number of horses were taken from the prairie, including Alex Cruikshank's entire herd.

In the circumstances, their appropriation of horses was justifiable. As Yellow Wolf said, "While we had many horses, it was good to have fresh ones. Best, too, that none be left for soldiers. It was aimed that no horses could be found by soldiers anywhere we passed."[6] The settlers may have been killed in resisting the seizure of their property; still, it was partly a case of wanton slaughter. When the Nez Perces appeared on Horse Prairie their tempers were still aroused by the recent brutal battle. Bitterroot settlers had betrayed their confidence, and this fact produced a vast change in their attitude toward all settlers. New commanders and forces continued to enter the field to hound them down. Thenceforth, all whites were likely to be regarded as enemies. Certainly all men directly in their path would be brushed aside. And yet, their behavior was not altogether consistent. One Indian simply said: "They are double-minded. . . . some boys are very bad. . . ."[7] It should be remembered that the young men ran in tribal factions and were not easy to control. Even so, they did not harm women and children, and no men were mutilated at any time.

A Circuitous Route

From Horse Prairie the Nez Perces crossed back over the Continental Divide through Bannock Pass, and then went down Cruikshank Canyon into Idaho. They hoped Howard would think that they intended doubling down the Mormon Fork (Lemhi) of the Salmon River, and that he would follow them. However, he had several Nez Perce scouts who assured him that the Clark Fork of the Yellowstone River was their true objective. For that reason, he refused to make the detour westward, even though a fervent appeal to do so reached him from Colonel George L. Shoup in Salmon City.[8] Instead, Howard hoped to intercept them by following the base line of the arc their route would describe. By following the stage and freight road over Monida Pass and down Beaver Canyon, Howard hoped to intercept the Indians near Beaver Creek station. However, he took still another precaution, lest the Nez Perces should outrun him to the point chosen. Lieutenant George Bacon, with a company of forty cavalry men, was ordered to go to Targhee Pass, above Henrys Lake, and hold the Indians at bay until Howard came upon their rear. By going up the Centennial Valley, this command was bound to reach Targhee Pass ahead of the Indians. As usual, Howard's plans were well conceived and promising. But before describing their execution, it is expedient to give an account of events incident to the Nez Perce detour upon the upper Lemhi River and Birch Creek areas.

Howard's refusal to pursue the Nez Perces across the Beaverhead Range threw the Salmon River country settlers entirely upon their own resources. Able leadership, combined with attitudes similar to those of the Bitterroot settlers, enabled them to cope with the Indians. Colonel Shoup had gained experience as an Indian fighter in the Southwest; he had served as a colonel under Colonel J. M. Chivington in the Massacre of Sand Creek in 1864. His associates, C. A. Woods and M. H. Andrews, also had fighting backgrounds. When they learned about the Big Hole battle these men and others made defense plans in case the Nez Perces should come into the Lemhi area. They decided to organize and fortify, but not to attack or provoke them. Special care was exercised in securing a pledge from Chief Tendoy that members of his band would remain on the Lemhi Indian Reservation and otherwise cooperate with the volunteers. It was reported that some of the Lemhis hoped for some excitement,[9] but in any case they confined themselves to a horse-stealing raid. It was reported that a group of Lemhis, led by Big Body, ran two hundred Nez Perce ponies onto the reservation.

Before this horse raid, Chief Tendoy pleaded with the Nez Perce chiefs to hurry through the country, and he may have sold cartridges to the refugees at excessive prices. Thus, these Shoshonis (Tendoy's Lemhi band), like the Bannocks, Flatheads, and (later) Crows, found it expedient to turn their backs on the beleaguered Nez Perces.

Although most of the Lemhi Valley settlers went down to Salmon City, some of the Junction men erected a stockade for their protection. It was made of timbers set on end in the ground and stationed in two rows, the space between being filled with earth. Portholes were made at intervals for use in case of attack. Some of the families were sent to Salmon, but a half dozen remained with the thirteen men who elected to defend the position. A level-headed man named Ed Swan acted as captain and managed to prevent any provocative action when Indians approached the stockade. The Nez Perces arrived at Junction at 10:00 A.M. on the morning of August 13. They set up their noon camp on the site of present-day Leadore. A friendly Indian from the Lemhi agency came to the stockade, and he was requested to enter the Nez Perce camp for information. A parley was arranged, and the chiefs assured the delegates that no harm was intended and that they could go to their homes. They returned to their posts, however, and awaited developments. At this juncture, a messenger was sent to Salmon with the following letter:

Junction, Lemhi, Aug. 13, 1877.

Geo. L. Shoup, Salmon City.

The Nez Perce Indians came in here at 10 A.M., about 60 in number with Looking Glass and White Bird. We have had a talk with them; they seem to be friendly disposed toward the citizens. They say for us to go home and attend to our business. They say that Joseph will be here today with 100 men. There are five lodges of Bannacks [sic] that came from Lost river this morning, they want to bring their squaws to our stockade. We shall be on the look out. If we get in trouble would be pleased to have help.

Very respectfully,
Jacob Yearian.

By midafternoon the Nez Perces were packed and the women and children were departing southward. The alert settlers recognized this as the critical hour, and H. C. McCreery recorded their reactions as he observed the scene from his battle station. A council of chiefs was held, in which there were three spokesmen. Then, every Indian mounted his horse and joined a line fronting the stockade. A charge was ordered and on they came, the men riding flat on the backs of their horses. But it was a mock maneuver; not a rifle was fired as the horsemen broke to the right and left and then circled back to the campground. On McCreery's order, "The gate was opened, and our crowd silently filed out and drew a long breath as we saw the line fade away and the sun disappear behind the mountains where they were going."[10] They struck south on the Old Mormon Missionary road toward the Birch Creek divide. McCreery wrote, "We could not help realizing the hardship and suffering, yes, and want that those poor human beings were enduring, all because of man's inhumanity to man. . . ."[11]

When the Indians moved southward from Junction, a man named John Clark volunteered to carry the news to Howard at Bannack City. In that way the general's judgment regarding their ultimate destination was confirmed. Al Linderman carried the good news that the chiefs had kept the truce to Colonel Shoup in Salmon City. On the morning of the fourteenth, three other settlers followed the Nez Perce trail to their campsite of the previous night. There they observed prepared positions of defense against attack, but no Indians were near. Although the Nez Perces had all left the area, the Junction settlers remained close to their stockade for several days. The efficacy of the stockade was later questioned when Lieutenant Albert G. Forse reported that it could have been enfiladed from higher ground within range on two sides.[12] Nevertheless, because of the good management of the settlers and the sufferance of the chiefs, no damage was inflicted upon the settlers of the Lemhi area. On the morning of the seventeenth, however, two Chinese reached Junction with the news of the Birch Creek Massacre.

The Birch Creek Massacre

All of the details of the Birch Creek Massacre will never be known, but the account given by the Chinese was later confirmed by Al Lyon, who also escaped. On the afternoon of August 15, an eight-wagon, three-team, freighting outfit serving Shoup and Woods and driven by Jim Hayden, Al Green, and Dan Combs entered Birch Creek Canyon. Two unnamed white men and two Chinese were passengers. A lonely horse herder named Albert Lyon saw the freight train from a distance and rode over to join it for the companionship of the night camp. These men had heard of the Nez Perce retreat, but their conception of the route was vague. While they were preparing their afternoon meal, an advance guard of Nez Perces arrived. Salutations were exchanged, and then the Indians demanded guns and supplies. Probably relations were peaceful until the whisky barrels were discovered and opened; after that, a wild spirit of horseplay developed. It appears that the Chinese were required to get down on all fours and run around like horses. The real trouble resulted from an attempt to force the same measure of humiliation upon the white men. Strenuous objections obviously inflamed the drunken Indians, and the five white men were slain. Lyon had requested a drink of water and an Indian guard had taken him to the creek. At that crucial moment, the wagons burst into flames and shots rang out, diverting the guard so that Lyon was able to dash into the willow-lined stream and hide.

During the night he emerged from the creek and made his way back to his neglected horse herd. Eventually, two of Shoup's cowboys rode up, and Lyon accompanied them to Salmon City, where he gave his account. The experience more than frightened him; for a time his mind was confused.[13]

Tradition holds, and Helen A. Howard also affirms, that these Indian scouts had no intention of committing murder at this time. It is also stated that the chiefs were disgusted with the behavior of the Indians who committed this atrocity.[14]

In the afternoon of the day the Chinese arrived at Junction, Colonel George L. Shoup, accompanied by about forty white men and as many friendly Lemhi Indians, appeared at the stockade. Alex Cruikshank has left an account of the volunteer activities in this instance. He was a Horse Prairie stockman whose horse herd was swept in by the fleeing Nez Perces, and he became a scout for General Howard and remained with him until they reached the final battlefield in the Bear Paw Mountains. Cruikshank contacted Colonel Shoup's forces at Junction. After appraising the situation, the colonel decided to return his volunteer force to Salmon City, but Chief Tendoy and fifteen Indians, together with William Falkner, joined Cruikshank's scouting detail and proceeded to the scene of the Birch Creek Massacre. Later, Colonel Shoup and Dave Wood, who owned the Hayden freighting outfit, and other men from Salmon arrived on the scene. The bodies of the five men were buried where they were found. Later in the fall the bodies of the three natives of the Lemhi Valley were removed to Salmon City. A monument now marks the spot where the Hayden party was massacred.

At this point, attention should be directed to the status of Bannock and Shoshoni Indians at the Fort

Hall Agency. On August 9, Agent W. H. Danielson reported a general restlessness resulting from rumors concerning the Nez Perce campaign. In fact, a young Bannock dressed for war deliberately committed depredations to arouse his tribesmen. They disciplined him, however, and affairs settled down. On August 13, Danielson wired Commissioner Smith that he could enlist two hundred warriors to fight the Nez Perces. He said, "They would do good service. It would be good for the Agency to have them thus employed."[15] His offer was forwarded to the War Department, and on the eighteenth General Sheridan authorized Danielson to enlist fifty scouts for thirty days and report to General Howard.[16]

On August 31, Commissioner Smith received the following offer from Agent James J. Patten in behalf of the Eastern Shoshonis located on the Wind River Reservation in Wyoming: "Chief Washakie says if they [officers] will give him a chance to mount his warriors when they [Nez Perces] come he can whip them in less than a day."[17]

On to Camas Meadows

From Birch Creek the Nez Perce cavalcade passed around the foothills in a southeastward direction. By the evening of the seventeenth their scouts reached the stage road a mile north of Hole-in-Rock stage station. The station was located on Dry, or Beaver, Creek, four miles above present-day Dubois. Myers Kaufman, stagekeeper, and other attendants, having been warned, hid in a lava cave. But the Indians did not raid the station, and the next morning, after Kaufman had made a quick reconnaissance, he assured his associates that "the danger is past; they went in by night."[18]

A camp was established on the north edge of the Snake River Plain, in a meadow bisected by Spring and

Camas creeks. Yellow Wolf said the Indians called the Dry, or Beaver, Creek Wewaltolkit Pah, meaning that it sank in the desert. None of the streams that originate in the mountains on the northeastern periphery of the Snake River Plain reach Snake River. The central part of Camas Meadows was situated about eighteen miles north of Hole-in-Rock station and an equal distance east of the mouth of Beaver Canyon. The Nez Perce name for their camp was Kamisnim Takin, meaning "camas meadows."

Howard's Race to the Crossing

Howard's forces reached the Montana Trail, or the old Corinne-Bannack stage route, at the mouth of Horse Prairie Creek on August 15. Two days later, as he was traveling south, he was overtaken by the Virginia City volunteers under the command of James E. Callaway, who were anxious to join his cavalry. On the same day Captain Randolph Norwood and fifty fresh cavalrymen, designated as Company 4 of the Second Infantry, from Fort Ellis, near Bozeman, also overtook Howard's command. Norwood was ordered to join Howard by General W. T. Sherman, who was a visitor at Fort Ellis in mid-August. The general was taken on a tour of Yellowstone National Park during the next week, escorted by a small detail of troops. Howard arranged to have the infantrymen transported in wagons along the freight road, and all energy was exerted to intercept the Nez Perces in the Dry Creek station area. Bannock Indian scouts were a day ahead of Howard's cavalry, and they observed the Nez Perce rear guard cross the road toward Camas Meadows on the evening of August 18. Chief Buffalo Horn, one of Howard's scouts, obtained a view of their camp in Camas Meadows.

Perhaps a few shots were exchanged between the two sets of Indian scouts. In any case, the Nez Perces were on the alert, and Howard's forces, having strained to intercept them, were still a day behind. While in camp near the present village of Spencer, Idaho, a settler Howard called "Uncle Mac" Carleton told Howard of the Birch Creek Massacre and offered to serve as a guide. His services were accepted. At this camp one of Howard's men stumbled upon two dead Nez Perce women lying in Dry Creek. Apparently wounded at the Big Hole, they had dropped out of the line of flight in this desolate spot.[19]

On August 19, Howard's command traveled the eighteen miles to Camas Meadows and made Camp Callaway between Camas and Spring creeks. It was a pleasant campsite, with ample grass for the horses and mules. The grass stood so thick in these meadows that the stage operators had cut and stacked it. These haystacks were not disturbed, as the horses preferred to eat the growing grasses. The men were disposed to relax by swimming, fishing, and hunting for grouse, and the Virginia City volunteers did not intend to bother about tethering their horses or posting guards. Howard and Captain Norwood gave all of their men orders to take both of these precautions,[20] and Major Edwin C. Mason attended to the confining and picketing of the stock with meticulous care. All of the horses were securely tethered, and the bell mares of the pack trains were hobbled. Sentinels were posted at points that covered every approach to the camp. Within this posted area two hundred mules were grazing at random. Upon receiving the major's report that the camp was in order, Howard expressed satisfaction over the situation:

From my tent I looked back to the parallel streams. Across the first one, the Callaway volunteers encamped. Norwood's Cavalry and the forty infantry occupied the west side. The other companies of cavalry covered all the approaches to my own, the central position which was upon a comparatively high lava pile, that, studded with bushes, constituted our castle-like defense. This position was strengthened by knolls and lava rocks on three sides, north, east, and south.[21]

Little wonder that Lieutenant Wood said, "Well, I'll take off my pants tonight, it is so safe a place." To this remark, Lieutenant Guy Howard laughingly replied: "I've loaned my pistol to a scout for tonight, so think likely the Indians will come back."[22] The quiet starlight night gave them promise of much-needed rest.

On the preceding night a wounded Nez Perce warrior named Black Hair had been disturbed by a dream as he lay upon this identical campsite. He saw himself and his companions escaping with General Howard's horses. The next morning he brought the message of his dream to the attention of the chiefs, and during the day they meditated upon it while their people moved fifteen miles to the north, where they camped.[23] The failure of Looking Glass to heed a warrior's dream medicine on the Big Hole made the chiefs susceptible to the horse-stealing suggestion. As a result, twenty-eight volunteers were organized under the leadership of Ollokot, Two Moons, Wottolen, and Peopeo Tholekt. By midnight, a column of horsemen started for Howard's camp, hoping there would be no sentries on the watch and that the stock would be grazing at random.

14. THE RAID AND BATTLE OF CAMAS MEADOWS

The exceptional precautions Howard had taken for the protection of Camp Callaway were observed by Nez Perce scouts. Upon returning to their own camp they reported what they had seen to the chiefs. The information did not diminish their resolution to carry out the plan. This tactic was designed to put Howard's cavalry on foot. The chiefs did not envision a battle.

Yellow Wolf described the movements of the little band:

We traveled slowly. No talking loud, no smoking. The match must not be seen. We went a good distance and then divided into two parties—one on each side of the creek. . . .

Chiefs Ollokot and Toohoolhoolzote were the outstanding leaders of my company. . . . Teeweeyounah and Espoowyes led the other company. . . .

Before reaching the soldier camp, all stopped, and the leaders held council. How make the attack? The older men did this planning. Some wanted to leave the horses and enter the camp on foot. Chief Looking Glass and others thought the horses must not be left out. This last plan was chosen—to go mounted. Chief Joseph was not along.[1]

The raiders reached the edge of the camp about 3:30 A.M. Several scouts dismounted and crept among the picketed horses to cut them loose. Then two things happened simultaneously. As a mounted column approached, a sentry shouted, "Who goes there?" At the same moment, a foot scout named Otskai accidentally discharged his gun in the midst of the camp. Thus, an alarm was sounded from two places before many horses had been released from their picket lines. However, two hundred mules were free, and the Indians concentrated upon stampeding them northward. This was accomplished by a "sharp, quick, multitudinous roaring, followed by the shrill Indian yell."[2] This terrible discordant war whoop, accompanied by a circling pattern of action and a lead-off horseman moving in the proper direction, enabled the raiders to control the loose stock. In spite of all the shouting, several men thought they heard "the great voice of Looking Glass" booming out orders.[3] Bullets were flying about and some of them struck the wagons, but only one man was hit, and his wound was slight. Darkness, noise, and surprise compounded the confusion, but the cavalry officers and men quickly dressed and mounted, while "Boots and Saddles" was sounded by Bugler Bernard Brooks.

Both Howard and Norwood reported that the Nez Perce horsemen approached their camp in a column of fours, thereby attempting to simulate the return of Bacon's absent cavalry. Nez Perce informants refused to take credit for this deception by stating that the Indians did not intentionally ride in such a formation. Obviously the sentry thought they resembled troopers and, on that account, his challenge came too late.

General Howard ordered Major George B. Sanford to organize a strong force, pursue the raiders, and recover the stock. In a few moments three companies of cavalry were assembled under Norwood, Captain Carr, and Captain Jackson. By dawn nearly a hundred horsemen were galloping northward in pursuit of the raiders,

Young Chief Joseph
(Historical Society
of Montana, Helena)

above:
Peopeo Tholekt

below:
Yellow Wolf,
Chief Joseph's nephew
(Historical Society
of Montana, Helena)

Big Hole battlefield,
sketch by Granville Stuart,
May 11, 1878
(Historical Society of
Montana, Helena)

A Nez Perce
woman drying
meat

Luther S.
"Yellowstone"
Kelley,
Chief Scout
for Colonel
Nelson A. Miles

Chief White Bird
(Historical Society
of Montana, Helena)

far left
Ollokot,
Chief Joseph's
brother

left center
Yellow Wolf in 1927

left
Captain S. G. Fisher

below
Chief Joseph's
camp at Nespelem,
Washington, 1902

Chief Joseph
(Historical Society
of Montana, Helena)

who had several miles' head start. Believing that Sanford's force could cope with the situation, Howard ordered breakfast for the reserves and proceeded to organize them with deliberation. According to his record, Callaway's volunteers needed plenty of time, because "not being used to sudden alarms . . . one take another's gun, some get the wrong belts, others drop their percussion caps, their horses get into a regular stampede and rush in the darkness toward the herd of mules, and all the animals scamper together, while the citizens plunge into water above their knees and cross to the regular troops at a double-quick."[4] A newspaper reporter named Tom Baker recorded his observations of their behavior in a more jocular vein:

> Our Volunteers
> Lay low boys, it is a general attack
> Down in the creek or you'll get shot in the back,
> I pledge you my word I wish I hadn't come,
> And I'll bet you ten to one we'll have to foot it home.
> Oh, I am one of the volunteers,
> Who marched right home on the tramp, tramp,
> When Joseph set the boys afoot,
> At the battle of Callaway's camp.[5]

Yellow Wolf describes the chagrin of the raiders as sunlight enabled them to see the stock: "Eeh! Nothing but mules—all mules. Only three horses among them. I did not know, did not understand why the Indians could not know the mules. Why they did not get the cavalry horses. That was the object the chiefs had in mind—why the raid was made."[6] Actually, about half of the horses belonging to the Virginia City volunteers were missing. It is recorded that the volunteers received $150 per head from the government for their mounts.[7]

An advance guard of Sanford's cavalry reached the end of the mule herd and managed to recover a few of them. This pressure produced a diversion in the tactics of the raiding party. Several warriors continued driving the mules on to camp, and the others deployed themselves in a thin skirmish line across the middle of a meadow that filled the narrow valley at this point, eight miles north of Camp Callaway.[8] A lava escarpment ten feet high formed a southern boundary five hundred yards from the Nez Perce position. This barrier stopped the progress of Sanford's cavalry, and some of the troopers dismounted and also formed a skirmish line.

The distance between these lines was too great for effective marksmanship, and when a shot struck Lieutenant Benson in the hip it was discovered that the Indians in the meadow were serving as a decoy, while others had been creeping forward on both flanks to enfilade the troops. Hence, Sanford ordered a bugler to call a retreat.

The retreat of those cavalrymen whose horses had been taken to the rear was an occasion of great excitement and confusion. A number were caught up by companions on horseback; this procedure caused the horses to buck. A horse's nosebag, filled with cartridges, was knocked out of a cavalryman's hand. In the confusion, Captain Norwood's company drifted so far to the east that the other units lost track of him. They continued retreating another mile or so, where they met General Howard advancing with his reserves. Quickly recognizing the absence of triumph on Sanford's face, Howard said, "What is the matter, Major?" Sanford then described the action. "But where is Norwood?" "That is what I am trying to find out." "Why, you haven't left him?" "No, I sent him the order [to draw back] at the same time as to Carr, but it seems that he has stopped." "Well, let us return to him at once."[9]

Howard took command and extended his lines as far east as possible. They moved forward through alternating stands of aspens and sagebrush, across a landscape broken by low ridges and small basins. Howard describes the terrain thus: "Here on the higher ground, acres upon acres, for ten miles or more, are thrown into curious lava-knolls, each knoll so much like another that you cannot fix your whereabouts by the distant and diverse features around you."[10]

By midafternoon Howard came upon Norwood and his men crouching in their lava rock rifle pits located a few rods apart along the top and on the edges of a series of ridges that enclosed a protected area for their horses.

Captain Norwood's Account

Since the principal part of the battle fell upon Norwood's company, his report of the action to Colonel Gibbon is the most satisfactory. He stated that obedience to Sanford's order to continue retreating would have imperiled his company. So he elected to seek cover upon the converging ridges, mentioned above, and make his stand. The Nez Perce sharpshooters pressed his position closely for four hours, but they could not dislodge him. Norwood praised Lieutenant Benson for exhibiting courage and coolness, in spite of a painful wound.[11] A sergeant named Hugh McCafferty rendered distinguished service by climbing a cottonwood tree, and, being concealed by the foliage, describing the shifting positions of the warriors to a soldier below, thereby contributing to the efficiency of Norwood's defense tactics.[12] Even so, Norwood attributed the survival of his company to the arrival of Howard's forces. Yellow Wolf implies that the warriors raised the siege on their own volition. He said, "Indians were on bluff, protected behind rocks. It was a sharp fight for some time. After a while I heard the warriors calling to each other. Chiefs say do no more fighting!"[13] Whereupon, these remarkable warriors withdrew from the battlefield and returned to their tribal camp without any fear of being followed. Their voluntary withdrawal is evidence that Norwood's position was strong, a fact duly noted and recognized by Howard.

Howard assembled his forces and returned to Camp Callaway, where the battle casualties and raid losses were calculated.

Casualties of the Battle

Yellow Wolf states that "no Indian was bad hurt, only one or two just grazed by bullets."[14] Wottolen was wounded in the side, and Peopeo Tholekt's head was creased.

Norwood listed the following casualties among the men in the Second Cavalry, Company 4:[15]

1st Lieut. H. M. Benson	wounded,	thigh
1st Sergt. H. Wilkins	"	head
Corpl. H. Garland	"	thigh
Blacksmith Samuel Glass	mortal (Died at Pleasant Valley)	
Private Harry Trevar	"	back (Died in Virginia City, Oct. 4, 1877)
Farrier Jones	wounded, leg	
Private William Clark (volunteer)	"	chin and shoulder

Bugler Bernard Brooks was killed, and his body was taken back to camp for burial by his comrades. Mason read the appropriate service, and farewell volleys were fired over a lonely grave among sagebrush and lava beds in the middle of a wilderness.

The Significance of Camas Meadows

Although Howard and his men did not realize the fact, they had now lost their chance to overtake the

Nez Perces; therein lies the significance of the raid and battle of Camas Meadows. At the very moment when a burst of energy and speed might have won a battle and closed the slender fifteen-mile gap that separated Howard from his quarry, the military force was stopped. No one could state the situation better than Yellow Wolf, when he said, "The soldiers did not hurry to follow us. They slowed after losing their pack mules."[16] Howard's means for fast pursuit had been taken away, and worse still, he would learn within two days that Lieutenant Bacon had failed to fulfill his blockade role at Targhee Pass.

It is probable that no other combination of grave, campground, and battlefield has been more neglected than Camas Meadows. This is partly due to its isolated location, the small numbers involved in the battle, and the few casualties. Although the area is quite attractive, the place has been all but forgotten. A homesteader found enough battle relics to locate the meadow where the Nez Perces stopped to engage the troops; a sheepherder noticed the rifle pits where Norwood's men took shelter; a stone marker was erected over the bugler's grave; but all of these places are hard to find today.

An Idaho association has designated a road that branches off from Route 91 near Mack's Inn as the Idaho Central. This third-rate, unimproved road attracts very few visitors, although some of the flavor of the Old West can be encountered. Along this road sheep and cattle can be seen grazing on the open range. Cowboys and sheepherders appear in their true roles of herding, wrangling, and trailing stock.

Perhaps highway markers will be placed to enable the passerby to locate Norwood's battlefield, Howard's Camp Callaway, and the grave of Bugler Bernard Brooks. Strangely enough, during World War II, the United States Navy conferred the name S.S. *Camas Meadows* upon a tanker.

15. ON TO YELLOWSTONE NATIONAL PARK

Chief Joseph, camp master during the entire flight, must have been confident that the mule raid would temporarily immobilize Howard. Accordingly, his people did not break camp on August 20. Undoubtedly they were busy gathering food all that day. Entirely without portable commissary, they were forced to provide along the way the nourishment they required. The area they were passing through was called "Shotgun," because sage grouse were often plentiful. No reference has been found to their hunting success at this time. However, they undoubtedly found edible roots and bulbs of various kinds. The soldiers noticed that bark had been stripped from many aspen trees along Camas Creek.

By midafternoon, the raiders reached camp with many mules and a few horses. These were distributed according to need, and the chiefs made arrangements for an early start the next morning. The band may have reached the meadow prairie southwest of Henrys Lake on August 21. This lake was well stocked with fish, and the forage for animals was excellent. Although the Indians rested here part of a day, they did not tarry. The next morning they again crossed the Continental

Divide at Targhee Pass without any interference from Lieutenant George Bacon, who had been ordered to blockade them.

Bacon's command had reached the pass on August 20, but, not seeing a Nez Perce camp at Henrys Lake, Bacon concluded that the Indians would not come that way after all. He decided that the tribe had skirted the northern rim of the Snake River Basin, penetrated the forests east of the Teton Range, and headed for Two Ocean Pass in the Wind River Mountains. Accordingly, he returned in search of Howard, but his route proved devious and he missed both the oncoming Indians and Howard's advance guard. Bacon's services, however energetic, were unavailing, because he did not wait at Targhee Pass. Howard had sent him messages of reassurance upon two occasions, but the messengers failed to overtake him.[1] It is clear today that Howard's entire command, or at least most of his cavalry, should have taken Bacon's route. Still, there is no guarantee that the Nez Perces would have blindly entered their ambuscade.

After crossing Targhee Pass, the Nez Perces trailed down to the Upper Madison River prairie and camped by that great fishing stream. No doubt their hunger was satisfied on the evening of August 22. From that point (present-day West Yellowstone, Montana), the Great Bannock Trail to the Clark Fork started to the northeast across the Gallatin Range, thence to the forks of the Yellowstone River at present-day Tower Junction, up the Lamar River, across the Absaroka Range, and down the Clark Fork of the Yellowstone River. Instead of crossing the Gallatin Range, the chiefs elected to follow the Madison River and thereby add another detour to their line of flight. This deviation was made in the hope that Howard would be confused. Of course, Nez Perce scouts "found each day the way to go."[2] Yellow Wolf and his cousin Otskai were attending to this scouting duty as they traveled toward Madison Junction, when they heard someone chopping wood. Dismounting, they crept toward the source of the sound and observed an elderly man feeding a campfire. He was a prospector named Shively, en route from the Black Hills to the Montana gold fields. Hoping that he knew Yellowstone Park, the scouts took him to the chiefs. They provided a horse for him and detained him for scouting purposes. He was treated in a civil and polite manner, and he stayed with them for a week.[3] The Indians were well oriented a day after finding Shively, and it is probable that he would have been released at any time after August 24, but he stayed with them until the night of August 31. Shively's observations concerning the number, manner of travel, and general demeanor of the Nez Perces were reported in the newspapers. He had an interesting experience, and he seemed to enjoy it.

On the night of August 23, the Nez Perce camp was located along a stream, since given their name, at the point of union with the Firehole River. After dark several scouts, who rode a little farther to the southeast, observed the flicker of campfires. Curious, and in need of supplies, they rode close to the camp under cover of darkness. There they waited for daylight in order to assess the situation. They were on the edge of a visitors' camp in the Lower Geyser Basin. The events that transpired here and elsewhere in Yellowstone National Park will be described in the next chapter. Meanwhile, Howard's progress should be described.

Howard's March to Henrys Lake

Shortly after Howard's command returned to Camp Callaway after the Battle of Camas Meadows on August 20, his infantry division arrived under the command of Captain Marcus P. Miller. They had traveled forty-eight miles in twenty-four hours. Howard's entire command was thereby united again. It consisted of two hundred cavalry, three hundred infantry, fifty scouts, and fifty Montana volunteers. Long, hard marches had taxed the endurance of the infantrymen, and the early morning horse raid, hot pursuit, and sharp fight had exhausted the rest of the command. Thus, everyone was in need of rest that night, and it was not interrupted. The loss of nearly one hundred mules and many of the volunteers' horses necessitated a revision of travel procedures. Many cavalry mounts were pressed into wagon service.

The next camp, which was on the Snake River, was named Benson in honor of the wounded lieutenant. That night Captain S. G. Fisher and a band of thirty Bannock Indian scouts arrived from the Fort Hall Indian Reservation. A score of Bannocks had joined Howard on the Clearwater, and they had been with him since that time. Their leader, Buffalo Horn, obtained Howard's permission to hold a dance that night. The enthusiasm the dancing generated impelled the chief to ask the general for permission to kill his three Nez Perce scouts and herders. Buffalo Horn affirmed that they were spies and traitors. Howard went so far as to secure their denials and have them face their accusers before refusing the bellicose demand. In less than a year Buffalo Horn was being pursued by Howard in what is called the Bannock War of 1878.

On the twenty-second, part of Howard's cavalcade made a long march and bivouacked at Henrys Lake. That evening two days' rations were issued to Captain S. G. Fisher and his Bannocks, and at 7:00 A.M. they crossed Targhee Pass.[4] These scouts followed the Nez Perce trail to their smouldering campsite on Madison River before a messenger returned to apprise Howard of the fact that Lieutenant Bacon had failed to contact the Indians. Howard's command, having had an early start, was toiling toward the pass along the creek that now bears his name.

In spite of his great disappointment the general wanted to press on, and he issued an order to move.[5] Doctor C. T. Alexander, his chief medical officer, remonstrated, "You can go no farther . . . your whole command is unfit to take the field again without a long rest."[6] This position was endorsed by the inspector, the aides, the quartermaster, and the officers. Perhaps the best evidence that Howard had done his utmost to overtake the Nez Perces is found in the absence of criticism from the Virginia City volunteers, other Montana teamsters, and the soldiers themselves. The only expressions of disapproval came from S. G. Fisher and his Bannock Indian scouts, who had joined the campaign just two days before.

The men lacked food, clothing, shoes, blankets, and medicine. Furthermore, they were short of horses and mules because of the Camas Meadows raid and the wear and tear of the campaign. In these circumstances, it was considered expedient to establish a four-day bivouac at Henrys Lake. While others rested, Howard, his son Guy, and an escort made a fast sixty-mile trip to Virginia City to secure the needed horses and supplies. Tom Farrell and several other citizens preceded them at top speed to buy several hundred horses.[7] All other Montana volunteers and teamsters returned to their homes at that time, except Fred K. Kohls, who continued to serve Howard as scout.[8]

Captain Norwood and Captain Cushing were sent to Fort Ellis with two companies of cavalry. They were advised to resupply their men and plan to resume the campaign if it should circle to the northeast of Yellowstone National Park. These men took Howard's worn-out horses and mules to Fort Ellis; in October the commanding officer of that post asked the Department Adjutant General for permission to sell "over one hundred and fifty broken down horses and mules Howard's people left here; about one half of them not worth feeding."[9]

Farrell and his assistants fulfilled their horse-buying assignment in respect to numbers, but when saddles were placed upon their backs many of the horses proved to be quite unbroken.

Howard's Virginia City Telegrams

Howard described the delight of the Virginia City merchants over the purchases he made during his visit. He telegraphed orders for military supplies to be delivered from Fort Ellis and sent communications to his superior officers. To General Sherman, at Fort Shaw, Montana, he reported the incidents that had transpired since his reports from Bannack City. Then, looking to the future, he said:

> What I wish is from some eastern force, the hostiles be headed off before they disaffect the Crows or unite with Sioux. . . .
> I heard that Miles, probably Sturgis, is on the Yellowstone, not far from my front. Is that true?
> My command is so much worn by over-fatigue and jaded animals that I cannot push it much further. If Miles, or Sturgis, is near by with Norwood's company, just sent to Ellis, and the 50 Indian scouts that I will send thither, or on the heels of the hostiles, I think I may stop near where I am, and in a few days work my way back to Fort Boise slowly, and distribute my troops before snow falls in the mountains.

General Sherman's reply of the same date, delivered at Henrys Lake, was stern and to the point:

> I don't want to give orders, as this may confuse Sheridan and Terry; but that force of yours should pursue the Nez Perces to the death, lead where they may. Miles is too far off, and I fear Sturgis is too slow. If you are tired, give the command to some young,

energetic officer, and let him follow them, go where they may, holding his men well in hand, subsisting them on beef gathered in the country, with coffee, sugar, and salt in packs. For such a stern chase infantry are as good as cavalry. Leave to Sturgis to head them off if he can. I will be at Helena on Tuesday next. No time should be lost. I don't know your officers, but you can select the commander and order accordingly. When the Indians are caught your men can march to the Pacific Railroad and reach their posts by rail and steamboat. They are not needed back in California and Oregon now, but are needed just where they are.

Howard replied, on August 27, as follows:

Yours of the 26th [24th] received. You misunderstood me. I never flag. It was the command, including the most energetic young officers, that were worn out and weary by a most extraordinary march. You need not fear for the campaign. Neither you nor General McDowell can doubt my pluck and energy. My Indian scouts are on the heels of the enemy. My supplies have just come, and we move in the morning and will continue till the end. I sent Cushing and Norwood, now en route, two days ago to operate from Ellis and Crow agency. Indians captured a party of eight gentlemen and two ladies on Lower Geyser Basin, Friday evening last. Hostiles will probably cross Stinking River about one hundred miles southeast from Crow agency.

General Sherman wired again on August 28:

Just back from Benton. Got your dispatch of 27th. Glad to find you so plucky. Have every possible faith in your intense energy, but thought it probable you were worn out, and I sometimes think men of less age and rank are best for Indian warfare. They have more to make. I think Sturgis will look out for your Indians at Clark's Fork, and that Sheridan will have another party at Camp Brown, and still another at the head of Tongue River. But my idea is that the Nez Perce expect to hide in the Big Horn Mountains, about Stinking Water, trusting to your stopping pursuit. Were your force to return to Idaho now, these Indians would surely return to Montana. I start on Thursday for Missoula and Walla Walla. Will report you all well.

Sherman had wired to General P. H. Sheridan, in Chicago, on August 24, as follows: "Dispatch received. I don't think Howard's troops will catch Joseph, but they will follow, trusting to your troops heading them off when they come out on the east of the mountains. Will be back to Helena next Tuesday."[10]

Howard also received a telegram from McDowell, in which he was advised to be less dependent upon what others at a distance might or might not do, and rely more on his own forces and plans. Howard was assured that Sheridan had ordered Terry to cooperate, even to the extent of placing Dakota Department troops temporarily under Howard's command. In fact, everything was in readiness for intercepting the hostiles if they reached the Yellowstone Valley.[11]

These telegrams disclose a part of the intricate strategy being contrived by officers in the Department of Dakota for the capture of the elusive Nez Perces. Other military documents record the desires, plans, and energies that were conspiring to throw a net around the fleeing Indians.

After Norwood and Cushing arrived at Fort Ellis, officials there hustled to secure scouts, supplies, and horses to enter the campaign. Lieutenant Gustavus C. Doane, who had been with the party of effective discovery of Yellowstone in 1870, hastened toward Mammoth Hot Springs with a company of Second Cavalry. Lieutenant De Rudio, with a company of Seventh Cavalry and a party of Crow Indian scouts, accompanied Doane. These units left Fort Ellis for the north entrance of the park on August 27, the same day Howard entered the west gate. Experienced scouts such as George Hernden, Jack Bean, Alex Anderson, J. R. King, and William Hamilton signed up to seek information about Nez Perce movements. They were expected to keep Howard, Sturgis, and Hart informed.[12] Commands under Sturgis and Hart were marking time at the eastern exits of Yellowstone National Park.

A letter from Sherman to Howard, from Helena, dated August 29, describes the disposition of forces ready to blockade the Nez Perces as they emerged from the park:

> General Sturgis, with six companies, was on Clark's Fork. Major Hart, with five companies and a hundred scouts, was on Stinking Water [Shoshoni River]. General Merritt, with ten companies was at Camp Brown. Yours as the pursuing force, requires much patience but not much chance of a fight.[13]

If Howard needed patience, so did the officers watching the passes. A letter from Colonel S. D. Sturgis to Governor Potts, written from a position between the mouths of the Clark Fork and the Stinking Water River on August 23, reveals that he was plagued by doubts and worries.[14] Colonel Nelson A. Miles, although far removed from the theater of activity, had a hand in the troop dispositions and movements. One line from his autobiography suggests his anxiety: "For weeks I anxiously watched for information from the West."[15]

The foregoing telegrams, letters, and activities also reveal the tension resulting from what many called Howard's dilatory pursuit. Memoranda from General McDowell to Sherman exhibit a mounting impatience with what he considered to be Howard's excuses. Perhaps these comments and criticisms caused Sherman to change his mind about releasing Howard from the onerous task of concluding the campaign. The day after his barbed telegram, he wrote Howard a friendly letter stating that he could return to his department with perfect propriety. In fact, Sherman authorized him to transfer the command in the field to Colonel C. C. Gilbert and join him in an inspection tour of the Department of Columbia.[16]

At the same time, Sherman sent Gilbert a letter to that effect and appointed him to take Howard's place. Gilbert and an escort left Fort Ellis on August 31, expecting to meet Howard in Yellowstone National Park. However, Gilbert's course passed Howard on the west, and although he doubled back and followed diligently he failed to overtake him. From this incident, it would appear that Colonel Gilbert was hardly the man to pursue the Nez Perces. All of the foregoing telegrams and letters had of course not reached Howard's headquarters on Henrys Lake by August 27. Still, enough had arrived to produce a salutary effect upon the morale of Howard's people. He described the reaction this way: "But the chafing stern order . . . worked like a charm upon the command. Officers and soldiers, now re-supplied, were ready, to a man, 'We will go with you to the death.' It was worthwhile to bear a little chagrin in order to awaken such a loyal spirit."[17]

Notwithstanding the diminution of Howard's cavalry resulting from the departure of Norwood and Cushing, the column appeared strong, and it moved briskly as it departed from Henrys Lake on the morning of August 27. After four days of rest they could follow the Nez Perce trail with enthusiasm. Upon reaching the west boundary of the park, the command came upon several men who had undergone a frightening experience with the Indians four days before. Since then they had been on foot and without food or bedding. While Howard supplied their needs, they described their encounter.

16. INDIANS AND SOLDIERS CROSS THE PARK

The area now known as Yellowstone National Park was discovered by John Colter in 1807. It was visited by trappers and miners until, by 1870, its phenomenal scenery had finally attracted the attention of official groups. The Washburn-Langford-Doane Expedition of 1870 and the Hayden Expedition of 1871 resulted in recommendations to Congress, which established Yellowstone National Park on March 1, 1872. The park was a peaceful domain when the Nez Perce campaign invaded its confines. For four years, Nathaniel P. Langford had served as superintendent without pay, and Philetus W. Norris, his successor in 1877, was serving on the same basis. No funds for any purpose had been made available; therefore, the park was no better endowed with roads and other facilities than the surrounding wilderness.

Notwithstanding the absence of improvements, five hundred people visited Yellowstone during the summer of 1873. There were fish in the streams, moose in the swamps, and elk in the meadows. No laws restricted taking them; people camped wherever they pleased, and the visitors were generally adventurous and resourceful.

The arrival of the Nez Perces, however, caused great consternation, and they proved to be the most unwelcome visitors in the history of the park. It was fortunate that only two single individuals and two camping parties encountered them.

The Radersburg Visitors

The Nez Perces spent the night of August 23 in a camp on the banks of the Firehole River, above the narrows. At daybreak the next morning several Indians appeared in the camp of some park visitors from Radersburg, Montana. The campers were Mr. and Mrs. George F. Cowan; Mrs. Cowan's brother and sister, Frank and Ida Carpenter; Charles Mann; William Dingee; Albert Oldham; A. D. Arnold; and Henry Myers. A prospector named Harmon was also associated with the Cowan party at this time.

These people were just preparing to break up the "home" camp located at the terminus of the wagon road. For the past week they had been enjoying themselves on horseback visits to the geyser basins, and several of them had been to the lake and canyon.

Dingee asked the Indians, "What are you?" "Snake Injun," one replied. Later they admitted they were Nez Perces and made a demand for coffee and bacon. Arnold began dealing out these supplies, but Cowan interfered and refused to give them any. Then, as one Indian who called himself "Charley" attempted to give a signal, Cowan peremptorily ordered him to keep his hands down, arousing the Indians' resentment. Frank Carpenter asked them if any harm was in store for the party. The spokesman said, "Don't know, maybe so." He gave them to understand that since the Big Hole battle the Nez Perces were suspicious of all white men.[1]

The worried little party held a hasty consultation, and in view of their limited arms and ammunition they decided, with serious misgivings, to make an appeal to the chiefs for their deliverance. They hooked up their team, saddled their horses, and, after going two miles, joined the Indian band, which turned eastward and journeyed up Nez Perce Creek. After a couple of miles the wagon was abandoned, its contents rifled and the spokes knocked out for whip handles.

By midday the case had come to the attention of the chiefs. A council was held at the base of Mary Mountain, in which it was decided that the tourists were to be liberated. Poker Joe spoke for the chiefs: "Some of our people [Looking Glass] knew Mrs. Cowan and her sister at Spokane House. The soldiers killed many Nez Perce women and children on the Big Hole. But we do not hurt Montana people. You may go. Take old horses and do not spy."[2] Their saddles, guns, and horses were taken, and they were given worn-out horses. The white men nodded acceptance of these extraordinary terms. They were glad to part with the tribe and retrace their course. Within a half hour, two of the men, Arnold and Dingee, abandoned their horses and ducked into the forest. Hidden Indian scouts were obviously expecting just such behavior. A few minutes later a number of braves stopped Cowan's party, demanding the missing members. Cowan pleaded ignorance, whereupon Charley said, "You will have to come back." The little band again turned eastward.

Angry Indians were milling around on all sides, each waiting for the other to start an attack. Suddenly Umtill-lilp-cown, one of the three Idaho murderers, fired at Cowan, hitting him in the thigh. At the same time Oldham was shot, a bullet passing through his face. Carpenter saw an Indian aiming at him, and thinking some of the Nez Perces might be Catholics he made the sign of the cross. His act may have disconcerted the warrior for he did not fire. Oldham managed to get away through a thicket, while Cowan was so stunned he fell to the earth. His wife jumped down from her horse and held him, but she was dragged away. Another shot, from close range, struck him in the forehead. His wounds were considered fatal, and he was left to die. At this juncture Poker Joe arrived from the chiefs, who had got word of the attack, and he stopped the onslaught.

In the shuffle and commotion that ensued, Myers, Harmon, and Mann escaped. Mann felt a bullet whiz through his hat as he ran among the trees. Each man went in a different direction and carried the impression that he was the sole survivor.

The other survivors, including Mrs. Cowan, her brother, and her sister, were again taken captives. Although their treatment during the next twenty-four hours was considerate, it was a period of great mental anguish for them. They spent the night by Chief Joseph's campfire, and Mrs. Cowan observed the chief.

> My brother tried to converse with Chief Joseph, but without avail. The Chief sat by the fire, sombre and silent, foreseeing in his gloomy meditations possibly the unhappy ending of his campaign. The "noble red man" we read of was more nearly impersonated in this Indian than in any I have ever met. Grave and dignified, he looked a chief.[3]

Mrs. Cowan was impressed by Chief Joseph's dignity and cares, but she also noted that the majority of the Nez Perces were lighthearted. She said that the chiefs were aware that Bannock Indian scouts were close upon their heels.

On the evening of the twenty-fifth the captives were provided with two horses and released near the Mud Volcano. Because the Indians wanted them to go slowly, they provided no saddle for Ida or horse for Frank. Poker Joe directed them to go down the river "quick." This they did as rapidly as their broken-down ponies would carry them. They made their way over Mount

Washburn and beyond Tower Falls, where they came upon a detail of soldiers who supplied their most urgent necessities and sent them to Bozeman.

While descending the Yellowstone Valley they received much sympathy from the settlers. As they entered Bozeman, Lieutenant Doane and a considerable number of Crow Indian scouts and soldiers were leaving for the park. Carpenter joined Doane's command, with the intention of returning to the scene of the attack and attending to the burial of his brother-in-law. In mourning, Mrs. Cowan and her sister continued on to Radersburg.

But Cowan was a sturdy being; he would not die. It was nearly sundown when he regained consciousness. Wounded in thigh and head, he yet pulled himself up from the ground. Unfortunately an Indian sentinel observed his movement and fired. Cowan fell with a fresh wound in his left side. He now felt that he was beyond all hope of recovery, but he remained conscious and lay motionless until darkness settled.

Then he started a crawling retreat toward Lower Geyser Basin, nine miles away.[4] About midnight he apprehended motion among the leaves. It was an Indian scout, raised to elbow posture, listening. Cowan remained quiet until the watchman relaxed; then he circled the danger zone by more than a mile. He finally reached the deserted wagon and found his bird dog waiting. There was no food to be found, but he gathered up the sheets of Carpenter's diary. Cowan pressed painfully on toward the campground in the Lower Geyser Basin. During the third day a band of Indians came by his hiding place. They were friendly Bannocks of Howard's command, but he did not know this and took no chance.

On the twenty-seventh he reached the old camp, found matches, and gathered spilled coffee grains and an empty can, to make coffee. He passed the night there and the next day crawled over to the road, where relief came in the form of two of Howard's scouts, Captain S. G. Fisher and J. W. Redington. The latter said, "Who in hell are you?" "I'm George Cowan of Radersburg." "You don't say! We've come to bury you."

They rendered first aid, provided food, and left Cowan by a roaring fire with the assurance that the main force would gather him up within two days. Chester Fee has deftly described Cowan's next misfortune:

> Cowan ate enough to keep himself alive and lay down in silent joy to sleep the night through. Towards morning he was awakened by awful heat, and found to his dismay that the vegetable mold he was lying on had taken fire and encircled him with flames. He rose on hands and knees and suffering terribly, crawled across the charred area to safety. His hands and legs were badly burned.[5]

In the meantime his scattered companions were being united. Harmon was the first to reach General Howard's command. Arnold and Dingee arrived after several days and nights of hardship. Myers and Oldham were found by Howard's scouts. The latter was in a pitiful state. His tongue was so swollen, as a result of his wound, that he could not speak. Shock and exposure to the cold nights, together with lack of food for four days, had left its mark upon them all.

Howard reluctantly took the survivors along, and on August 29 they reached Cowan in the Lower Geyser Basin. Arnold said Cowan was a "most pitiful looking object. He was covered with blood, which had dried on him, and he was as black as a negro." Here Cowan learned of his wife's safety, and that news, together with his friend Arnold's care, pulled him through. The army surgeon ministered to the physical wounds of the men, but there was no time for sympathy. The Radersburg men desired to return home by way of Henrys

Lake, but they were bundled along through the park with the command, over roads that were "simply horrible and almost impassable for wagons. At times we were compelled to lower them over precipices with ropes, and again we would hitch a rope to a wagon and pull it up the hill by man power."[6]

In the meantime Frank Carpenter, along with Lieutenant Doane's command, pressed toward the park. They found Henderson's ranch buildings in flames. A band of renegade Nez Perces were spreading terror in their wake. Camp was established at the ranch, and a courier arrived, directing Lieutenant Doane to mark time until joined by Colonel Charles C. Gilbert and the Seventh Infantry. Carpenter's plan to return and bury Cowan was thus frustrated. A frontiersman named George Houston promised to bury Cowan's body, and Carpenter was induced to return to Bozeman. There he learned that all members of the party were safe and accounted for except Cowan. The news that Cowan was still alive reached him a few days later when he met the two scouts who had found Cowan just a week before. Perhaps no one else could have convinced him his friend was alive.

A telegram to Mrs. Cowan brought her from Radersburg. She reached Bottler's ranch, having come 175 miles in thirty-one hours, and the Cowans were reunited on September 24, exactly one month from the date of the attack.

The Helena Visitors

As the Nez Perces crossed the park, the chiefs generally maintained discipline and restraint, but there were unprincipled factions under less responsible leadership that could not be controlled. While the main tribe was slowly weaving its course through the park, some of the reckless young men were foraging far and wide.

On August 25, a man named Irwin was captured by a band of Nez Perces. He had just been discharged from the army at Fort Ellis. In questioning him the Indians learned that a party of Helena tourists was camping in the Hayden Valley area. Irwin escaped from the Nez Perces on the night of September 1. The next day he reached Howard, who benefited from his knowledge concerning the Nez Perce course and situation. Meanwhile the Indians encountered the visitors from Helena. There were ten men in this company: A. J. Weikert, Richard Dietrich, Frederick Pfister, Joseph Roberts, Charles Kenck, Jack Stewart, August Foller, Leslie Wilkie, L. Duncan, and a Negro cook named Benjamin Stone.

On the morning of August 25 this party was traveling between Sulphur Mountain and Mud Volcano when they observed a body of horsemen fording the river. They guessed that the mounted men were hostile Nez Perces, and hastily formed a camp in the timber near the forks of Otter Creek.[7] It was a well-chosen position and might have been defended effectively if the natural advantages had been utilized.

No harm came to them that day or night. The next morning Weikert and Wilkie went reconnoitering in the vicinity of Alum Creek where they encountered a band of the marauders. The white men retreated, but Weikert was hit in the shoulder in the exchange of fire.

In the meantime the camp on Otter Creek was raided. Instead of posting a lookout the campers had huddled together, hoping they would continue to escape notice. Kenck's mind was active with forebodings; addressing the elderly cook, he said, "Stone, what would you do if the Indians should jump us?" Stone replied, "You all take care ob yoursel' and I'll take care ob me."[8] At that instant the raiders struck. Kenck was hit and killed; Stewart was shot, fell, and was overtaken. He pleaded so earnestly for his life that he was spared. Dietrich fell in the creek and remained there for hours.

Ben Stone ran as fast as he could, but in midstream his legs gave out, and he lay prone in the water. The raiders left as suddenly as they came. When Wilkie and Weikert arrived they joined some of the others and started for Mammoth. Joseph Roberts and August Foller had slipped away, and as it later transpired they went west to Madison River and thence to Virginia City and home. The other seven reached Mammoth, where Dietrich and Stone unfortunately decided to remain to await the arrival of Roberts and Foller. Dietrich had promised young Roberts' mother that he would be responsible for his safe return.

On August 31, Weikert and McCartney, the Mammoth hotel owner, left for Otter Creek campground to look for the two missing men and to bury Kenck's body. They were returning when a score of raiders, who had just committed a fresh deed of vengeance at Mammoth, met them at the falls of the East Gardner River. This chance encounter produced a skirmish in which Weikert's horse was killed and the other horses got away before the white men could reach a sheltered position. The Indians withdrew, and the white men pursued a cautious course to Mammoth.

Upon reaching Mammoth they learned of Dietrich's death. On August 31 he and Stone saw a band of Indians pass McCartney's place. They were Nez Perces on their way to Henderson's ranch, which they ransacked and burned. The next day, when they returned, Ben Stone ran from the cabin and hid in Clematis Gulch. Dietrich, evidently believing the Indians friendly, stood in the doorway. They shot and killed him. Lieutenant Hugh L. Scott, who had accompanied Doane, his company of cavalry, and thirty Crow Indian scouts, was the first man to reach Dietrich. The Helena musician's body was still warm. This situation interrupted Scott's pursuit of the raiders.

At this time word arrived that Roberts and Foller were in Virginia City. Dietrich's body was taken to Helena by Weikert, who also took Kenck's body there for final interment.

Naturally these raids caused great excitement in Montana and elsewhere. Newspapers printed reports of the tourists' adventures. In fact, one reported that nine of the Helena tourists were killed, instead of two. The *Helena Herald* issued an extra concerning the killing of Dietrich.

The Activities of Howard's Scouts

It has been mentioned that Howard's scouts, Fisher and Redington, with about fifty Bannocks, kept close to the retreating Nez Perces. They followed them over Mary Mountain into Hayden Valley, where they crossed the Yellowstone River near Mud Volcano. From there they went upstream to Yellowstone Lake, thence northeast up Pelican Creek. On September 5, Fisher made this entry in his journal:

> Madison John and the balance of the boys got in at daylight this morning. I sent an Indian back to the command with a letter to General Howard. We stayed in camp today and rested our horses, cleaned up our guns, etc.; had nothing to eat but beans. . . . I am becoming tired of trying to get the soldiers and the hostiles together. "Uncle Sam's" boys are too slow for this business.[9]

Fisher states that his Bannocks occasionally came within hearing distance of the Nez Perces. Indeed, the hostiles offered them friendship, saying, "We don't want to fight you. Let us talk and smoke together."[10] Then a few shots were exchanged, but distance and timber prevented any serious damage. Fisher's Fort Hall Bannocks were becoming weary of the chase, and several days later most of them deserted him and started for home. Near Mud Volcano they attempted to steal some of Spurgin's horses. Howard induced several of them to join a detail under Scout Redington, return to Fisher, and obtain a fresh report upon the Nez Perce position. This unit rode along the Yellowstone River and up Pelican and Cache creeks, where they located Fisher. Then Redington returned and overtook Howard as he ascended the Lamar River Valley.

Howard's Course in the Park

From the west entrance Howard took the Madison Plateau road to Nez Perce Creek, which he followed to the base of Mary Mountain. He crossed Mary Mountain, followed by Spurgin and his men, who widened the trail into a road for their wagons as they traveled. When Howard reached the Yellowstone River where the Indians crossed, he talked to Irwin and decided not to follow their rough trail. Howard left to Fisher and his scouts the task of tracking the Nez Perces up the Pelican-Cache creeks toward the Clark Fork. Instead, Howard headed north down the west side of the Yellowstone River toward its junction with the Lamar. At that point he could cross the Yellowstone on the Baronett Bridge and ascend the Lamar River and Soda Butte Creek to the Clark Fork. This route would save a hundred-mile jaunt in a heavily timbered country.

It was a good plan, and by pursuing it he cou'd ~ve both time and distance, but there was no road fo. his wagons. The lack of a road was, however, no obstacle to Captain W. F. Spurgin's Twenty-first Infantry and the corps of fifty Idaho frontiersmen who had helped him bring his pack string over the Lolo Trail and take wagons over the hogback from the Bitterroot

Valley into the Big Hole Basin. These skilled laborers demonstrated their energy and resourcefulness in crossing a deep ravine two miles above the Upper Falls of the Yellowstone. A narrow corridor was cut through the timber, and the wagons were lowered six hundred feet with ropes wound around successive pairs of trees. The tree burns produced by friction were clearly visible when Park Naturalist Wayne Replogle rediscovered "Spurgin's Beaver Slide" in 1936.

A pathway for the wagons was cleared over Dunraven Pass, across the Washburn Range, down Carnelian Creek, over Tower Creek, and into Pleasant Valley to the Baronett Bridge. From that point Spurgin took his wagons and men down the Yellowstone River to Fort Ellis, where they were discharged. Tributes have been paid to the indomitable Spurgin for the will, energy, and work required to bring Howard's pack trains and wagons from the Clearwater River to Fort Ellis, over mountains and plateaus where roads were practically nonexistent.

When Howard's command reached the Baronett Bridge on September 5, they found it partly burned. This was the work of the Nez Perce raiders who stole horses from Henderson's ranch and killed Dietrich at Mammoth on August 31. Repairs were made, and Howard's forces crossed the Yellowstone and rapidly proceeded up the Lamar. At that time the command recruited an excellent guide, named George Houston, from a score of miners who were developing a mine at the head of Soda Butte Creek. This was the natural passage to the Clark Fork, but the miners had not seen the Indians. Worried and anxious, Howard sent scouts in quest of information.

Chief Joseph's scouts had reported the presence of the miners on the Lamar and Howard's spies in the area. The scouts further noted that Colonel Samuel Sturgis and eight troops of the Seventh Cavalry from the Crow Agency on the Little Rosebud were in position at the regular Absaroka Pass near Hart (Heart) Mountain. Joseph was now cut off between the commands of Howard and Sturgis.

FLIGHT TOWARD CANADA

17. ESCAPING THE ABSAROKA BLOCKADE

The Absaroka Range forms the east boundary of Yellowstone National Park. It is a lofty granite barrier with thirty peaks towering above ten thousand feet. Small headwater tributaries appertaining to the Shoshone River (Stinking Water) and the Clark Fork of the Yellowstone have carved slight depressions above the eight-thousand-foot level that are used as passes. Any body of horsemen seeking an eastern exit would be channeled into one of these passageways. Accordingly, the military officials of the Dakota Department distributed their considerable troops at strategic transition points where the hostiles might be pocketed.[1]

Colonel Sturgis was guarding the Clark Fork, Major Hart was on the Shoshone River, Colonel Merritt was on the Wind River to the southeast, and Captain Cushing was near the Crow Agency to the northwest. General Howard, backed by detachments under Colonel Gilbert and Lieutenant Doane, was pressing from the rear, and Scout Fisher and his Bannocks were tracking the Nez Perces closely.[2] Considering terrain and logistics, this was a vast concentration of power in the midst of the northern Rockies.

The Nez Perces discovered that they were

surrounded. Fisher's Bannocks used the term "trap" to describe the Nez Perce position as of September 8.[3] Newspaper correspondents had informed the public about these moves, and reports from the park were eagerly awaited. On August 31, the *New Northwest* prematurely exulted over the promise of victory:

In view of the bad effect their success and escape would have on other Indians, and in view of the evil they would probably hereafter do Montana, this concentration of forces, and the determination to destroy them, is in the highest degree gratifying. We are largely indebted for it to the presence of General Sherman in Montana, who has had the lion in him roused by the defiant progress of the Nez Perces and by personal attention to the movement of troops has raised up an army on the four sides of Joseph just when it seemed most probable that he was about to escape, scot free, except for the blow Gibbon struck him, and laden with booty, into the great open country of the hostiles. We wait now hopefully for news that the Nez Perces have been struck hard and fatally. They are too brave and dangerous a foe to escape, for their escape unscathed means still darker days for the border.

The forces of nature and man had combined to interpose a seemingly invulnerable blockade upon the Indians from Idaho.

The Chiefs Overcome All Obstacles

One author suggests that the Nez Perces escaped from this predicament in a supernatural fashion. "At a sign from the red man, the barriers had rolled away; the trap, so carefully adjusted to ensnare him [Joseph], had been folded up and put aside; the white man had been outwitted; the quarry had made good his escape."[4]

Actually, the Nez Perces were delivered by a simple combination of factors that worked to their advantage. The principal mistake was made by Colonel Sturgis. After taking a position at the mouth of the Clark Fork, from which he could swing a powerful blockade (360 troops) across the canyon, he was persuaded to depart. This decision resulted from the reports of three different scouting details he had sent up the Clark Fork to look for the Indians. Like Bacon at Targhee Pass, Sturgis was several days early, and he abandoned watchful waiting in favor of moving the command. His reconnoitering detachments convinced him that the hostiles had chosen the Shoshone River thoroughfare. In fact, Lieutenant Ezra B. Fuller and a guide climbed a ridge and got a glimpse of a receding Indian column as it wound around a hill in that direction. The guide affirmed that having gone that far south, the hostiles could not possibly find a pass leading into the Clark Fork drainage. He failed to realize that they might double back under a timber cover.

Foreseeing such a prospect, Howard sent several sets of scouts to Sturgis, warning him to stand fast, but none of them reached him. Because of both the rugged wilderness and the vigilant Nez Perces, no intelligence was ever passed between these officers. In fact, several prospectors caught in the area were killed, as well as several scouts.[5] These murders by the Nez Perces struck terror throughout the area and supported the charge that the hostiles condoned wanton murder. Actually, every man destroyed was either a messenger at the time or he was bound to become one in a matter of moments. The circumstances warranted drastic action against any who were found in this no man's land between the military forces. Measures taken in behalf of self-preservation demand little justification. Thus, Yellow Wolf made a statement rather than an apology in saying, "Every white man in those mountains could be counted our enemy."[6]

Although Howard lacked certain knowledge of Sturgis' position, he was sufficiently confident to send a messenger to Fort Ellis with a reassuring telegram to General McDowell.[7] On September 12, Howard was obliged to wire McDowell that the Clark Fork net had collapsed and the hostiles had fled. His explanation was simple: "While Sturgis was scouting toward Stinking Water (Shoshone River), the Indians with my force in close pursuit passed his right, turning to Clark's Fork after short detour and made a double march, avoiding him completely."[8]

Whether the Nez Perce maneuver toward the Shoshone River was deliberate or accidental, the result was the same. Sturgis was lured away into a futile forty-mile game of hide-and-seek, which placed him two days behind the fleeing enemy.

Nez Perce records concerning the precise method of their escape are few. Yellow Wolf remembered that the soldiers missed them. He said, "We had gone down the creek while they came along the hillside."[9]

Perhaps Howard's scout, S. G. Fisher, left the most accurate account in his journal, dated September 10. This entry describes what the Nez Perces had accomplished the day before:

To the east, from the top of the divide, the enemy's trail bore off towards the south-east, which direction my Indians told me would take them onto the Stinkingwater, to the south of Hart Mt., which are in plain sight from the top of the divide we passed over this morning. After leaving the summit the enemy followed the trail towards the Stinkingwater about two miles, and then attempted to elude pursuit by concealing their trail. To do this, the hostiles "milled," drove their ponies around in every direction, when, instead of going out of the basin in the direction they had been traveling and across an open plain, they turned short off to the north, passing along the steep side of the mountain through the timber for several miles.

When we reached the point where the enemy had endeavored to cache their trail, we scattered out in every direction looking for it. At first the scouts were at a loss to know which way they had gone but after spending some time in the search I was so fortunate as to stumble onto the trail. I then went back to apprise the command of this new change of direction, leaving the other scouts to follow after the Indians. Returning, we followed through a very narrow and rocky canon down to Clarks Fork, at a point about two miles below where it comes out of a canon.[10]

These maneuvers disclose that Nez Perce scouting was excellent and their skill in deception and camouflage superb. Furthermore, the passage of their caravan through the rugged Absarokas was an outstanding feat in horsemanship. General Howard characterized the total performance as an example of consummate generalship.[11]

The baffling Nez Perce route across the Absarokas was probably this: from Cache Creek they crossed Sunlight Pass and descended the Sunlight River for a dozen miles. Then, they quartered northward to Trail Creek, which they ascended to Lodgepole Divide. They descended Lodgepole Creek to its point of confluence with Crandall Creek, which they followed to the Clark Fork. It was a rough hunters' trail, wholly unsuited for the passage of nearly seven hundred people with all their possessions and herds of horses.

Lieutenant Wood said the canyon through which the Indian cavalcade filed was like a gigantic railroad tunnel. Howard described it as "a strange canyon, where rocks on each side came so near together that two horses abreast could hardly pass."[12] He further stated that many horses and mules fell as his command slid down this canyon. His men were forced to "admire the quick wit of an Indian who had the hardihood to try the experiment, and break the almost impassable roadway."[13]

The Military Commands Unite

The Nez Perces made their precipitous exit from the Absarokas on September 9. Howard struggled through the same defile and emerged late the next day. By then Sturgis had discovered his mistake, and he returned to the Clark Fork, where he came upon Howard's trail. He overtook Howard on the eleventh, and the two established a camp in the valley. Of course both officers were greatly chagrined over the chieftains' success in eluding the trap that had been contrived. They considered it wise to send two messengers, one by water and one by land, to Colonel Nelson A. Miles at Fort Keogh (Miles City) on the Tongue River. In this message, Howard explained how the Nez Perces escaped and where they would probably go. He urged Miles to make every effort to intercept and detain them until he could overtake them again.[14]

By now the Indians were probably fifty miles ahead of Howard and Sturgis, but the commanders decided on pursuit. Howard allowed Sturgis to take the lead in an attempt to overtake the Nez Perces. Howard's officers were opposed to this arrangement, but Sturgis' horses were in better condition to make a fast march down the valley toward the plains. Howard realized better than anyone that durable horses and men would be needed to overtake the hard-riding hostiles. Besides, Sturgis was eager to redeem his command from the blunder he had recently made. Indeed, when he first discovered that the chiefs had escaped, he swore that he would overtake them before they crossed the Missouri River if he had to go on foot and alone.[15] Howard gave him additional scouts, artillery, and cavalry; and at daylight on the twelfth the Seventh Cavalry was eagerly pursuing the Indian trail. They traveled sixty miles in the rain that day without seeing fresh Indian

signs. The next morning an early march took them to
the Yellowstone River, near present-day Laurel. Men
and horses were stiff and dispirited from their strenuous
exertions. After fording the river, Sturgis called a halt
and issued a welcome order to unsaddle and put the
horses on stake ropes. All indications pointed to a
weakening of the resolution to press the pursuit at that
time. Actually, they were within a few miles of the Nez
Perces, who were leisurely breaking camp.

Upon reaching the Clark Fork, Looking Glass, who
had boasted of his close bonds with the Crow Indians,
went ahead to seek friends and allies. He succeeded in
contacting leaders of both segments of the Crow nation,
the Mountain and the River clans. Neither clan could be
persuaded to join the hostiles. The Crows evidently considered Nez Perce resistance a lost cause. The Mountain
chiefs declared strict neutrality, but the more sedentary
River Crows were definitely partial to the whites. Governed by expediency and cupidity, they were ready to
despoil the Nez Perces as opportunity afforded. This
attitude, added to the positions previously taken by
treaty Nez Perces, Flatheads, Bannocks, Tendoy's Lemhis, and Washakie's Shoshonis, caused Yellow Wolf to
exclaim:

> I do not understand how the Crows could think to
> help the soldiers. They were fighting against their best
> friends! Some Nez Perces in our band had helped
> them whip the Sioux who came against them only
> a few snows before. This was why Chief Looking
> Glass had advised going to the Crows, to the buffalo
> country. He thought Crows would help us, if there
> was more fighting.[16]

The Nez Perces in the Yellowstone Valley

The Nez Perce retreat down the Clark Fork to the
Yellowstone River Valley, and thence northwestward up

Canyon Creek, describes an arc. Parts of these valleys were sparsely populated, resembling the Horse Prairie and Lemhi areas in that respect. Unfortunately, Nez Perce conduct toward the white men encountered was also similar to their earlier conduct. Lacking facilities for handling prisoners, too many of their scouts were disposed to kill the whites and take their horses. Several miners were killed on the Clark Fork. In one instance a man named J. M. V. Cochran and his companions were spared when his ranch was raided. However, two trappers, named Clint Dills and Milton Summers, temporarily staying there, were killed. An account by Cochran, printed in the Billings *Gazette,* June 30, 1927, describes the attack by several warriors upon the P. W. McAdow sawmill and their "annexation" of the horses on the premises. The article also states that a band of Nez Perces dashed into Coulson and burned the saloon. These acts impelled Cochran and his friend, the notorious John Johnson ("Liver-eating Johnson"), to become members of a band known as George Houston's Yellowstone Scouts.

In spite of the hardships that characterized their retreat, the Nez Perce braves were inclined to enjoy themselves whenever possible. Such an opportunity was provided by the arrival of a stagecoach at the Bill Brockway ranch on the Yellowstone, two miles below its junction with the Clark Fork. The three passengers aboard, including Fanny Clark, a vaudeville performer, were able to hide before the young men spied the vehicle. Seizing the reins, they had great sport in weaving back and forth and scattering the contents of the mailbags.

By this time, Pawnee Tom, one of Sturgis' best scouts, had located the Nez Perces. He hurried upstream to tell the colonel, and a few moments later he approached the relaxing troops, wildly shouting, "Indians! Indians!" Only a few miles separated the command from its quarry. Within fifteen minutes the troopers reached the crest of a ridge, hoping to catch the Nez Perces in camp. But the Indians were in motion and pushing toward the mouth of Canyon Creek. Yellow Wolf remembered that the traveling camp was nearly surprised, but the attention of scattered scouts was attracted by a blanket signal, meaning "Soldiers coming close!"[17] Such were the circumstances in which Colonel Sturgis and the Seventh Cavalry undertook to capture the Nez Perces after several days of forced marching.

18. THE BATTLE OF CANYON CREEK

From the area of its union with the Clark Fork, the Yellowstone River constitutes a line of transition between the Rocky Mountains and the High Plains. The river bisects a massive country that once sustained an abundance of game. This was the region the nontreaty Nez Perces had chosen when war forced them from their Idaho homeland. They believed the Crow Indians would welcome them and that the white men would allow them to make the long journey in peace. They had chosen to travel through the least settled areas, hoping thereby to avoid trouble. They had bypassed the military force in Lolo Canyon and made a truce with the Bitterroot settlers. In the Big Hole Basin they were surprised by Colonel Gibbon. They were not looking for battles; rather, they were attempting to avoid them. To that end they had kept moving relentlessly. The pace was so rapid that Howard never quite caught them, although their occasional detours failed to deceive him.

Aware of the presence of troops on the Clark Fork, the chiefs had tried again to avoid battle. Now Colonel Sturgis, with over four hundred cavalrymen and two howitzers, was bearing down upon them.

The Nez Perces Strive to Avoid Battle

There are no records disclosing the thoughts and plans of the chiefs in this situation. When Looking Glass discovered that the Crows were undependable, the Nez Perces must have realized that their continued presence in this area was unwise. Howard and Sturgis were bound to attack them in order to restore military prestige, and the Crows would steal their horses if they possibly could. It was doubtful whether the Nez Perces had enough vitality, manpower, and ammunition to make a determined and effective stand against the forces at hand, not to mention those under Merritt and Cushing, in position nearby or approaching. Continued flight was the only possibility.

This strategy, together with a resurgence of energy and determination, definitely reflect Chief Joseph's increasing influence. Although he had been the foremost champion of nontreaty Nez Perce rights, still he had deplored the outbreak of war and entered the campaign reluctantly. Then he had favored a major effort in Idaho, but Looking Glass had persuaded the council to retreat to Crow territory. Looking Glass's leadership was dominant until the Battle of the Big Hole; then it declined. On the Clark Fork his prestige fell again, because the Crows proved untrustworthy. On the other hand, Joseph had demonstrated an unwavering concern for the well-being of all the people. This was natural, because he was chief of the largest faction; but his sense of responsibility encompassed them all. He possessed an inherent understanding of their hardships and suffering that constantly enlarged his stature as the guardian of the people. The miscalculations of others had placed the tribe in great and continuing danger. At this point, and henceforth, the speed and endurance necessary for their survival must be truly heroic. The campaign could only be won by the pervading influence and leadership of an exceptional character.

The Canyon Creek setting was conducive to flight and the Nez Perces took advantage of the environment, racing across a prairie to the canyon as the cavalry quartered toward them from the south. Canyon Creek is not a narrow defile, easily protected. Its lower reaches are broad and open, and the rimrock guarding the flanges does not extend far upon the interior sides. The canyon trail gradually ascended between rolling hills to the uneven plateau west of the Yellowstone Valley. Therefore, the terrain did not preclude the possibility of pursuit by exceptionally resolute men.

Skirmishing on Canyon Creek

Colonel Sturgis and his command first sighted the Indians from a ridge two miles away. The hostiles were moving toward the mouth of Canyon Creek. Major Lewis Merrill's battalion and Lieutenant Wilkinson's L Company took the lead. Captain Bell and Captain Nowlan, with Companies F and I, moved along rapidly in support of the advance guard. Captain F. W. Benteen and Captain French, commanding Companies H and M, were held in reserve for a while; then they were ordered to strike the warriors on the southwest wall of the canyon.

When the troops raced forward, Nez Perce sharpshooters began firing from the rimrock flanges. Other warriors, directed by Looking Glass, formed a rear guard and fired steadily at the approaching troops. These fusillades caused a slackening of speed; indeed, the advance troops were ordered to dismount, deploy, and advance on foot. A. F. Mulford, a member of the regiment, claims that this was a serious tactical error, insuring the Indians' escape. He said that many troopers wept with frustration over the command to dismount.[1]

Obviously the chiefs did not intend to do anything beyond covering their retreat, whereas Sturgis mistakenly assumed that they would accept this challenge and join in a close-range battle against the approaching line. Yellow Wolf described the maneuvers of Nez Perce horsemen: "We did not line up like soldiers. We went by ones, just here and there entering the canyon."[2] He further stated that toward the end of the skirmish, when the people were all in the canyon, "Only one warrior, Teeto Hoonod, was there doing the fighting. His horse hidden, he was behind the rocks holding a line of dismounted soldiers back. He was shooting regularly, not too fast."[3]

What started out as a vital and promising action bogged down because of effective fire power from a few Nez Perce sharpshooters ensconced in the rimrock and a counterattack by a few warriors with long-range rifles. Captain Benteen made two charges in an attempt to dislodge the warriors from the rimrock, but Nez Perce fire compelled him to withdraw. Merrill's failure to inflict any real punishment upon the Nez Perce rear guard, followed by Benteen's inability to gain entrance to the canyon without considerable risk, enabled the people to reach security in the canyon. Sturgis did not press the attack but viewed the action through field glasses from a position a half-mile behind the line. A soldier named Jacob Horner expressed appreciation for the fact that Sturgis mounted the wounded and sent them down to the Yellowstone River under escort, but he thought this humanitarian action contributed to the escape of the hostiles. Mulford states that Lieutenant Hare requested permission from Major Merrill to lead a charge into the canyon, but the request was refused.

Accordingly, the skirmishing at the mouth of Canyon Creek was lively but short-lived. The Nez Perces were only interested in covering their retreat, and Sturgis was unwilling to risk close pursuit up the canyon. Many troopers believed that more prompt, daring, and resolute action would have been rewarding. As it turned out, the Nez Perce warriors succeeded in holding the troops back by gradually vacating their battle stations and then reassembling as a rear guard. Meanwhile, the chiefs kept the tribe moving until after dark. This effort enabled them to pass through Canyon Creek and camp among the hills beyond.

After following the Nez Perces up the canyon until dusk, Sturgis decided to return and form a camp at the mouth of Canyon Creek. The next morning, when the pursuit was resumed, Sturgis found narrow places in the trail, "so choked with rocks, trees, and brush that any attempt on our part to have followed them by night march would have resulted in disaster."[4]

Howard Reaches the Battlefield

Upon hearing of the battle on the afternoon of September 13, Howard picked a company of fifty cavalrymen and pushed ahead of his command. He reached the mouth of Canyon Creek early the next morning. His impressions of the situation were vividly recorded:

It was the most horrible of places,—sage-brush and dirt, and only alkaline-water, and very little of that! Dead horses were strewn about, and other relics of the battlefield! A few wounded men and the dead were there. To all this admixture of disagreeable things was added a cold, raw wind, that, unobstructed, swept over the country. Surely if anything was needed to make us hate war such after-battle scenes come well in play.[5]

Although the descriptions of the battle and the battleground were satisfactory, the reports issued by Sturgis concerning Indian casualties proved to be greatly exaggerated. He placed their loss at sixteen, and added that "nine hundred ponies had been dropped by the hostiles. . . . I am going ahead this morning [September 15] and propose to push them until they drop their whole herd."⁶

Howard's Bannock Scouts and Sturgis' Crows searched the canyon, but they did not find any dead Nez Perces. Scout Fisher confirmed this report and it agrees with Yellow Wolf's declaration that only three Indians were wounded in this fight.⁷ Howard reduced the estimate of stolen horses to four hundred, whereas Yellow Wolf remembered that the number actually stolen by the Crows at that time was nearer forty. However, he said a good many worn-out ponies were abandoned.

Sturgis lost three killed and eleven wounded. Forty-one horses were either killed or abandoned by the cavalry as a result of this skirmish.⁸ Obviously the Nez Perce warriors had made an effective defense for people trying their best to avoid a battle.

Howard spent September 14 at the battleground camp awaiting the arrival of his command. That evening, Captain Cushing also arrived with supplies from Fort Ellis. Even so, the rations of both commands were so low that captured Indian ponies were killed for food. The general had been expecting Cushing and Norwood to arrive with reinforcements for some time, but Colonel Gibbon had given Norwood another assignment. Therefore, Cushing confined his efforts to bringing in the supplies.⁹ At this point, Howard's cavalry, under Sanford, and Otis' battery and scouts, under Fletcher, joined Sturgis.

Pursuit by Colonel Sturgis

Meanwhile, Sturgis continued pursuing the hostiles for several days. During that time his cavalry traveled a hundred and fifty miles. This brought them to the Musselshell River, where a halt was called. The Nez Perce pace was too fast for Sturgis. His men and horses were in desperate need of rest and supplies. Hence, for the second time he was planning to give up the chase. His letter to Howard, explaining this decision, is revealing: "I find it impossible for my command to gain upon them, and their direction is taking me further and further from supplies. I have . . . reluctantly determined to abandon a hopeless pursuit before my horses are completely destroyed or placed beyond recuperation. . . ."[10] In one week Sturgis discovered what Howard had been contending with for two months: the Nez Perces were an exceptionally fleet, resolute, and resourceful band of people.

Notwithstanding the colonel's confession of inadequacy, the *Helena Weekly Independent,* on September 27, stated that Sturgis had a fight with the Indians on the Musselshell and that skirmishing was a daily occurrence. Yellow Wolf flatly declared that no soldiers ever caught up with them after they entered Canyon Creek.

The Role of the Crow Indians

Perhaps part of the exceptional Nez Perce speed in this terrible flight should be attributed to the cunning and persistence of the horse-stealing Crows. Lieutenant Theodore W. Goldin, of the Seventh Cavalry, declared that a band of them held a frenzied war dance in Sturgis' camp after the Canyon Creek Battle. They served as scouts, and in so doing they tantalized and molested the Nez Perces as opportunity afforded.[11] Yellow Wolf estimated that a hundred Crows and Bannocks attacked the Nez Perce rear on September 14. He said they darted in close to the rear of the cavalcade, hanging low on the sides of their horses, "doing under-neck shooting. . . . Only when we were moving would they come after us. When we met them, they ran from us." His "heart was just like fire" with indignation, and he charged them in his anger and received a slight wound in the thigh before retreating.[12]

Although these tactics were annoying, the chiefs could not afford to stop and fight the pursuers. At least three Nez Perces were killed by the Crows and Bannocks in this area. They were Teeweeyounah (Yellow Wolf's friend), Tooklecks (Fish Trap), and Wetyetmas Hapima (Surrounded Goose). Only one of the three was a warrior. On September 21, the *Benton Record* carried an account of a Crow warrior who was captured by the Nez Perces. They whipped and ridiculed him, then sent him away.

A man named Langhorne sent a message to the *Helena Daily* on September 15, stating, "The Crows are harassing them and stealing a good many horses." On September 29, the *Bozeman Times* printed the following memorandum from George W. Frost, United States Indian Agent, Crow Agency: "Please give information to the papers from me that the Crows are loyal and fighting every time with the whites. . . . They have taken all the Nez Perces' pack animals with packs . . . say 200."[13]

It is apparent that friendly Indian scouts inflicted more damage during this protracted extension of the Canyon Creek Battle than Sturgis had done in the beginning.[14]

19. FROM THE MUSSELSHELL TO THE BEAR PAW RANGE

On September 16, General Howard's command was assembled in a campground on the Yellowstone River, just below its confluence with Canyon Creek. There Lieutenant Robert H. Fletcher gave Howard a full account of the recent battle and other incidents pertaining to the Sturgis command. Howard was then able to resupply his troops before resuming the pursuit of Sturgis and the hostiles.

On September 20, Howard's command reached the Musselshell River and camped within a few miles of Sturgis. He and Sturgis held several consultations, and during one of them a messenger from Colonel Nelson A. Miles arrived announcing that he had received their communication of the twelfth and that he was preparing to enter the campaign on the morning of the eighteenth.[1]

This news was welcome to the officers, and Major Lewis Merrill predicted that Miles would surely succeed in capturing the hostiles. His judgment was based upon what he knew about the colonel's ambitions, competence, and knowledge of the country. Merrill cautiously suggested that Miles was "something of a glory chaser like Custer. . . ."[2] Howard agreed with Merrill's prediction, and, speaking to Colonel Mason, he said, "Colonel, I believe that we shall capture these Indians yet."[3] Others were less optimistic; indeed, Dr. Alexander thought Miles had not one chance in a million. Nonetheless, the spirits of the men were lightened and they resumed the pursuit with enthusiasm. In fact, the outlook became sufficiently promising to permit the release of Sanford and his cavalry unit, and Robbins and several other scouts. This was done on September 27, when the force reached the Missouri River.

Joseph's Route and Progress

When Sturgis stopped on the Musselshell to recuperate and wait for Howard, the Nez Perces had little to fear. They knew nothing about Miles, but even so they traveled as fast as they could toward the Missouri. In order to reach the Cow Island ford on the Missouri, they headed almost due north through Judith Gap, thereby avoiding both the Judith and Snowy ranges. The plains country through which they passed was generally uninviting, but there were several basins and grasslands where bison, elk, and antelope were abundant. The Judith Basin was such a place, and there they encountered Chief Dumb Bull's band of Crows drying bison meat. The Nez Perce chiefs evidently permitted the young warriors to seize the Crows' ponies. This addition of several hundred fresh mounts enabled the Nez Perces to abandon worn-out horses.[4]

The unremitting speed that enabled the Nez Perces to outrun Sturgis and the Crows also cost them some of their own numbers. The seriously ill and the tired elders continued to fall by the way. The facts of a case involving a woman who fell behind to give birth to a baby have been preserved. Friendly Crows discovered her and persuaded her to stay with them until her son was strong and both were better able to travel. She did so, dwelling with them contentedly until her presence was disclosed to the Crow Agency officials. When that happened she and the child were compelled to return to her people, who had by then been exiled to Kansas Indian Territory.[5]

On September 21, the band camped near the Reed and Bowles Stockade on Big Spring Creek, near Lewistown. By this time it is doubtful if there were more than 650 left. It does not appear that any atrocities or thefts were committed upon the settlers in this particular area.[6] Generally paralleling the Carroll Trail, the Nez Perces followed the Snowy Mountain foothills to Dog Creek, which they descended to the site of the present town of Winifred. From there they headed northeast along the route followed by a present-day automobile road to Cow Island, which they reached on the morning of September 23. They covered the last seventy miles of this lap in thirty-six hours.

The Cow Island Affair

The Cow Island crossing was the head of steamboat navigation at that season of the year. Therefore, Cow Island Landing was a place of deposit, where supplies were stored for northern Montana forts and settlements and frontier posts in Canada.[7]

Since there were supplies for Fort Benton, a detachment of a dozen soldiers under Sergeant William Moelchert from Company B, Seventh Infantry, was on guard. In addition, three civilian employees who were responsible for private supplies were stationed there. Colonel George Glendennin was the Cow Island freight agent for the Josephine line of steamboats.

The soldiers, having been warned that the Nez Perces might arrive, had improvised breastworks around a tented area. The men took such refuge as these defenses afforded, and awaited developments.

Meanwhile, the Nez Perces swam their horses across the Missouri and established camp two miles up Cow Creek. While this was being done, some of the warriors held back and two of them rode to the supply area and asked for a parley with the leader. When Moelchert appeared the scouts asked for supplies from the stockpile. He refused and would not reconsider when they offered to pay, although he did give them a side of bacon and a half-sack of hardtack. Since this gift fell far short of their requirements, the chiefs decided to help themselves. At this juncture, a note was drafted by one of the guards and sent to Colonel Glendennin, who was in Fort Benton:

> Rifle Pit at Cow Island
> September 23, 1877, 10 A.M.
>
> Colonel:
> Chief Joseph is here, and says he will surrender for two hundred bags of sugar. I told him to surrender without the sugar. He took the sugar and will not surrender. What will I do?
>
> Michael Foley[8]

In another communication, Foley explained that a coulee just north of the pile of freight enabled the Indians to carry away the supplies without being exposed to rifle fire.

Yellow Wolf stated that the chiefs had told the warriors to refrain from fighting. Nevertheless, a shot was fired by someone, and a desultory exchange ensued. The breastworks were not charged, but one warrior and two of the civilians were wounded as a result of the shooting. Obviously the Nez Perces were only interested in the food; otherwise the supply defenders would have been destroyed. Instead, according to Peopeo Tholekt, "We took whatever we needed. . . . Some took pans and pots for cooking. We figured it was soldier supplies, so set fire to what we did not take. We had privilege to do this. It was war."[9] Other informants remembered that the chiefs were opposed to the destruction of supplies that took place during the night. At dawn the journey was resumed.

On the morning of September 24, shortly after the Nez Perces had departed, Major Guido Ilges and Lieutenant E. E. Hardin, of Fort Benton, arrived at Cow Island Landing with thirty-six mounted volunteers and one enlisted man. Ilges decided to pursue the Nez Perces, and by noon he overtook their rear-guard scouts. A band of the hostiles had encountered a freighter train, killed three of the teamsters, and were still ransacking the contents. As Ilges approached, the wagons were burned and a few shots were exchanged. One of the citizen volunteers was killed and the major decided to return to Cow Island.[10] He certified that the Nez Perce sharpshooters were excellent marksmen at long range.

The Nez Perces Slow Down

During September 24, the Nez Perces made a change in leadership and policy that was to lead to their defeat. Lean Elk was replaced by Looking Glass as leader of the caravan. Looking Glass was in favor of a slower pace. Howard was several days in the rear, the people and ponies were nearly exhausted, fresh supplies had been obtained, and bison were within reach. Besides, the weather was turning cold and stormy. Lean Elk advocated that the rapid flight continue, but his demands were considered unreasonable. Several informants certified to McWhorter that Looking Glass upbraided Lean Elk for his haste; it was causing too much weariness. The latter replied, "All right, Looking Glass, you can lead. I am trying to save the people, doing my best to cross into Canada before the soldiers find us. You can take command, but I think we will be caught and killed."[11]

Notwithstanding the solemnity of this warning, the council consented to the changes and short marches were made during the next four days. On the morning of the twenty-ninth, an advance guard killed some bison on Snake Creek about eight miles above its mouth, near a northern spur of the Bear Paw Range. This creek is a tributary to the Milk River, which flows into the Missouri east of Fort Peck. When the caravan reached this place at noon, Looking Glass advised making a night camp, although the place, being without trees, lacked wood for fuel. However, bison chips were plentiful and there was a maze of ravines and coulees along the creek bed that would partially protect them from the cold wind blowing from the north. Except on the south, where a ridge protected it, the campsite was vulnerable to a sweeping approach by horsemen on three sides. The position was not well chosen from the standpoint of defense.

The proposal to establish camp there was specifically opposed by a warrior named Wottolen, who had received an impression of impending danger. Looking Glass scoffed at this protest as he had done when similarly warned on August 8 in the Big Hole,[12] and the group made the fatal mistake of establishing camp at midday and relaxing, within forty miles of the International Boundary and safety.

Many authors have stated that the chiefs stopped on Snake Creek because they thought they had reached Canada. Yellow Wolf denied this in saying, "We knew the distance to the Canadian line. Knew how long it would take to travel there."[13] Joseph remembered sending runners in search of Sitting Bull's camp, but he did not admit to ignorance of the geographical situation.

The controlling factors in the delay were an imperative need for rest and food and a sense of security against surprise by Howard. Since crossing the Missouri the warriors had found excellent hunting, and they knew Howard was far behind them.

Howard's Pursuit to Snake Creek

On September 20, when Howard learned Miles had entered the campaign, he and Sturgis agreed to follow the hostiles with deliberation. Sturgis wrote, "We must not move too fast lest we flush the game."[14] Accordingly, the officers shortened their daily marches between the Musselshell and Missouri rivers, hoping the chiefs would act similarly. Howard gave Joseph credit for quickly detecting his design in thus delaying. In any case, the Nez Perces moved rapidly in this area, and Howard experienced some difficulty in following their trail through the Judith Basin.[15] However, both commands emerged from the basin in good order.

On September 25, Howard was pleased to meet two messengers from Fort Benton. They bore the news that the Indians had forded the Missouri at Cow Island, taken stored supplies, and seized a freighting outfit. The messengers also stated that a strong command, under Miles, had crossed the Missouri near its junction with the Musselshell and was moving rapidly.

Howard quickly accelerated his pace. He wrote, "It did not take us long to pass the next fifty or sixty miles to Carroll."[16] At that point he secured the steamer *Benton* and, taking his two aides, several scouts, and Captain Marcus P. Miller and his artillery battalion on board, went upstream to Cow Island. The rest of the soldiers remained at Carroll with Sturgis and Mason, awaiting new orders from Howard or Miles. At Cow Island, Howard received another message from Miles assuring him that his movements had not been discovered by the hostiles. Howard and his escort of seventeen mounted men hastened north along the Nez Perce trail. Upon reaching the bluff at the north end of the Bear Paw Range on October 4, they intercepted Miles's trail, and toward evening they met two of his scouts. Before darkness descended, they arrived at the Bear Paw camp, where Miles gave Howard an account of his march to that place.

SEVENTH CAVALRY SUCCESS

20. COLONEL NELSON A. MILES ENTERS THE CAMPAIGN

When Howard and Sturgis found themselves trailing the Nez Perces down the Clark Fork on September 12, they realized that they needed assistance in capturing the rebels. Fort Keogh, where Colonel Nelson Miles had a strong command, was several hundred miles to the northeast. There was a chance that a messenger might reach Miles in time, however, and Howard sent an appeal for Miles to march rapidly "to prevent the escape of this hostile band, and at least hold them in check until I can overtake them."[1]

Meanwhile, Miles was becoming increasingly anxious to receive some word of the campaign from the west. Upon receiving Howard's dispatch on September 17, Miles proceeded forthwith to carry out his orders, and by morning his troops had been ferried across the Yellowstone River. Forty wagons and a pack train with a month's supplies had been assembled and loaded. The colonel's report to the Assistant Adjutant General, Department of Dakota, states: "The command left Cantonment on the morning of the 18th, the different orders regarding escort for the Commission had already put enroute the Battalion 2d Cavalry and one (1) Company, (Hale's) 7th Cavalry; these were taken on the march."[2] Miles's total force included three troops of the Second Cavalry, three of the Seventh Cavalry, six companies of the Fifth Infantry (mounted upon Sioux ponies), and thirty Cheyenne Indian scouts. There were two pieces of artillery, a breech-loading Hotchkiss, and a twelve-pound Napoleon cannon.[3] The entire command included 383 men.

Miles sent couriers to Fort Peck and Fort Buford on the Missouri River, ordering a steamerload of supplies to go up the river, for the relief of Howard and Sturgis and to supply his own needs when he reached the mouth of the Musselshell River.

The Colonel's Line of March

From the Tongue River, Miles proposed to quarter his course northwestward across the headwaters of the Big Dry, to the junction of the Musselshell and Missouri rivers. He hoped to intercept the fugitives somewhere between that point and Cow Island before they crossed the river. On September 23, the day the Nez Perces crossed at Cow Island, Miles camped within six miles of the confluence of the Missouri and Musselshell rivers.

That evening the colonel sent Lieutenant Biddle to the Missouri in search of a steamboat, and he succeeded in overtaking the last one of the season. The next morning Captain George L. Tyler and a battalion were ferried across the river with instructions to go upstream while Miles followed a parallel course on the south bank. This distribution of forces would assure quicker initial action if the Nez Perces had already crossed the Missouri. Miles doubted that they had crossed. He sent a dispatch to General Alfred H. Terry that morning which read: "The reports from Howard and Sturgis are encouraging, and I will move upon the South side of the Missouri to Carroll, and possibly Judith Basin, to intercept any, if possible, prevent any of the Nez Perces from going north."[4] Miles further stated that in his opinion the hostiles had by then been exhausted by the rigors of their long campaign.

Half an hour after the steamboat was released, three men came downstream in a small boat, bearing the news that the Nez Perces had crossed at Cow Island on the twenty-third. Glancing downstream, the colonel estimated the distance to the steamer at three miles. If Sergeant McHugh could throw a shot from his Napoleon into the side of the headland the boat was approaching, the captain might understand that her return was desired. The plan worked, and within the hour the troop-ferrying procedure was resumed. Some of the wagon supplies were transferred to the pack train in anticipation of a fast race against the Nez Perces for the Canadian boundary. During the next four days the Indian and the white forces moved northward, with the Nez Perces a day ahead and the Little Rocky Mountains between them. Miles had not seen any sign of the hostiles by the twenty-ninth of September. He had expected to overtake them at a pass between the Little Rockies and the Bear Paws.

A courier named Charles Buckrum, sent by Major Ilges, arrived on the twenty-ninth with information concerning the position of the Indians.[5] Scouting parties had been fanning out ahead of Miles as his command advanced, and at six o'clock on the morning of the thirtieth a detail of Cheyenne scouts, under Louie Shambow, discovered the Nez Perce trail. Lieutenant O. F. Long of the Fifth Infantry relayed this information back to Miles.

Miles hastened forward, and he believed that his arrival completely surprised the Indians. He wrote:

The Nez Perce were quietly slumbering in their tents, evidently without a thought of danger, as they had sent out scouts the day before to see if there were any troops in the vicinity, and the scouts had reported "none discovered," but that they had seen vast herds of buffaloes, deer, elk, and antelopes quietly grazing on the prairie undisturbed, and no enemy in sight.[6]

Although the chiefs had neglected to send out scouts or post sentinels around the camp, they had a few minutes notice in which to strike a defense posture. Perhaps several Nez Perce buffalo hunters observed the troops with field glasses as they approached between two coulees at the southeast corner of the campground.[7] Actually, preparations were under way for continuing the flight to Canada. Many Indians were seen running toward their horses, and there was no time for Miles to reconnoiter their position. The circumstances required action, and Miles decided to attack.[8]

21. THE BATTLE OF THE BEAR PAWS

The Nez Perce campground was located at the base of a crescent-shaped cove on the east side of Snake Creek. Although the upper end of the crescent on the southwest was only twenty-five feet higher than the bottom land, it prevented an effective approach from that angle. The other three sides were open, undulating, grasslands. Therefore, the camp did not offer much in way of protection from an assault by cavalrymen.

Although the campground was not chosen because of its defensibility, it did possess several strategic advantages. Snake Creek not only provided water, but it had carved several coulees in the alluvial soil. Between the mouths of two coulees a triangular bar, with its base along the creek, provided room for action; and the coulees, nearly six feet deep, served as natural trenches. Even so, after Miles established his siege, the Indians excavated many jug-shaped fox holes with connecting tunnels.[1] The tools used in digging included trowel bayonets taken from the Big Hole battlefield, and knives and pans from Cow Island supplies. Shelter pits were dug for the old people, women, and children; rifle pits for the fighters. Small rocks from the creek bed were

237

placed above the firing pits to deflect bullets. There were no rocky crags or windfalls of timber, behind which the besieged Indians might find shelter.

Miles Attacks

As Miles surveyed the Indian position from the distance, he could not see the Nez Perce lodges or observe the details of their position. He knew where the camp was, however, from the activities his scouts had reported. He also noted commotion among the thousand or so horses, grazing on the northeast side of the creek beyond the village. Obviously, his presence had been reported and Indian horsemen were moving toward their mounts. Perhaps a hundred ponies were already loaded with squaws and papooses. At least that many, accompanied by an escort of about sixty braves, were able to escape.[2] Lacking time to catch and load their horses, the rest of the Indians rushed back to the coulees, where the warriors crouched with rifles in hand and waited.

Miles arranged his attack as follows: Captain Hale and his Seventh Cavalry command moved in on the southern flank of the village; Captain Snyder, with the Fifth Infantry, attacked the front; Lieutenant Maus supported Snyder's movement with his scouts; Captain Tyler encircled the Indians' horses with another cavalry unit; Lieutenant McClernand pursued the Indians who had fled; McHugh wheeled forward the Hotchkiss and prepared the four-pound howitzer; and the main body of cavalry began a frontal assault, while the infantry spread out and followed the cavalry charge.[3]

The force of at least six hundred horses charged forward with the same speed and precision that had broken the power of the Sioux and Cheyenne nations. Yellow Wolf said he heard "a rumble like stampeding buffaloes. . . . Hundreds of soldiers were charging in two, wide, circling wings. They were surrounding our camp. . . . I saw soldiers firing at everybody."[4] At a hundred yards the warriors opened fire, and the battle began.

Captain Carter's charge upon the edge of the village was repulsed with the loss of a third of his command. A half-dozen soldiers were cut off, but they defended their position in a ravine and withdrew after dark. Captain Hale was killed instantly, and his comrades remembered his recent response to Miles's order to advance on the Indian camp: "My God, have I got to go out and get killed in such cold weather!"[5] Lieutenant Biddle was also mortally wounded; Hale's K Troop was therefore leaderless, and it was almost annihilated. Other units fared little better, and when Lieutenant Eckerson, covered with blood, rushed back to Miles and shouted, "I am the only damned man of the Seventh Cavalry who wears shoulder straps alive!" the colonel ordered a change of tactics.[6] The Nez Perces' accurate fire made an advance on foot too costly, and the soldiers found and enlarged depressions, thereby automatically effecting a transition from charging strategy to siege tactics.

Although greatly disappointed, Miles gave direction to this change. He had hoped that his combination of surprise and numbers, momentum, and precision would overwhelm the Nez Perces. Miles had commanded an impressive attack, but to a degree he had charged an invisible foe. He had understood that the Nez Perces were exceptional marksmen, and he knew that ordering an assault would be taking a risk, but he probably hoped to achieve a decisive victory before Howard arrived with reinforcements. Within an hour he began to realize that storming the stronghold would produce unacceptable casualties, and at 3:00 P.M. he reluctantly imposed a siege upon the entrenched Indians.

The Character of Nez Perce Defenses

Meanwhile, the Nez Perces were confused. Many warriors were unable to catch their ponies, because Captain Tyler's soldiers and Cheyennes were pressing down upon them. Chief Joseph managed to catch a pony for his daughter and send her north with the fleeing column, but then the horses were stampeding and he was forced to run for his life. He described his feelings and reactions about this emergency in these words:

> I thought of my wife and children, who were now surrounded by soldiers, and I resolved to go to them or die. With a prayer in my mouth to the Great Spirit Chief who rules above, I dashed unarmed through the line of soldiers. It seemed to me that there were guns on every side, before and behind me. My clothes were cut to pieces and my horse was wounded, but I was not hurt. As I reached the door of my lodge, my wife handed me my rifle, saying: "Here's your gun. Fight!"
>
> The soldiers kept up a continuous fire. Six of my men were killed in one spot near me. Ten or twelve soldiers charged into our camp and got possession of two lodges, killing three Nez Perces and losing three of their men, who fell inside our lines. I called my men to drive them back. We fought at close range, not more than twenty steps apart, and drove the soldiers back upon their main line, leaving their dead in our hands. We secured their arms and ammunition. We lost, the first day and night, eighteen men and three women.[7]

As Chief Joseph stated, some of the warriors were killed in their flight toward the coulees. Others sought the protection of shallow lateral ravines close at hand, where they remained until nightfall, when they returned to the camp under cover of darkness. In these circumstances, with the Nez Perce warriors separated and fighting singly or in pairs, mistakes were made. Four braves, including Lean Elk, met death at the hands of their own comrades. Joseph's brother Ollokot, Pile of Clouds, Toohoolhoolzote, Hahtalekin, and many others were slain by the attackers. Surrounded by soldiers and bereft of all but a few of their ponies, the Indians were desperate. The loss of their herd was catastrophic. Without horses there was no prospect of a successful flight.

Several soldiers and scouts have left records of the fighting during the first afternoon. Jacob Horner stated that after the soldiers dismounted, "the Fifth Infantry charged toward the village on foot, but the withering fire of the Indians soon proved too severe, and attempts to capture the village by such means had to be abandoned."[8] Louis Shambow stated that he used his dead horse as bulwark until the odor resulting from repeated hits forced him to wiggle into a new position behind a rock. Here he was joined by Luther S. "Yellowstone" Kelley and Corporal John Haddo. They exchanged shots with the nearly invisible sharpshooters until the corporal was mortally wounded. He died while they were carrying him away. Shambow later said, "Those Indians were the best shots I ever saw. I would put a small stone on the top of my rock and they would get it every time."[9]

On the other hand, the soldiers and scouts pinned the warriors down in their rifle pits. Any reckless Indian was sure to draw a volley of accurate shots. Thus, marksmen on both sides exercised great caution in these exchanges. The most terrifying weapons in this battle were the artillery pieces. This was particularly true on the evening of October 1, after Captain Brotherton's wagon train arrived with tents, supplies, and a twelve-pound cannon. At first the artillerymen experienced difficulty in placing their shots in the coulees, but by sinking the tailpiece they elevated the muzzle and thereby converted the cannon into a mortar. Exploding shrapnel proved to be deadly in the rifle pits and tunnels. Indeed, a woman and child were buried alive in a shelter as a result of such an explosion. Other Indians were partially buried from time to time, but no deaths were attributed to direct hits. Surely Miles had the Nez Perces corralled, and their surrender was inevitable. He decided, nevertheless, to send a courier to inform Howard and Sturgis about the siege and urge them to hasten forward with reinforcements. The messenger missed Howard, but he reached Sturgis on the evening of October 2, and Sturgis moved forward rapidly.

Conditions in the Coulees during the Siege

The soldiers were quite comfortable in camp on the evening of October 1, but the Nez Perces were suffering in their cold, dismal coulees. An unnamed woman left this record of her experience:

> We digged the trenches with camas hooks and butcher knives. With pans we threw out the dirt. We could not do much cooking. Dried meat . . . would be handed around . . . given to the children first. I was three days without food. Children cried with hunger and cold. Old people suffering in silence. Misery everywhere. Cold and dampness all around.[10]

Ollokot's wife, Wetatonmi, added: "We slept only by naps; sitting in our pits; leaning forward or back against the dirt wall. Many of the warriors stayed in their pits all the time."[11]

Yellow Wolf gave an account of their forlorn situation at the beginning of the third day of battle:

> Morning came, bringing the battle anew. Bullets from everywhere! A big gun throwing bursting shells. From rifle pits, warriors returned shot for shot. Wild and

stormy, the cold wind was thick with snow. Air filled with smoke of powder. Flash of guns through it all. As the hidden sun traveled upward, the war did not weaken. . . . Cooking facilities in the besieged camp were piteously meager. The dead brush along the creek—a species of undersized willow—afforded scant kindling. Buffalo chips, though abundant, became buried the first night of the siege beneath a blanket of snow and were available only under cover of darkness. . . . A young warrior, wounded, lay on a buffalo robe dying without complaint. Children crying with cold. No fire. There could be no light. Everywhere the crying, the death wail. . . . All night we remained in those pits. The cold grew stronger. The wind was filled with snow. Only a little sleep. There might be a charge by the soldiers. The warriors watched by turns. A long night. . . . I felt the coming end. All for which we had suffered lost![12]

At one time there were a few moments of exultation among the Indians, accompanied by corresponding depression in the colonel's camp; then the reactions were completely reversed. The Nez Perces thought they had seen Indians coming to their aid, but then realized they were mistaken. They had sent a plea for help to Chief Sitting Bull and were still awaiting his answer. The defeat of General George A. Custer's forces in the Battle of the Little Big Horn on June 25, 1876, brought great pressure upon the Sioux nation. In order to escape retaliation, a large tribe, under Chief Sitting Bull, had sought a sanctuary in Canada. They occupied an area directly north of the Bear Paws, and occasionally their presence was reported on the United States side of the border. The Nez Perces knew they were near Sitting Bull, and six warriors were sent out of camp during the night of September 30, with a message for Sitting Bull. These messengers unfortunately came upon an Assiniboine village, where they were murdered. Sitting Bull received the message from other escapees, but he quickly moved his camp forty miles in the opposite direction.

Apparently he did not choose to increase his unpopularity in the United States by assisting the Nez Perces.

Meanwhile, the imprisoned Nez Perces waited and hoped. Then, on the afternoon of October 3, they saw many dark objects in the distance, moving toward their camp, and a joyful shout rang out that Sitting Bull's warriors were coming. Further observation disclosed that what looked like mounted Indians and their trappings was a herd of partially snow-covered bison. This discovery produced gloom in the coulees and relief among the soldiers.

The death of Chief Looking Glass was another disaster for the Indians. While he stood partly exposed in order to observe the approach of a mounted Indian whom he supposed to be a courier from the Sioux, a bullet struck him in the forehead.[18] His death was instantaneous and it had a profound effect upon the people.

Like Young Joseph, Looking Glass was the son of a renowned chief who bore the same name. Both father and son had been strong leaders, proud, independent, eloquent, and forceful. Looking Glass was the fifth chief killed on Snake Creek, and his passing symbolized the end of the old order of Nez Perce culture. The Nez Perces had always been governed by a dynasty of chiefs. The tribal solidarity that had united the generations was being torn asunder with the deaths of Lean Elk, Hahtalekin, Ollokot, Toohoolhoolzote, and Looking Glass. Although Looking Glass had entered the war more reluctantly than some other chiefs, his responsibility for tribal misadventures was great. His vote for flight from the Clearwater was decisive. His determination to unite with the Crow Indians and to travel leisurely over a circuitous route in reaching them was not wise. His confidence at the Big Hole, and again in the Bear Paws, had overcome the anxieties of more restless warriors. He had been a strong chieftain, but now leadership and responsibility must be shared by Chief Joseph and Chief White Bird.

Gestures toward Peace

In his report to the Assistant Adjutant General, Colonel Miles stated that "the Indians had from time to time displayed a white flag, but when communicated with had refused to surrender their arms, but on the morning of the 5th they surrendered. . . ."[14] Mc-Whorter's informants affirm that the first gesture toward cessation of hostilities came from Miles on the morning of October 1. According to Yellow Wolf, a white flag went up and an Indian voice shouted in Chinook that Miles would like to see Joseph. The chiefs delegated a half-blood Nez Perce named Tom Hill to go to Miles. This version is probably correct, because, as one historian reasoned, with victory within his grasp,

> Miles feared reinforcements for his own troops almost as much as he feared allies for the Nez Perces. Any hour might bring Sturgis, his equal in rank and anxious for promotion. Even worse, Howard might arrive and take command of all the troops, because of his superior rank, and thus get the lion's share of the credit for the capture. To forestall such a calamity, Miles began negotiating with Joseph, whom he regarded as the head chief of the hostiles.[15]

Meanwhile, Looking Glass, White Bird, Joseph, and others attempted to formulate a course of action. Concerning this issue, as upon other occasions, Looking Glass assumed an arbitrary position. In his view, white men could not be trusted. He prophesied that surrender would entail disillusionment, sorrow, and death. Chief White Bird expressed similar opinions and flatly declared he would never surrender. Joseph, as the guardian of the people, was somewhat disposed to accept honorable terms of surrender.

Upon returning, Hill conveyed the impression that Miles was honorable and sincere, as well as able to force a surrender. A parley was arranged, and Joseph and two other warriors went forth to meet Miles and several of his officers at a halfway point marked by a bison robe.

The terms of surrender were explained to Joseph's interpreters. Miles demanded the surrender of all firearms, but Joseph insisted that his people should retain half of them to shoot game. Upon this point Miles was adamant and Joseph would not yield. This disagreement broke up the parley, and the Indians started back toward their entrenchments. Then, upon some pretext known only to Miles, Joseph was taken into custody. Once again it was the white commander who violated the truce flag in dealing with the Nez Perces.

Miles referred to this matter by saying simply that he "detained" Joseph at his camp overnight. Later, when Lieutenant Lovell Jerome was asked why Joseph was held captive, he said, "That was Miles' way. When he could get hold of a chief or some prominent person he would hold him on some pretext. He also did this with Geronimo in the Apache affair.[16] Whatever the motivation, this act nearly cost Jerome his life.

While Joseph was being detained, Miles ordered Jerome to reconnoiter the boundaries of the Nez Perce camp and ascertain if the Indians were stacking their arms in compliance with his instructions to Joseph's associates. Instead of stopping on the edge, Jerome rode into the middle of the stronghold. Yellow Bull seized the bridle reins of the lieutenant's horse and pulled the rider from the saddle. Joseph's failure to return had convinced some of his young men that Miles was treacherous, and some of the warriors wanted to kill Jerome. Yellow Bull and Wottolen restrained them by agreeing to investigate the reason for Joseph's detention. Meanwhile, Jerome was held in one of the better underground shelters, where he was allowed to retain his side arms and communicate with Miles. He was also permitted to receive warm food from the officers' mess.

As he promised, Yellow Bull entered "Bear Coat's" (the Nez Perce name for Miles) camp to see Joseph and secure his release. Joseph described their meeting:

> General Miles would not let me leave the tent to see my friend alone.
>
> Yellow Bull said to me: "They have got you in their power, and I am afraid they will never let you go again. I have an officer in our camp, and I will hold him until they let you go free."
>
> I said: "I do not know what they mean to do with me, but if they kill me you must not kill the officer. It will do no good to avenge my death by killing him."[17]

Although Miles directed the artillery fire upon the Indian stronghold that evening, on the following morning, October 2, he exchanged Chief Joseph for Lieutenant Jerome.

Yellow Wolf stated that Joseph was subjected to indignities during his detention: "Chief Joseph was hobbled hands and feet. They took a double blanket. Soldiers rolled him in it. . . . He was put where there were mules, and not in the soldier tent. That was how Chief Joseph was treated all night."[18] Yellow Wolf further stated that Jerome sent a message to the officers informing them of the hospitality accorded to him: "I am treated like I was at home. I hope you are treating Chief Joseph as I am treated."[19] Presumably, this note had a bearing upon the decision to release the chieftain. When the two prisoners were exchanged on the halfway ground, they shook hands. The truce flag came down and the siege was resumed.

Joseph must have realized that unless the Sioux came

soon their case was hopeless. Later he said, "We could have escaped from the Bear Paw Mountains if we had left our wounded, old women, and children behind. We were unwilling to do this. We never heard of a wounded Indian recovering in the hands of white men."[20]

It should be noted that this time Joseph employed the plural pronoun. After Looking Glass was killed and White Bird escaped, Joseph spoke in the first person singular when referring to his role of leadership. This usage did not signify a change in the man, but rather in the circumstances.

On the evening of October 4, after their hopes of help from Sitting Bull waned, Joseph and White Bird reached an understanding. Each would act as he saw fit, in respect to himself and in behalf of his tribesmen. Actually, that had been the basis of their alliance from the beginning. White Bird's disillusionment concerning white men was intense and of long duration. Then, too, the war had been started by members of his band. He really feared that he would be executed if he surrendered. However, he found no fault with Joseph for attempting to make peace. As the time for decision approached, White Bird said, "What Joseph does is allright; I have nothing to say."[21] Their agreement came when General Howard and his escort reached the battlefield at dusk on the evening of October 4.

The Effect of Howard's Arrival

Having been without word of Miles's progress since he left Cow Island on September 29, Howard was becoming increasingly apprehensive. Then, on the evening of October 4, his detachment came upon Miles's trail after passing the gap between the Little Rockies and the Bear Paws. As the men were preparing to make camp, the two couriers who had successfully carried Miles's message to Sturgis rode up. Explaining that they had found Sturgis and Mason, they assured Howard that their joint command was rapidly marching toward the Bear Paws. They also described the first day of the Bear Paws battle and the location of the battleground. Resuming their march, Howard's men soon heard the slow but steady rifle fire, and, as they topped a ridge, they saw the military encampment in the semidarkness.

Colonel Miles, observing the general's approach, quickly organized an escort consisting of his adjutant, Lieutenant Oscar Long, an orderly, and several soldiers, and rode out on the prairie to meet Howard. Both parties dismounted and Howard said, "Hello, Miles! I'm glad to see you. I thought you might have met Gibbon's fate. Why didn't you let me know?"[22] Since the reason for this failure had been given by the messengers, Howard's question was given scant attention. In fact, Lieutenant C. E. S. Wood, Howard's aide, wrote that Miles exhibited a formal and reserved attitude toward the general until after Howard had generously assured him that he could proceed with the surrender. Then, "Colonel Miles' entire manner changed; he became cordial, thanked the General for all he had said."[23] This version is supported by Howard's official report, in which he stated, "I had no desire to assume immediate command of the field, but would be glad to have him finish the work he had so well begun."[24]

The two officers made plans for implementing a surrender the next day. It was agreed that Howard's Nez Perce scouts, Captain John (Jokais) and Old George (Meopkowit), should serve as messengers. Each of these Indians had a daughter with the nontreaty group —a fact partly responsible for their scouting role, and one that was bound to assure them entry to the camp.

Later, when Howard was alone with his aide, Lieutenant Wood registered an objection over Howard's promise to occupy a secondary role in the conclusion of the campaign. Wood and his fellow officers on Howard's staff felt that their exertions and hardships in pursuing the Nez Perces over thirteen hundred miles of wilderness were being ignored in this gesture by Howard. The general had given his word, however, and he obviously believed that there would be enough credit and praise for all.[25] As always, Wood was impressed by Howard's character, integrity, and soldierly ethics; but he distrusted Miles, and events were to confirm his suspicion.

Thus, in two simultaneous councils, on opposite sides of the battleground, it was decided that the principal roles in the impending negotiations would be played by Joseph and Miles. Their ascendancy was due to a combination of fate and the magnanimity of their peers. Each was to stand out above his fellow warriors in the surrender scene the next afternoon and afterwards, in accounts of the scene.

Chief Joseph was invited to surrender at the point marked by the bison robe, midway between the camps. Howard's Nez Perce scouts were on hand to establish the necessary contact and confidence.

22. "I WILL FIGHT NO MORE FOREVER"

In midforenoon of October 5, Howard's Nez Perce interpreters approached the siege trenches waving a white flag. Yellow Wolf recorded Captain John's salutation: "All my brothers, I am glad to see you alive this sun! . . . We have traveled a long ways trying to catch you folks. We are glad to hear you want no more war, do not want to fight. We are all glad."[1]

These words were not entirely acceptable to the warriors. In fact, Chuslum Hihhih wanted to shoot the spokesman, but a warrior restrained and rebuked him. Then Old George spoke:

> We have come far from home. You now see many soldiers lying down side by side. We see Indians, too, lying dead. I am glad today to be shaking hands. We are all not mad. We all think of Chief Joseph and these other brothers. We see your sons and relations lying dead, but we are glad to shake hands with you today. I am glad to catch up with you and find my daughter, too, alive.[2]

In this fashion, a proper liaison was established. Speaking in turns, Captain John and Old George offered assurances: Miles was an honest-appearing man who

251

could be trusted to be just and considerate. After listening to these assurances and promises Joseph and White Bird counseled with the warriors.

Final Peace Negotiations

Several warriors distrusted the officers and feared hangings and firing squads under Howard's supervision. Yet the messengers had promised that their horses and rifles would be returned in due course and that food, blankets, and good treatment were awaiting them. Many were persuaded that their lives would be spared and their property restored.

While the warriors were deliberating, the messengers returned. They explained that the generals were becoming impatient. Chief Joseph replied: "We will council over this. We will decide what to do!"[3] Then, the messengers emphasized the point that the army wanted no more fighting: "Those generals said tell you 'We will have no more war!'" This provided a way for the Indians to agree to the cessation of the battle without giving the appearance of yielding to a forced surrender. Joseph said: "You see, it is true, I did not say 'Let's quit.' You see, it is true enough! I did not say 'Let's quit!'"[4]

Yellow Wolf said this line of argument convinced most of the warriors. They said, "Yes, we believe you now." He then stated his own viewpoint: "We were not captured. It was a draw battle. . . . We expected to be returned to our own homes. This was promised us by General Miles. This was how he got our rifles from us. It was the only way he could get them."[5]

White Bird opposed surrender. What Joseph said and did was all right; he had spoken, and he would act as he saw fit, but unanimity was not an important consideration in Nez Perce policy. Tribal law accorded each chief, faction, and individual the right of decision, and White Bird would follow his own judgment. Joseph, as guardian of the shivering, starving non-combatants and the wounded braves, said, "It is for them I am going to surrender."[6]

Chief Joseph thought then, and later, that he actually had a choice at that time of surrendering or continuing the battle. Some doubt the reality of this position. They honor him for his courage in holding out until October 5, but by then defeat was practically inevitable. His people were starving, freezing, and dying, and Howard's cavalrymen, under Mason and Sturgis, were only thirty miles away.[7] Joseph was not unaware of these facts; yet he said: "General Miles said to me in plain words, 'If you will come out and give up your arms, I will spare your lives and send you back to the reservation.' . . . General Miles had promised that we might return to our country with what stock we had left. . . . I believed General Miles, or I never would have surrendered."[8]

That is obviously an accurate statement of Joseph's belief. No one has ever suggested that he was given to exaggeration, and indeed, his statements and actions were always characterized by restraint. General Howard recorded his recognition of this fact in a significant line: "And even at the last, the natural resources of his mind did not fail him."[9]

Joseph's Understanding of the Surrender Terms

Therefore, when Chief Joseph rode out to meet Howard and Miles at the halfway point on the afternoon of October 5, he did so confidently, knowing his cause was a good one. He was proud of his people's record in the war and sure of receiving justice. He understood that a full surrender of his people, that is, all who chose to follow him, would lead to their return to the Clearwater country. They could hardly expect to regain their ancestral homelands, but he believed that the terms originally governing their removal to the Lapwai reservation would be met. He and his warriors had reached this understanding as a result of a parley with Colonel Miles on October 1. This viewpoint was further confirmed during the extended consultations with Captain John and Old George, the two Nez Perces who had been with General Howard since the beginning of the campaign. Furthermore, if the foregoing conditions were improperly understood, there would be ample opportunity for clarification upon the surrender spot.

Although aware that surrender would terminate the existence of the Nez Perces as an independent nation, Chief Joseph pointed out the positive elements in the situation. The Clearwater Valley was pleasant, overgrown with the familiar camas and cowish roots. They would soon become accustomed to the new land.

In such a fashion, Joseph conducted a persuasive argument, and his melodious voice and optimistic manner won the confidence of nearly all.

Finally the messengers were summoned to the coulees, and Chief Joseph told them what had been decided. Then, as an act of faith, he uttered an avowal to the effect that he would fight no more. He based this resolution upon the desperate plight his people were in. At this point in Joseph's deliberation he gave extemporaneous expression to the thoughts he so eloquently delivered to the generals an hour later: "Most of the old men and the chiefs are dead." Speaking of his beloved brother, Ollokot, he said, "He who led the young men is dead." "It is cold and we have no blankets. The little children are freezing to death." He wondered what had happened to those of his people who had fled: "Maybe I shall find them among the dead."[10] Then he disclosed the peaceful nature of his inner soul: "I am tired; my heart is sick and sad."[11] Greetings were then sent to the generals, with a promise to surrender.

The two Nez Perce messengers returned to the camp,

impressed with the solemnity of Joseph's words and manner. Captain John's eyes were filled with tears as he delivered the surrender message to Howard and Miles.[12]

These officers, flanked by three other officers and interpreter Arthur Chapman, then took their stance upon the parley ground. Toward evening, Joseph rode out from the coulees, followed by several warriors on foot. A snow-filled wind swirled down from the Bear Paws and swept the prairie, adding to the gloom of the occasion.[13]

The Surrender

Lieutenant Wood, one of the officers who witnessed the surrender, wrote the most satisfactory account of the proceedings. His description follows:

Joseph's hair hung in two braids on either side of his face. He wore a blanket ... and moccasin leggings. His rifle was across the pommel in front of him. When he dismounted he ... walked to General Howard and offered him the rifle. Howard waved him to Miles. He then walked to Miles and handed him the rifle. Then Chief Joseph stepped back and began his formal speech.[14]

Chief Joseph spoke as follows:

Tell General Howard I know his heart. What he told me before I have in my heart. I am tired of fighting. Our chiefs are killed. Looking Glass is dead. The old men are all killed. It is the young men who say yes or no. He who led the young men is dead. It is cold and we have no blankets. The little children are freezing to death. My people, some of them, have run away to the hills and have no blankets, no food; no one knows where they are, perhaps freezing to death. I want time to look for my children and see how many of them I can find. Maybe I shall find them among the dead. Hear me, my chiefs, I am tired; my heart is sick and sad. From where the sun now stands, I will fight no more forever.[15]

Joseph's bearing was dignified, and Howard spoke to him in a kindly manner: "You have your life. I am living. I have lost my brothers. Many of you have lost brothers, maybe more than on our side. I do not know. Do not worry more."[16] Colonel Miles said: "No more battles and blood. From this sun, we will have a good time on both sides, your band and mine."[17] In accordance with Joseph's understanding of the surrender terms, Miles assured the chief that his people would be returned to the Idaho reservation in the spring.[18]

Miles won the confidence of the Nez Perces, who thereafter regarded him as their protector. They understood that he would take them to Fort Keogh for the winter; when spring came they could go home. Their reaction to this prospect was expressed by Yellow Wolf: "Now we understand these words, and will go with General Miles. He is head man. We will go with him."[19]

The Nez Perce delegates returned to the coulees, where they confidently urged the people to surrender their arms. Chief Joseph's courage and care for his people won the admiration of both Indians and white men. J. J. Healy reported his activities in the *Benton Record* of October 12, 1877, as follows: "Joseph was walking round about his people talking to the wounded and occasionally addressing the warriors by signs and seemed quite unconcerned about his defeat." Healy observed that the people quickly responded to his leadership.

Meanwhile, White Bird and his followers had been preparing to leave for Canada when opportunity afforded. Later in the night, "when deep darkness came, Chief Whitebird and his people walked out from that camp."[20] It was reported that fourteen men and a comparable number of women constituted this band, w'.ich planned to go to Chief Sitting Bull's camp. Only six of White Bird's warriors cast their lot with Chief Joseph. These six were Yellow Bull, his two brothers, and three additional men.[21]

Condition and Enumeration of the Nez Perces

Meanwhile, the surrender had been effectuated. In Howard's words, "The lame, maimed, halt, and blind (Nez Perces) came crawling up the hill."[22] Of course there were also many able-bodied refugees. Estimates concerning the number that surrendered vary from 410 to 431. Perhaps McWhorter's estimate is the most reliable one. He states, "In all, Joseph surrendered eighty-seven (87) men, one hundred eighty-four (184) women and one hundred forty-seven (147) children."[23] That made a total of 418. A large proportion of the men were elderly, and some forty were wounded.

An officer who examined the Indians' arms said that "he did not see one worth having."[24] Arthur I. Chapman, Nez Perce interpreter, stated that 1,531 horses, 300 saddles, bridles, ropes, camp equipment, and blankets were surrendered. The Nez Perces understood that seven hundred horses would be returned to them.[25]

The Misfortunes of Many Escapees

Approximately 150 Nez Perces had escaped from the Bear Paws camp just as Miles launched his attack. Chief Joseph's daughter and his sister were in this band. Others probably escaped between then and White Bird's departure on the night of October 5. One of White Bird's companions, named Black Eagle, estimated that a total of 233 escaped from the battlefield.[26]

Of this number, 140 were men and boys and 93 were women and girls.

Perhaps Yellow Wolf was the last one to leave the coulees. He was Chief Joseph's nephew, and his mother and Joseph's daughter (Kapkap Ponmi, meaning "noise of running feet") were among the escapees. Toward morning on October 6, Chief Joseph said to Yellow Wolf, "You better go and find your mother and my daughter. Bring them here!"[27] Yellow Wolf succeeded in reaching Canada, but not in fulfilling Joseph's request.

The following statement by Colonel Miles describes his effort to intercept the escapees. It also reveals a misfortune that befell many of the escaping Nez Perces. Miles erred in stating that White Bird escaped in the beginning of the battle.

During the siege Lieutenant Maus had been sent north with a detachment to, if possible, overtake White Bird and any other Indian that had been able to escape. In this he was to some extent successful, and brought back several. He also brought back the information that when the Indians who had escaped reached the Assinniboine camp, the friendly Assinniboins, instead of coming to the assistance of their beleaguered brethren, killed the two Nez Perces and left their bodies on the prairie.[28]

J. J. Healy and George Croft confirmed this report: "We met Bull's Lodge, a Gros Ventre chief, who told us that the Assiniboins and Gros Ventres, assisted by three white men, had attacked a Nez Perce camp . . . and had captured two women and two boys, and killed several warriors. They had one fresh scalp with them. . . ."[29] Healy and Croft gave Major Ilges credit for securing pledges from the above-mentioned tribes to attack and plunder the fleeing Nez Perces. A man named John Samples reported that more than thirty Nez Perces, who appealed for refuge, were slain and robbed by the

Assiniboins and Gros Ventres.[30] This report was no doubt exaggerated, but a Gros Ventre named Moccasin also gave testimony to the effect that seven Nez Perces were killed and four captured by a band of his people. Obviously, the lives of detached Nez Perce escapees were in jeopardy. Even so, nearly two hundred of them succeeded in reaching Canada, where the Sioux welcomed them.

Newspaper Reports of Chief Joseph's Surrender

Howard and Miles prepared separate reports for their superior officers. According to Howard's aide, Lieutenant Wood, Miles showed Howard the message he had prepared for General Alfred H. Terry. In this version, Howard's arrival and presence at the surrender ceremony were mentioned. The courier left on schedule and the message he bore duly reached General Terry and finally General Philip H. Sheridan, for release to the press in Chicago. The message was dated October 5, and came from Colonel Nelson A. Miles. Although brief, it was exulting, if not egotistical: "We have had our usual success. We made a very direct and rapid march across country, and after a severe engagement and being kept under fire for three days, the hostile camp under Chief Joseph surrendered at two o'clock today."[31]

This message made no mention of Howard, but Howard did not know this until he reached Fort Lincoln a week later. Howard's officers had cautioned him against such an event when he so generously allowed Miles to conduct the peace negotiations. They all felt betrayed. Being thus ignored by their superior officers and the press, after pursuing the hostiles for so long, was worse than the ridicule the same sources had poured upon them all summer.

No doubt the influence of Howard's officers had a

bearing upon the surrender report he authorized Lieutenant Wood to give the Chicago newspapers on October 25. Wood justified this issuing of a new account by what he regarded as Miles's disloyal and unsoldierly conduct in deleting the mention of Howard's role from the first report. Miles had sent a second report on October 6 that contained more details pertaining to the surrender and gave Howard the recognition he deserved, but the news value was minor. In the meantime, Howard's account of the surrender had reached General Sheridan's desk; indeed, he read both Wood's newspaper account and Howard's report the same morning. The appearance of Wood's article in the Chicago *Tribune,* without his permission as division commander, made Sheridan angry. Upon meeting Howard, he was so angry and spoke so vehemently that Howard left his presence indignantly.[32] Contrary to Howard's expectations, events had revealed that there was not enough glory in Joseph's surrender to go around.

Before Howard left Chicago for the Columbia River Department, he wrote a note of apology to Sheridan stating that he was "very sorry to have compromised you in any way."[33] The note was forwarded to Sherman, bearing Sheridan's endorsement: "I do not feel much compromised. It seems to me that General Howard compromised himself."[34]

Battle Casualties and Evaluations

Twenty-five Nez Perces were killed in the Bear Paw battle, all but three of them on the first day. Miles reported that forty-six Nez Perces were wounded, and that may be the most accurate figure.

Miles's report of October 6, from the Bear Paw camp to the Assistant Adjutant General, listed twenty-three dead and forty-five wounded. A later list of fatalities, certified by the War Department, included the name of

Private William Randall. The following soldiers were killed:

Captain Owen Hale	7th Cavalry
2nd Lieut. Jonathan W. Biddle	"
1st Sergt. George McDermott	"
1st Sergt. Michael Martin	"
1st Sergt. Otto Wild	"
Sergt. James H. Alberts	"
Sergt. Otto Durselow	"
Sergt. Max Mielke	"
Sergt. Henry W. Raichel	"
Private John E. Cleveland	"
Private David I. Dawsey	"
Private George F. Hurdick	"
Private Frank Knaupp	"
Private Lewis Kelly	"
Private Samuel McIntyre	"
Private Francis Roth	"
Private William Randall	"
Private William Whitlow	"
Private Thomas Geohegan	5th Infantry
Corporal John Haddo (Heddo)	"
Private Joseph Kohler	"
Private Richard M. Peshall	"

Private Kohler died October 1, 1877, of wounds.

Analysis of the casualties disclosed the fact that both sides sustained almost identical losses. In each case, most of these casualties occurred during the morning assaults upon the Indian situation. At that time, as Miles reported, "the fighting was very severe and at close quarters."[35] Upon surveying the battleground four days later, General Howard stated, "The work was bravely done, though the gallant charge cost the lives of many men, and disabled many more."[36]

Perhaps Louis Shambow was the only man on the field who thought Miles resorted to siege tactics prematurely. He said, "I have been in harder fights than that and will always believe that if we had not hesitated we would have ended that fight in fifteen minutes, as there were twice as many white men as there were Indian warriors."[37]

Shambow was a frontiersman, however, and the responsibility for the men's lives was not his. Will Cave also held the opinion that "General Miles could have wiped them out in a few hours, but he took three days to force their surrender rather than to destroy them entirely."[38] He attributes Miles's restraint to a consideration for Nez Perce lives. Perhaps Miles was governed by both caution and admiration of the Indians. He wrote, "[The Nez Perces] were the boldest men and best marksmen of any Indians I have ever encountered. And Chief Joseph was a man of more sagacity and intelligence than any Indian I have ever met."[39]

The Status of the Bear Paws Battlefield

Upon the conclusion of the surrender, food, blankets, and medicine were issued to the Indians. During the next two days the soldiers and Indians buried their dead. With a few exceptions, the bodies were left there until the fall of 1903, when Quartermaster McDonald at Fort Assiniboine received orders to transfer the soldiers' bodies to the fort burial ground. Eight years later, when Fort Assiniboine was abandoned, they were again disinterred and taken to the Fort Custer National Military Cemetery.[40]

For decades little interest was exhibited in the battlefield, and its existence was forgotten by all but a few. L. V. Bogy was chiefly responsible for getting a section, including the battleground, withdrawn from homestead entry.

In 1928, Montana residents sponsored a project of staking the Indian situation on the battlefield. L. V. McWhorter, Many Wounds, Peopeo Tholekt, and

Yellow Wolf marked many points of interest. They also placed a monument upon the spot where Chief Looking Glass fell. In 1929, the battleground was further memorialized by the erection of a monument from rocks gathered on the battleground.[41]

On April 15, 1930, Congress appropriated funds that provided for the erection of another monument. It included a bronze plaque designed by Jessie S. Lincoln, which depicts Colonel Nelson A. Miles and Chief Joseph in the central positions of the surrender scene.[42] This plaque was embedded in a huge boulder mounted upon a concrete base. The plaque bears this inscription:

"From where the sun now stands I will fight no more forever"

October 5, 1877

Surrender of Chief Joseph to Colonel Nelson A. Miles
To the valor and devotion of those
Both Red and white who struggled here
Erected by the Congress of the United States
Under the authority of an Act approved April 15, 1930.

The stakes driven by McWhorter and his associates in 1928 had by then been lost or destroyed. Therefore, arrangements were made for McWhorter and several Nez Perce warriors to return in 1935. This time the stakes were re-established and a sketch of the area was made. On September 30, 1936, another monument was placed upon the battleground, upon which an embedded plaque bears this legend:

BEAR PAWS BATTLE GROUND

In grateful remembrance of the officers and enlisted men killed in action in the last decisive armed conflict between the white men and the Red men in the Northwest.

September 30–October 6, 1877

7th U.S. Cavalry	Pvt. Lewis Kelly
Captain Owen Hale	Pvt. Samuel McIntyre
2nd Lieut. Jonathan W. Biddle	Pvt. William J. Randall
1st Sergt. George McDermott	Pvt. Francis Roth
1st Sergt. Michael Martin	Pvt. William Whitlow
1st Sergt. Otto Wild	
Sergt. James H. Alberts	2nd U.S. Cavalry
Sergt. Otto Durselow	Pvt. John Irving
Sergt. Max Mielke	
Sergt. Henry W. Raichel	5th U.S. Infantry
Pvt. John F. Cleveland	Corporal John Haddo
Pvt. David I. Dawsey	Pvt. Thomas Goehegan
Pvt. Charles F. Hurdick	Pvt. Joseph Kohler
Pvt. Frank Knaupp	Pvt. Richard M. Peshall

Erected by the
Daughters of the American Revolution
and the
Citizens of Blaine County, Montana,
September 30, 1936

Since then, occasional efforts have been made to secure additional funds from Congress to enlarge and beautify the battleground. Perhaps the existing elemental atmosphere of desolation provides a proper setting for a memorial to the men who fought here from September 30 to October 5, 1877.

23. A SUMMARY OF THE NEZ PERCE CAMPAIGN

Many graphic and eloquent accounts have been written about the Nez Perce campaign. The official reports alone comprise more than one hundred thousand words. Perhaps the gist of this bulk has been compressed into the following paragraph, which appears in the Army R.O.T.C. manual:

In 11 weeks, he (Joseph) had moved his tribe 1,600 miles, engaged 10 separate U.S. commands in 13 battles and skirmishes, and in nearly every instance had either defeated them or fought them to a standstill. General Sherman rightly termed the struggle "one of the most extraordinary Indian wars of which there is any record.[1]

Nevertheless, it is expedient to record additional commentaries and observations. In "An Indian's View of Indian Affairs," Chief Joseph described the Nez Perce side of the campaign quite accurately. These are the highlights in his narration:

At White Bird, we numbered sixty men, and the soldiers a hundred. The fight lasted a few minutes. They lost thirty-three killed, and had seven wounded.

Seven days after White Bird Battle, General Howard arrived in the Nez Perce country. We crossed over Salmon River, hoping he would follow. He did follow us and we got between him and his supplies, and cut him off for three days. He sent out two companies to open the way. We attacked them killing one officer, two guides, and ten men. [On Camas Prairie] we killed four and wounded seven or eight. On the Clearwater River, Howard attacked us with three hundred and fifty soldiers and settlers. We had two hundred and fifty warriors. The fight lasted twenty-seven hours. We lost four killed and several wounded. General Howard's loss was twenty-nine men killed and sixty wounded.

Finding that we were outnumbered we retreated to the Bitter Root Valley. Here another body of soldiers came upon us and demanded our surrender. We then made a treaty with these soldiers. We agreed not to molest anyone. We understood that there was to be no more war.

Gibbon's soldiers surrounded our Big Hole camp. He charged us while some of our people were still asleep. We had a hard fight, but we finally drove General Gibbon back. In the fight with General Gibbon we lost fifty women and children and thirty fighting men.

We retreated as rapidly as we could toward the Buffalo country. After six days General Howard came close to us, and we attacked him, and captured nearly all of his horses and mules. We then marched on to the Yellowstone Basin.

On the way we captured one white man and two white women. They were treated kindly and released at the end of three days.

We also captured two more white men. One of them stole a horse and escaped. We gave the other a poor horse and told him he was free.

Beyond Clarks Fork, General Sturgis, a new war-chief, attacked us. We held him in check, leaving a few men to cover our retreat.

Several days passed, and we heard nothing of General Howard, or Gibbon, or Sturgis. We had repulsed each in turn, and began to feel secure, when another army, under General Miles, struck us. This was the fourth army, each of which outnumbered our fighting force, that we had encountered within sixty days.

We had no knowledge of General Miles' army until a short time before he made a charge upon us, cutting our camp in two, and capturing nearly all of our horses. About seventy men, myself among them, were cut off.

I dashed unarmed through the line of soldiers. It seemed to me that there were guns on every side. We fought at close range and drove the soldiers back upon their main line. We lost, the first day and night, thirteen men and three women. General Miles lost twenty-six killed and forty wounded.

On the fifth day I went to General Miles and gave up my gun and said, "From where the sun now stands I will fight no more."[2]

A similar compression of General Howard's voluminous accounts would be impractical. However, he made a summary of the campaign strategy at a gathering in Portland, Oregon, on November 11, 1877.

I may venture a single remark in our own behalf. However the rewards and the criticisms concerning this last Indian war may be distributed, it is indeed true that there has been one campaign continuous, and we claim systematic, extending from the time the savage murderers of Idaho forced the unequal battle of White Bird Canyon and bedewed the steep slopes and neighboring ravines with the precious blood of our slain, to the last scene when Col. Miles stood at my side to receive the surrendered rifle of the Indian chief—a campaign begun in the treachery, murder and fearful outrages of the non-treaty Nez Perces, but continued beyond the line of this military department in precise conformity to Gen. Sherman's order, and with General McDowell's generous support and more specific direction.[3]

Howard's statement as patently disclosed his defensive attitude as it concealed his charitable disposition. Nonetheless, he brought out the fact that, after all, this devious and protracted campaign had not been prosecuted in a wholly haphazard fashion. Indeed, there had been a unified pattern of operation, and it finally succeeded.

On November 13, 1877, a United States Senate resolution requested information from President Hayes concerning the causes and costs of the Nez Perce war. In turn, Secretary of War George W. McCrary called upon various officials in his department. General William T. Sherman wrote a summary of the war, which appeared in a document entitled "Message for the President of the United States," A.G.O. 3464-77. The account was printed in the *United States Senate Executive Documents,* Volume I, covering the first and second sessions of the Forty-fifth Congress. The following represents a brief abstract of Sherman's seven-page description of the campaign:

The recent war with the Nez Perces was so unexpected, and has been attended with so varied and interesting incidents, covering a vast surface of country utterly regardless of boundary lines, that I find it necessary to embrace it more at length and in detail than is ordinarily called for where an Indian war is usually confined to a smaller area, generally to a single department.

On June 15, General Howard dispatched two cavalry companies under Captain Perry, numbering ninety-nine men, to the scene of disorder.

Captain Perry proceeded rapidly by night to the head of White Bird Canon, making seventy miles, with the loss of two nights' sleep. There he found the Indian camp, and assisted by eleven citizen volunteers, proceeded at once to attack. The Indians seemed well prepared, for they repulsed the attack and compelled the command to fall back, losing Lieutenant Theller and thirty-three enlisted men.

Reinforcements were promptly dispatched by the division commander, General McDowell from the small frontier posts along the Pacific coast as far south as Yuma; and the Second Infantry under Colonel Wheaton was sent from South Carolina.

By the 8th of July, General Howard had collected a force of about four hundred men; and on the 11th he discovered the enemy on Clearwater and attacked them. General Howard reports twenty-three warriors killed, twice as many wounded, twenty-three warriors taken prisoners, and seventeen women and children made captive. His own loss was thirteen men killed, two officers and twenty-two men wounded. This battle was chiefly important because it prevented other Indians from joining the hostile Nez Perces. Howard reorganized his command, sending one force up north into the Spokane country; another was held in reserve near the Indian reservation, and he himself started in pursuit across the Lolo Trail.

Hearing of the approach of these Indians, Captain Charles C. Rawn, located at Fort Missoula, entrenched himself on Lolo Creek with forty enlisted men and quite a force of citizen volunteers. The Indians reached Rawn's fort July 28, passed around it into the Bitter Root Valley in such numbers that he was not justified in attacking them outside his entrenchments, and with a large herd of horses passed deliberately up the Bitter Root Valley (which is well settled), doing little comparative damage to the inhabitants.

Colonel Gibbon, with one hundred forty-six men, afterwards increased by thirty-four citizens, overtook the enemy on a branch of the Big Hole, surprised them at daybreak of August 9th and for a time had the Indians at his mercy; but their numbers so far exceeded his own, that he in turn was compelled to seek cover in a point of timber where he fought on the defensive 'til the Indians withdrew at 11 p.m. on the 10th.

Colonel Gibbon reports his loss at two officers, six citizens, and twenty-one enlisted men killed; five officers, four citizens, and thirty-one men wounded. And on the part of the enemy, eighty-nine were buried. It is otherwise known that the Indians sustained a very heavy and nearly fatal loss in wounded in this fight, and could Colonel Gibbon have had another hundred men, the Nez Perces War would have ended right there.

From Gibbon's battlefield, Howard resumed the pursuit. He followed to Horse Prairie, then threw a force of forty cavalry and some scouts towards Henrys Lake, designing to intercept and hinder the enemy, but this party, after waiting a few days, returned, leaving the route open to the Indians.

On August 19th General Howard made camp at Camas Prairie. Here the Indians turned on him, stampeded and ran off at daylight of the 20th his pack-train, which was partially recovered by his cavalry. In this fight Captain Norwood's company made a handsome fight. General Howard was compelled to give his men and animals some rest at Henrys Lake. I recognize the full measure of the labors, exposure, fatigue, and fighting of General Howard and his command, having personally seen much of the route over which he passed. It is simply impossible for infantry or even cavalry with their single horses, to overtake Indians who drive along a whole herd, changing from a tired horse to one comparatively fresh at pleasure; knowing the country as these Indians do, ready to hide in the many rocky canons, ravines and dense woods and able with a small rear guard to hold at bay any number in pursuit, who often for miles must follow trails in single file. Happening to be in Montana at the time, I gave up my cavalry escort and was pleased to learn that it was of material assistance to General Howard at Camas on the 20th of August.

From Henrys Lake to Bear Paw Mountains, all Howard could do was follow where the Indians led, and this he did with praiseworthy zeal and perseverance. On others devolved the task of "heading off" and "capture." The Indians were in General Sheridan's division, and he promptly gave the necessary orders. He caused a force of six companies of the Seventh Cavalry, under its colonel, Sturgis, to watch the outlet by Clarks Fork of the Yellowstone; another of five companies of cavalry, under Major Hart, of the Fifth on the Stinking Water, which is a branch of the Big Horn; and still another of ten companies of cavalry, under Merritt, of the Fifth, on Wind River. One or other of these bodies was sure to intercept them, with General Howard's command on their heels.

They successfully evaded General Sturgis' command but he made a fast pursuit and engaged them in a running battle at Canon Creek on September 13th. The Nez Perces then passed north across the Musselshell, through Judith Basin, to the Missouri River at Cow Island. Here on September 23rd, the Indians lightly skirmished with a small guard of the Seventh Infantry; burned some supplies, forded the river and pushed on north toward Milk River and the British boundary.

On the morning of September 30, Colonel Miles found the Nez Perce camp on Eagle Creek. The result of his attack was complete, viz., the capture of Joseph and the surviving remnant of his brave but dangerous body of Indians. The Indians in this fight lost in killed six of their leading chiefs and twenty-five warriors, with forty-six wounded.

Colonel Miles reports his own loss at two officers

and twenty men killed, four officers and forty-one men wounded.

General Howard, with a small escort, arrived on the field a short time before the surrender, but did not exercise any command. Of course Colonel Miles and his officers and men are entitled to all honor and praise for their prompt, skillful, and successful work; while others, by their long, toilsome pursuit are entitled to corresponding credit, because they made the success possible.

Thus has terminated one of the most extraordinary Indian wars of which there is any record. The Indians throughout displayed a courage and skill that elicited universal praise. They abstained from scalping; let captive women go free; did not commit indiscriminate murder of peaceful families, which is usual, and fought with almost scientific skill, using advance and rear guards, skirmish lines, and field fortifications. Nevertheless, they would not settle down on lands set apart for them, ample for their maintenance; and, when commanded by proper authority, they began resistance by murdering persons in no manner connected with their alleged grievances. With your approval, these prisoners are now en route by the most economical way to Fort Leavenworth, to be there held as prisoners of war until spring, when, I trust, the Indian Bureau will provide them homes on the Indian reservations near the modocs, where, by moderate labor, they can soon be able to support themselves in peace. They should never again be allowed to return to Oregon or to Lapwai.

Atrocities Committed

Each side was guilty of committing cruel and wanton acts against the lives of others. Perhaps the military officers can be held more accountable, because their mores, disciplines, and authority were presumed to be much higher, firmer, and more clearly invested. While Nez Perce behavior reached extreme cruelty in the wanton murders on the White Bird, Horse Prairie, Birch Creek, and the Clark Fork, and in Yellowstone Park, their conduct was predominantly praiseworthy. Their meticulous adherence to the agreement with the Bitterroot settlers and their considerate treatment of several captives in Yellowstone National Park were exceptional.[4]

The most reprehensible acts committed under military auspices were those of the Indian scouts employed by Howard, Sturgis, and Miles. Bannocks, Crows, Cheyennes, Assiniboines, and Gros Ventres scouts scalped the Nez Perce dead and killed their aged and wounded whenever they had a chance. The morality of Gibbon's and Miles's surprise attacks upon villages, including noncombatants, is still a controversial issue. Both Perry and Miles violated the flag of truce.

Distances, Strategy, and Tactics

General Howard's official estimate of the distance traveled by his command follows:

From the beginning of the Indian pursuit across the Lolo trail, until the embarkation on the Missouri River for the homeward journey, including all halts and stopages, from July 27th to October 10th, my command marched one thousand three hundred and twenty-one miles in seventy-five days. Joseph, the Indian, taking with him his men, women, and children, traversed even greater distances, for he had to make many a loop in his skein, many a deviation into a tangled thicket, to avoid or deceive his enemy.

So that whichever side of the picture we examine we find there evidence of wonderful energy, and prolonged endurance.[5]

Actually, the command's starting point was Fort Lapwai, not Kamiah. Therefore, his forces had traveled about two hundred miles before Howard started his count.[6]

In their attempts to throw Howard off the trail, the Nez Perces made several detours, traveling an additional two hundred miles. The over-all distances covered by Howard's command and the Nez Perces were fifteen hundred and seventeen hundred miles, respectively.

The cardinal point of Nez Perce strategy was defensive. When Howard mounted a superior force they placed their trust in the speed of their horses. The major battles were fought from fixed positions, but even within such a framework the Nez Perces exercised great mobility. At both White Bird Canyon and the Clearwater River, they were in proper defensive postures. In both the Big Hole and the Bear Paws battles they fought under considerable disadvantages. When closely pressed, they were well served by scouts and they even constructed rifle pits. Howard's guiding principle was to arrange an advanced military blockade and then strike from the rear. Colonel Miles ultimately executed the forward facet of the plan with token assistance from Howard, coming up from the rear. A combination of physical elements favorable to his purpose, together with the power and valor of his command, enabled Miles to achieve a surrender.

Total Fighting Forces and Casualties

The various responsible estimates of the Nez Perce fighting men ranged from Howard's excessive 325 to Yellow Wolf's scant 100. Chief Joseph stated that there were 70 warriors in the White Bird battle and 250 in the Clearwater battle. A half-dozen were lost in the latter battle, thirty more at the Big Hole, and fifty escaped before the Bear Paws battle. That formula would give the Nez Perces an average of 188 fighting men in the four major battles.

L. V. McWhorter estimated that the combined military and organized volunteer forces who participated in the campaign totaled fourteen hundred.[7] The *Dictionary of American History,* quoting Cyrus Townsend Brady, lists the total number as five thousand, and states that two thousand were actually engaged in battle.[8] Some of the contradictory elements in these statements may be reconciled by the fact that the following officers had commands in motion that were not joined in battle: C. C. Gilbert, G. C. Doane, Major Hart, and Wesley Merritt. In addition, a total of several hundred Indians served the military force as scouts, raiders, and fighters, and many civilian scouts were attached to the different commands.[9] All told, the military probably averaged 282 fighting men in the four major battles of the campaign.

Estimates of Indian casualties sustained during the campaign vary considerably. Official military reports state that approximately 151 Indians were killed and 88 were wounded. A summary of the casualties disclosed in this history would support the tabulation of 122 killed and about 93 wounded.[10] The official casualty report listed 127 soldiers killed and 147 wounded, and about 50 civilian fatalities.[11]

The total casualties, Indian, civilian, and military, reported officially were 328 killed and 235 wounded. The record compiled in this history approximates 292 killed and 248 wounded.

Material Costs and Losses

Perhaps the material losses involved in the war may be more accurately assessed than any other. At the Treaty of 1863 the Indians were offered $262,500 to facilitate their establishment upon the reservation. Although that was an unacceptable sum for the five tribal provinces under consideration, it was at any rate lost to them because of their subsequent action.

Apart from this, more tangible property was involved, such as many horses and cattle lost during their removal from the ranges. Then, there was the seizure and destruction of Looking Glass's village by Colonel Whipple. On July 12, the village of the combined tribes was abandoned under pressure of Howard's pursuit. Much property loss was sustained in the Big Hole battle. Finally, the horses Miles secured at the Bear Paws surrender were never returned to the Indians. Joseph said, "We gave up all our horses—over eleven hundred—and all our saddles—over one hundred—and we have not heard from them since. Somebody has got our horses."[12] Before the war, the nontreaty Nez Perces were prosperous, even wealthy, by Indian standards; upon its conclusion, they were wholly destitute.

An appraisal of the white men's material losses would include individual damages and state and federal costs. A Lewiston, Idaho, newspaper listed destruction or damage to sixteen dwellings, fourteen barns, and many minor buildings on Camas Prairie. Settlers in Horse Prairie and on the Clark Fork lost many horses. George L. Shoup's wagon train was burned, and several buildings in the Clark Fork–Yellowstone area were damaged. Fifteen tons of supplies at Cow Island and a wagon train north of the Missouri crossing were seized or destroyed.

The governors of Idaho and Montana each called forth volunteers, and the expenses for these activities amounted to many thousands of dollars. United States Army reports indicate that the extra expense the campaign entailed, beyond normal maintenance, was $931,329.02.[13]

In response to the question of whether the territory gained was worth the price paid, various answers have been given. General Howard's attitude was clear: "One hundred and eleven comrades have been killed and buried between Oregon and Minnesota, and as many have been sorely wounded, but yet success has perched upon our banners and we can come back to you rejoicing. The results have been dearly purchased, but those results are good."[14]

General Miles was equally affirmative: "What was at one time a vast plain, wilderness and mountain waste, has been transformed into a land of immeasurable resources, a realm rivaling in extent and resources the empire of the Caesars."[15] He further explained that the nontreaty Nez Perces stood in the path of civilization and progress. In his view, their removal to the Lapwai reservation was both necessary and justifiable. Defenders of the position upheld by the nontreaty chiefs base their case upon the criterion of resource utilization. They hold that the grazing areas involved were not suitable for any other purpose. Actually, substantial improvements have not been made by white men. In brief, bands of Nez Perce stockmen were disposed of to make room for white ranchers.

Chief Joseph's Role

Frequent references have been made to the resolutions and actions taken in council by the Nez Perce chiefs. The status and roles of the principal leaders should be reviewed.

The duration, distance, and deviousness of the Nez Perce campaign attracted wide attention. The Indians' skill in eluding capture, and the valor they disclosed when battles were joined, captured the public imagination. Many experienced observers supposed that a native military genius was conducting the retreat. Actually, the clans did not invest a single chief with general permanent powers. No one was made a total war chief. Instead, decisions were made in council and executed in concert.

The military officers, however, assumed that Joseph was the dominant chieftain. General Howard confessed that they lacked factual proof. He said, "It is a difficult matter to ascertain the doings and sayings of Indians after they have gone on the 'war path.' As soon as Joseph's Indians had passed Kamiah to traverse the Lolo trail, I had but few opportunities to gain knowledge from inside their lodges."[16] No other officer learned as much as Howard concerning Nez Perce leadership. Perhaps Lieutenant Wood, Howard's aide, made the most positive statement upon this point by writing, "He (Joseph) was, in council, at first probably not so influential as White Bird and the group of chiefs that sustained him, but from first to last he (Joseph) was preeminently their 'war-chief.' Such was the testimony of his followers after his surrender, and such seems to be the evidence of the campaign itself."[17] Obviously, Wood's conclusion was primarily based upon the fact of Joseph's survival, and he was unduly influenced by the testimony of Joseph's followers. Other chiefs were unable to speak for themselves. Other officers also certified by inference that Joseph planned and controlled the flight.

On the other hand, L. V. McWhorter expresses the Indian viewpoint: "Joseph, the war chief, is a creature of legend; Joseph, the Indian Napoleon, does not emerge from the Nez Perce chronicles of their great fight for freedom. Why he has received credit for engineering the great retreat is something of a mystery, symptomatic perhaps of the white man's great ignorance of his Indian adversaries."[18]

McWhorter thus explained the legend. Even so, it is not likely to diminish, because, as time passed, many tributes were paid by men who served in the campaign, and many authors have written in glowing terms of Chief Joseph.

H. Hamlin wrote, "Considering the tools with which he (Joseph) had to work, and what he did, he is the matchless wonder of all time, notwithstanding Napoleon, or those who preceded or followed him."[19] Chester A. Fee extolled Joseph's generalship:

> As a guerilla leader Joseph stands as high as any known in history: Forrest, Morgan de la Reye, T. E. Lawrence, Von Vorbeck-Littlow, Abd-el-Krim. ... Joseph ranks with Lee, Jackson and Grant as one of the best generals this country has produced. ...
>
> Had Joseph led thousands and had he been born of a people and in a place less remote from the main currents of history, his name would resound in our ears like thunder.[20]

Nelson C. Titus spoke of the chief in this fashion: "Chief Joseph, ... as a human being, a warrior and a leader and the representative of his people, ranks high above King Philip or Pontiac; superior to Osceola, Black Hawk and Sitting Bull, and the equal of Tecumseh, and the noblest of them all in times of disaster, peril and misfortune."[21]

In this history, Joseph has been represented as the highest embodiment of Nez Perce manhood. He was tall, stalwart, massively framed. He possessed exceptionally large, brilliant, black eyes. In expression, he was calm, impassive, and sedate. Joseph was disposed to bend with the storm, instead of defying it. He was diplomatic, just, and courageous. He became chief of the Wallowas in 1871. There were about fifty-five ablebodied men in his band. Chief Joseph was not classed as a warrior before 1877. During the Nez Perce war he filled the role of guardian of the people, as well as that of fighter.[22]

Alvin M. Josephy placed Joseph's status in focus by saying:

> The fact that neither Joseph nor any other individual chief had been responsible for the outstanding strategy and masterful success of the campaign is irrele-

vant. The surrender speech, taken down by Howard's adjutant and published soon afterwards, confirmed Joseph in the public's mind as the symbol of the Nez Perces' heroic, fighting retreat.[23]

Chief White Bird

White Bird was born about 1807. His Indian name was Peopeo Kiskiok Hihih, meaning White Goose. In his younger years, White Bird became noted as a bison hunter and warrior against the Cheyennes and Sioux.

Howard described White Bird as a demure-looking Indian. Nonetheless, he was so constituted as to attract attention. He was five feet nine inches tall, with broad shoulders and sinewy limbs. His cranium was advanced, his face was longer than average, and its features were impressive.

White Bird was hostile to white invaders upon his domain, and he no doubt influenced his younger tribesmen, but he was mild in temper, manner, and speech. He was opposed to war, because he feared the consequences would be disastrous.

White Bird's influence and prestige extended beyond his tribe, and his views carried weight in council. He helped formulate the campaign plans, but he took no part in the fighting until the last battle. At the Bear Paws, he occupied a rifle pit.

Refusing to surrender, White Bird sought asylum in Canada, where he lived for about five years. His ministrations as a medicine man were believed to have caused the deaths of two young men. Therefore, their father, a member of Joseph's band, killed the old chief.

Chief Looking Glass

The name Ippakness Wayhayken, meaning Looking Glass Around Neck, was given to the father of the

Looking Glass who fought in the war of 1877. Perhaps the name was derived from a tin looking glass worn by the elder chieftain. Old Looking Glass was a noted bison hunter, and tribal warrior. He participated in the treaty council of 1855.

Young Looking Glass was born about 1832. In 1877, although his hair was streaked with gray he was exceptionally active. He was almost six feet tall, rather heavily muscled, and somewhat flat-faced. His band included about forty able-bodied men.

Although Chief Looking Glass was aggressive in nature, he was definitely opposed to the war. Indeed, he deliberately separated his tribesmen from the other clans as a precaution against involvement. However, he proposed to stay in his homeland on the Middle Fork of Clearwater. Colonel Whipple's attack upon his village on July 1 forced him into the camp of the belligerents.

Looking Glass was bright, decisive, opinionated, and persuasive. A natural leader of men, his influence and confidence gave him an outstanding role in the direction of the retreat. He had often traveled to the bison country and was familiar with the Lolo Trail and its connecting trails east of the Bitterroots. He was also acquainted with the leading chiefs among the Flathead, Bannock, and Crow tribes. Hence, he strongly counseled retreat, and he led the march more than any other chief. His errors in strategy and a tendency to move too slowly were primarily responsible for the failure to reach Canada.

He was killed in the Bear Paws battle. Otherwise, he would probably have fled from the camp with White Bird, rather than join Joseph in the surrender.

Chief Toohoolhoolzote

Toohoolhoolzote means "sound"; it was probably a Flathead name. He was a broad-shouldered, deep-chested man, five feet ten inches tall. A hunter and warrior in his youth, he was a man of great strength. Tradition affirms that he could carry a deer on each shoulder. In his later years he became a Dreamer. It was said that he was a homely man, with a heavy guttural voice that enhanced his oratorical power. Haughty in demeanor, resentful of the white man's invasion, he was determined to go where he pleased and live where he wished. General Howard called him a "cross-grained growler." He regarded him as insolent, abrupt, and provocative in manner and address. Surely, in defense of his hereditary rights, he proved to be fierce and implacable. His attitude no doubt influenced the young men who started hostilities in June, 1877. Toohoolhoolzote was greatly revered as a leader and patriot. His influence extended far beyond his small band. For an old man, he was extremely active in the campaign. His band consisted of 183 people, of whom about 30 were able-bodied men. He was killed in the Battle of the Bear Paws.

Lean Elk, or Poker Joe

A French half blood, Lean Elk owned fast race horses and was clever in other sports and games. An intelligent, restless man, he was well qualified to take a leading part in an adventure of this kind. Yellow Wolf said Lean Elk was a great leader and warrior. He was returning to Idaho from a long bison hunt when he met the fleeing Nez Perces upon the Lolo Trail. After the Big Hole battle, he took Looking Glass's place as the leader of the march, a position he held until they reached the Bear Paws. Lean Elk's insistence upon speed was responsible for the change in command there and the resulting battle. He was killed in the charge upon the camp.

Chiefs Hahtalekin and Husishusis Kute

The name Hahtalekin has no English translation. However, Hahtalekin was also known as Taktsoukt Ilppilp, which means "echo." He was only about thirty-four years old, but he had achieved considerable experience as a hunter. He was the principal chief of the Palouse band, which included about sixteen able-bodied men. As the leader of the smallest contingent, his influence in council and strategy was probably minor. Chief Hahtalekin was killed in the Battle of the Big Hole.

Husishusis Kute, also spelled Hush-Hush-cute, means "bald head." A subleader under Hahtalekin, he was about thirty-seven years old. He was a Dreamer, and being a good orator, he spoke for the Palouse band in the Lapwai council. He survived the campaign and went into exile with Joseph.

Ollokot and Yellow Wolf

The name Ollokot, meaning "frog," may have been derived from Cayuse or Umatilla. Son of Old Chief Joseph and brother of Chief Joseph, Ollokot was sometimes called "Young Joseph." In his relations with others, including the whites, Ollokot was always friendly. His countenance was more open and his features more mobile than Joseph's.

He was six feet two inches tall, very nimble and strong; a great athlete. Animated and amusing, he was very popular with the young men, and was the principal warrior in Joseph's band. Chief Joseph trusted and confided in Ollokot, and in some ways the latter was Joseph's mentor and guide.

Yellow Wolf, Heinmot Hihhih, was also known as

Hermene Moxmox; the first name means "white thunder" or "white lightning," the second, "yellow wolf." Yellow Wolf was twenty-one years old when the Nez Perce war started. He was nearly six feet tall, and he weighed 187 pounds. He was strong and quick in movement. His special ability was breaking and training horses. L. V. McWhorter characterized Yellow Wolf as a man of sensitive nature, with tragedy written in every lineament of his face. His laughter was infrequent, and never more than a soft, scarcely audible chuckle. He was a keen observer and his memory was good.[24]

He played an active part in the campaign of 1877 as a scout and warrior. He did not surrender after the Battle of the Bear Paws, but escaped to Canada. In the summer of 1878 he returned to Lapwai and gave himself up. He was sent to the Indian Territory for six years, until the survivors were returned to the Northwest. Yellow Wolf lived at Nespelem in company with his uncle, Chief Joseph.

L. V. McWhorter became acquainted with Yellow Wolf in 1908 and found him to be an excellent reporter of the history of his people. His record of the war was published in 1940, and he thus served as historian as well as warrior. He died at the Colville Indian Reservation on August 21, 1935, at the age of seventy-nine.

Great Nez Perce Warriors

Next to the chiefs and subchiefs came the renowned bison hunters and tribal warriors. There were probably a score who had achieved fame as bison hunters and leaders in tribal forays against the plains Indians. A list of these marksmen, who also understood battle tactics and strategy, would include Five Wounds, Rainbow, Pahkatos, Two Moons, Red Moccasin Tops, Wounded Head, Otstotpoo, Yellow Bull, Peopeo Tholekt, Passing Overhead, Jeekunkun, Iskatpod (Black Trail), Tewit

Toitoi, Lakochets Kunnin, and Light in the Mountain.

From these veterans the younger Nez Perces learned the arts of Indian fighting, and many of the young men became experienced and effective warriors during the course of the campaign.

General Oliver Otis Howard

Howard was born in Leeds, Maine, November 8, 1830. He graduated with an A.M. from Bowdoin College in 1850 and from the United States Military Academy in 1854. In 1865, Waterville College, Maine, and Shirtliff College, Illinois, conferred the LL.D. degree upon him.

Howard commanded a brigade in the first and second battles of Bull Run. He had command of a division in the Fredericksburg and Chancellorville battles. He was wounded twice in the Battle of Seven Pines (Fair Oaks), where he lost his right arm. Howard was in full command of the Battle of Gettysburg for a short time on July 1. Later, he commanded the Fifteenth and the Seventeenth corps in the campaign of Atlanta and in Sherman's March to the Sea.[25] He achieved the rank of major-general in December, 1864.

Howard was, therefore, an experienced commander, and the Nez Perce campaign gave him a full opportunity to apply his energy, tactics, and strategy. Critics find fault with his management, and he did make some mistakes. He was too abrupt in dealing with Chief Toohoolhoolzote in the May council; he failed to follow the hostiles after demoralizing their forces in the Clearwater battle; he has been condemned by many for abandoning Chief Joseph to his fate after the Bear Paws surrender.

Howard's officers, regulars, and scouts found him diligent, energetic, considerate, and determined. One of the scouts, Joseph Wall, said, "Howard wore a faded blue overall suit, and only his military hat with a star in front proclaimed his rank."[26] Perhaps Howard's common appearance would symbolize his actual stature in respect to the prosecution of the Nez Perce campaign. It was a hardy man's task, and he performed in a workmanlike manner. No flashes of brilliance or strokes of ingenuity were disclosed. Howard's generalship during the Bannock War of 1878 was far more decisive and impressive. Yet, as far as can be determined, Howard's conduct of the Nez Perce war was probably the best one possible.

Colonel Nelson A. Miles

Miles was born in 1840 of a well-known family in Westminster, Massachusetts. When the Civil War started, he became a volunteer, and in 1861 he had become a lieutenant. Before the war ended, Miles was commissioned a colonel and brevet major general. He served as General Howard's aide-de-camp, and the two men were therefore friends.

By 1877 Miles had acquired wide experience in conducting Indian warfare, campaigning against many tribes throughout the west, and he was well acquainted with the upper Missouri River country. Although he preferred diplomacy to war in contacts with the Indians, he believed strongly that the west was soon to become white men's territory, cultivated by farmers and crossed by railroads, and that the Indians must be moved.

In 1876 Colonel Miles was appointed post commander of the newly constructed Fort Keogh, situated at the junction of the Tongue and Yellowstone rivers. His soldiers of the Fifth Infantry were equipped and trained rigorously for campaigning in the coldest weather, and Miles, who was an ambitious man, kept himself and his men prepared for immediate action.

Miles's decision to attack at the Bear Paws, rather than merely to conduct a siege and wait for Howard's arrival, reveals his belief in all-out measures and prompt action. He felt that a quick, decisive victory would restore military prestige and bring honor to his command.

The Bear Paws victory enhanced the colonel's prestige and had a direct bearing upon his subsequent promotions.[27] He eventually became chief of staff, and he served in that capacity during the Spanish-American War. In June, 1900, he was promoted to lieutenant general in the United States Army.

Colonel John Gibbon

John Gibbon was born in Philadelphia on April 20, 1827. Graduating from the Military Academy in 1857, Gibbon served in the war with Mexico. His next assignment was to capture and remove the Seminole Indians from Florida to the Indian Territory. Subsequent frontier service in Utah and Kansas resulted in his promotion to the rank of captain.

Gibbon served as a Union division commander during the Civil War. He was wounded at Fredericksburg and Gettysburg, and the unit he commanded was called the "Iron Brigade."[28] Gibbon was promoted four times for "Gallant and Meritorious Services," and in 1865 he achieved the rank of brevet major general.

After the war, Gibbon returned to the frontier with the rank of colonel. He served in Utah, Dakota, and Montana territories. He was in charge of a column of 450 men during the Sioux campaign in 1876. His command buried the dead at the Little Big Horn. Gibbon was a vigorous, experienced, and sagacious officer.

When the Nez Perce war started, Gibbon was in command of the Seventh Infantry at Fort Shaw, Montana. From that post he moved toward the Nez

Perces with characteristic energy and confidence. He exercised great skill in overtaking the Indians and surprising them at the Big Hole, although the ethics of his surprise attack upon a village of sleeping Indians has been criticized.

After the Nez Perce campaign, Gibbon was in command of the departments of Dakota, Platt, and Columbia. He was detached from service in April, 1891. Gibbon died at Baltimore, Maryland, on February 6, 1896.

Colonel Samuel D. Sturgis

Samuel D. Sturgis was born in Shippensburg, Pennsylvania, on June 11, 1822. Upon graduating from the Military Academy in 1846, he entered the war with Mexico. He was captured at Buena Vista and was held there as a prisoner of war for a short time.

During the decade of the fifties, Sturgis served in Missouri, Kansas, California, New Mexico, and Texas. In these tours he campaigned against Apache, Cheyenne, Comanche, and Kiowa Indians.

Sturgis entered the Civil War on the side of the Union with the rank of captain. As a result of his extraordinary services at Manassas, Fredericksburg, South Mountain, Antietam, and elsewhere, Sturgis was promoted to the rank of lieutenant colonel, Sixth Cavalry, on October 27, 1863. In addition, upon three other occasions Colonel Sturgis commanded full divisions.

After the war, Sturgis resumed service upon the Texas frontier. Later, as colonel, Seventh Cavalry, he was in command of a regiment at Fort Lincoln in the Dakota Department. From that post he participated in the Yellowstone expedition designed to capture the fleeing Nez Perces.

Colonel Sturgis displayed energy and determination

during this phase of the Nez Perce Campaign. Perhaps he erred in being overly eager to intercept the Indians. Instead of waiting at the mouth of the Clark Fork, he was drawn into the baffling Absaroka foothills, where the chiefs eluded him. Once they were beyond him, no amount of energy and speed on his part could overtake the Nez Perces.

Colonel Sturgis later served as governor of the soldiers' home near Washington, D.C., and finally, as commandant at Fort Meade, Dakota. He retired from active service in 1886, at the age of sixty-four. He died three years later at St. Paul, Minnesota.[29]

Captain Charles C. Rawn

Charles C. Rawn was born in Pennsylvania about 1843. He enlisted in the Civil War as a private in May, 1861. During his first year he became a second lieutenant. In 1863, he was advanced to the rank of captain.[30]

Rawn entered frontier military service, and he was supervising the construction of Fort Missoula when the Nez Perce War started. He exercised restraint and prudence in refusing to attack the Nez Perces in the Lolo Canyon.

Other high-ranking officers connected with the Nez Perce Campaign, who had achieved distinction in the Mexican and Civil Wars, included General Irwin McDowell and Colonel Charles C. Gilbert.

Disposal of the Campaign Forces

Chief Joseph and his 418 people joined the long procession that Miles started at the Bear Paws on October 7. They understood that their destination would be

Fort Keogh, and that they would spend the winter there. Howard's order to Miles on this point read:

> On account of the cost of transportation of the Nez Perces to the Pacific Coast, I deem it best to retain them all at some place within your district, where they can be kept under military control until spring. Then, unless you receive military instructions from higher authority, you are hereby directed to have them sent under proper guard to my department, where I will take charge of them and carry out the instructions I have already received.[31]

The Cheyenne Indian scouts, each given five Nez Perce ponies, were allowed to go in advance of the command. Miles moved slowly because he was encumbered by the captives and wounded. It was a heterogeneous caravan, consisting of three battalions of troops, 418 prisoners, their ponies and travois, a wagon train, and ambulances.

On October 13, Miles reached the confluence of the Missouri and Musselshell rivers. There he met Howard and his command, which the general had assembled near Carroll. He had secured enough steamboat space to take his infantrymen on board. These troops were transported to Saint Louis on the *Benton*. From that station they returned to Fort Vancouver by rail. The cavalry units returned to their respective posts overland. Howard and Miles held their final interview at this time. It was agreed that the general would make a personal report of their plans for the Nez Perces to General Philip Sheridan in Chicago. An account of Howard's altercation with Sheridan over the Bear Paws battle newspaper reports has been given.

Colonel Samuel D. Sturgis and his command remained in the field to watch the Sioux and capture as many runaway Nez Perces as possible. The feelings of these men, and others in the Department of Dakota, were described by Major James S. Brisbin in his report to the Assistant Adjutant General from Fort Ellis, Montana, on October 29, 1877: "Many of the old soldiers say the year 1877 was the hardest they ever experienced, and if I may be allowed to judge, I will say, I never saw, even during the Civil War, harder or more dangerous service."

The thirty fast-riding Sioux and Cheyenne scouts arrived at Fort Keogh on October 13. For half a day their garbled accounts of the battle caused considerable anxiety at the fort. Then a white scout, named John Brughier, arrived with more details of the battle and information about the casualties.

On October 15, Miles reached the Yellowstone River directly opposite the cantonment.

EXILE DECREED, APPLIED, AND ABANDONED

24. TRAILS OF TRIUMPH AND TEARS

A phase of the reception given the commandant of Fort Keogh and his men was recorded by Colonel Miles:

> The families of the officers and soldiers and all the other people at the garrison, including the band of the Fifth Infantry, citizens and Indians, lined the bank of the Yellowstone; and as some of the principal Indians stepped into the boat, and it moved from the northern shore, the band struck up "Hail to the Chief," and then as we neared the other shore, it suddenly changed to "O, no! no! not for Joseph," which it played for a short time, and then went back to the former strain.[1]

Colonel Miles was considered a hero, and the little town developing in juxtaposition to the fort was subsequently named in his honor. Several weeks later, when he visited Fort Buford, Fort Lincoln, and the town of Bismarck, Dakota Territory, he was again honored and feted, by the people residing in those places.[2]

General Howard's frustration over the subordinate position accorded him in the newspapers and his attempt to place the record in balance in Chicago have been described. Perhaps Howard's emotional state upon that occasion prevented him from reaching a firm understanding with General Sheridan in regard to the fate of the Nez Perce captives. In any case, Howard's superiors had already overruled the surrender terms he and Miles had made with Chief Joseph.

From Chicago Howard took the train to San Francisco, where he made a full report of the campaign to General Irwin McDowell. He then returned to Portland by boat, arriving on November 11.

As Howard and his wife came ashore they were greeted by a committee carrying banners. Posters and mastheads announced a celebration in honor of his success. A Portland *Daily Bee* supplement, November 11, 1877, contained an account of the tributes and responses given at the meeting. At the conclusion, J. W. Walley delivered the following eulogy:

> We are here also, I apprehend, to show that republics, so far as Oregon is concerned, are not ungrateful, and that ridicule and misrepresentation, come from what source they may, when applied to those whose courage and patriotism have been proved on many a well-fought field in preserving the liberty we enjoy, merit and receive our unqualified disapprobation. We are also here to show that Oregonians, in estimating the meed of praise due to final success, consider the means by which success was rendered possible; and in awarding their tribute, forget not those who have borne the heat and labor of the day, whilst justly treating all who did their duty from the eleventh hour.

Thus, General Oliver Otis Howard was finally accorded a fair measure of recognition and praise for his considerable exertions in dealing with the Nez Perces during the preceding five months.

Countermanding the Surrender Terms

Meanwhile, Miles quartered his captive Nez Perces at Fort Keogh and began making preparations for their sustenance until spring, at which time he planned to return them to the Northwest in accordance with the surrender terms. Having received no reply to his requests for information or orders, Miles was governed by the original design of placing the Nez Perces on the Lapwai reservation. However, higher authorities had been assessing the facts of the Nez Perce case, and they decided to countermand the terms and pursue a different course from that which had been originally contemplated. It has been noted that on July 20, 1877, Erwin C. Watkins, Indian Bureau Inspector, proposed sending the nontreaty Nez Perces to the Indian Territory.[3] The idea obviously had merit, because Idaho citizens who had sustained losses in lives and property were bound to harbor bitterness toward the hostiles. Treaty Nez Perces and Lapwai reservation officials entertained reasonable doubts concerning the integration of the former nontreaty Dreamer stockmen and hunters with the steady reservation farmers.

Of course, if that prospect posed a problem, then there was still less logic in attempting to merge the captives with a miscellany of other tribes in the Indian Territory. But Indian Bureau officials were governed by vacillating policies. Even a consistent policy and uniform procedure failed to achieve salutary results, because Indian tribes were so diverse in character. During the decade of the seventies the officials were committed to a centralized reservation system, and it seemed expedient to establish these Nez Perces upon it. General Sherman and General Sheridan were in accord with this policy.[4] On August 31, Sherman instructed Sheridan to withhold terms from the hostiles if, and when, they were captured. They were to be treated with extreme severity, as the Modocs had been. In a telegram dated October 10, Sherman flatly stated that the Nez Perces "must never be allowed to return to Oregon, but should be engrafted on the Modoc in Indian country." That these developments were repugnant to Miles is disclosed in a telegram to E. A. Hayt, Commissioner of Indian Affairs, registering a strong objection: ". . . the Nez Perce trouble was caused by the rascality of their Agent, and the encroachments of the whites; and [I] have regarded their treatment unusually severe. Joseph can tell you his own story. . . ." Miles then reminded Hayt that the Department of Interior had ordered Howard to place the Indians upon the Idaho reservation. Therefore, "acting upon the only information I had at the time of the surrender, I informed the Nez Perces the object of the war, and, as I supposed, the design of the Government. I should have started them immediately, except for the lateness of the season."[5]

Instead of coming to Miles's support, the Department of Interior officials started an investigation of his charge of Monteith's rascality. Meantime, Sherman convinced Secretary of War McCrary to confirm Sheridan's recommendation to hold the Nez Perces as prisoners of war at Fort Leavenworth until the Indian Bureau could provide them a permanent home near the Modocs, "or elsewhere not in Oregon."[6]

By November most of the officials were in favor of settling the Nez Perces upon the Quapaw reservation near the Modocs. General Sherman thought that was an excellent place for them, "where by moderate labor they can soon be able to support themselves in peace. They should never again be allowed to return to Oregon or Lapwai."[7] Sherman realized that this decision conflicted with his order to Howard before he had left the Department of the Columbia, wherein he had said: "Pursue the Indians until captured or driven out of the country. If captured care for them in your own department. . . ."[8] He was also aware that Howard and Miles had promised to send their captives to the Lapwai reservation in the spring of 1878. Nevertheless, he invoked the exile sentence upon them, because "there should be extreme severity, else other tribes alike situated may imitate their example."[9] In supporting this policy of reprisal, General Sherman, General Sheridan, and General Terry affirmed that both Howard and Miles had lacked even a "shadow of authority" to receive anything except an unconditional surrender from Joseph.[10]

As a general, Sherman admired the fighting and tactical qualities the Nez Perces had exhibited in the campaign. Indeed, he paid tribute to their prowess:

Thus had terminated one of the most extraordinary Indian wars of which there is any record. The Indians throughout displayed a courage and skill that elicited universal praise; they abstained from scalping; let captive women go free; did not commit indiscriminate murders of peaceful families and fought with almost scientific skill, using advance and rear guards, skirmish lines and field fortifications.[11]

Even so, Sherman's admiration for an honorable foe did not blind him to the dangers of returning them to the Northwest. Restlessness still existed among many tribes, and Sherman did not propose to make any Nez Perce leadership available to potential enemies.

The Secretary of the Interior, Carl Schurz, concurred in these views, and by November 1 Miles received notice from General Sheridan that he should transport his prisoners down the Yellowstone River to Fort Buford, thence on the Missouri to Fort Lincoln. It was four hundred miles from Fort Keogh to Fort Buford and another four hundred miles to Fort Lincoln.

The full import of this order was not disclosed to Chief Joseph until he reached Fort Lincoln on November 16. In fact, General Sheridan's first order simply implied that the cost of supplying the prisoners would be much less at Fort Lincoln. Even if Miles suspected that a long-range plan was on foot, he had no alternative. Winter was pressing in upon the Yellowstone, as evidenced by the appearance of slush ice in the water. The transportation of 431 people (some had been rounded up since the surrender), including the wounded and ill, eight hundred miles through a wilderness region would be a difficult task.

Accordingly, Colonel Miles organized a wagon train and arranged to march the warriors and most of the able-bodied women prisoners overland under military escort. The rest, consisting of the wounded, ill, old people, and children, could be transported more expeditiously by water. Steamboats were not available for service at that season of the year. An alternative was presented by the arrival of a fleet of flatboats from Livingston, with winter food supplies for Fort Keogh. Miles requisitioned fourteen flatboats and their operators to transport his prisoners to Fort Buford, which was situated at the junction of the Yellowstone and the Missouri rivers.

Down the Yellowstone and the Missouri Rivers

An account of this flatboating operation was written by one of the steersmen named Fred G. Bond.[12] The following paragraphs represent a compression of his twenty-two-page monograph concerning the voyage.

The flatboats were about thirty-two feet long and eight feet wide, tapering slightly at each end, with four long sweeps. Twenty-two Nez Perces were turned over to Mr. Bond, together with the following rations: dried salt pork, Rio green coffee, brown sugar, hard tack, rice, navy beans, flour, and baking powder. Stones were arranged on the boat for the accommodation of an Indian fire.

In hopes of a fast voyage, Colonel Miles offered a prize to the first flatboatman who arrived at Fort Buford. Mr. Bond accepted the challenge, and in order to strengthen his prospects he held a council and organized his prisoners in this fashion:

> I stood up and told them I was there Chief on this journey of wha-wha meaning Far-Far, that we was going through a hostile country of the dog cutthrout of Sioux and the flaping Crows giving them the signs that hereafter they was my people to watch for safety and I expected them to do my commands quickly and with respect. I then turned towards the aged Chief who had repeated all I said in this counsel I said I name this Chief George Washington because of his noble appearance. You will do his bidding from me at all times and places on this journey. I then turned to a very aged Indian woman who hair was snow white, she was tall slender and very dark with folded wrinkles on her face that would put to shame an age allegator of the Florida glades. This lady I said we will call her Shades of Night, she will be our boat figure head and pilot and in command of all women with us, also the two children. Then I turned to a middle age woman and said you will make and care for the coffee at all times also its roasting and help geather dry willow wood for the boat fire. The other Indian women I told them to cook, wash and tend to sick and wounded. The young Indian men I did not give them a task for I needed them when the time come for them to act.

The young men were often needed as oarsmen, and sometimes as pullers and pushers when sandbars were encountered. Otherwise, they were permitted to make and use bows and arrows. Their skill as archers, together with George Washington's prowess in using

Bond's rifle, adequately supplemented their rations with fresh game of many kinds.

Bond tied up his boat on an island, whenever possible, for an hour at noon. This respite gave his people an opportunity to exercise and relax. They averaged four miles an hour, or forty miles a day. Precautions were taken each night against mishaps or theft of rations by animals or roving Sioux bands.

An evidence of Bond's spiritual stewardship is found in this statement:

> After tieing up for the nights and our feast was over I would explain to my people about our head chief (Great Father) at Washington, D.C. How they held consol's there to run so large white nation. The city were the white people lived so thick they would fight for space to live and air to breath, the great Iron horse that had the speed of a hundred ponies that lived on wood and water and how many sun it would take his Iron horse to reach Washington, D.C. Washington would help me translate and by signs my people understood. We seat there and talk till the moon would throw its silver rays on the frozen river mist on the drift wood. All then would be hushed when Washington gave a prayer.[18]

Obviously, Bond established an exceptional rapport with these Nez Perce people.

The weather was generally pleasant, with bright days and frosty nights, and fish and game were abundant. In a stretch of the Badlands, the Yellowstone River was lined by bullberry bushes. The Indians relished the berries, but in so doing, they made "it sad for our sugar ration."

When Bond reached the Missouri River the slush ice made his crossing difficult, but he reached Fort Buford in good order. There the military personnel took over his twenty-two Nez Perces, placed them under guard, and treated them as prisoners. The other flatboats arrived during the next few days, and the wagon train with prisoners and escort, under command of Colonel Miles, also came in.

On November 9, Special Order No. 225 directed the release of five companies from Fort Buford to escort the Nez Perce prisoners to Bismarck.[14] However, Colonels Miles and Moore decided to extend the waterborne operation to Fort Lincoln. After all, only one flatboat out of fourteen had been wrecked, with few lives lost. The operators were offered high wages to undertake the navigation of the rapidly flowing Missouri. Again, speed was important, because the slush was congealing into ice blocks.

Fred Bond's description of the voyage from Fort Buford to Fort Lincoln discloses certain changed conditions:

Day after day we sailed, drifted, and pushed ice packs from our bow and at times the ashpoles acting like runners to slip over some half hidden cake of ice that now was wirling in a jam crouding and crushing on their voige to perish in the warm waters of the South. Once in a while a deer or antelope would fall befor the never failing shot of Washington and the twang of the youth Indian bow with steel pointed arrows would furnish a beaver tail for replenish our feast, for beaver tail is good food if it cooked proper. And yet among my people I noticed a blank "now and anon" a blank turned up face to mine. Try as I could I could not find a spark of who had sown a word of evel among my people. What was it? they appeared all alike.[15]

Bond accurately suspected that contact with the military force and certain "hangers on" at Fort Buford had greatly depressed his Nez Perces. They were losing confidence in Miles and becoming fearful for their lives.

These fears were partially confirmed from a different

source as they approached the Mandan Indian villages. These people regarded the Nez Perces as interlopers and treated them accordingly. They threw rocks at the captives and attempted to upset their flatboats. However, the unarmed Nez Perces responded to these hostile gestures with vigor. Their real fears were centered upon powers and principalities that surpassed their understanding.

Upon reaching Fort Lincoln, they were greatly frightened by Northern Pacific Railroad engine whistles and the firing of salutes by the fort artillery. These blasts and volleys were regarded as the signals of their fate. Bond said, "They became so helpless I had to work the boat across the river all alone to the Fort Landing. They sat up a moaning chant no dout their death chant."[16]

The flatboats and the wagon train, with the prisoners and their escort, reached Fort Lincoln on November 16. Colonel Miles received orders to requisition a passenger train to transport the Nez Perces from Fort Lincoln to Fort Leavenworth. That the War Department might have chosen a better location was disclosed in a telegram from Sheridan to Sherman: "Your dispatch about the Nez Perces received. I have directed the Nez Perce prisoners to be held at Fort Leavenworth instead of Fort Riley until further orders. The reason alleged by Gen. Pope for desiring to send them to Fort Riley was the abundance of comfortable quarters for them there."[17]

At this juncture, Miles earnestly asked Sheridan for authority to take a delegation of Nez Perce leaders to Washington, D.C. This official request received negative endorsements from McCrary, Schurz, Sherman, Sheridan, and Hayt.[18]

Meanwhile, the citizens of Bismarck organized a celebration to honor Colonel Miles, his escort, and Chief Joseph on the evening of November 19. Bond's description of the preparation for the affair follows: "The little city was by now on the buzz getting ready to give a grand ball and supper in honor of Chief Joseph. The ladies of the Fort joined in. There were no printed tickets. The tickets were $10.00 gold coin, ladies free, and oppen to all."[19]

When Colonel Miles, his escort, and the prisoners entered Bismarck they were greeted by the Fort Lincoln band and practically all of the citizens in the area. Food was provided in the town square for the military guards and prisoners. As Bond observed the dress and over-all status of the Nez Perces, he remarked: "The appearance of all was heart rending sad."[20] By that time the prisoners had learned that they were to be exiled in the Indian Territory and had lost all hope of seeing their homes again. Chief Joseph's only comment was, "When will the white man learn to tell the truth."[21] Besides the general reception accorded the Miles cavalcade, a special banquet was held in honor of Chief Joseph and two of his aides. The invitation appeared in the *Bismarck Tri-Weekly Tribune* on November 21, 1877:

To Joseph, Head Chief of the Nez Perces.
Sir:
   Desiring to show you our kind feelings and the admiration we have for your bravery and humanity, as exhibited in your recent conflict with the forces of the United States, we most cordially invite you to dine with us at the Sheridan House in this city. The dinner to be given at 1½ p.m. today.

While Joseph and his friends were being honored by a select committee in the Sheridan Parlors, Fred Bond treated George Washington to a farewell dinner. Mr. Bond recorded that although salmon was available his friend Washington "was too sad to eat and the Irish waitress said, 'The Devils to put those people under soldiers guard.' "[22] An Irish waitress in a rough, raw

Missouri River town thus expressed the latent American sympathy for these misplaced people.

The high military and civil authorities were making a mistake which was apparent to common citizens dwelling far beyond the area of hostilities. Even so, the officials were probably exercising some restraint. They might have heeded the radical demands from some Idaho citizens. One author expressed such sentiment as follows: "These prisoners should have been tried for their offenses by the courts, should have been brought back where they could have been identified and, where found guilty, should have been hanged till they were dead, as other murderers!"[23]

Several officials had called attention to certain hazards inherent in the removal of the Nez Perces. In fact, on November 1, 1877, E. A. Hayt, the Commissioner of Indian Affairs, wrote as follows to Secretary of the Interior Schurz: "Experience has demonstrated the impolicy of sending northern Indians to the Indian Territory. To go no further back than the date of the Ponca removal, it will be seen that the effect of a radical change of climate is disastrous. . . ."[24] He then cited casualty rates incident to the removal of both Poncas and Cheyennes. Since the Nez Perce removal involved still greater climatic variations, proportionately higher death rates could be anticipated. Nevertheless, as Miles continued his own journey to St. Paul on November 19, arrangements were being made for the Nez Perces to leave for Fort Leavenworth four days later. Concerning this and subsequent moves, Chief Joseph said: "We were not asked if we were willing to go. We were ordered to get into railroad cars."[25]

The Reactions of Miles and Howard

Colonel Miles declared that he exerted all possible influence to prevent the removal of the Nez Perces to the Indian Territory. Surely, his report to Secretary of War McCrary discloses a genuine solicitude for their welfare:

> As these people have been hitherto loyal to the government and friends of the white race from the time their country was first explored, and in their skilful campaigns have spared hundreds of lives and thousands of dollars' worth of property that they might have destroyed, and as they have, in my opinion, been grossly wronged in years past, have lost most of their warriors, their homes, property, and everything except a small amount of clothing. I have the honor to recommend that ample provision be made for their civilization, and to enable them to become self-sustaining. They are sufficiently intelligent to appreciate the consideration which, in my opinion, is justly due them from the government.[26]

In explaining the removal order to Chief Joseph, Colonel Miles said: "You must not blame me. I have endeavored to keep my word, but the chief who is over me has given the order, and I must obey it or resign. That would do you no good. Some other officer would carry out the order."[27] Joseph believed Miles and did not blame him. He said, "I do not know who to blame . . . but there are some things I want to know, which no one seems able to explain. I cannot understand how the government sends a man out to fight us, as it did General Miles, and then breaks his word. Such a government has something wrong about it."[28] Later, as Joseph became better acquainted with the federal system and its political and military hierarchy, he said, "White men have too many chiefs."

Lieutenant C. E. S. Wood was unimpressed by Miles's exertions. He obviously felt that the colonel could have prevented the removal if he had tried harder. However, the lieutenant was critical of Colonel Miles for reasons disclosed in connection with the surrender.

Lieutenant Wood was even less charitable toward Howard for his course in regard to the removal issue. He said:

> I differed with General Howard, who took the ground that no promise had been made Joseph, that the surrender was unconditional, and that he had no right to make terms. I thought this too technical and a moral wrong, and thought that the general's understanding was so clear as to be a part of the surrender, and that we were morally bound; also that, technically, Sherman's wire warranted a promise to return the prisoners to the Department of the Columbia, and the order Howard gave to Miles, after the surrender, to return the prisoners to his department, showed his own interpretation and intention.[29]

Lieutenant Wood properly criticized General Howard for insisting that Chief White Bird's flight made the surrender terms with Joseph null and void. As previously noted, Joseph had no power to control the older chief or his followers. Wood affirmed that there was only one opinion at that time, namely, that the Nez Perces would be taken back to the Lapwai reservation in the spring of 1878. Nevertheless, Howard shrugged off the injustice of the Nez Perce exile by saying, "Let them settle down and keep quiet in Indian Territory, as the Modocs have done and they will thrive as they do."[30] The general thereby conceded that his honor was not at stake. Colonel Miles, however, continued to be uneasy.

Winter at Fort Leavenworth

On November 23, when the Nez Perce train was leaving Bismarck, General Sherman sent a report to the Secretary of War: "The prisoners are now enroute by the most economical way to Fort Leavenworth, to be held there as prisoners of war until spring when I trust the Indian Bureau will provide them homes on the Indian Reservation. . . ."[31]

Upon reaching their temporary destination on November 27, the Nez Perces were placed upon a campground between a swampy slough and the Missouri River, two miles above the fort. One observer said the spot must have been selected for the express purpose of decimating the Indians. The fort physician reported that half of the Indians were soon afflicted by malaria. Of the 431 prisoners recorded on December 4, 1877, 410 were alive the following July, when the Bureau of Indian Affairs finally assumed jurisdiction.

On December 10, Chief Joseph and seven members of his band addressed a petition to the government and submitted it to Captain George M. Randall. The petition pleaded their case to be returned to Idaho. However, as an alternative, they requested the right to select a tract of land in the Indian Territory. The area was to include room enough for the Canadian and other scattered members of the tribe. These requests were considered reasonable by Captain Randall; therefore, he endorsed them and forwarded the petition to General Sherman. On January 12, 1878, Sherman wrote "Disapproved" on the document and reminded Randall that much concern over the wishes of his prisoners was improper. The Nez Perces should be handled and located at the convenience of the government, without reference to their desires. The Nez Perce position received the sympathetic attention of President R. B. Hayes and Secretary Carl Schurz, however, and this fact impelled General Sherman to send the following telegram to Sheridan, McDowell, Howard, and Miles: "Influence is brought on President to restore the Nez Perce prisoners now at Fort Leavenworth back to Lapwai. I want your [McDowell] and General Howard's opinion thereof." Sherman's request elicited negative opinions from all except Miles.[32]

Living conditions in the camp were tolerable during the cold winter months, but when spring came the lack of proper sanitation, together with the ravages of malaria, weakened the Nez Perces. Accustomed to living in a healthful climate with horses and cattle to keep them busy and happy, the inactive prisoners became dispirited. Joseph graphically described their dismal situation: "Many of our people sickened and died, and we buried them in this strange land. . . . The Great Spirit Chief who rules above seemed to be looking some other way, and did not see what was being done to my people."[33]

The matter of providing a permanent home for the exiles was explored by Congress in the spring of 1878. The idea of fulfilling the Bear Paws surrender terms did not receive any consideration. Congressmen from the Northwest were opposed to such a course. On the other hand, those who represented states and territories in proximity to the Indian Territory were reluctant to provide homes for additional Indians there. Thus, while the fate of these misplaced people was debated, they sickened and died upon Fort Leavenworth swampland. The political interplay between the western and middlewestern Congressmen eventuated in proposals to (1) return the Nez Perces to Idaho, and (2) secure their consent before sending them to the Oklahoma Indian Territory. Both measures were defeated in favor of locating them on the Quapaw reserve in Kansas Territory.[34] The bill, approved on May 27, 1878, provided that the sum of twenty thousand dollars might be expended under the direction of the Secretary of the Interior for moving the Nez Perces from Fort Leavenworth to a suitable location in the Indian Territory and for their settlement thereon. Therefore, on July 9, 1878, Indian Commissioner E. A. Hayt requested the War Department to deliver the prisoners to his jurisdiction.

Accordingly, Indian Inspector John McNeill and Agent Hiram W. Jones of the Quapaw reserve arrived at Fort Leavenworth to escort the Nez Perces to their new home. They were taken to Baxter Springs on the train, thence by wagons to a seven-thousand-acre tract of Miami and Peoria lands. Several Indians died en route, and by October forty-seven more had died.[35]

This heavy death rate was the aftermath of exposure to a cold winter and a hot summer in different climates, without sanitation or proper living facilities. No preparations had been made to receive them at either Fort Leavenworth or the Quapaw reserve. Upon arriving on the Quapaw in late July, they were wholly without shelter. No quinine was available to provide relief from malaria. The Nez Perces called the Quapaw reserve Eeikish Pah, meaning "hot place."

In spite of their exertions to wrest a livelihood from the soil, little progress was achieved in a year. Joseph expressed the general feeling of his people in saying, "I think very little of this country. It is like a poor man; it amounts to nothing."[36] That attitude was bound to complicate their ordeal of acclimatization.

25. SURVIVAL IN EXILE

In his surrender speech at the Bear Paws, Chief Joseph had expressed the hope of finding those of his people who had escaped or been left along the trail. In exile, he could not search for the lost ones, but eventually some of them were brought to him. The motivation of the government in rounding up the runaway Nez Perces, however, was more punitive than humanitarian.

Escaped Nez Perces Return

Eloosykaset, meaning "standing on a point," also known as John Pinkham, related his experience in the campaign and as an exile. He and five other Nez Perce boys, ranging in age from twelve to seventeen, fled during the Battle of the Big Hole. Hiding and frightened, they did not succeed in rejoining the fleeing Indians. Instead, they made their way back to the Clearwater River. During several weeks, with only one gun among the six, they were kept busy: "Dodging, keeping away from where might be whites, our traveling was slow. Most of the time we had nothing to eat. We suffered terribly from hunger. For days we did not know where we were. We were always afraid of our lives. After long wandering, we crossed the Rockies and other wild ranges, and reached the Nez Perce Reservation."[1] The officials at the reservation sent them to Fort Leavenworth along with thirteen nontreaty adults who had returned from a bison-hunting expedition. This policy of seizing nontreaty Nez Perces, wherever found, and sending them to the Indian Territory was applied consistently.

Reference has been made to the woman left behind, because of childbirth, in the Musselshell country. Friendly Crow Indians adopted her and her baby, but, when discovered by agency officials, they were sent to the Indian Territory. All fort commandants and agency officials received orders to send all nontreaty Nez Perces to the Indian Territory. Indian tribal chiefs were sternly warned not to harbor any stray Nez Perces, and the plains tribes were more than cooperative in bringing the hostiles to the forts. One citizen who lived near the Bear Paws described the brutal treatment of the Nez Perces who fled from the last battle and were caught. She observed that they did not receive "the protection of a stray dog. . . . I will always remember this cruel thing with horror."[2]

On October 28, 1877, Colonel Miles dictated a memorandum from his camp on the Tongue River, to the Assistant Adjutant General of the Department of Dakota at St. Paul, that describes the procedure employed in handling these matters: "I have the honor to report that I have sent two Nez Perces Indians, Um-Tock-Multin (Five Hat) and Sup-Pu-Innos (Bugle), under charge of Capt. A. S. Bennett, 5th Infantry, to Ft. Lincoln, there to be held subjects to orders from Dept. Headqrs."[3]

Eighty prisoners were added to the 418 who originally surrendered on Snake Creek. Even some of those who escaped into Canada were finally sent to Kansas. Yellow Wolf was among these.

When Yellow Wolf's party of escapees approached the Sioux village in Canada, they were met by members of that tribe, who "mixed us up. They took us one by one. . . . They gave me everything I asked, just as if I was one of their children. In the spring, one Sioux made himself a brother to me."[4] Yellow Wolf stated that the Nez Perces got along well with the Sioux and that they remained all winter in the same camp, about five hundred miles north of the Canadian border. In the spring of 1878, the Nez Perces heard that they might return to their ancestral hunting grounds.

The rumor was false, as those attempting to return soon discovered. However, in May, 1878, military arrangements were made for three members of Joseph's band, an interpreter, and Lieutenant C. W. Baird to extend an invitation to the Nez Perces in Canada to join Chief Joseph. At Fort Walsh the necessary legal permission was obtained from Colonel J. T. McLeod of the Northwest Mounted Police. On June 30, contact was made by the delegation with White Bird and others. Although the exiles disclaimed all interest in war and expressed a strong desire to return to Idaho, they refused to go to the Indian Territory.[5]

Small parties were organized from time to time, which started for Idaho. There were thirteen men, nine women, and several children in Yellow Wolf's band. All were mounted and about half of the men had guns. They resolved that trouble would not be sought, but they realized that it would be difficult to avoid. Having no funds, they were obliged to forage along the trail. In the circumstances, theft of livestock might become imperative for survival. However, they felt justified in appropriating food because of the losses they had sustained the previous year. Actually, these hunters were generally able to secure enough wild game to meet their requirements.

Whenever possible, they would bypass the white man's habitations. Twice, reservation Indians attempted to lure them into captivity. Once, the Nez Perces helped themselves to a rancher's cattle, then decided to find him, offer a settlement, and get some flour. Three white men then threatened them with rifles and shouted, "Get out of there!" In the ensuing altercation Yellow Wolf killed one of the three men.

Farther on, Yellow Wolf committed still another brutal act in a crude effort to secure food and friendship. Inadequacy in the use of English made Nez Perce communication of their peaceful intentions almost impossible. In one instance, a white man exercised a salutary approach by saying, "Come on, friends! Come on! Get off! Tie up your horses! . . . We will give you one sack of flour."[6]

On Rock Creek, about twenty miles from Philipsburg, Montana, they had another rough episode with several miners. Mutual suspicions and inability to communicate resulted in the deaths of John Hays, Amos Elliott, and Billy Jory. One J. H. Jones was in the kitchen preparing food for the unwelcome visitors, but when he heard they had shot his friends he dropped his pans and fled. The Nez Perces chased him, but he managed to elude them. The account of this hazardous flight made such an impression upon his Philipsburg auditors that they promptly dubbed him "Nez Perce" Jones.[7] In going up Lolo Creek, Yellow Wolf clubbed one citizen and disarmed three others, because he interpreted their menacing gestures with rifles to mean, "Come on! We want trouble!"[8]

Reports of these depredations reached the officials at Fort Missoula, and a detail of thirteen soldiers, under Lieutenant Thomas S. Wallace, trailed the Nez Perces across the Lolo Trail. They eventually caught up with them on July 25, and shots and horses were exchanged in a series of raids and counterthrusts. As Yellow Wolf stated, "We had a little war."[9]

An account of these affairs also reached the officers at Fort Lapwai, and a joint delegation of soldiers and agency officials met the returning exiles when they reached the Clearwater River in late July. The older men, women, and children gave themselves up promptly. Yellow Wolf expressed his personal feelings in saying, "For me, I will stay in the prairie like a coyote. I have no home!"[10]

A few warriors attempted to avoid the inevitable by roaming about in their most sequestered haunts. Homeless, disheartened, hungry, and classed as renegades, they were ultimately forced to give themselves up. Otherwise they would have been hunted down and shot. A report dated August 2, 1878, from Major D. P. Hancock at Camp Howard, describes the excitement, however groundless, that existed among the Idaho settlers over the return of these few Nez Perces.[11]

The women and children from Canada were distributed among the people at Lapwai, but Yellow Wolf and his associates were placed in custody at Fort Lapwai. This precaution was necessary in the interest of safety, but it was also taken in preparation for their removal to the Indian Territory.

Yellow Wolf learned that eleven men and one woman of White Bird's band had reached their old home on the Salmon River in mid-July. Their leader, Tahmiteahkun, described their journey from the Sioux camp to the Salmon River, and the experiences of this group and those of other exiles who returned to Idaho generally conformed to the pattern described.

Yellow Wolf's account of his life in exile in the Indian Territory was characterized by brevity and simplicity. He said:

> I was sent to the Territory with nine other of Chief Joseph's band. There we united with our old friends and relations—those left of them. . . .
> We were not badly treated in captivity. We were

free so long as we did not come towards Idaho and Wallowa. We had schools. Only the climate killed many of us. All the newborn babies died, and many of the old people too. . . . All the time, night and day, we suffered from the climate. For the first year they kept us all where many got shaking sickness, chills, hot fever. We were always lonely for our old-time homes. ... No mountains, no springs, no clear running rivers. Thoughts came of the Wallowa where I grew up. Of my own country when only Indians were there. Of tepees along the bending river. Of the blue clear lake, wide meadows with horse and cattle herds. From the mountain forests, voices seemed calling. I felt as dreaming. Not my living self.[12]

This description of Nez Perce life in exile was confirmed by the lengthy reports of four different agents who supervised their seven years of captivity.

Chief Joseph's Leadership in Exile

As guardian of the Nez Perces, Chief Joseph had struggled to retain the Wallowa homeland by negotiation. When that means failed, he had reluctantly waged war in defense of their rights and liberties, and had surrendered under terms that were acceptable. When these terms were undone, he turned his intelligence, energy, and resources to the task of survival and ultimate liberation from what he considered to be bondage in exile. In achieving these ends this dedicated chieftain exhibited great talent in the field of politics and diplomacy.

His dissatisfaction with the Nez Perce allotment on the Quapaw reservation in Kansas has been disclosed. These complaints proved sufficient to impel Indian Commissioner E. A. Hayt and Ezra M. Kingsley to make an investigation. Upon observing the distress and forlorn character of the people, Hayt concluded that he and his colleagues had erred in assuming that these mountain Indians would be easily acclimated in Kansas Territory. The same conclusion was reached by Senator Thomas C. McCreery, a member of a congressional investigating committee, who visited the Nez Perces in October, 1878.

In mid-October, therefore, Hayt, Kingsley, Joseph, and Husishusis Kute made a 250-mile trip in search of an area more suitable and acceptable to these badly misplaced people. The two chiefs chose an area situated at the junction of the Salt Fork of the Arkansas and the Chikaskia rivers, in the vicinity of present-day Tonkawa. This region, consisting of 90,710 acres of fertile bottom land, well timbered near the boundaries, was within the boundaries of the Ponca agency.

Joseph's legal talent was disclosed by an astute move that was conceived as he pondered the prospect of removing to a permanent home. It should be remembered that he had lost the Wallowa Valley, and, later, his rights under the Bear Paws surrender, from the want of formal treaties. In January, 1879, Joseph, Yellow Bull, and Arthur Chapman, their interpreter, went to Washington, D.C. On the fourteenth, the chiefs presented their case in Lincoln Hall to a gathering that included congressmen, cabinet members, and diplomats. Close attention was given to their appeals and they were accorded a considerable ovation at the conclusion. Impressed by their reception, Joseph and Yellow Bull filed a proposition with the office of Indian Affairs on January 31. They offered to relinquish all claims to lands in Oregon and Idaho for four townships to be selected by them from lands in the Indian Territory, plus a bonus of a quarter of a million dollars and the expenses of moving them to the new reservation. Commissioner Hayt considered the offer as just and proper, and Schurz transmitted the plan to the House Committee on Indian Affairs, with a request for favorable consideration. But Congress failed to take any action. Therefore, in the summer of 1879, Hayt made arrangements for the removal of the Nez Perces to the 90,710-acre tract in the Ponca country. No title of land ownership was issued at the time for the area, known as the Oakland Reservation, where they were settled.[13] Having made a special concession to Joseph, Commissioner Hayt hoped the chief would abandon all hope of returning to the Northwest and would, from this time on, devote his efforts and leadership to the development of the new reserve.[14]

Accordingly, in June, 1879, 370 Nez Perces were moved to the Oklahoma reserve.[15] Their principal settlement was established at a point on the Salt River which they named Yellow Bull Crossing (present-day Tonkawa, Oklahoma). Since they lacked sufficient horses to effectuate the 180-mile journey, the Indian Bureau provided twenty-five additional teams. Several Nez Perces died en route, and others succumbed during subsequent weeks of difficult adjustment. As at Fort Leavenworth and Quapaw, no preparations of any sort had been made to receive them at Ponca. Hence, their habitations for over a year were primitive. Fall rains and subsequent cold weather caught most of the people without adequate shelter. Medical attention for the ill was nonexistent, and even quinine was always in short supply.

Nez Perce Endeavors toward Subsistence

As plows and harrows came to hand, some of the men clumsily turned to gardening. Others devoted their attention to starting a cattle herd. One of the Indian agents observed that the Nez Perces were natural herdsmen, but their capacity in this regard was never fully tested because they had so few cattle. This lack enabled them to rent some of their range to encroaching white cattlemen. The Nez Perces had formerly been successful as horse breeders, but horses were even harder to get than cattle; they finally acquired 189 horses, 10 mules, and 183 cattle. Actually, they did not lack means for the acquisition of brood stock and bare necessities. Despite Joseph's dissatisfaction, the Indian Bureau expended about one hundred thousand dollars upon the Nez Perces during a five-year period. With this support, the exiles began to recover from the abject poverty and total dependence to which they had been reduced by the war.

They made some progress in respect to education and Christian endeavor. In 1879, three Nez Perces from Lapwai joined the exiles for the purpose of preaching and teaching. They were Archie Lawyer, Mark Williams, and James Reuben. Lawyer and Williams were both weakened by the climate and returned home, but Reuben served as a teacher until May, 1883.[16]

Successive reports from Indian agents indicate that, although the Nez Perces were gradually improving economically and socially, the death rate remained abnormally high. Dr. George Spinning, who visited the reserve, counted the graves of one hundred children. He reported, and other sources concurred, that practically all of the children born in this land died there.[17] Many children who had survived the hardships of the campaign also passed away; Chief Joseph's daughter, born at Tolo Lake in mid-June, 1877, was among these.[18]

Joseph Works and Yearns for the West

Joseph continued to hope and work for a return to Idaho. In 1878, Indian Inspector General McNeill visited Joseph on the Quapaw reserve. The inspector's observations led him to suggest that a direct appeal to President Rutherford B. Hayes might prove fruitful, and he made arrangements for such an interview. In March, 1879, Joseph, Yellow Bull, and their interpreter, Arthur Chapman, went again to Washington, D.C. Joseph's description of his political contacts follows: "I have seen the Great Father Chief (the President); the next Great Chief (Secretary of the Interior); the Commissioner Chief (Hayt); the Law Chief (General Butler), and many other law chiefs (Congressmen), and they all say they are my friends, and that I shall have justice."[19]

Although Joseph conferred at length with the officials mentioned, he was unable to achieve any substantial results, and he became increasingly aware of the fact that there was strong opposition to his proposal of restoration. Western Congressmen were not willing to support such a plan. Joseph became disheartened over his failure to obtain a solid promise of support, and he spoke the following words to a reporter representing the *North American Review:*

> I have heard talk and talk, but nothing is done. Good words do not last long until they amount to something. Words do not pay for my dead people. They do not pay for my country, now over-run by white men. They do not pay for my horses and cattle. Good words will not give me back my children. Good words will not make good the promise of your War Chief, General Miles. Good words will not give my people good health and stop them from dying. Good words will not get my people a home where they can live in peace and take care of themselves.[20]

In April, 1879, the *North American Review* published Chief Joseph's story under the title "An Indian's Views of Indian Affairs." Joseph gave "His Own Story," as it was popularly called, in a calm, forthright, and insistent style, and it pricked the consciences of many readers. He reviewed the history of his people from the time of Lewis and Clark to 1879. He described their early independence and prosperity; their acceptance of missionaries, settlers, and miners; the adjustments they willingly made in the Treaty of 1855; their refusal to surrender tribal homelands under the terms of the Treaty of 1863; the pressures that resulted in forcing them upon the Lapwai reservation in June, 1877; the unfortunate Indian raids and the eventual war. He explained the avowals governing his surrender and their subsequent repudiation. He described the harmful effects of the climate upon his people.

His appeal for help was pathetic. Joseph and his people would have preferred annihilation in the Battle of the Bear Paws rather than suffer gradual tribal extinction in the Oklahoma Territory. An uprising would be unrealistic; besides, Joseph had given his word at the Bear Paws "to fight no more forever." Now, he could only appeal to the honor and justice of his masters. In his view, this effort was proving futile, because of duplicity. Even Leonard Grover, a former governor of Oregon who had helped drive Joseph out of the Wallowa Valley, now as United States senator proffered influence and friendship if Joseph would forget about his claim to the Wallowa Valley.[21] In July, 1879, A. B. Meacham, formerly Superintendent of Indian Affairs in Oregon, and a party of well-wishers visited the Nez Perces. Their presence elicited the following remarks from Joseph:

> You come to see me as you would a man upon his death-bed. The Great Spirit above has left me and my people to their fate. The white men forget us, and death comes almost every day for some of my people. He will come for all of us. A few months more and we will be in the ground. We are a doomed people.[22]

It was after interviews with such men that Joseph made the following observations: "I am tired of talk that comes to nothing. . . . I cannot understand why so many white chiefs are allowed to talk so many different ways, and promise so many different things." When promises were lightly made, Joseph said, "Look twice at a two-faced man." When someone circulated a resolution, he commented, "Big name often on small legs."[23] In reflecting upon his contacts with many officials he said, "It makes my heart sick when I remember all the good words and all the broken promises,"[24]

As the public became increasingly aware of Joseph's story, he emerged as a champion of freedom. Every interview was reported by a favorable press. It was recognized that many of his statements, such as the following appeal, with which he concluded his article in the *North American Review,* came from a wise and penetrating mind.

All men were made by the same Great Spirit Chief. They are all brothers. The earth is the mother of all people, and all people should have equal rights upon it. You might as well expect the rivers to run backward as that any man who was born a free man should be contented penned up and denied liberty to go where he pleases. If you tie a horse to a stake, do you expect he will grow fat? If you pen an Indian up on a small spot of earth, and compel him to stay there, he will not be contented nor will he grow and prosper. I have asked some of the great white chiefs where they get their authority to say to the Indian that he shall stay in one place, while he sees white men going where they please. They cannot tell me.

I only ask of the Government to be treated as all other men are treated. If I cannot go to my own home, let me have a home in some country where my people will not die so fast. . . .

Whenever the white man treats the Indian as they treat each other, then we shall have no more wars. We shall be all alike—brothers of one father and one mother, with one sky above us and one country around us, and one government for all. Then the Great Spirit Chief who rules above will smile upon this land, and send rain to wash out the bloody spots made by brothers' hands upon the face of the earth.

For this time the Indian race are waiting and praying.[25]

The Nez Perce Cause Gains Momentum

Finally, the seeds Joseph had planted during his visits in Washington began to take root. The Indian Rights Association and the Presbyterian Church both recommended the return of the Nez Perces to a mountain environment. C. E. S. Wood, having resigned from the army, began a letter campaign in their behalf. He also went to Boston, where he enlisted the support of Moorefield Storey and other humanitarians.[26] Scores of letters and telegrams supporting the removal of the Nez Perces to the Northwest reached Congressmen, and on April 14, 1884, Senator Henry L. Dawes presented a petition to that end, sponsored by the Presbyterians of Cleveland, Ohio, and bearing over five hundred signatures, including the name of Mrs. James A. Garfield.

There were still opponents of the project, in Washington and in the Northwest. However, by 1884, Indian tribes generally had been reduced to a status of military impotency, and a concession to the Nez Perces was finally accepted as an expedient. On July 4, 1884, Senator Dawes secured the passage of an act which gave the Secretary of the Interior discretionary power over the disposition of Joseph's band. The Nez Perces hailed this news with great joy and feasting, and their hopes for return were at last realized in May of the following year.[27]

26. EPICAL TWILIGHTS

By 1880 most of the Indian tribes of the West had been subjugated and were scattered or confined on reservations. The skill and persistence of veteran Civil War officers and men had overwhelmed the last of the large bands, and white migration had covered the continent. Many Americans were now beginning to question the justice of the government's Indian policy, and the Nez Perce tragedy received wide publicity. Chief Joseph's appeals for justice were heeded, and, without exception, Indian agency officials who contacted the Nez Perces became convinced that their survival depended upon their return to the mountains.

On January 19, 1881, General Miles made a fervent appeal to President Hayes in behalf of returning the Nez Perces to Idaho. The President referred the matter to Secretary Schurz, who agreed to the removal after Miles became established as Commanding General in the Department of the Columbia and had assured himself of the wisdom of the plan. Schurz wanted to be certain that Miles could ensure their safety from persecution.[1]

After Miles became oriented in his new position as commanding officer in the Department of Columbia, he renewed his campaign for the return of the Nez Perces. In a letter to Assistant Adjutant General McDowell, dated October 24, 1881, he said, "I still adhere to my opinion that to punish a village of people, many of them innocent, is not in accordance with any law or just rule, and I therefore recommend that that portion of the tribe not charged with crime be allowed to return to their reservation."[2] He feared no trouble, because practically all of the Nez Perce "criminals" were either in confinement or dead. Miles was convinced that the return of the exiles would be beneficial to all concerned.

Meanwhile, as of September 6, 1881, Agent Thomas Jordan reported that there were only 328 survivors from the original total of nearly five hundred captives. He said the death rate continued to be so high that "the tribe, unless something is done for them, will soon be extinct." Furthermore, Agent Jordan absolved the Nez Perces from carelessness in regard to health. He wrote, "They are cleanly to a fault. . . . They keep their stock in good order, and are hard working, painstaking people."[3] Thus, successive agents and the Indian Commissioner concurred upon the central fact that the Nez Perces were simply not becoming acclimated in Oklahoma.

The First Refugees Return to Idaho

In May, 1883, the War Department approved a proposal by the Indian Bureau to close the Nez Perce school and permit twenty-nine people to return to Idaho. Congress appropriated $1,625 to meet the expenses incident to their removal. James Reuben took charge of the group, which consisted almost entirely of widows and orphans. These people were transported by railroad from Arkansas City to Kelton, Utah. Before leaving, Reuben wrote to the Lapwai reservation officials requesting men and horses to meet the train at Kelton.

Accordingly, Agent Monteith organized a band of Nez Perces to take the necessary horses to meet Reuben's party at Kelton, Utah. Upon reaching Camas Prairie, the expedition from Lapwai was turned back by incensed settlers. A telegram from Monteith to Commissioner Hayt produced an order from Secretary of War Robert T. Lincoln, instructing the proper military officers "to protect from molestation or interference the Indians who are en route from the Indian Territory to the Nez Perce Agency."[4]

Thus, after weeks of travel, they finally reached the reservation. Kate C. McBeth described their appearance: "After him [James Rueben], rode the weariest, dustiest, most forlorn band of women with blankets and belongings behind each woman on her horse. . . . But they were well drilled. A half circle was formed by them facing the agent's office."[5] Then Reuben addressed those assembled for the occasion. He described the hardships the refugees had endured, the suffering and death that had afflicted and decimated them. Consideration and sympathy were shown the little band, and no untoward threats or demonstrations were made against them. Reverend A. L. Lindsley made a partial survey of public feeling in the Salmon River district that might serve as a guide in future restorations. Some people were in favor of the restorations and some were strongly opposed. Judge Leland advocated legal procedures: "There is only one way of prevention: to surrender to the authorities of Nez Perce County the survivors of the Indians who were indicted for outrage and murder committed before the war began."[6] The United States Attorney General had previously recommended suspension of such legal action and Idaho courts had complied. However, a suspension only had been granted, and there were claims that if the war criminals were restored to Idaho they must be tried. Otherwise, it was affirmed that they would be shot on sight. Actually, the young warriors who had begun the White Bird raids had been killed during the campaign. In the circumstances, demands for trials and threats of summary action seemed more vindictive than rational. Still, it was a matter that confronted the federal officials, and they resisted the growing demand for the return of the Nez Perces for two more years.

On June 14, 1883, the Cherokees conveyed title to the Oakland tract in Oklahoma to the Nez Perces. A lear later, their appropriation of more than eighteen thousand dollars was made available for improvements. Neither of these facts changed their attitude toward the country, and the reports from the Ponca Agency included records of still more illness and death. The number of survivors in 1884 had dropped to 282. Agent John W. Scott reported that "there is a tinge of melancholy in their bearing and conversation that is truly pathetic. I think they should be sent back, as it seems clear they will never take root and prosper in this locality."[7]

In May, 1884, fourteen petitions were presented in Congress, demanding action upon the repatriation of the Nez Perces. Foreseeing the prospect of even more insistent appeals, the Senate amended an Indian Appropriation Bill to provide funds for such a move if the Secretary of Interior authorized it. The bill became a law on July 4. Secretary Henry M. Teller and Commissioner of Indian Affairs H. Price decided to authorize the removal. To that end they formulated a plan of distribution under which the White Bird and Looking Glass Indians would be settled on the Lapwai reservation, and Joseph and most of his followers would be placed upon the Colville reservation in northern Washington.

On September 16, Agent Scott received this information, and he presented it to the Nez Perces the next day. In general, they were delighted with the message, but Chief Joseph and many of his followers objected to the Colville proposition. They held that they had been punished enough and, therefore, they would not voluntarily consent to further humiliation. In their view, the proposed segregation would brand them as "wild." Said Joseph, "If I could, I would take my heart out and hold it in my hand and let the Great Father and the white people see that there is nothing in it but kind feelings and love for Him and them." Since these objections and scruples were minor in comparison to the main objective, Joseph and his associates reconciled themselves to the plan. Apprehension among Indian Bureau officials dwelling in Washington, D.C., and the Northwest held the removal in abeyance for seven months. Finally, by April of 1885, the necessary steps had been taken to restore the surviving 268 Nez Perces to the Northwest. The sale of their livestock netted the tribe $2,860.50, which was little enough for so many people, and a far cry from the wealth they owned in the spring of 1877. Before boarding the train at Arkansas City on May 22, 1885, four Nez Perce chiefs signed a document wherein they relinquished all claims to the Oakland reservation.

Distributing the Exiles

Upon arriving at Pocatello, Idaho, the Nez Perces were greeted by Captain Frank Baldwin, Acting Judge Advocate of the Columbia Military Department. He separated them into two groups according to the assigned destinations. Captain Baldwin explained that federal officials had formed this policy for the protection and welfare of all concerned. Accordingly, 118 were sent to Lapwai, while 150 were shipped farther on to Colville, Washington.

Chief Joseph had agreed to this arrangement before the band left Oklahoma. In his view, this was a proper temporary expedient as a concession to the officials who were disturbed by threats from Idaho citizens. He also realized that it would take time to negotiate for the restoration of part of the Wallowa Valley; but he was now hoping for a complete diplomatic triumph.

This policy had been designed to preclude violent action and revenge by white settlers. The Indians who were to be exiled from Idaho by this act were, however, those least responsible for the war. Therefore, this double exile appears to have been a final punitive measure against Chief Joseph as the symbol of the entire Nez Perce controversy and war.[8] Actually, the reasons for this discrimination were never clearly defined. As a result, various interpretations have been made concerning the motives that governed the officials in this matter. Yellow Wolf stated flatly that he was given a choice. He said that when they reached Walla Walla the interpreter asked, "Where you want to go? Lapwai and be a Christian, or Colville and just be yourself?"[9] Both Francis Monteith and Kate C. McBeth admit that the Lapwai officials and mission workers were anxious to receive the more progressive exiles. They wanted those who would respond to the program of civilization rather than adhere to tribal traditions and the teachings of the old Dreamer cult. In any case, the line of demarcation does not appear to have been absolutely rigid. A partial mixture eventuated, and this amalgam probably proved salutary for both groups.

A boat from Walla Walla deposited the Lapwai contingent at Lewiston on June 1, 1885. No untoward gestures of hatred were made by white men, although one person stated, "A group of men were at the landing . . . to meet the boat. They had intended to take him [Joseph] away from the officers and hang him."[10]

The Nez Perce refugees soon became accustomed to the Lapwai reservation. F. D. Fleming, head clerk of the agency, wrote, "Not once did these forlorn outcasts prove recreant to the trust placed in their promises. . . . Returning broken in spirit and in purse they stoically accepted the inevitable burying the dead past."[11] Fleming also stated that all official influences upon the reservation were opposed to Chief Joseph's return to Lapwai. Kate C. McBeth reported his position thus: "For a few years at first Joseph was afraid to come down upon the Nez Perce reserve—afraid of the surrounding whites, and because of the many indictments against him—but this fear wore off. Then he visited his friends—too often for their good, for he held to his heathenism with all the tenacity with which he had clung to his beloved Wallowa Valley."[12]

Missionary McBeth was not explicit concerning the influence Joseph's visits had upon the steady Lapwai reservation Indians. Actually, the disturbing factor was related to Joseph's increasing prestige and popularity. Lapwai Indians, and others, were still eager to rally around the hero of the great campaign. They wanted to hear him describe incidents of valor and deeds of heroism. In this regard Joseph was quite reticent, but the veterans who always accompanied him could be induced to recite accounts that produced nostalgia for the former Nez Perce unity and power. In fact, the people finally recognized that the war of 1877 was the greatest epic in Nez Perce history.

The negative influence, if any, that Kate McBeth deplored proved to be evanescent. Every society stands in need of traditions of leadership in the field of independence and valor. Surely Joseph and the other nontreaty chiefs and warriors endowed the Nez Perce people with praiseworthy examples in that regard. But those were not the virtues reservation and church officials considered paramount at that time. However, the war and exile had largely eliminated the hunters, and in their passing the last vestiges of anti-reservation sentiment disappeared. Administrators gradually minimized, and finally eradicated, the role of chieftainship in reservation procedures. In time, the exiles mingled with the other Lapwai Indians and made progress toward becoming a self-sufficient farming population.

Chief Joseph's Band at Colville

When Joseph's band arrived at Colville in June, they were met by an unsympathetic Indian agent named Major Gwydir. His supplies were inadequate to meet Nez Perce requirements, and the military officials at Fort Spokane provided some rations.

Taking his cue from the agent, Chief Skolaskin of the San-poil tribe refused to admit the Nez Perces to their assigned area on the Colville reservation. In fact, Major Gwydir was forced to employ troops from Fort Spokane before Joseph's people could be settled. Characteristically, Chief Joseph attempted to improve conditions. He observed that the land at Nespelem appeared more promising than that at Colville, and he requested the privilege of relocating his people there. Permission was received, and a move was made in December, 1885. Then it was discovered that the land settled upon had already been assigned for other purposes. This development necessitated another move within the Nespelem area during July, 1886. Because of these frequent moves, no crops were raised and available rations proved inadequate. Low morale expressed itself in gambling and other nonconstructive activities.

Some crops were finally planted in 1887, and within three years thirty heads of families were classed as farmers. Others were gradually building up horse and cattle herds. The value of horses, in which they took inordinate pride, was relatively small. Ownership of great numbers yielded prestige, however low the market value. Joseph was much more interested in horses than in crops.

Therefore, progress came slowly; indeed, the Nespelem Nez Perces were far from self-supporting in 1890. At that time the government furnished 75 per cent of their living costs; they produced 10 per cent and gath-

ered 15 per cent from their traditional occupations.[13]
By 1900, the government reduced their allowance to
half-rations in food and clothing, to encourage greater
effort in production.

The climate at Nespelem was healthful. The exiles
were surrounded by a great complex of mountains, forests, prairies, lakes, and streams. Their village was situated on the banks of a rapid river named Nespelem.
As Yellow Wolf stated:

> On the Colville we found wild game aplenty. Fish,
> berries, and all kinds of roots. Everything so fine
> many wanted to remain there, after learning that Wal-
> lowa was not to be returned to us. Chief Moses ad-
> vised Joseph to stay. The Indians were good to us.
> Gave us horses, and other useful property and goods.
> Deer everywhere, and good salmon at Keller. It was
> better than Idaho, where all Christian Nez Perces and
> whites were against us.[14]

At Nespelem, the Nez Perces were permitted to wor-
ship in their own ways, whereas at Lapwai the pressures
of religion and progress were greater. Under the Severalty Act of 1887 Joseph's people might have received
allotments of land at Lapwai, but they declined.[15] Acceptance would have forever precluded any prospect of
receiving comparable allotments at Wallowa, an event
for which they were still hoping.

Nespelem proved to be a satisfactory homeland, and
by the turn of the century the Nez Perces began to
prosper. Many have become substantial cattlemen and
farmers, and those who do not care to work their own
land lease it to others.

Tribal Life at Nespelem

Having lost his first wife, Joseph married two widows
of fallen Nez Perce warriors. When a missionary sug-

gested that he should abandon one, he replied: "I fought through the war for my country and these women. You took away my country; I shall keep my wives."[16]

Joseph had nine children, but all except one died before reaching maturity. This daughter, who was exiled from him, died in early womanhood. Joseph maintained a large, patriarchal household, however, by inviting nephews and others to be his lodge companions.

An account of Chief Joseph's life in 1892 was recorded by Erskine Wood, the thirteen-year-old son of C. E. S. Wood, aide-de-camp to General Howard during the Nez Perce war. As an expression of friendship, Joseph invited this young man to be his guest, and Wood spent two three-month periods at Nespelem and then wrote down his observations. According to him, Joseph preferred a tent to the house provided by the government. His main interest was in raising horses. He liked to race and bet cautiously upon his favorites. The races were sometimes conducted with considerable fanfare. Hunting deer was an important fall activity in which nearly all the people participated. Joseph distributed the meat according to need, but the hide became the sole property of the killer. Curing meat and tanning hides were integral parts of the hunting business.

In winter the people established communal lodges for mutual comfort and pleasure. Attention was given to the instruction of the young in tribal history, religion, and arts. Joseph advised the youth to learn both the old and the new ways.

Young Wood stated that Joseph was considerate and kind toward all, and that he was highly revered. He had no official authority, but his personality enforced his decisions. He presided upon all festival occasions, and he spoke eloquently. When dressed in full ceremonial regalia, his bearing was majestic. Erskine Wood was greatly impressed by Joseph's regard for the son of a former enemy. A half-century later, in the *Wenatchee Daily World* of June 13, 1956, Wood's feelings were recorded: "He took me into his tepee and into his heart and treated me as a son. . . . We ate together, hunted deer together, and slept together. I can say truthfully, knowing him was the high spot of my entire life."

Joseph's Last Journeys and Honors

In 1897, Joseph observed that white squatters were encroaching upon open lands within the Colville reservation. Appeals to local authorities were futile, and Joseph went to Washington, D.C., for help. He explained the situation to President William McKinley and others, and he also met General Miles. These officials assured Joseph that his grievance would be given prompt attention.

While Joseph was in the East the dedication of U. S. Grant's tomb took place. General Miles sponsored Joseph's appearance for the occasion and arranged to have him ride in the procession of honor, where both he and William F. "Buffalo Bill" Cody were admired and applauded. General Howard and General Miles also attracted considerable attention, and the appearance of the three principals in the Bear Paws surrender scene reanimated the controversy concerning the relative parts the generals had played in the chieftain's capture.[17] Joseph also visited an Indian camp exhibition being held in Brooklyn.

Joseph's desire to remove his people from Nespelem to the Wallowa Valley was given expression and publicity on this trip. Indeed, he met with members of the Indian Commission in Washington, D.C., and submitted a petition to that effect. Although his request received support from General Miles and others, the commissioners were reluctant to take any action. However, they authorized United States Indian Inspector James McLoughlin to make an investigation.

In June, 1900, McLoughlin visited the Nez Perces at

Nespelem. Then, accompanied by Joseph, he made a reconnaissance of the Wallowa and Imnaha valleys. This was now white man's country. Fences and irrigation ditches circumscribed the landscape, and four little hamlets had sprung up along the Wallowa River. Joseph presented his proposition to purchase part of the Wallowa Valley from the people of Enterprise if they would allow the Nez Perces to return, but McLoughlin did not recommend this transaction. The Nespelem agent concurred with the inspector, and the Indian Commissioners decided that such a move would be impractical.

Joseph still felt that the Wallowa Valley belonged to his people. On March 27, 1901, while Professor Edmond S. Meany was interviewing him, he dictated this statement: "My home is in the Wallowa Valley, and I want to go back there to live. My father and mother are buried there. If the government would only give me a small piece of land for my people in the Wallowa Valley, with a teacher, that is all I would ask."[18] He made a final effort to achieve his objective. In the late winter of 1903, Joseph made another journey to Washington, D.C. General Miles was his host, and he visited President Theodore Roosevelt. The chief's conduct, as always, was discreet and proper.

Officials of the Carlisle Indian School invited Joseph to stop in Pennsylvania en route to the Northwest. There he met General Howard, and the former enemies expressed mutual good will. James J. Hill became interested in Chief Joseph's cause, and in September, 1904, he sponsored his appearance in Seattle. A public meeting was held in which Professor Meany reviewed the history of the campaign and then presented Joseph and his nephew Red Thunder to the audience.

Whatever hopes Hill may have entertained of restoring Joseph to the Wallowa country were shattered by the latter's death on September 21, 1904.[19] Dr. Latham, the agency physician, reported that Joseph died of a broken heart while sitting before his tepee fire.

At that time Joseph was buried without fanfare, but on June 20, 1905, an impressive monument was provided by the Washington State Historical Society, and his remains were disinterred and redeposited with great ceremony. White and Indian orators praised Joseph's character and record, and the sentiments expressed then have persisted. A Chief Joseph Memorial and Historical Association was organized, and, by the mid-thirties, a considerable legend had evolved in which Joseph became a great war chief, a majestic symbol.

In 1939, Representative Compton I. White introduced a bill, H. R. 4331, requesting an appropriation of twenty-five thousand dollars to provide a monument in memory of Chief Joseph and a museum for Indian relics and records at Lapwai, Idaho. The bill was not acted upon, but a public controversy was started concerning its merits. J. W. Redington, one of General Howard's scouts, wrote a protest on the ground that Joseph was an outlaw. A rebuttal in Joseph's defense was made by F. M. Redfield, a Lapwai Agency official in 1877.[20] Mrs. C. F. Manning, professing to represent the settler viewpoint, said flatly, "A memorial to Joseph is unthinkable!"[21] As veneration for Joseph increased, so did antipathy.[22] Obviously, the time for a memorial in Idaho had not arrived in 1939.

In 1943, a movement for the removal of Chief Joseph's remains to the Wallowa Valley began in eastern Oregon. Archie Phinney, Superintendent of the Lapwai Indian Agency, supported the move. He said, "While reburial of Joseph's remains in his Wallowa home cannot be expected to undo the historical wrongs his people suffered, his cause can be revitalized in the nation's consciousness by return of his body."[23] However, Superintendent C. L. Graves of the Colville agency characterized the proposal as a publicity stunt sponsored by the citizens of Joseph, Oregon.

On June 12, 1956, the Chief Joseph Dam, on the Columbia below Bridgeport, Washington, was officially named and dedicated. The speakers included federal and tribal leaders. A special tribute to Chief Joseph by Erskine Wood included this statement: "He ruled by the sheer force of his character. The people were happy in their leader. . . . There was no hatred in his soul in spite of the wrongs our race had done him. . . . He was a man of true magnanimity."[24]

NOTES

Chapter 1

1. John R. Swanton, *The Indian Tribes of North America* (Washington, D.C.: Government Printing Office, 1953), p. 401.

2. Kate C. McBeth, *The Nez Perce Since Lewis and Clark* (New York: Fleming H. Revell, 1908), p. 19.

3. L. V. McWhorter, *Hear Me, My Chiefs* (Caldwell, Ida.: The Caxton Printers, 1952), p. 9. Also McWhorter, *Yellow Wolf: His Own Story* (Caldwell, Ida.: The Caxton Printers, 1940), p. 22.

4. Reuben G. Trwaites, *The Original Journals of the Lewis and Clark Expedition* (New York: Dodd, Mead, 1905), III, 105; p. 29.

5. McWhorter, *Hear Me, My Chiefs*, p. 2.

6. Nelson A. Miles, *Personal Recollections and Observations of General Nelson A. Miles* (New York: The Werner Co., 1897), p. 279.

7. Francis Haines, *The Nez Perce Tribesmen of the Columbia Plateau* (Norman, Okla.: University of Oklahoma Press, 1955), p. 5.

8. Robert D. Leeper, The Soul of a Pioneer, lecture delivered to the Sons and Daughters of the Pioneers in 1932 (MS in Idaho State College Historical Archives, Pocatello, Idaho).

9. McWhorter, *Yellow Wolf*, p. 43.

10. H. J. Spinden, *The Nez Perce Indians* (Memoirs of the American Anthropological Association, Vol. II, Part 3 [Lancaster, Pa.: New Era Print Co., 1908]), p. 197. This is the basic work upon Nez Perce culture. It is not only authoritative, but it is artistic in concept and portrayal as well.

11. Sven Liljeblad, Indian Peoples of Idaho (MS in Idaho State College Historical Archives), p. 26.

12. A Shoshoni chief named Arimo owned hundreds of horses. Dr. Sven Liljeblad asked his grandson why he had so many. The reply was immediate and conclusive: "To put his brand on!" See Liljeblad, Indian Peoples of Idaho, pp. 31, 32.

13. U.S. Commissioner of Indian Affairs, *Annual Report to the Department of the Interior,* 1879–1880 (Washington, D.C.: Government Printing Office, 1881), p. 85.

14. McWhorter, *Yellow Wolf,* p. 35.

15. Liljeblad, Indian Peoples of Idaho, pp. 31, 32.

16. McBeth, *The Nez Perce Since Lewis and Clark,* p. 77.

17. Otis W. Freeman and Howard H. Martin, *The Pacific Northwest* (New York: John Wiley and Sons, 1947), chaps. i and iii.

Chapter 2

1. W. A. Goulder, Personal Recollections (MS No. 395, Idaho State College Historical Archives, Pocatello, Idaho).

2. Kate C. McBeth, *The Nez Perce Since Lewis and Clark* (New York: Fleming H. Revell, 1908), p. 37.

3. In 1842, Father Nicholas Point established a mission among the Coeur d'Alene Indians. First located on the south end of Coeur d'Alene Lake, but later moved to Cataldo, the mission had an influence upon some of the Nez Perces.

4. This was a logical choice, because Spalding was a Presbyterian. However, the law certainly voided the principle of religious liberty.

5. Clifford M. Drury, *Henry Harmon Spalding* (Caldwell, Ida.: The Caxton Printers, 1936), p. 414.

6. P. W. Norris, *Annual Report of the Superintendent of Yellowstone National Park* (Washington, D.C.: Government Printing Office, 1877), p. 842.

7. Francis Haines, *The Nez Perce Tribesmen of the Columbia Plateau* (Norman, Okla.: University of Oklahoma Press, 1955), p. 114.

8. Years later, Yellow Wolf recognized this fact in saying, "The discovery of gold on our reservation brought thousands of white men. That was the beginning of our trouble." L. V. McWhorter, *Yellow Wolf: His Own Story* (Caldwell, Ida.: The Caxton Printers, 1940), p. 43.

9. Benjamin F. Manring, *The Conquest of the Coeur d'Alenes, Spokanes and Palouses* (Spokane, 1912), pp. 133–34.

10. *Idaho Semi-Weekly World* (Idaho City), August 28, 1877.

Chapter 3

1. Dan E. Clark, *The West in American History* (New York: Thomas Y. Crowell Co., 1947), pp. 221–22.

2. Granville Stuart, Recollections (MS in Montana Historical Society, Helena).

3. George Dangerfield, *The Era of Good Feelings* (New York: Harcourt, Brace and Co., 1952), p. 27.

4. Francis Haines, "Problems of Indian Policy," *Pacific Northwest Quarterly*, XLI (July, 1950), 203–12.

5. Hazard Stevens, *The Life of Isaac Ingalls Stevens* (Boston: Houghton Mifflin Co., 1900), II, 39.

6. *Ibid.*, p. 46.

7. *Ibid.*, p. 50.

8. *Ibid.*, p. 54.

9. Francis Haines, *The Nez Perce Tribesmen of the Columbia Plateau* (Norman, Okla.: University of Oklahoma Press, 1955), p. 144.

10. These were both squaw men as well as agency officials.

11. Haines, *The Nez Perce Tribesmen of the Columbia Plateau*, p. 205. L. V. McWhorter, *Yellow Wolf: His Own Story* (Caldwell, Ida.: The Caxton Printers, 1940), p. 64.

12. Haines, *The Nez Perce Tribesmen of the Columbia Plateau*, pp. 168–70.

13. Chief Joseph, "An Indian's View of Indian Affairs," *North American Review*, Vol. CXXVIII (April, 1879), p. 419.

14. *Ibid.*

15. *Ibid.*, p. 16.

16. Lindsley to Howard, Document No. 3597-76; A.G.O. 3464-77, National Archives.

17. Henry Clay Wood, *Status of Young Joseph and His Band of Nez Perce Indians* (Portland, Ore.: Assistant Adjutant General's Office, 1876), p. 45.

18. *Ibid.*

19. Albert G. Forse, "Chief Joseph as a Commander," *Winners of the West*, No. 12 (November, 1936), p. 3.

20. Mrs. John B. Monteith, *Lewiston Morning Tribune*, January 22, 1933.

21. General Howard asked Secretary of War J. D. Cameron to allow Captain Stephen G. Whipple, Captain David Perry, Major H. Clay Wood, and himself to serve on the commission. The secretary refused, saying that he saw no need of the commission. Later, he permitted Wood and Howard to serve. (Document No. 6177-76; A.G.O. 3464-77, National Archives.)

22. Oliver O. Howard, *Nez Perce Joseph* (Boston: Lee and Shepard, 1881), p. 31.

23. Document No. 128-77; A.G.O. 3464-77, National Archives.

24. U.S. Commissioner of Indian Affairs, *Annual Report to the Department of the Interior* (Washington, D.C.: Government Printing Office, 1877), p. 212.

25. Secretary of War George W. McCrary specifically reminded Secretary of Interior Carl Schurz that the role of "the military authorities was merely protecting and aiding them in the execution of their instructions." (Document No. 1364-77; A.G.O. 3464-77, National Archives.)

26. *Ibid.* In a letter to J. Q. Smith, Agent Monteith recommended that the Wallowa Nez Perces be granted permission to hunt and fish in the Imnaha Valley for six weeks each year. J. Q. Smith approved the suggestion and the prospect of official adoption was good.

27. Letter from J. B. Monteith to J. Q. Smith, March 19, 1877. Document No. 2196-77; A.G.O. 3464-77, National Archives.

28. Letter from Howard to Kelton, from Lapwai, May 3, 1877. Document No. 3003-77; A.G.O. 3464-77, National Archives.

29. The *Walla Walla Statesman,* March 24, stated, "We have a right to demand that no half way measure be adopted by the officer in command. Send out a large force at first, and not in small details, and let the question be settled forever." The *Daily Oregonian,* February 28, stated, "The case of Joseph is in many respects similar to that of Captain Jack, out of which the Modoc massacre arose. . . . The government should act with promptness and energy. . . . Temporizing will only make matters worse. Having determined upon a policy to be pursued toward this defiant band, the way to prevent its numbers from increasing till it becomes formidable is to break its power at once."

30. Wood, *Status of Young Joseph . . . ,* p. 213. Henry Clay Wood's description of Joseph follows: "Joseph wore leggings, moccasins and a blanket. His face, manners, and general appearance are calculated to impress one favorably. He wears no smile, but seems thoroughly absorbed in the business under consideration. His speech is fluent and impressive; his action energetic, yet graceful." (Document No. 3597-77; A.G.O. 3464-77, National Archives.)

31. Howard, *Nez Perce Joseph,* pp. 64–65. Also, Document No. 3394-77; A.G.O. 3464-77, National Archives.

32. *Ibid.* Howard had previously placed a Dreamer leader named Skimiah, of the Celilo band, in the guardhouse at Fort Vancouver.

33. James Reuben, *Lewiston Morning Tribune,* March 24, 1877. This item was reprinted in the *Lewiston Morning Tribune,* March 27, 1927.

34. U.S. Department of War, *Annual Report of the Secretary of War,* 1877, p. 115.

35. General Howard relates the case of Chief Thomas, who promised to move his clan of fifty to the Umatilla Reservation by the first of September, and states, "He kept the promise in No-

vember." (*Nez Perce Joseph*, p. 83.) But he came. Chief Joseph said, "I blame General Howard for not giving my people time to get their stock away from Wallowa. . . . Why are you in such a hurry? . . . Our stock is scattered, and Snake River is very high. . . . We want time to gather our stock and gather our supplies for the winter." ("An Indian's Views," pp. 19–21.) Howard had been repeatedly advised by his superiors, General Sherman and General McDowell, that the removal of Joseph's band was a delicate matter. His work was to be done in "the interest of peace . . . merely protecting and aiding them in the execution of their instructions." (Letter from Samuel Breck, for McDowell, to Howard, March 24, 1877. Document No. 1824-77; A.G.O. 3464-77, National Archives.)

Chapter 4

1. The *Army and Navy Journal*, July 7, 1877, contains an article entitled "The Indian War," based upon H. Clay Wood's report. This statement appears: "A solitary case of manslaughter in the year 1863 by an Indian named Sapoonmas, in a quarrel with a frontiersman named Varble, is the only recorded case of trouble between the two races." (Document No. 3597-76; A.G.O. 3464-77, National Archives.)

2. The Nez Perces claim that Wallowa settlers took advantage of the opportunities incident to this migration to stampede horses and steal them.

3. L. V. McWhorter, *Hear Me, My Chiefs* (Caldwell, Ida.: The Caxton Printers, 1952), p. 190.

4. *Ibid.*, p. 191.

5. *Ibid.*, p. 202.

6. *Ibid.*

7. L. V. McWhorter, *Yellow Wolf: His Own Story* (Caldwell, Ida.: The Caxton Printers, 1940), pp. 44–45. General Howard states that Chief White Bird avowed that they would not go on the reservation, thereby stirring the people to action. (U.S. Department of War, *Annual Report of the Secretary of War*, 1877.)

8. McWhorter, *Yellow Wolf*, pp. 46–47.

9. Chief Joseph, "An Indian's Views of Indian Affairs," *North American Review*, CXXVIII (April, 1879), 425. In 1879, Joseph thought of himself as guardian of all nontreaty Nez Perces; hence, he referred to members of White Bird's band as "my young men."

10. Charlotte M. Kirkwood, *The Nez Perce Indian War under Chiefs Joseph and Whitebird* (Grangeville, Ida.: Idaho County Free Press, 1928), p. 35. E. C. Watkins, Inspector of Indian Affairs, held this view. (Document No. 4018-77; A.G.O. 3464-77, National Archives.)

11. Oliver O. Howard, *Nez Perce Joseph* (Boston: Lee and Shepard, 1881), p. 99.

12. *Ibid.* At this place, with a daughter of six and a babe in arms, Mrs. Samuel Benedict, whose husband had been killed by the avengers, emerged from hiding. Two volunteers escorted them to Mount Idaho.

13. Will Cave, "Interesting Narratives of Historical Period in Idaho, Montana, and the Northwest," *Wallace Press Times* (Wallace, Idaho), August 21, 1921.

Chapter 5

1. Oliver O. Howard, *Nez Perce Joseph* (Boston: Lee and Shepard, 1881), p. 116. The general described the battle as "a kind of Bull Run on a small scale."

2. Cyrus Townsend Brady, *Northwestern Fights and Fighters* (Garden City, New York: Doubleday, Doran and Co., 1928), p. 116.

3. Howard, *Nez Perce Joseph*, p. 118.

4. Brady, *Northwestern Fights*, p. 102. Parnell's estimate of the number of Indians filtering to the rear approximates the total number involved in the battle.

5. *Ibid.*, p. 102.

6. *Ibid.*, p. 95. Daily target practice was held on the basis of ten rounds of ammunition per man. In critical periods, the amount of ammunition for target practice was expanded. (Document No. 3855-77; A.G.O. 3464-77, National Archives.)

7. The *Idaho Statesman* (Boise), September 13, 1931. A statement made by John P. Schorr to A. F. Parker of Grangeville, Idaho.

8. Some writers have stated that scalps were taken and bodies otherwise mutilated at White Bird, but it seems that deformations were due to days of exposure before burial.

9. Francis M. Redfield, "Reminiscences of Francis M. Redfield, Chief Joseph's War," ed. Floy Laird, *Pacific Northwest Quarterly*, XXVII (January, 1936), 72-73.

10. *Idaho Statesman* (Boise), September 4, 1927.

Chapter 6

1. Oliver O. Howard, *Nez Perce Joseph* (Boston: Lee and Shepard, 1881), p. 121. Howard's account of the companies at Fort Lapwai, available to him on June 22, follows:
Whipple's ("L") and Winters' ("E") companies of calvary, . . . Pollock's ("D"), Eltonhead's ("I"), Miles' ("E"), Jocelyn's ("B"), Haughey's ("H") companies of 21st infantry. . . . The second force, Throckmorton's, Rodney's and Morris' company, 21st Infantry . . . joined the advance—making in all an effective

force of four hundred men. (General Howard's Annual Report, August 27, 1877, Document No. 5405-77; A.G.O. 3464-77, p. 3.) In a telegram dated June 20, McDowell informed Sherman that a total of 960 men would soon be en route to Lewiston, Idaho. (Document No. 3505-77; A.G.O. 3464-77.)

2. Telegram from Brayman to the War Department, Document No. 3473; A.G.O. 3464-77. Only July 2, the Boise City Council asked the War Department to garrison two companies of cavalry at Fort Boise. Five days later, the county commissioners requested similar action. (Documents No. 4030-77 and No. 4188-77; A.G.O. 3464-77. Telegram from Sherman to McDowell, June 20, 1877, Document No. 3468-77; A.G.O. 3464-77.)

3. *Lewiston Teller,* July 21, 1877.

4. Volunteer leaders in these companies were D. B. Randall, Arthur Chapman, Luther P. Wilmot, James L. Cearley, and William D. Bloomer.

5. Donald Wells, Governor Brayman and the Nez Perce War (MS in Idaho Historical Society, Boise, Idaho), p. 16.

6. Howard to McDowell, Document No. 3703-77; A.G.O. 3464-77, National Archives.

7. L. V. McWhorter, *Yellow Wolf: His Own Story* (Caldwell, Ida.: The Caxton Printers, 1940), p. 68.

8. Francis Haines, *The Nez Perce Tribesmen of the Columbia Plateau* (Norman, Okla.: University of Oklahoma Press, 1955), p. 231.

9. Stress was placed upon this and subsequent use of red blankets by the hostiles.

10. Francis M. Redfield, Letter, available in the Idaho State College Library, Pocatello, Idaho.

11. L. V. McWhorter, *Hear Me, My Chiefs* (Caldwell, Ida.: The Caxton Printers, 1952), p. 276.

12. U.S. Department of War, *Report of the Secretary of War,* 1877. In another place Howard describes Salmon River as being "swift, deep and difficult." (Document No. 3778-77; A.G.O. 3464-77, National Archives.)

13. McWhorter, *Hear Me, My Chiefs,* p. 266.

14. Howard, *Nez Perce Joseph,* pp. 148–49. General Howard justified this attack upon the basis of reports from his scouts that Looking Glass tribesmen were joining the hostiles. The Nez Perce informants deny the charge. Hence, it is a case of the word of scouts and perhaps some friendly Christian Nez Perces against that of nontreaty warriors. Howard also claims that Looking Glass agreed to surrender, but the Nez Perces affirm the contrary. Monteith supported Howard in a telegram to Commissioner J. Q. Smith. (Document No. 3936-77; A.G.O. 3464-77, National Archives.)

15. *Idaho Semi-Weekly World* (Idaho City), August 7, 1877.

An appropriate reminder of this skirmish, called the Foster Monument, marks the area of encounter. A poem expressed the settlers' feelings for the lieutenant and his men:

> The news has come, and we have read
> That brave Lieutenant Rains is dead;
> Who entered with such fearless zeal
> The wild and dangerous battlefield.
> With courage all unchecked by fear
> He saw the red foe drawing near;
> But not one quiver of his face
> Showed that he feared this death to face. . . .

16. George M. Shearer, "The Skirmish at Cottonwood," *Idaho Yesterdays,* II (1958), 6–7. Before going to the rescue of the Randall party, George Shearer exclaimed: "The man who goes down there is a d——d fool, but he's a d——d coward if he don't." See George Hunter's *Reminiscences of an Old Timer* (San Francisco: H. S. Crocker and Co., 1887), p. 338.

17. Colonel J. C. Kelton investigated the charges against the army officers and described them as wicked falsifications. (Telegrams from Kelton to McDowell, July 18, 1877, Document No. 4109-77; A.G.O. 3464-77, National Archives.) The charges persisted and Captain Perry demanded a court of inquiry. The court rendered an opinion on November 30, 1877, that exonerated Captain Perry completely. (Document No. 7782-77; A.G.O. 3464-77, National Archives.)

18. General Howard was quite diplomatic in dealing with volunteers. His reports do not disparage, but rather commend them. This was not true of Captain Keeler, who wrote, "Volunteers of the character and status of those with General Howard would be worse than useless." (Telegram from Keeler to McDowell, July 20, 1877, Document No. 4117-77; A.G.O. 3464-77, National Archives.)

19. Letter from E. C. Watkins to J. Q. Smith, July 8, 1877. (Document No. 4499-77; A.G.O. 3464-77, National Archives.)

20. Charlotte M. Kirkwood, *The Nez Perce Indian War under Chiefs Joseph and Whitebird* (Grangeville, Ida.: Idaho County Free Press), p. 38.

21. Luther P. Wilmot, An Account of White Bird, Cottonwood, Misery Hill and Clear Water Battles (MS in Yellowstone National Park Library).

22. *Lewiston Teller,* June 26, 1877.

Chapter 7

1. Oliver O. Howard, *Nez Perce Joseph* (Boston: Lee and Shepard, 1881), p. 20. Also Documents No. 3973-77, No. 4107; A.G.O. 3464-77, National Archives. There were seventy-two tepees

in the village, according to Luther P. Wilmot, who made a careful count.

2. L. V. McWhorter, *Yellow Wolf: His Own Story* (Caldwell, Ida.: The Caxton Printers, 1940), pp. 88–89. Other sayings Yellow Wolf learned from his uncle were: "If you go to war and get shot, do not cry! . . . In wartime man cannot sleep with woman. Might get killed if he does. . . . Do not think to eat when in dangerous places."

3. Albert G. Forse, "Chief Joseph as a Commander," *Winners of the West*, No. 12 (November 30, 1936).

4. Howard, *Nez Perce Joseph*, p. 164.

5. Oliver O. Howard, *Supplementary Report*, Document No. 5405-77; A.G.O. 3464-77, National Archives.

6. Howard, *Nez Perce Joseph*, p. 165. On July 12, General McDowell's aide-de-camp, Captain Keeler, sent the following telegram concerning the Battle of Clearwater: "I consider this a most important success. Joseph in full flight westward. Nothing can surpass the vigor of General Howard's movement and action." (Document No. 3874-77; A.G.O. 3464-77, National Archives.)

7. McWhorter, *Yellow Wolf*, p. 101.

8. Lieutenant Forse states that Howard later censured Perry for not pursuing the warriors but that Perry proved before a court of inquiry that he followed orders.

9. Colonel H. L. Bailey states that, although the order was "Burn everything," the execution did not preclude the acquisition of great plunder, particularly by packers and citizens. "It was marvelous how many citizens seemed to arrive," he said. See L. V. McWhorter, *Hear Me, My Chiefs* (Caldwell, Ida.: The Caxton Printers, 1952), p. 322.

10. John A. Carpenter, "General Howard and the Nez Perce War of 1877," *Pacific Northwest Quarterly*, *XLIX* (October, 1958), 134–35.

11. *Ibid.*, p. 133. In a telegram, July 4, 1877, Sherman expressed the same thought to General Vincent. (Document No. 3840-77; A.G.O. 3464-77, National Archives.)

12. Yellow Wolf listed the names and others confirmed his record. See McWhorter, *Hear Me, My Chiefs*, p. 323. Later, Howard's count of twenty-two wounded soldiers was raised to twenty-seven, two of them fatally.

13. McWhorter, *Yellow Wolf*, p. 101.

14. Howard left no record concerning the arrival of a Nez Perce messenger seeking information concerning peace terms, but Agent Monteith states that one appeared. He affirms that Howard stipulated unconditional surrender, to be followed by trials and punishment. (Letter from Monteith to Smith, July 31, 1877, Document No. 5259-77; A.G.O. 3464-77, National Archives.)

15. Luther P. Wilmot, An Account of White Bird, Cottonwood,

Misery Hill and Clear Water Battles (MS in Yellowstone National Park Library).

16. Howard, *Nez Perce Joseph*, p. 170.

17. Letters from Watkins to Smith, Smith to Watkins, and McCrary to Smith, Document No. 5219-77; A.G.O. 3464-77, National Archives.

18. *Ibid.*

19. C. T. Stranahan, article in *Idaho Statesman* (Boise), June 18, 1933.

Chapter 8

1. L. V. McWhorter, *Yellow Wolf: His Own Story* (Caldwell, Ida.: The Caxton Printers, 1940), p. 112.

2. Sherman to McDowell, Document No. 5044-77; A.G.O. 3464-77, National Archives.

3. McWhorter, *Yellow Wolf*, p. 112.

4. Oliver O. Howard, *Nez Perce Joseph* (Boston: Lee and Shepard, 1881), p. 172.

5. Lieutenant C. E. S. Wood said the criticism of the Sunday delay for prayers originated among saloon loafers, far from the battlefield. Eastern newspapermen then took up the theme without considering the reasons that made pursuit move slowly.

6. Oliver O. Howard, *Supplementary Report*, p. 66. A.G.O. 3464-77, National Archives.

7. John E. Rees states that the name Lolo is a derivative from the Flathead word "Loulou," which resulted from their attempt to say Lawerence. Lawerence was a half-breed trapper who was buried on the creek since known as Lolo Creek. *Idaho Chronology, Nomenclature Bibliography* (Chicago: W. B. Conkey Co., 1918), p. 90.

8. Olin D. Wheeler, *The Trail of Lewis and Clark, 1804–1904* (New York: G. P. Putnam's Sons, 1904), II, 82–84.

9. Bernard DeVoto, *The Journals of Lewis and Clark* (Boston: Houghton Mifflin Co., 1955), p. 233.

10. *Ibid.*, p. 402.

11. Wheeler, *The Trail of Lewis and Clark*, p. 101.

12. Amos Buck, "The Nez Perce Campaign," *Great Falls Tribune*, December 31, 1944.

13. Howard, *Nez Perce Joseph*, p. 178.

14. Howard had been warned that the hostiles might leave the trail, let his troops pass by and then return to the Kamiah area. Document No. 5259-77; A.G.O. 3464-77, National Archives.

15. Howard, *Nez Perce Joseph*, pp. 179–80.

Chapter 9

1. Peter Ronan to Commissioner J. Q. Smith, August 1, 1877. Document No. 3531 DD 1877, National Archives.

2. *Ibid.*

3. W. B. Harlan, letter to Governor B. F. Potts, in "The Battle of the Big Hole," *Historical Reprints,* ed. Paul C. Phillips (Sources of Northwest History, No. 8 [Missoula: University of Montana, 1929]), Item No. 6[a], p. 6.

4. L. V. McWhorter, *Yellow Wolf: His Own Story* (Caldwell, Ida.: The Caxton Printers, 1940), p. 107.

5. *Helena Weekly Independent,* August 2, 1877. Potts's telegram to Secretary McCrary, Document No. 4643-77; A.G.O. 3464-77, National Archives.

6. Telegram from Sherman to Potts, Document No. 5045-77; A.G.O. 3464-77, National Archives. A telegram from Sheridan to General E. D. Townsend, August 2, 1877, states that General Alfred H. Terry opposed raising Montana volunteers. (Document No. 4692-77; A.G.O. 3464-77, National Archives.)

7. Charles C. Rawn, *Annual Report to the Assistant Adjutant General,* Department of Dakota, September 30, 1877. Document No. 4085 DD 1877, National Archives.

8. Charles C. Rawn to Adjutant Burnett in *Early Days at Fort Missoula,* ed. A. E. Rothermich (Missoula: University of Montana, 1936).

9. T. J. Kerttula, *Dillon Examiner,* October 23, 1940. A state highway sign upon the barricade site bears this inscription:

FORT FIZZLE

Here Captain Charles C. Rawn 7th Infantry, with four officers and twenty-five enlisted men from Fort Missoula, approximately 150 citizen volunteers, 25 Flathead braves, erected and occupied a redoubt from July 25 to 28th, 1877, to challenge the passage of the hostile nontreaty Nez Perces Indians under Chief Joseph.

On July 28th, the Nez Perces evaded the troops by ascending a gulch on north side of Lolo Creek ½ mile above this place and going down Sleeman Creek into the Bitterroot Valley.

A forest fire on Sept. 30th, 1934, destroyed the last visible sector of the old log redoubt which is now marked by five cement piers.

10. Samuel L. Cappius, A History of the Bitter Root Valley to 1914 (Master's thesis, University of Washington, 1939). Lieutenant C. E. S. Wood informed General McDowell that 150 Bitterroot volunteers left Rawn after they understood that the Indians would let them alone in the valley. (Telegram from Wood to McDowell, August 11, 1877, Document No. 6718-77; A.G.O. 3464-77, National Archives, p. 10.)

11. Chief Joseph, "An Indian's Views of Indian Affairs," *North American Review,* CXXVIII (April, 1879), 426.

12. McWhorter, *Yellow Wolf*, p. 108.

13. *Historical Reprints,* Item No. 20, p. 12.

14. *Ibid.,* Item No. 25, p. 14.

15. *Ibid.,* Item No. 21, p. 13. A telegram from Assistant Adjutant General R. C. Drum, Division of Missouri, Chicago, dated July 21, ordered Gibbon into the campaign. (Document No. 4392-77; A.G.O. 3464-77, National Archives.)

Chapter 10

1. Different statements have been made about this vendor of liquor. McWhorter states that he was a blacksmith; Amos Buck states that some liquor was purchased in the stores owned by Jerry Fahy and a Mr. Reeves.

2. Amos Buck, "The Nez Perce Campaign," *Great Falls Tribune,* January 14, 1945.

3. Report from James L. Clearly to the *Idaho Semi-Weekly World* (Idaho City), August 21, 1877. Amos Buck states that some of the settlers who visited a Nez Perce camp saw a white girl about sixteen years old living with them.

4. L. V. McWhorter, *Yellow Wolf: His Own Story* (Caldwell, Ida.: The Caxton Printers, 1940), p. 109.

5. *Ibid.,* p. 110.

6. John H. Raftery, *The Story of Yellowstone* (Butte, 1912), p. 67.

7. A letter by A. Plummer, written to the editor of *Recreation* and published in that magazine in July, 1923.

8. *Wallace Press Times* (Wallace, Ida.), September 4, 1921.

9. A statement given to the author by Moses Chaffin on July 11, 1945.

10. Alva J. Noyes, The Battle of the Big Hole as I Saw It (MS in Montana Historical Society, Helena).

11. The story was related to the author by Moses Chaffin on July 11, 1945.

12. Ella C. Hathaway, "Battle of the Big Hole as Told by T. C. Sherrill," Yellowstone National Park Library, Mammoth, Wyoming.

13. Oliver O. Howard, *Nez Perce Joseph* (Boston: Lee and Shepard, 1881), p. 184.

14. *Ibid.,* p. 196.

Chapter 11

1. Alva J. Noyes, The Battle of the Big Hole as I Saw It (MS in Montana Historical Society, Helena), p. 4. Sherrill also related this conversation to Will Cave, who quoted it in his account in the *Wallace Press Times,* September 4, 1921.

2. L. V. McWhorter, *Yellow Wolf: His Own Story* (Caldwell,

Ida.: The Caxton Printers, 1940), p. 111; also, L. V. McWhorter, *Hear Me, My Chiefs* (Caldwell, Ida.: The Caxton Printers, 1952), p. 368; Angus McDonald, The Nez Perce Campaign (MS in Montana Historical Society, Helena).

3. McWhorter, *Hear Me, My Chiefs*, p. 369.

4. *Ibid.*

5. Cyrus T. Brady, *Northwestern Fights and Fighters* (New York: The McClure Co., 1907), p. 173. Although no documentary proof has been found, the charge persists that some of Gibbon's men secretly fortified themselves with liquor against the cold and the impending battle.

6. C. A. Woodruff, *The Battle of the Big Hole* (Contributions to the Historical Society of Montana, Vol. VII [Helena, 1910]), p. 189. Also, McWhorter, *Yellow Wolf*, p. 127.

7. In a telegram to Terry, Gibbon stated, "The surprise was complete and many were killed in the tepees or running out. Forty (40) dead Indians were counted on about one-half the battlefield." (Document No. 4989-77; A.G.O. 3464-77, National Archives.)

8. Woodruff, *The Battle of the Big Hole.*

9. McWhorter, *Yellow Wolf*, pp. 120, 125.

10. McWhorter, *Hear Me, My Chiefs*, p. 383. A Nez Perce poet wrote a song concerning the Rainbow-Pahkatos incident:

> Gone is the Rain-bow, my War-time brother,
> Bravest in Battle, kindliest in Peace.
> Falling where the fighting raged,
> Why was I not there?
> By compact, both our fathers died in war,
> And likewise this day their sons.
>
> Changed as water is my warrior-power,
> And I, "Pah-ka-tos," now yearns for death.
>
> From the Night-trail my "war-mate" calls me,
> And I answer, "YES!"
>
> Tis well. Better this than bondage;
> For the oppressor's hand is iron.
>
> I go, again not to return.
>
> Sad Brothers, Weeping Sisters, Farewell!

11. Noyes, The Battle of the Big Hole, p. 7.

12. Brady, *Northwestern Fights*, p. 25.

13. C. R. Noyes, "Details of the Indian War," *Great Falls Tribune*, February 16, 1936. Also, Will Cave, "Interesting Narratives," *Wallace Press Times*, September 11, 1921.

14. This information was given to the author on July 11, 1945, by Moses Chaffin in Corvallis, Montana.

15. J. T. Van Orsdale, *Annual Report to the Assistant-Adjutant General*, Department of Dakota, September 30, 1877. Document No. 4085, Box 13, National Archives.

16. John Gibbon, Report of the Battle of the Big Hole, with the List of Killed and Wounded, Document No. 3595 DD 1877, National Archives.

17. John B. Catlin, *The Battle of the Big Hole* (Montana State Historian's Annual Report [Missoula, 1927]), p. 12.

18. Colonel Rice invented the trowel bayonet while he was serving in the Department of Dakota. This rifle attachment was just as effective in battle as the saber bayonet, and it could be used almost as well as a small shovel in digging rifle pits.

19. Depressions tracing the trench lines constitute an interesting evidence of the siege ground. Trees marked by bullets formerly attracted attention, but they have mostly died and been removed.

20. Charles E. S. Wood, "Chief Joseph, the Nez Percé," *The Century Magazine*, XXVIII (May, 1884), 139.

21. McWhorter, *Yellow Wolf*, p. 151.

22. John Gibbon, "The Battle of the Big Hole," *Harper's Weekly*, Vol. XXXIX (December 28, 1895).

23. Noyes, The Battle of the Big Hole, p. 26.

24. McWhorter, *Yellow Wolf*, p. 129. T. C. Sherrill concurs with Yellow Wolf in saying, "I could see that they were badly crippled up from the number of wounded they had tied to the horses. The squaws were very busy." (Noyes, The Battle of the Big Hole, p. 117.)

25. Noyes, The Battle of the Big Hole, p. 10.

26. Gibbon, Report of the Battle of the Big Hole.

27. Woodruff, *The Battle of the Big Hole*. Also described in Brady, *Northwestern Fights*, p. 186. L. V. McWhorter could not get any information from Nez Perce sources confirming the fire incident. On September 4, 1943, the author received this statement from him: "The 'Death Song,' the attempted 'Burning Out,' and several other items of that day's fight, *was not!*" In spite of this positive statement, the author believes that a fire was started. He cannot disregard the statement from several sources.

28. McWhorter, *Yellow Wolf*, p. 156.

29. *Ibid.*, p. 157.

30. *Helena Weekly Independent*, August 9, 1877.

31. *Montana Standard* (Butte), March 1, 1931. John M. Evans describes seeing Edwards ride into Deer Lodge.

32. Oliver O. Howard, *Nez Perce Joseph* (Boston: Lee and Shepard, 1881), p. 203.

33. *Ibid.*, p. 208.

Chapter 12

1. John Gibbon, Report of the Battle of the Big Hole, Document No. 5884-77; A.G.O. 3464-77, National Archives.

2. Albert G. Forse, "Chief Joseph as a Commander," *Winners of the West*, No. 12 (November, 1936).

3. Chief Joseph, "An Indian's Views of Indian Affairs," *North American Review*, CXXVIII (April, 1879), 427.

4. L. V. McWhorter, *Yellow Wolf: His Own Story* (Caldwell, Ida.: The Caxton Printers, 1940), p. 159.

5. L. V. McWhorter, *Hear Me, My Chiefs* (Caldwell, Ida.: The Caxton Printers, 1952), p. 403.

6. Chief Joseph, "An Indian's Views," p. 427.

7. J. A. Harrington told this to the author in an interview on September 4, 1958, basing his report upon information received from Howard, Stevens, Ed Cramer, and others. Big Lake Creek camp was located eighteen miles from the battlefield and a mile from the mouth of Nez Perce Canyon.

8. McWhorter, *Yellow Wolf*, p. 159.

9. In 1923, when Thorn Christensen visited this area, there were seventy-five stone-pile rifle pits. Twenty years later, the author found thirty-three intact. The author visited the area and took pictures of these stone-pile pits in August, 1945.

10. McWhorter, *Hear Me, My Chiefs*, p. 405.

11. *Ibid.* Also, Oliver O. Howard, *Nez Perce Joseph* (Boston: Lee and Shepard, 1881), p. 251.

12. Gibbon, Report of the Battle of the Big Hole. The officers were Captains Charles C. Rawn, Richard Comba, George L. Browning, J. M. J. Sanno, Constant Williams (wounded twice), and William Logan (killed); First Lieutenants C. A. Coolidge (wounded three times), James H. Bradley (killed), J. W. Jacobs, Regimental Quartermaster, Allen H. Jackson, George H. Wright, and William L. English (mortally wounded); and Second Lieutenants C. A. Woodruff, Acting Adjutant J. T. Van Orsdale (wounded three times), E. E. Hardin, and Francis Woodbridge.

A singular fact noted was that all of the officers who were killed or wounded were married. *Montana Standard* (Butte), August 10, 1958, stated that Congress awarded Medals of Honor to the following men for distinguished service in the Battle of the Big Hole: Captain James Jackson; Sergeants William D. Edwards and Milden H. Wilson; Privates Wilfred Clark, Lorenzo Brown, and John McLennon.

13. Howard, *Nez Perce Joseph*, p. 203. After being briefed upon the battle, Howard referred to the hostiles as "this most enterprising band of Indians." (Document No. 6718-77; A.G.O. 3464-77, National Archives.)

14. The doctors were Mitchell, Deer Lodge; James W. Wheelock and O. B. Whitford, Butte; and Reese and Steele, Helena.

15. *Wallace Press Times* (Wallace, Idaho), August 14, 1921.

16. Gibbon, Report of the Battle of the Big Hole.

17. McWhorter, *Hear Me, My Chiefs*, p. 382.

18. Gibbon, Report of the Battle of the Big Hole.

19. John B. Catlin, *The Battle of the Big Hole* (Montana State Historian's Annual Report [Missoula, 1927]), p. 14.

20. *Wallace Press Times* (Wallace, Idaho), September 11, 1921.

21. McWhorter, *Yellow Wolf*, p. 133.

22. *Montana Standard*, March 1, 1931.

23. *New Northwest* (Deer Lodge), August 21, 1877.

24. Angus McDonald, The Nez Perce Campaign (MS in Montana Historical Society, Helena), p. 4.

25. Catlin, *The Battle of the Big Hole*, p. 14.

26. Alva J. Noyes, The Battle of the Big Hole as I Saw It (MS in Montana Historical Society, Helena), p. 25.

27. *Butte Miner*, August 21, 1877. It should be noted that many volunteers were favorably impressed by Howard. The following statement, signed by ten men led by Thomas Stuart, appeared in the *New Northwest*, August 24, 1877: "In our intercourse with Gen. Howard, we found him thoroughly kind, courteous and gentlemanly. We regret that any reports should have been circulated to the contrary and trust that this statement may have the effect of preventing any such in the future."

28. *Helena Weekly Independent*, August 23, 1877.

29. *New Northwest* (Deer Lodge), August 17, 1877.

30. A telegram from Sherman to McDowell, sent to Howard on June 26, 1877. See U.S. Congress, Senate, Claims of the Nez Perce Indians (Washington, D.C.: Government Printing Office, 1900), 56th Congress, 1st Session, Senate Document No. 257, p. 10.

31. Howard to Assistant Adjutant General, Military Division of the Pacific, August 14, 1877.

32. Forse, "Chief Joseph as a Commander."

33. Howard, *Nez Perce Joseph*, p. 210.

34. Noyes, The Battle of the Big Hole, p. 24.

35. Frank H. Garver, A Visit to the Big Hole Battlefield Told by Amede Bassette (MS in Montana Historical Society, Helena).

36. Charlotte M. Kirkwood, *The Nez Perce Indian War under Chiefs Joseph and Whitebird* (Grangeville, Ida.: Idaho County Free Press, 1928), p. 23. Toohoolhoolzote was killed in the Battle of the Bear Paws.

37. *Early Days at Fort Missoula*, ed. A. E. Rothermich (Missoula: University of Montana, 1936), p. 7.

38. L. V. McWhorter to Mrs. Flora Hirschy, November 23, 1938.

Chapter 13

1. Bloody Dick Creek was named for an Englishman whose byword was "bloody." Obviously his first name was Dick. Alva J. Noyes, who gave this explanation, did not mention a surname.

2. *Dillon Examiner*, October 23, 1940.

3. Mattie T. Cramer, "Sky Pilot Turns Scout," *Dillon Examiner*, March 27, 1940.

4. Mrs. James Mansfield, Sr., related this detail to Merrill D. Beal on August 28, 1945.

5. James Mansfield and Mike Herr eluded the scouts. The latter hid in a beaver dam.

6. L. V. McWhorter, *Yellow Wolf: His Own Story* (Caldwell, Ida.: The Caxton Printers, 1940), p. 162.

7. *Ibid.*, p. 174.

8. Colonel Shoup not only kept in close touch with Howard, he also sent and received messages from Con Brag, Sheriff of Beaverhead County, Bannack City, Montana. Copies of these messages are filed in the Idaho Historical Society, Boise, Idaho.

9. A note from Egbert Nasholds, at the Lemhi agency, to Colonel Shoup, August 13, 1877. Captain Augustus Bainbridge, who visited the Lemhi Reservation on June 27, 1877, found the Indians anxious but loyal. (Letter from Bainbridge to Assistant Adjutant General, Document No. 4140-77; A.G.O. 3464-77, National Archives.)

10. H. C. McCreery, Reminiscences of the Nez Perce War in 1877 in Idaho Territory (MS No. 398, in Idaho State College Historical Archives), p. 6.

11. *Ibid.*, p. 5.

12. Albert G. Forse, "Chief Joseph as a Commander," *Winners of the West*, No. 12 (November, 1936).

13. This account was related to Merrill D. Beal by George F. Shoup on February 26, 1950. Shoup heard Lyon's report in August, 1877.

14. Helen Addison Howard and Dan L. McGrath, *War Chief Joseph* (Caldwell, Ida.: The Caxton Printers, 1935), p. 225.

15. Letter from Danielson to J. Q. Smith, Document No. 5390-77; A.G.O. 3464-77, National Archives.

16. Document No. 5081-77; A.G.O. 3464-77, National Archives. Telegram from Sheridan to Townsend, August 18, 1877, Document No. 5164-77; A.G.O. 3464-77, National Archives.

17. Telegram from Patten to Smith, Document No. 5593-77; A.G.O. 3464-77, National Archives.

18. *New Northwest* (Deer Lodge), August 24, 1877. Also, *Salt Lake Tribune*, August 16, 1942.

19. Charles E. S. Wood, "Indian Epic Is Re-told," *The Spectator,* September 14, 1929.

20. *Helena Daily Independent,* June 15, 1896. A report written to Frank T. Conway.

21. Oliver O. Howard, *Nez Perce Joseph* (Boston: Lee and Shepard, 1881), p. 225.

22. *Ibid.*

23. Present-day Sheridan Creek. General Sheridan visited this area on August 30, 1881, and the creek was named in his honor at that time.

Chapter 14

1. L. V. McWhorter, *Yellow Wolf: His Own Story* (Caldwell, Ida.: The Caxton Printers, 1940), p. 166.

2. Oliver O. Howard, *Nez Perce Joseph* (Boston: Lee and Shepard, 1881), p. 226.

3. *Dillon Examiner,* September 3, 1941.

4. Howard, *Nez Perce Joseph,* p. 226.

5. *Helena Daily Independent,* June 15, 1896. An account of the "Indian War," dealing with the service of the Virginia City volunteers in the fight at Camas Meadows, appeared in *The Madisonian* published at Virginia City, August 25, 1877. This account contains a roster of those who composed the company. (Document No. 5816-77; A.G.O. 3464-77, National Archives.)

6. McWhorter, *Yellow Wolf,* p. 168. Various estimates exist concerning the number of mules taken. Howard states that about one hundred were driven away, but about one-third were recovered. (Document No. 5282-77; A.G.O. 3464-77, National Archives.)

7. *Helena Daily Independent,* June 15, 1896.

8. Randolph Norwood, Report to Colonel John Gibbon, written on Upper Madison River, August 24, 1877. (Document No. 3754 DD 1877, National Archives.)

9. Howard, *Nez Perce Joseph,* p. 228.

10. *Ibid.,* p. 224. When Howard found Norwood, heard his report and surveyed the situation, he seemed satisfied with what had been done. In a letter to Gibbon, Howard states, "Captain Norwood behaved most gallantly and did grand service." (Document No. 6154-77; A.G.O. 3464-77, National Archives.)

11. Norwood, Report.

12. Elvin W. Henninger homesteaded the meadow tract in which the battle started. He has done more than anyone else in rescuing this battle situation from near oblivion. He is also the source of a legend that a Nez Perce woman named Ta-ha-ya-ya, although in pain from a wound received at the Big Hole, joined in the battle of Camas Meadows.

13. McWhorter, *Yellow Wolf,* p. 168.

14. *Ibid.*

15. Norwood, Report.
16. McWhorter, *Yellow Wolf*, p. 169.

Chapter 15

1. Major Charles Moody gave this information to the author on August 26, 1923.

2. L. V. McWhorter, *Yellow Wolf: His Own Story* (Caldwell, Ida.: The Caxton Printers, 1940), p. 189.

3. The *New Northwest*, September 14, 1877.

4. S. G. Fisher, *Chief of Scouts to General Howard during the Nez Perce Campaign* (Contributions to the Historical Society of Montana). Helena: State Publishing Co., 1896, II, 270. This pass has been called Tasher, Tagie, Ti-gee, and Targhee. It was named for the Bannock Chief Tagi. An Idaho village is also named for him, but it is spelled Tyhee.

5. Howard was greatly disappointed over Bacon's failure to blockade the Nez Perces at Targhee Pass. On August 16, he had sent a telegram to McDowell from Red Rock Station, Montana, stating, "Think I shall be able to intercept the Indians for I am now nearer than they to the pass near Henry's Lake." (Document No. 6718-77; A.G.O. 3464-77, National Archives.)

6. Oliver O. Howard, *Nez Perce Joseph* (Boston: Lee and Shepard, 1881), p. 234.

7. *Bozeman Times*, August 30, 1877.

8. *Dillon Examiner*, September 3, 1941. Also, *Great Falls Tribune*, January 25, 1945.

9. Brisbin, commanding at Fort Ellis, to Assistant Adjutant General, Department of Dakota, October 23, 1877, Document 4263 DD 1877, Box 23, National Archives.

10. Telegrams from Howard to Sherman; also Sherman to Sheridan. Nez Perce Claims 66, Box 1181, National Archives.

11. Telegrams from McDowell to Howard; Sheridan to McDowell; Sheridan to Terry; and Williams to McDowell. Documents No. 6718-77 and No. 5233-77; A.G.O. 3464-77, National Archives.

12. Fort Ellis, Headquarters, August 26, 1877. Document 3479 DD 1877, National Archives.

13. Document 3983 DD 1877, Box 23, National Archives.

14. A letter from Sturgis to Potts, from a camp on Yellowstone River, near the mouth of the Still-Water (*sic*), August 23, 1877. Paul C. Phillips, *Historical Reprints* (Sources of Northwest History, No. 8 [Missoula: University of Montana, 1929]), Item No. 30, p. 19.

15. Nelson A. Miles, *Serving the Republic* (New York: Harper and Brothers, 1911), p. 172.

16. Letter from Sherman to Howard, written in Helena, August

29, 1877, to be delivered to Howard by Colonel Gilbert. Document 3983 DD 1877, Box 23, National Archives.

17. Howard, *Nez Perce Joseph*, p. 237.

Chapter 16

1. Heister D. Guie and L. V. McWhorter (eds.), *Adventures in Geyser Land* (Caldwell, Ida.: The Caxton Printers, 1935), p. 279. George F. Cowan was born in Ohio in 1842. He was with the first volunteers during the Civil War and attained the rank of sergeant. At this time he was one of Montana's leading attorneys.

2. Chester A. Fee, *Chief Joseph: The Biography of a Great Indian* (New York: Wilson-Erickson, 1936), p. 218.

3. Guie and McWhorter, *Adventures in Geyser Land*, p. 223.

4. Edwin J. Stanley, *Rambles in Wonderland* (New York: D. Appleton and Co., 1878), p. 166.

5. Chester A. Fee, *Chief Joseph*, p. 223.

6. Guie and McWhorter, *Adventures in Geyser Land*, p. 225. George F. Cowan's experiences were so peculiar that one is puzzled to know whether he was the most lucky or unlucky of men. A train of incidents followed his suffering in the park. Near Fort Ellis the neck yoke broke, and the Cowan party was thrown out of the carriage. At Bozeman, when Mr. Arnold was dressing Cowan's wounds in the hotel room, the bedstead gave way and down went the injured man.

7. Andrew J. Weikert, *Journal of a Tour through Yellowstone National Park in August and September 1877* (Contributions to the Historical Society of Montana, IV [Helena, 1900]), 185–99.

8. H. M. Chittenden, *Yellowstone National Park*, p. 142. Stewart was relieved of $260 and a watch.

9. S. G. Fisher, "A Scout for General Howard." Ogden *Daily Pilot*, October 18, 1891. This article and Fisher's diary are in the possession of Mrs. Robert Gregg, Dillon, Montana.

10. *Ibid.* Fisher's services are also described in an article entitled *Chief of Scouts to General Howard during the Nez Perce Campaign* (Contributions to the Historical Society of Montana). Helena: State Publishing Co., 1896.

Chapter 17

1. Sturgis had six companies, Hart had five, and Merritt had ten.

2. On August 29, Sherman sent Howard a letter from Helena confirming these assignments and positions. The letter also included this advice: "I don't want to order you back to Oregon, but I do say you can with perfect propriety return to your command, leaving the troops to continue 'till the Nez Perces have been destroyed or captured, and I authorize you to transfer to him, Lt.

Col. Gilbert, your command in the field. . . ." Since Colonel Gilbert failed to overtake Howard, the matter did not come to a head. (Document No. 6436-77; A.G.O. 3464-77, National Archives.) A telegram from Sheridan to Townsend, Chicago, August 28, gives further details upon the position of troops: "Merritt at Camp Brown nine (9) companies of cavalry; Major Hart on Tongue River five (5) companies of Fifth (5) Cavalry. . . . Hart will move toward Stinking Water (Shoshone River) if Nez Perces do." (Document No. 5398-77; A.G.O. 3464-77, National Archives.)

3. S. G. Fisher, *Chief of Scouts to General Howard during the Nez Perce Campaign* (Contributions to the Historical Society of Montana). Helena: State Publishing Co., 1896, II, 270.

4. P. E. Byrne, *Soldiers of the Plains* (New York: Minton, Balch and Co., 1926), p. 198.

5. Two of Sturgis' scouts, named Groff and Leonard, and a Crow Indian boy were killed. Fisher discovered the bodies of two miners he identified as Oleson and Anderson from the Black Hills. Fisher also tells of a Nez Perce scout killed and scalped by members of his own scouting party. Redington came upon three dead miners, and one who was wounded.

6. L. V. McWhorter, *Yellow Wolf: His Own Story* (Caldwell, Ida.: The Caxton Printers, 1940), p. 184.

7. Helen Addison Howard and Dan L. McGrath, *War Chief Joseph* (Caldwell, Ida.: The Caxton Printers, 1935), p. 253.

8. General Sheridan expressed the ranking military opinion concerning this incident in a telegram to General Townsend, dated Chicago, October 1: "The Nez Perces should have been caught on the Clarks Fork trail, but there was blundering which enabled them to escape." (Document No. 6075-77; A.G.O. 3464-77, National Archives.)

9. McWhorter, *Yellow Wolf*, p. 183.

10. Fisher, *Chief of Scouts*, p. 277.

11. Oliver O. Howard, *Nez Perce Joseph* (Boston: Lee and Shepard, 1881), p. 255.

12. Oliver O. Howard, *My Life and Experiences among Our Hostile Indians* (Hartford, Conn.: A. D. Worthington and Co., 1907), p. 295.

13. Howard, *Nez Perce Joseph*, p. 255.

14. Howard's *Supplementary Report*, pp. 622–23, Document No. 6137-77; A.G.O. 3464-77, National Archives. Charles Erskine Scott Wood wrote the order to Colonel Miles to this effect: "The hostiles are regulating their speed by ours. I [Howard] will pace my march to not exceeding ten miles a day to enable you to get ahead of them. When you have done this, notify me immediately, and I will close up and support you." See *The Spectator*, September 14, 1929. Howard's insight concerning the Nez Perce plans is disclosed by this statement to Miles: "They will in all probability

. . . make all haste to join a band of hostile Sioux. . . . I earnestly request that you make every effort in your power to prevent the escape of the hostile band, and at least hold them in check until I can overtake them."

15. Theodore W. Goldin, "The Seventh Calvary at Canon Creek," in Cyrus Townsend Brady, *Northwestern Fights and Fighters* (New York: The McClure Co., 1907), p. 214.

16. McWhorter, *Yellow Wolf*, p. 194.

17. *Ibid.*, p. 185.

Chapter 18

1. A. F. Mulford, *Fighting Indians* (Corning, N.Y.: Paul L. Mulford, no date), p. 115.

2. L. V. McWhorter, *Yellow Wolf: His Own Story* (Caldwell, Ida.: The Caxton Printers, 1940), p. 185.

3. *Ibid.* On July 13, 1958, Lloyd Golden, a native of Laurel, Montana, told the author that considerable lead was found along the base of the rimrock, and the ledge had many holes where bullets had struck. Perhaps Teeto Hoonod was using Poker Joe's long-range Sharps rifle. It is said that this gun was buried at the night camp after this battle, because there was no more ammunition for it and the rifle weighed fifteen pounds. The warriors also had several long-range needle-guns with telescope sights, and one heavy Creedmore. H. M. ("Muggins") Taylor claimed that these rifles could shoot 1,300 yards.

4. Theodore W. Goldin to L. V. McWhorter. See McWhorter, *Yellow Wolf*, p. 187, note.

5. Oliver O. Howard, *Nez Perce Joseph* (Boston: Lee and Shepard, 1881), p. 257.

6. Tom Stout, *Montana, Its Story and Biography* (Chicago: American Historical Society, 1921), p. 362.

7. Yellow Wolf named Silooyan, Eeahlokoon, and Elaskolatat as the warriors who sustained wounds in this battle. L. V. McWhorter, *Hear Me, My Chiefs* (Caldwell, Ida.: The Caxton Printers, 1952), p. 465.

8. On July 13, 1958, Charles Zimmerman told the author that the bodies of two soldiers were uncovered in 1907 by a Northern Pacific Railroad crew building a line from Billings to Rapelje. The graves were at the mouth of Canyon Creek. The remains were removed to the Custer Battlefield.

9. McWhorter, *Hear Me, My Chiefs*, p. 466.

10. Sturgis to Howard, September 15. *Supplementary Report*, p. 627.

11. McWhorter, *Yellow Wolf*, p. 189.

12. *Ibid.*, p. 187. Howard sent a telegram to McDowell on September 16, stating: "Five Nez Perces killed and left on the field, indicating many wounded carried along. Compelled hostiles

to drop over six hundred horses." (Document No. 5938-77; A.G.O. 3464-77, National Archives.)

13. On August 30, 1877, Frost reported of his Indians "the prospect of capturing their (Nez Perces) fine ponies makes them willing to fight their former friends." (Document No. 6087-77; A.G.O. 3464-77, National Archives.)

14. On July 13, 1958, a sandstone monument was dedicated upon the Canyon Creek Battlefield, under the auspices of the Yellowstone Historical Society. Speakers for the occasion included Walter C. Nye, Fred C. Krieg, Campbell Calvert, Peter Yegen, William M. Kirkpatrick, and Dr. Merrill D. Beal. Each explained a facet of the campaign or battle. A bronze plaque bears the following legend:

CANYON CREEK BATTLE
September 13, 1877

Soldiers were elements from the Seventh and First Cavalry and the Fourth Artillery. Col. Samuel D. Sturgis, commanding. Casualties: Three dead, eleven wounded.

Indians engaged were the Nez Perce tribe, escaping from their reservation and fleeing to Canada. Leader, Chief Joesph.

The Indians crossed the Yellowstone River, east of Laurel, burned a stage station on Canyon Creek and cut spokes from a stagecoach's wheels for use as quirt handles. They proceeded to this point, where they met and fought the Sturgis command in the area south of this marker.

Yellowstone Historical Society, 1958

Chapter 19

1. Letter from Miles to Howard, dated September 17, 1877. After describing the line of march he proposed to follow, Miles stated: ". . . request that the movement of my command be kept as secret as possible. . . ." (Howard's *Supplementary Report,* A.G.O. 3464-77, National Archives, p. 53.)

2. Francis Haines, *The Nez Perce Tribesmen of the Columbia Plateau* (Norman, Okla.: University of Oklahoma Press, 1955), p. 271.

3. Oliver O. Howard, *Nez Perce Joseph* (Boston: Lee and Shepard, 1881), p. 264.

4. J. W. Redington, "Scouting in Montana in the 1870's," *Frontier,* XIII (November, 1932), 62.

5. C. T. Stranahan, "Aftermath of the Nez Perce War," *Lewiston Morning Tribune,* April 16, 1933.

6. Oscar O. Mueller, "Surrender of Nez Perces," *Lewiston Daily News,* March 2, 1948. Yellow Wolf had an unfortunate experience in the Judith Basin area while hunting mountain sheep, accidentally wounding his own horse. This put him on foot, and

in returning to the caravan, he came upon four white campers. In quest of hospitality, he received a command to stop, which he disregarded. His forward movement caused the men to shoot at him. One bullet grazed his arm. He charged them, injured two, and took four horses. He justified his conduct in saying: "Those men spoke war when they drew their guns. I understood that meaning." L. V. McWhorter, *Yellow Wolf: His Own Story* (Caldwell, Ida.: The Caxton Printers, 1940), p. 197.

7. The Indians called this Missouri River ford "Seloselo Wejanivais," meaning a kind of colored paint.

8. *New Northwest*, October 12, 1877.

9. Narrative of Peopeo Tholekt, McWhorter Northwest Pacific 16, State College of Washington, Pullman, Washington, p. 62.

10. Gibbon to Sheridan, Document No. 6126-77; A.G.O. 3464-77, National Archives.

11. L. V. McWhorter, *Hear Me, My Chiefs* (Caldwell, Ida.: The Caxton Printers, 1952), p. 473.

12. *Ibid.*, p. 478.

13. McWhorter, *Yellow Wolf*, p. 204. Yellow Wolf said, "We knew General Howard was more than two suns back on the trail. It was nothing hard to keep ahead of him."

14. Howard, *Nez Perce Joseph*, p. 263.

15. *Ibid.*

16. *Ibid.*, p. 264. Nothwithstanding Howard's display of energy, speed, and determination during this phase of the pursuit, the *Helena Weekly Independent* of October 4 stated: "The impression is strengthening that the sword is too horny an implement for Howard to handle."

Chapter 20

1. Letter from Howard to Miles, September 12, 1877. Howard's *Supplementary Report*, A.G.O. 3464-77, National Archives, p. 45.

2. Letter from Miles to the Assistant Adjutant General, Department of Dakota, written October 6, 1877, from camp in the Bear Paw Mountains. National Archives.

3. Letter from J. J. Healy to *Benton Record*, from the Bear Paws battlefield. Published October 12, 1877. Also, L. A. Noblett, letter concerning the Bear Paws battle (in Montana Historical Society, Helena).

4. Letter from Miles to Terry, September 24, 1877, from camp at the mouth of Squaw Creek on Missouri River.

5. *Helena Weekly Independent*, October 11, 1877.

6. Nelson A. Miles, *Personal Recollections and Observations of General Nelson A. Miles* (New York: The Werner Co., 1897), p. 271.

7. C. R. Noyes, *Great Falls Tribune*, February 16, 1936.

8. J. J. Healy, *Benton Record*, October 12, 1877.

Chapter 21

1. C. R. Noyes, The Last Stand, or The Battle of the Bear Paws (MS in Yellowstone National Park Library, Mammoth, Wyoming), p. 9.

2. Francis Haines, *The Nez Perce Tribesmen of the Columbia Plateau* (Norman, Okla.: University of Oklahoma Press, 1955), p. 274.

3. Helen Addison Howard and Dan L. McGrath, *War Chief Joseph* (Caldwell, Ida.: The Caxton Printers, 1935), pp. 271–72. Also, Miles's Report to the Assistant Adjutant General, Department of Dakota, October 6, 1877. (Document No. 6646-77; A.G.O. 3464-77, National Archives.)

4. L. V. McWhorter, *Yellow Wolf: His Own Story* (Caldwell, Ida.: The Caxton Printers, 1940), pp. 205–6.

5. Howard and McGrath, *War Chief Joseph*, p. 271.

6. *Ibid.*

7. Chief Joseph, "An Indian's Views of Indian Affairs," *North American Review*, CXXVIII (April, 1879), 428.

8. Usher L. Burdick and Eugene D. Hart, *Jacob Horner and the Indian Campaigns of 1876–1877* (Baltimore: Wirth Brothers, 1942), p. 23.

9. Noyes, "Shambow's Story," in The Last Stand, p. 11.

10. L. V. McWhorter, *Hear Me, My Chiefs* (Caldwell, Ida.: The Caxton Printers, 1952), p. 485.

11. *Ibid.*, p. 486.

12. McWhorter, *Yellow Wolf*, p. 212.

13. McWhorter, *Hear Me, My Chiefs*, p. 495. The sharpshooter who received credit for killing Looking Glass was a scout named Milan Tripp. C. R. Noyes said he received information from a warrior named Many Wounds that Looking Glass was struck down by a piece of shrapnel. See the *Great Falls Tribune*, February 16, 1936. Chester A. Fee stated that Looking Glass was killed by the sentinels while attempting to get by them and escape to Canada. (*Chief Joseph: The Biography of a Great Indian* [New York: Wilson-Erickson, 1936], p. 259.)

14. Miles, Report to the Assistant Adjutant General, October 6, 1877.

15. Francis Haines, *Nez Perce Tribesmen*, p. 277. McWhorter reached the same conclusion: "The Nez Perces had little to gain by opening negotiations for surrender; their salvation lay in holding out until help could arrive from the Sioux in Canada. Miles, impatient to terminate the fight successfully, probably asked for the parley." (*Hear Me, My Chiefs*, p. 488.)

16. McWhorter, *Hear Me, My Chiefs*, p. 489.

17. Howard and McGrath, *War Chief Joseph*, p. 278.

18. McWhorter, *Yellow Wolf*, pp. 217–18.

19. *Ibid.*

20. Chief Joseph, "An Indian's Views," p. 429.

21. U.S. Department of War, *Report of the Secretary of War, 1877*, I, 630. (Quoting General O. O. Howard.)

22. Chester A. Fee, *Chief Joseph*, p. 324.

23. *Ibid.*, p. 326.

24. General Howard's official report, December 27, 1877, in U.S. Department of War, *Report of the Secretary of War, 1877*, I, 630.

25. Concerning his remonstration to Howard, Lieutenant Wood wrote the following for *The Spectator*, September 14, 1929: "I stood in Howard's tent (which I shared) while he told Miles: 'I have not come to rob you of any credit. I know you are after a star, and I shall stand back and let you receive the surrender, which I am sure will take place tomorrow.' When Miles left the tent, I told General Howard I thought he made a mistake, for the regulations required the senior officer to assume command—that it was not fair to leave his own command out of the surrender. He laid his one hand on my shoulder and said: 'Wood, Miles was my aide-de-camp in the Civil War; as you all know I got him his first command. I trust him as I would trust you.'"

Chapter 22

1. L. V. McWhorter, *Yellow Wolf: His Own Story* (Caldwell, Ida.: The Caxton Printers, 1940), p. 222.

2. *Ibid.*

3. *Ibid.*, p. 223.

4. *Ibid.*, p. 224.

5. *Ibid.*, p. 225.

6. Alvin M. Josephy, Jr., "The Last Stand of Chief Joseph," *American Heritage*, IX (February, 1958), 80.

7. Oliver O. Howard, *Supplementary Report*, A.G.O. 3464-77, National Archives, p. 62.

8. Chief Joseph, "An Indian's Views of Indian Affairs," *North American Review*, CXXVIII (April 1, 1879), 429.

9. Oliver O. Howard, *Nez Perce Joseph* (Boston: Lee and Shepard, 1881), p. 273.

10. L. V. McWhorter, *Hear Me, My Chiefs* (Caldwell, Ida.: The Caxton Printers, 1952), p. 498. By this time Joseph had lost two wives and his brother Ollokot. His daughter had fled to Canada.

11. *Ibid.*

12. Francis Haines, *The Nez Perce Tribesmen of the Columbia Plateau* (Norman, Okla.: University of Oklahoma Press, 1955), pp. 279–80.

13. Character of Indian surrenders: The surrender of armies has often been the occasion for elaborate military protocol and fanfare. However, Indian capitulations were inevitably characterized by a lack of pomp and ceremony. Such surrenders were bound to be one-sided affairs. The hostiles lacked uniformity of dress, and their colorful ceremonial costumes were not likely to be available at the conclusion of an arduous campaign. Thus, surrendering Indians usually presented a nondescript, ragged appearance. Chief Joseph's surrender on the Bear Paw prairie was no exception, taking place among the shambles of a battlefield. Dead horses were both seen and smelled. A generally disheveled and grimy appearance was presented by all except a knot of officers who carried extra wearing apparel. The dead and wounded on both sides disclosed the stark misery of war. Resentment, frustration, defiance, and resignation produced an atmosphere of tremendous pathos. One of the spectators on this occasion was a wounded Cheyenne former chieftain named Hump. He had served Miles in this campaign, having killed two Nez Perces with his own hands. As he viewed Chief Joseph's surrender, he may have remembered the occasion when he made the following statement to Colonel Miles: "Alas! Alas! For my race, it is passing away." Then, after meditating a few moments, he took off his belt and gun and handed them to Miles. Then he pointed to his ponies and said, "Take them, I am no longer either a chief or a warrior." (*Avant Courier* [Bozeman, Montana], June 21, 1877.)

14. C. E. S. Wood, "An Indian Epic Is Re-told," *The Spectator,* September 14, 1929, p. 4. Also, letter from Wood to McWhorter, January 31, 1936, McWhorter NP 29, State College of Washington Archives, Pullman, Washington, pp. 19–20. Several versions of Joseph's actions incident to the surrender were given by persons whose lack of proximity to the scene render their statements somewhat unreliable. Private Charles A. Smith and citizens William Bent, John Samples, and Frank J. Parker may have received the impression that Joseph deliberately insulted Howard in either refusing to tender his rifle to him or else offering it to him, muzzle first, in a menacing manner. These reports, unsupported by reference from the principals, are not very convincing. Wood's account is much more in keeping with Joseph's character.

15. McWhorter, *Hear Me, My Chiefs,* p. 498.

16. McWhorter, *Yellow Wolf,* p. 225.

17. *Ibid.,* p. 224.

18. In a letter to President Hayes, dated January 19, 1881, Miles wrote, "At the time of their surrender they (Nez Perces) were informed by me that it was the design of the Government to place them upon the small reservation in Idaho." (Document No. 1565-81; A.G.O. 3464-77, National Archives.)

19. McWhorter, *Yellow Wolf,* p. 224.

20. *Ibid.,* p. 229.

21. *Ibid.,* p. 226.

22. Howard, *Nez Perce Joseph,* p. 269.

23. McWhorter, *Hear Me, My Chiefs,* p. 499.

24. Albert G. Forse, "Chief Joseph as a Commander," *Winners of the West,* No. 12 (November, 1936).

25. Letter from Chapman to Commissioner E. A. Hayt, December 19, 1878, Document No. 8978-78; A.G.O. 3464-77, National Archives.

26. McWhorter, *Hear Me, My Chiefs,* p. 499.

27. McWhorter, *Yellow Wolf,* p. 229.

28. Nelson A. Miles, *Personal Recollections and Observations of General Nelson A. Miles* (New York: The Werner Co., 1897), p. 276.

29. *Benton Record,* October 12, 1877.

30. Charlotte M. Kirkwood, *The Nez Perce Indian War under Chiefs Joseph and Whitebird* (Grangeville, Ida.: Idaho County Free Press, 1928), p. 27. Mrs. James Dorrity recorded an example of Gros Ventre cruelty toward three Nez Perce men and two women escapees. She stated that an Indian named Long Horse and his associates took the Nez Perces captive and killed them. This crime was committed on a sandbar in the Milk River several miles west of present-day Chinook, Montana.

31. Miles to Terry, October 5, 1877, Document No. 6260-77; A.G.O. 3464-77, National Archives.

32. *Chicago Tribune,* October 25, 1877. Also, C. E. S. Wood, *The Spectator,* September 14, 1929.

33. Howard to Sheridan, October 25, 1877, Box 1183, National Archives.

34. Document No. 7113-77; A.G.O. 3464-77, National Archives.

35. Letter from Miles to the Assistant Adjutant General, Department of Dakota, written October 6, 1877, from camp in the Bear Paw Mountains, National Archives.

36. Howard, *Nez Perce Joseph,* p. 270.

37. C. R. Noyes, "Shambow's Story," in The Last Stand, or The Battle of the Bear Paws (MS in Yellowstone National Park Library, Mammoth, Wyoming).

38. *Wallace Press Times,* September 18, 1921.

39. Nelson A. Miles, *Serving the Republic* (New York: Harper and Brothers, 1911), p. 181.

40. *Butte Miner,* November 19, 1931.

41. *Great Falls Tribune,* February 16, 1936. The Lions Club, Daughters of the American Revolution, Emil Kopac, and James Griffin were the leaders in these projects.

42. *Boise Capital News,* November 19, 1931.

Chapter 23

1. U.S. Army *American Military History, 1607–1953* (R.O.T.C. Manual [Washington, D.C.: Government Printing Office, 1956]), p. 287.

2. Chief Joseph, "An Indian's Views of Indian Affairs," *North American Review*, CXXVIII (April, 1879), 429.

3. *Daily Bee Supplement* (Portland), November 11, 1877.

4. Cyrus Townsend Brady, *Northwestern Fights and Fighters* (New York: The McClure Co., 1907), p. 4.

5. Oliver O. Howard, *Nez Perce Joseph* (Boston: Lee and Shepard, 1881), pp. 273–74. Also *Supplementary Report*, A.G.O. 3464-77, National Archives, p. 68. Howard's average rate of travel was 17.61 miles per day. Exceptional marches included: Cavalry, 70 miles in two days, 155 miles in four days. Infantry, 31 miles in one day, 46 miles in one day. Entire command, 160 miles in seven consecutive days.

6. *Daily Bee Supplement* (Portland), November 11, 1877.

7. L. V. McWhorter, *Hear Me, My Chiefs* (Caldwell, Ida.: The Caxton Printers, 1952), p. 501.

8. James Truslow Adams, *Dictionary of American History* (New York: Charles Scribner's Sons, 1940), IV, 129.

9. U.S. Department of Interior, *Annual Report of the Secretary of Interior*, 1877, II, 108.

10. In this history, the casualties have been recorded as follows: White Bird battle: 2 Indians wounded; 34 whites killed and 4 wounded. Clearwater and Camas Prairie skirmishes: 3 Indians killed and 3 wounded; 14 whites killed and 3 wounded. Clearwater battle: 4 Indians killed and 6 wounded; 13 whites killed and 40 wounded. Big Hole battle: 87 Indians killed and about 30 wounded; 30 whites killed and 40 wounded. Camas Meadows skirmish: 2 Indians wounded; 3 whites killed and 5 wounded. Canyon Creek battle: 2 Indians wounded; 3 whites killed and 11 wounded. Deaths from Musselshell to Missouri: 3 Indians killed and 1 wounded. Cow Island skirmish: 1 Indian wounded; 1 white wounded. Bear Paws battle: 25 Indians killed and 46 wounded; 24 whites killed and 45 wounded. Total casualties: 122 Indians killed (including about 57 women and children), and about 93 wounded; 121 whites killed and 149 wounded. No one can ever know exactly how many Indians were killed and wounded, and yet one must place confidence in their own estimates because military estimates were never conclusive.

11. An accurate record of civilian deaths incident to the Nez Perce war is also elusive. For example, estimates concerning the settlers killed in the White Bird raids vary from 14 to 22. The names of 12 were listed in this monograph. Other civilians killed

during the campaign included: about 10 on Camas Prairie; 6 at the Big Hole and 4 wounded; 5 on Horse Prairie; 5 on Birch Creek; 2 in Yellowstone National Park, and 2 wounded; about 6 on the Clark Fork; and 3 north of Cow Island Crossing. Total killed, 49; total wounded, 6.

12. Chief Joseph, "An Indian's Views," p. 430.

13. Report of Henry C. Hodges, Deputy Quartermaster General to the Secretary of War, December 18, 1877. U.S. Congress, Senate, Report (Washington, D.C.: Government Printing Office, 1878), 45th Congress, 2nd Session, Senate Executive Document No. 14, p. 10. A cursory examination of the *Congressional Record* index covering 1878, 1879, and 1880 disclosed the fact that several bills were introduced pertaining to damages and expenses sustained by the people of Idaho and their government. Mr. Cockrell introduced a bill on April 29, 1878, "to provide for ascertaining and reporting the expenses incurred by the Territory of Idaho, and the people thereof, in defending themselves from attacks and hostilities of the Nez Perce Indians in the year 1877. . . ." On February 9, 1880, H.R. No. 4391 was introduced, to provide "for the relief of the citizens of Idaho and Washington Territories who served in connection with the United States troops in the war with the Nez Perce Indians, and for the relief of the heirs of such as were killed in such service." This bill was reported favorably on May 21, 1880.

14. *Daily Bee Supplement* (Portland), November 11, 1877.

15. Nelson A. Miles, *Personal Recollections and Observations of General Nelson A. Miles* (New York: The Werner Co., 1897), p. 51.

16. Howard, *Nez Perce Joseph*, p. 272.

17. C. E. S. Wood, "Chief Joseph, the Nez Percé," *The Century Magazine*, XXVIII (May, 1884), 142.

18. McWhorter, *Hear Me, My Chiefs*, pp. 501–2.

19. H. Hamlin, "The Chief Joseph Trek and Surrender," *The Pony Express*, September, 1947. Herbert Ravenel Sass wrote, "This Chief Joseph, whose face was curiously like Napoleon's, proved himself probably the most brilliant soldier the red race ever had." ("The Man Who Looked Like Napoleon," *Collier's*, September 21, 1940.)

20. Chester A. Fee, *Chief Joseph: The Biography of a Great Indian* (New York: Wilson-Erickson, 1936), p. 272.

21. *Ibid.*, p. 289.

22. *Ibid.*, p. 303. Joseph has had many detractors. It appears that as his prestige increased, especially after his own article was published, many citizens certified that he was a bad Indian. Arthur Chapman, who had posed as Joseph's friend, circulated the false story that Joseph participated in the White Bird raids. Indeed, he said that he killed Mrs. J. J. Manuel with his own hands.

23. Alvin M. Josephy, Jr., "The Last Stand of Chief Joseph," *American Heritage,* IX (February, 1958), 81.

24. L. V. McWhorter, *Yellow Wolf: His Own Story* (Caldwell, Ida.: The Caxton Printers, 1940), pp. 13–18.

25. Ned Bradford, *Battles and Leaders of the Civil War* (New York: Appleton-Century-Crofts, Inc., 1956), pp. 36, 54, 308, 326, 491, 506, 596.

26. *Dillon Examiner,* September 14, 1938.

27. The *Miles City Daily Star,* May 24, 1934, printed this item: "Nelson A. Miles was Commandant at Fort Keogh from 1876 to 1880. He was honored by the conferring of the military title of Brigadier General in recognition of his painstaking and successful campaigns against the wandering bands of Indians in the northwest, forcing them to surrender and return to their reservations. Miles City was named in his honor."

28. *Dictionary of American Biography* (New York: Charles Scribner's Sons, 1928), VII, 236.

29. George W. Cullum, *Biographical Register of the Officers and Graduates of West Point* (Boston: Houghton Mifflin Co., 1891), II, 280.

30. Francis B. Heitman, *Historical Register and Dictionary of the United States Army* (Washington, D.C.: Government Printing Office, 1903), I, 817.

31. Howard to Miles, October 7, 1877. U.S. Department of War, *Report of the Secretary of War, 1877,* I, 631. Also, Howard's *Supplementary Report,* A.G.O. 3464-77, National Archives, p. 63. Also, Document No. 8076-77; A.G.O. 3464-77, National Archives.

Chapter 24

1. Nelson A. Miles, *Personal Recollections and Observations of General Nelson A. Miles* (New York: The Werner Co., 1897), pp. 278–79.

2. On October 10, Sherman telegraphed this commendation from San Francisco: "Assure General Miles that we all fully approve the skill and activity of his command, which has brought to a favorable conclusion one of the most perplexing of our Indian wars." (Document No. 6286-77; A.G.O. 3464-77, National Archives.)

3. E. C. Watkins to J. Q. Smith, July 20, 1877. On September 3, 1877, Watkins wrote another letter to Smith, reaffirming the virtue of his exile plan. His word to the peaceful Nez Perces was at stake; they had been promised that all hostiles would be exiled. He said that white people would kill the warriors. On December 21, 1877, the United States Attorney General received notice from the Idaho Attorney General that indictments had been drawn against thirty Nez Perces for murders committed in Idaho. At-

torney General Devens sought Secretary McCrary's opinion and received this reply: "I do not suppose the Nez Perces are exempt from prosecution by the terms of their surrender in battle, but their understanding was that they were. As a tribe they have been severely punished." (Documents No. 180-78 and No. 6170-77; A.G.O. 3464-77, National Archives.)

4. Sherman to Sheridan, August 31, 1877, Box 1182, A.G.O. 5558, National Archives.

5. Miles to Hayt, Fort Keogh, October 10, 1878, Document No. 7688-78; A.G.O. 3464-77, National Archives.

6. Document No. 6564-77, A.G.O. 3464-77, National Archives.

7. Letter from Sherman to Sheridan, August 31, 1877: "Many of their leaders should be executed preferably by sentence in civil courts for their murders in Idaho and Montana, and what are left should be treated like the Modocs, . . ." (Document No. 5558-77; A.G.O. 3464-77, National Archives.)

8. C. E. S. Wood, "Chief Joseph, the Nez Percé," *The Century Magazine*, XXVIII (May, 1884), 142.

9. Sherman to E. D. Townsend, October 10, 1877, Box 1182 and Document No. 6286-77; A.G.O. 3464-77, National Archives.

10. Document No. 8978-78; A.G.O. 3464-77, National Archives. In fact, General Terry asserted that Howard lacked authority to assume command or issue orders to Miles, because their commands were not united. Howard claimed that they were actually united in terms of over-all situation. A heavy controversy was developing until Sherman intervened. (Documents No. 1579-78 and No. 1233-78; A.G.O. 3464-77, National Archives.)

11. Sherman to Townsend, Box 1182, A.G.O. 6286-77, National Archives.

12. Fred G. Bond, *Flatboating on the Yellowstone, 1877* (New York: New York Public Library, 1925).

13. *Ibid.,* p. 10.

14. Document No. 4753 DD 1877; Box 24, National Archives.

15. Bond, *Flatboating on the Yellowstone*, p. 15.

16. *Ibid.,* p. 19.

17. Document No. 7295-77; A.G.O. 3464-77, National Archives.

18. Documents No. 7266-77 and No. 7053-77; A.G.O. 3464-77, National Archives.

19. Bond, *Flatboating on the Yellowstone*, p. 21.

20. *Ibid.,* p. 22.

21. Chester A. Fee, *Chief Joseph: The Biography of a Great Indian* (New York: Wilson-Erickson, 1936), p. 274. Joseph's statement resembles one made by Red Cloud during his visit to the Black Hills, where he was hospitably entertained by his white friends. In bidding them good-bye he expressed the hope that, if they did not meet again on earth, they might meet beyond the

grave "in a land where white men ceased to be liars." See Helen Hunt Jackson, *A Century of Dishonor* (Boston: Roberts Brothers, 1887), p. 9.

22. Bond, *Flatboating on the Yellowstone*, p. 22.

23. Charlotte M. Kirkwood, *The Nez Perce Indian War under Chiefs Joseph and Whitebird* (Grangeville, Ida.: Idaho County Free Press, 1928), p. 35.

24. Chester A. Fee, *Chief Joseph*, p. 274.

25. Chief Joseph, "An Indian's Views of Indian Affairs," *North American Review*, CXXVIII (April, 1879), 430.

26. Miles to McCrary, U.S. Department of War, *Report of the Secretary of War, 1877*, p. 529.

27. Chief Joseph, "An Indian's Views," p. 430.

28. *Ibid.*

29. C. E. S. Wood, *The Spectator*, September 14, 1929.

30. Chester A. Fee, *Chief Joseph*, p. 276.

31. Sherman's Annual Report, U.S. Department of War, *Report of the Secretary of War, 1877*, I, 15. On December 4, 1877, General Pope certified that there were 87 men, 184 women and 147 children, making a total of 418 Nez Perces at Fort Leavenworth.

32. Colonel Rufus Saxton, though not solicited, wrote a strong letter supporting Miles's position. (Document No. 3507-78; A.G.O. 3464-77, National Archives.)

33. Chief Joseph, "An Indian's Views," p. 430. The deleterious effect of Nez Perce idleness was called to Sheridan's attention by General John Pope, Commanding at Fort Leavenworth, in a letter dated April 30, 1878. (Document No. 3173-78; A.G.O. 3464-77, National Archives.)

34. *Congressional Record*, May 7–8, 1878, 45th Congress, 2nd Session, VII, 3233–66. By March, 1878, Sherman was demanding action from the Bureau of Indian Affairs in regard to locating the Nez Perces. The army was paying more than two thousand dollars per month for their sustenance. (Documents, No. 1690-78 and No. 394-78; A.G.O. 3464-77, National Archives.)

35. Helen Addison Howard and Daniel McGrath, *War Chief Joseph* (Caldwell, Ida.: The Caxton Printers, 1935), pp. 296–97. By July 21, 21 Nez Perces had died, 260 were ill, and shortly thereafter the total number of fatalities exceeded 100.

36. U.S. Congress, Senate Report (Washington, D.C.: Government Printing Office, 1878), 45th Congress, 3rd Session, Senate Miscellaneous Document No. 53, II, 77.

Chapter 25

1. L. V. McWhorter, *Yellow Wolf: His Own Story* (Caldwell, Ida.: The Caxton Printers, 1940), pp. 135–36.

2. Mrs. James Dorrity, Mrs. James Dorrity's Story concerning

the Battle of the Bear Paws (MS in Idaho State College Historical Archives, Pocatello, Idaho).

3. Colonel Miles to the Assistant Adjutant General, Document No. 4352 DD 1877, National Archives. An unspecified number of warriors turned back on the Lolo Trail. Howard's men apprehended them when the war ended, and they were taken to Fort Vancouver as prisoners. Assured of their reform, Howard returned them to their families at Lapwai in April, 1878. In July, 1878, Miles discovered seven Nez Perces in a Crow camp at Terry's Landing. They were sent to the Indian Territory.

4. McWhorter, *Yellow Wolf*, pp. 234–36. This description of conditions does not agree with reports that reached Colonel Gibbon in December, 1877. He heard that the Nez Perces were being badly treated by the Sioux and they wished to return to Idaho. Gibbon wired Sheridan for instructions. (Document No. 7974-77; A.G.O. 3464-77, National Archives.)

5. The men who accompanied Baird were Yellow Bull, Bald Head, Eo-paw-yez, and Ben Clark. Concerning the Canadian Nez Perces, Baird wrote, "If I had had authority to promise to return them to Idaho, I think I could have brought in the entire band—twenty-five lodges." (Documents No. 5994-78 and No. 2608-78; A.G.O. 3464-77, National Archives.)

6. McWhorter, *Yellow Wolf*, p. 252.

7. *Ibid.*, p. 255. Also, see John K. Standish's account entitled "Hazardous Race of Nez Perce Jones," *Fallon County News*, Nov. 24, 1930.

8. McWhorter, *Yellow Wolf*, p. 253.

9. *Ibid.*, p. 263. See John Gibbon's account as it appears in U.S. Department of War, *Report of the Secretary of War, 1878*, p. 68. Eric Thane stated that Wallace and his men killed six of these Nez Perces and that the others were "hunted to death." This does not agree with Yellow Wolf's version in respect to the casualties. (*Dillon Examiner*, December 14, 1938, and Document No. 5835-78; A.G.O. 3464-77, National Archives.)

10. McWhorter, *Yellow Wolf*, p. 272. Also, Document No. 5578-78; A.G.O. 3464-77, National Archives.

11. Hancock to the Assistant Inspector General, August 2, 1878, in U.S. Department of War, *Report of the Secretary of War, 1878*, pp. 181–82. A party of nine, attempting to return to Idaho under the leadership of Tom Hill, a Delaware, was taken into custody by the Blackfoot Indian agent on August 17, 1878. These Indians were then taken to Fort Shaw and, finally, to the Indian Territory by Monteith. (Documents No. 7995-78, No. 7238-78, No. 7078-78; A.G.O. 3464-77, National Archives.)

12. McWhorter, *Yellow Wolf*, pp. 212, 289.

13. This tract of land was ceded to the Nez Perces in June, 1883. See Berlin B. Chapman, "Banishment of the Nez Perces,"

Daily Oklahomian, May 10, 1936, and November 20, 1910. Also, "Nez Perces in Indian Territory: An Archival Study," *Oregon Historical Quarterly,* Vol. I (June, 1949). This tract consisted of Townships 25 and 26 North, Range 1 West, and Townships 25 and 26, Range 2 West. The Cherokee Indians conveyed title to the government by deed on June 14, 1883.

14. U.S. Commissioner of Indian Affairs, *Annual Report of the Commissioner of Indian Affairs to the Department of the Interior, 1878,* pp. 33–34. Hayt became well acquainted with Joseph during the October tour. Hence, his opinion of him was well conceived. He said, "Joseph is one of the most gentlemanly and well-behaved Indians I ever met. He is bright and intelligent and is anxious for the welfare of his people."

15. L. V. McWhorter, *Hear Me, My Chiefs* (Caldwell, Ida.: The Caxton Printers, 1952), p. 534.

16. Clifford M. Drury, *Lewiston Morning Tribune,* October 18, 1936. Drury describes this as a thrilling episode in an otherwise barren period of Babylonian captivity.

17. Kate C. McBeth, *The Nez Perce Since Lewis and Clark* (New York: F. H. Revell, 1908), pp. 96–97.

18. L. V. McWhorter, *Research Studies of the State of Washington* (Pullman: Washington State University), XXVI, No. 4 (December, 1958), 217. A "Calendar of the McWhorter Papers" pertaining to the Nez Perces was printed in four issues of the *Research Studies:* June, 1952, No. 2; September, 1958, No. 3; December, 1958, No. 4; and March, 1959, No. 1 of Vol. XXVII.

19. Chief Joseph, "An Indian's Views of Indian Affairs," *North American Review,* CXXVIII (April, 1879), 431–32.

20. *Ibid.*

21. Chester A. Fee, *Chief Joseph: The Biography of a Great Indian* (New York: Wilson-Erickson, 1936), pp. 277–78.

22. *Council Fire,* Washington, D.C., October, 1879.

23. Chester A. Fee, *Chief Joseph,* p. 282.

24. Chief Joseph, "An Indian's Views," p. 432.

25. *Ibid.*

26. C. E. S. Wood, *The Spectator,* September 14, 1929.

27. J. Stanley Clark, "The Nez Percés in Exile," *Pacific Northwest Quarterly,* XXXVI (July, 1945), 229.

Chapter 26

1. Letter from Secretary Schurz to President Hayes, February 21, 1881. This was an important issue, because indictments were still pending against seventeen Nez Perces on docket of the First Judicial District Court in Idaho. (Documents No. 1945-82, No. 825-82; A.G.O. 3464-77, National Archives.)

2. Major Pearson, Post Commander at Fort Lapwai, concurred

in this opinion. (Document No. 6202-81; A.G.O. 3464-77, National Archives.)

3. U.S. Commissioner of Indian Affairs, *Annual Report of the United States Commissioner of Indian Affairs to the Department of the Interior, 1881*, p. 94.

4. Telegrams and letters from John B. Monteith, Henry M. Teller, H. Price, and Robert T. Lincoln, Document No. 2650-83; A.G.O. 3464-77, National Archives.

5. Kate C. McBeth, *The Nez Perce Since Lewis and Clark* (New York: F. H. Revell, 1908), pp. 99–100.

6. Chester A. Fee, *Chief Joseph: The Biography of a Great Indian* (New York: Wilson-Erickson, 1936), p. 287.

7. *Ibid.*, p. 285. Yellow Bull was quoted as saying, "Every time sun rises another Indian dead."

8. It should be noted that Joseph's twelve-year-old daughter, Kapkap Ponmi, escaped into Canada. She returned to Lapwai, where she entered the agency school. She was not permitted to live with Joseph at Nespelem. See L. V. McWhorter, *Yellow Wolf: His Own Story* (Caldwell, Ida.: The Caxton Printers, 1940), p. 288.

9. *Ibid.*, p. 290.

10. Mrs. C. F. Manning, The Nez Perce Indian War as I Knew It (MS in Idaho State College Historical Archives, Pocatello, Idaho).

11. McWhorter, *Yellow Wolf*, p. 292.

12. McBeth, *The Nez Perce*, pp. 97–98.

13. L. V. McWhorter, *Hear Me, My Chiefs* (Caldwell, Ida.: The Caxton Printers, 1952), p. 545.

14. McWhorter, *Yellow Wolf*, p. 290.

15. Francis Haines, *The Nez Perce Tribesmen of the Columbia Plateau* (Norman, Okla.: University of Oklahoma Press, 1955), p. 297.

16. Fee, *Chief Joseph*, p. 291.

17. *Ibid.*, p. 296.

18. *Ibid.*, p. 300.

19. *Montana Standard*, August 10, 1958.

20. *Idaho Statesman*, December 5, 1926.

21. Manning, The Nez Perce War as I Knew It.

22. Haines, *Nez Perce Tribesmen . . .*, pp. 297–99. Even Arthur Chapman was impelled to circulate falsehoods, wherein Joseph was accused of participating in the White Bird raids that started the war.

23. *Lewiston Daily News*, March 12, 1948.

24. *Wenatchee Daily World*, June 13, 1956.

BIBLIOGRAPHY

The description of the Nez Perces before the campaign of 1877 was based principally upon the following works: Francis Haines, *The Nez Perce Tribesmen of the Columbia Plateau;* Kate C. McBeth, *The Nez Perce Since Lewis and Clark;* Lucullus V. McWhorter, *Yellow Wolf* and *Hear Me, My Chiefs;* Archie Phinney, *Nez Perce Texts;* Henry Harmon Spalding, *The Diaries and Letters of Henry Harmon Spalding and Asa Browen Smith relating to the Nez Perce Mission, 1838–1842;* Herbert J. Spinden, *The Nez Perce Indians;* and H. Clay Wood, *The Status of Young Joseph and His Band of Nez Perce Indians, 1876.*

The McWhorter titles are also indispensable sources of Indian data concerning the campaign of 1877. Other valuable histories of the war include Cyrus Townsend Brady, *Northwestern Fights and Fighters;* Helen A. Howard and Dan L. McGrath, *War Chief Joseph;* and Oliver O. Howard, *Nez Perce Joseph,* together with his annual reports to the Assistant Adjutant General, Military Division of the Pacific, for 1877 and 1878.

The National Archives and Record Services supplied xerox reproductions of the Consolidated Correspondence File 3464-77, Adjutant General's Office, 1877–1878, which included miscellaneous documents relating to events during 1878–1885. Four rolls, including 312 documents (about 2,000 pages), are now available at the Idaho State College Library, Pocatello, Idaho.

Major Published Sources

Bruffey, George A. *Eighty-one Years in the West*. Butte: The Butte Miner Co., 1925.

Fee, Chester A. *Chief Joseph: The Biography of a Great Indian*. New York: Wilson-Erickson, 1936.

Ferris, Warren A. *Life in the Rocky Mountains*. Denver: Old West Publishing Co., 1940.

Howard, Oliver O. *My Life and Experiences among Our Hostile Indians*. Hartford, Conn.: A. D. Worthington Co., 1907.

Hunter, George. *Reminiscences of an Old Timer*. Battle Creek, Mich.: Review and Herald, 1889.

Marquis, Thomas B. *Memoirs of a White Crow Indian*. New York: The Century Co., 1928.

Miles, Nelson A. *Personal Recollections and Observations of General Nelson A. Miles*. New York: The Werner Co., 1897.

————. *Serving the Republic*. New York: Harper and Brothers, 1911.

Noyes, Alva J. *The Story of Ajax*. Helena: State Publicity Co., 1914.

Palmer, Joel, *Journal and Travels over the Rocky Mountains*. Cleveland: Arthur H. Clark, 1906.

Quaife, Milo M. *Yellowstone Kelley's Memoirs*. New Haven: Yale University Press, 1926.

Spalding, Henry Harmon. *The Diaries and Letters of Henry Harmon Spalding and Asa Browen Smith relating to the Nez Perce Mission, 1838–1842*, ed. Clifford M. Drury. Glendale, Calif.: Arthur H. Clark, 1958.

Thwaites, Reuben Gold. *The Original Journals of the Lewis and Clark Expedition, 1804–1806*. New York: Dodd, Mead, and Co., 1906.

Warren, Eliza Spalding. *Memoirs of the West*. Portland, Oregon: March Printing Co., 1916.

Special Books and Pamphlets

"Battle of the Big Hole, The," *Historical Reprints,* ed. Paul C. Phillips. (Sources of Northwest History, No. 8.) Missoula: University of Montana, 1929.

Bond, Fred G. *Flatboating on the Yellowstone, 1877.* New York: New York Public Library, 1925.

Bradford, Ned. *Battles and Leaders of the Civil War.* New York: Appleton-Century-Crofts, Inc., 1956.

Brady, Cyrus Townsend. *Northwestern Fights and Fighters.* New York: Doubleday, Doran Co., 1928.

Burdick, Usher L., and Eugene D. Hart. *Jacob Horner and the Indian Campaigns of 1876–1877.* Baltimore: Wirth Brothers, 1942.

Crawford, Mary M. *The Nez Perces Since Spalding.* Berkeley: Professional Press, 1936.

Cullum, George W. *Biographical Register of the Officers and Graduates of West Point.* Boston and New York: Houghton Mifflin Co., 1891.

Dictionary of American Biography. Vol. XVIII. New York: Charles Scribner's Sons, 1936.

Early Days at Fort Missoula, ed. A. E. Rothermich. Missoula: University of Montana, 1936.

Fisher, S. G. *Chief of Scouts to General Howard during the Nez Perce Campaign.* (Contributions to the Historical Society of Montana.) Helena: State Publishing Co., 1896.

Haines, Francis. *The Nez Perce Tribesmen of the Columbia Plateau.* Norman, Okla.: University of Oklahoma Press, 1955.

————. *Red Eagles of the Northwest.* Portland, Oregon: The Scholastic Press, 1939.

Howard, Helen Addison, and Dan L. McGrath. *War Chief Joseph.* Caldwell, Ida.: The Caxton Printers, 1935.

Kip, Lawrence. *Indian Council at Walla Walla, 1855.* Eugene, Oregon: Star Job Office, 1897. (Available at the Clark Memorial Library, Los Angeles.)

Kirkwood, Charlotte M. *The Nez Perce Indian War under Chiefs Joseph and Whitebird.* Grangeville, Ida.: Idaho County Free Press, 1928.

Lipps, Oscar H. *Laws and Regulations Relating to Indians and Their Lands.* Lewiston, Ida.: Lewiston Printing Co., 1913.

McBeth, Kate C. *The Nez Perce Since Lewis and Clark.* New York: Fleming H. Revell, 1908.

McWhorter, Lucullus Virgil. *Hear Me, My Chiefs.* Caldwell, Ida.: The Caxton Printers, 1952.

————. *Yellow Wolf: His Own Story*. Caldwell, Ida.: The Caxton Printers, 1940.

Norris, P. W. *Annual Report of the Superintendent of Yellowstone National Park*. Washington, D.C.: Government Printing Office, 1877.

Phinney, Archie. *Nez Perce Texts*. (Columbia University Contributions to Anthropology, No. 25.) New York: Columbia University, 1934.

Romeyn, Henry. *The Capture of Chief Joseph and His Nez Perce Indians*. (Contributions to the Historical Society of Montana, Vol. II.) Helena, 1896.

Spinden, Herbert Joseph. *The Nez Perce Indians*. (Memoirs of the American Anthropological Association, Vol. II, Part 3.) Lancaster, Pa.: New Era Print Co., 1908.

Wood, Henry Clay. *The Status of Young Joseph and His Band of Nez Perce Indians*. Portland, Ore.: Assistant Adjutant General's Office, 1876.

Woodruff, C. A. *The Battle of the Big Hole*. (Contributions to the Historical Society of Montana, Vol. VII.) Helena, 1910.

Periodicals

Burns, R. Ignatius. "The Jesuits, the Northern Indians, and the Nez Perce War of 1877," *Pacific Northwest Quarterly*, XLII (January, 1951), 40–76.

Carpenter, John A. "General Howard and the Nez Perce War of 1877," *Pacific Northwest Quarterly*, XLIX (October, 1958), 129–45.

Catlin, J. B. *The Battle of the Big Hole*. (Montana State Historian's Annual Report.) Missoula, 1927.

Chaffee, Eugene B. *Nez Perce War Letters*. (Idaho Historical Society Fifteenth Biennial Report.) Boise, 1936.

Chief Joseph. "An Indian's Views of Indian Affairs," *North American Review*, CXXVIII (April, 1879), 412–33.

Clark, J. Stanley. "The Nez Percés in Exile," *Pacific Northwest Quarterly*, XXXVI (July, 1945), 213–32.

Drury, Clifford M. "The Nez Perce Delegation of 1831," *Oregon Historical Quarterly*, XL (September, 1939), 283–87.

Forse, Albert G. "Chief Joseph as a Commander," *Winners of the West*, No. 12 (November, 1936), pp. 1–6.

Gibbon, John. "The Battle of the Big Hole," *Harper's Weekly*, XXXIX (December 28, 1895), 2036.

Haines, Francis. "Northward Spread of Horses to the Plains Indians," *American Anthropologist*, V (July, 1938), 429–37.

———. "Problems of Indian Policy," *Pacific Northwest Quarterly*, XLI (July, 1950), 203–12.

———. "Chief Joseph and the Nez Perce Warriors," *Pacific Northwest Quarterly*, XLV (January, 1954), 1–7.

Hamlin, H. "The Chief Joseph Trek and Surrender," *The Pony Express*, September, 1947.

Horner, J. H., and G. Butterfield. "The Nez Perce–Findley Affair," *Oregon Historical Quarterly*, XL (March, 1939), 40–51.

Hunt, Fred A. "The Battle of the Big Hole, Montana," *The Pacific Monthly*, XVIII (December, 1907), 700–7.

Hunt, Garret. "Sergeant Sutherland's Ride: An Incident of the Nez Perce War," *Mississippi Valley Historical Review*, XIV (June, 1927), 39–46.

Josephy, Alvin M., Jr. "The Last Stand of Chief Joseph," *American Heritage*, IX (February, 1958), 36–43, 78–81.

Kearns, William E. "The Nez Perce War," *Yellowstone National Park Nature Notes*, Vol. XII (May–June, 1935).

Kelly, Matt J. "Trail Herds of the Big Hole Basin," *Montana Magazine of History*, II (July, 1952), 57.

Mesplie, Rev. Father. "Report of Chaplain Mesplie of Fort Boise," *Army and Navy Journal* (April 6, 1878).

Miles, Nelson A. "The Indian Problem," *North American Review*, CXXVII (April, 1879), 304–14.

———. "Chief Joseph's Surrender," *New York Tribune Supplement* (August 4, 1907).

Pennypacker, I. R. "Military Historians and History," *Pennsylvania Magazine of History and Biography*, LII (April, 1928), 141–61; continued in following issue.

Phillips, Paul C. "Battle of the Big Hole," *Frontier*, X (1926), 63–80.

Pinkerton, Robert E. "The Indian Who Beat the U.S. Army," *True Magazine* (April, 1953), 55, 56.

Pond, George E. "Major-General Nelson A. Miles," *McClures Magazine*, V, No. 6 (November, 1895), 562–74.

Redfield, Francis M. "Reminiscences of Francis M. Redfield,

Chief Joseph's War," ed. Floy Laird, *Pacific Northwest Quarterly*, XXVII (January, 1936), 66–77.

Redington, J. W. "Scouting in Montana in the 1870's," *Frontier*, XIII (November, 1932), 55–68.

Sass, Herbert R. "The Man Who Looked Like Napoleon," *Colliers* (September 21, 1940), 23, 60, 62.

———. "The Future of the Indian Question," *North American Review*, CLII (January, 1891), 1–10.

Shearer, George. "The Skirmish at Cottonwood," *Idaho Yesterdays*, II (1958), 1–7.

Titus, Nelson C. "The Last Stand of the Nez Perces," *Washington Historical Quarterly*, VI (July, 1915), 145–53.

Wood, Charles E. S. "Indian Epic is Re-told," *The Spectator* (September 14, 1929).

———. "Chief Joseph, the Nez Percé," *The Century Magazine*, XXVIII (May, 1884), 135–42.

General Secondary Sources

Adams, James Truslow. *Dictionary of American History*. New York: Charles Scribner's Sons, 1940.

Allen, William. *Chequemegon*. New York: The Wm. Frederick Press, 1949.

Bailey, Robert G. *Nez Perce Indians*. Lewiston, Ida.: Bailey Publishing Co., 1943.

Beal, Merrill D. *The Story of Man in Yellowstone*. Caldwell, Ida.: The Caxton Printers, 1949.

Britt, Albert. *Great Indian Chiefs*. New York: Whittlesey House, 1938.

Brown, Mark H., and W. R. Felton. *Before Barbed Wire*. New York: Henry Holt and Co., 1956.

———. *The Frontier Years*. New York: Henry Holt and Co., 1950.

Burlingame, Merrill G. *The Military-Indian Frontier in Montana, 1860–90*. Iowa City: University of Iowa Press, 1938.

———. *Montana Frontier*. Helena: State Publishing Co., 1942.

———, and K. Ross Toole. *A History of Montana*. New York: Lewis Historical Publishing Co., 1957.

Byrne, P. E. *Soldiers of the Plains*. New York: Minton, Balch and Co., 1926.

Catlin, George. *North American Indians.* London: Published by the author, 1841.

Chittenden, Hiram M. *Yellowstone National Park.* Palo Alto: Stanford University Press, 1933.

Clark, Dan E. *The West in American History.* New York: Thomas Y. Crowell Co., 1947.

Clark, Thomas D. *Frontier America.* New York: Charles Scribner's Sons, 1959.

Collier, John. *Indians of America: The Long Hope.* New York: New American Library, 1951.

Cullum, George W. *Biographical Register of the Officers and Graduates of the U.S. Military Academy.* Boston: Houghton Mifflin Co., 1891.

Dangerfield, George. *The Era of Good Feelings.* New York: Harcourt, Brace and Co., 1952.

DeVoto, Bernard. *The Journals of Lewis and Clark.* Boston: Houghton Mifflin Co., 1955.

Drury, Clifford M. *Nez Perce Indian Missions.* Caldwell, Ida.: The Caxton Printers, 1936.

Federal Writers' Project. *Montana, A State Guide Book.* New York: Hastings House, 1939.

Ferris, Warren Angus. *Life in the Rocky Mountains.* Salt Lake City: Rocky Mountain Book Shop, 1940.

Finerty, John F. *War-path and Bivouac.* Chicago: M. A. Donohue and Co., 1890.

Francis, Bertha Agnes. *The Land of Big Snows.* Caldwell, Ida.: The Caxton Printers, 1955.

Freeman, Otis W., and Howard H. Martin. *The Pacific Northwest.* New York: John Wiley and Sons, 1947.

Garst, Shannon. *Chief Joseph of the Nez Perces.* New York: Julian Messer, 1953.

Glassley, Howard. *Pacific Northwest Indian Wars.* Portland, Ore.: Binfords and Mort, 1953.

Guie, Heister D., and Lucullus Virgil McWhorter (eds.). *Adventures in Geyser Land.* Caldwell, Ida.: The Caxton Printers, 1935.

Heitman, Francis B. *Historical Register and Dictionary of the United States Army.* Washington, D.C.: Government Printing Office, 1903.

Howard, Oliver O. *Famous Indian Chiefs I Have Known.* New York: The Century Co., 1907.

————. *My Life and Experiences among Hostile Indians.* Hartford: A. D. Worthington Co., 1907.

————. *Nez Perce Joseph.* Boston: Lee and Shepard, 1881.

Hunter, George. *Reminiscences of an Old Timer.* San Francisco: H. S. Crocker and Co., 1887.

Idaho Chronology, Nomenclature, Bibliography. Chicago: W. B. Conkey Co., 1918.

Jackson, Helen Hunt. *A Century of Dishonor.* Boston: Robert Brothers, 1882.

Judson, Katharine B. *Montana, the Land of Shining Mountains.* Chicago: A. C. McClurg Co., 1909.

Kastner, George Charles. *Riders from the West.* Portland, Ore.: Metropolitan Press, 1932.

Leeson, Michael A. *History of Montana.* Chicago: Warner, Beers and Co., 1885.

Lowe, Martha Perry. *The Story of Chief Joseph.* Boston: D. Lothrop and Co., 1881.

McWhorter, Lucullus Virgil. *A Calendar of the McWhorter Papers.* (Research Studies of the State College of Washington, Vol. XXVI, Nos. 2–4; Vol. XXVII, No. 1.) Pullman, Wn.: Washington State College.

Madsen, Brigham D. *The Bannock of Idaho.* Caldwell, Ida.: The Caxton Printers, 1958.

Mangam, William D. *The Clarks of Montana.* Privately published, 1939.

Manring, Benjamin F. *The Conquest of the Coeur d'Alenes, Spokanes, and Palouses.* Spokane, Wn.: The Inland Printing Company, 1912.

Miller, Joaquin. *An Illustrated History of the State of Montana.* Chicago: Lewis Publishing Co., 1894.

Mulford, A. F. *Fighting Indians.* Corning, N.Y.: Paul L. Mulford, no date.

Noyes, Alva J. *In the Land of the Chinook.* Helena: State Publishing Co., 1917.

Parker, Francis. *Winding Waters, the Story of a Long Trail and Strong Hearts.* Boston: C. M. Clark Publishing Co., 1909.

Payne, Robert. *The Chieftain, a Story of the Nez Perce People.* New York: Lewis Publishing Co., 1913.

Pollack, Dean. *Joseph, Chief of the Nez Perce.* Portland, Ore.: Binfords and Mort, 1950.

Priest, Loring B. *Uncle Sam's Stepchildren*. New Brunswick: Rutgers University Press, 1942.

Raftery, John H. *The Story of Yellowstone*. Butte, 1912.

Raymer, Robert G. *Montana, the Land and the People*. New York: Lewis Publishing Co., 1930.

Ross, Alexander. *The Fur Hunt of the Far West*. London: Smith and Elder, 1855.

Sanders, Helen Fitzgerald. *A History of Montana*. New York: Lewis Publishing Co., 1913.

Schmitt, Martin F., and Dee Brown. *Fighting Indians of the West*. New York: Charles Scribner's Sons, 1948.

Scott, Hugh Lennox. *Some Memories of a Soldier*. New York: The Century Co., 1928.

Seymour, Flora. *The Story of the Red Man*. New York: Longmans, Green and Co., 1929.

Silloway, Perley M. *History of Central Montana*. Lewiston, Mont.: *Fergus County Democrat*, 1935.

Stanley, Edwin J. *Rambles in Wonderland*. New York: D. Appleton and Co., 1878.

Steele, Matthew Forney. *American Campaigns*. Harrisburg, Pa.: The Telegraph Press, 1946.

Stevens, Hazard. *The Life of Isaac Ingalls Stevens*. Boston: Houghton Mifflin Co., 1900.

Stout, Tom. *Montana, Its Story and Biography*. Chicago: American Historical Society, 1921.

Stranahan, C. T. *Pioneer Stories*. Lewiston, Ida.: The Lewiston Chapter Idaho Writers League, 1942.

Stuart, Granville. *Forty Years on the Frontier*. Cleveland: Arthur H. Clark, 1925.

Sutherland, Thomas A. *Howard's Campaign against the Nez Perce Indians, 1877*. Portland, Ore.: Watling Co., 1878.

Swanton, John R. *The Indian Tribes of North America*. (Smithsonian Institute, Bureau of American Ethnology, Bulletin No. 145.) Washington, D.C.: Government Printing Office, 1953.

Toole, K. Ross. *Montana, an Uncommon Land*. Norman, Okla.: University of Oklahoma Press, 1959.

Townsend, John K. *Westward to Oregon*. Philadelphia: Henry Perkins, 1839.

Warner, Frank W. *Montana Territory*. Helena: Fisk Brothers Printers, 1879.

Wellman, Paul I. *Death on Horseback*. New York: J. B. Lippincott Co., 1945.

Wheeler, Olin Dunbar. *The Trail of Lewis and Clark, 1804–1904*. New York: G. P. Putnam's Sons, 1904.

Wissler, Clark. *Indians of the United States*. Garden City, N.Y.: Doubleday and Co., 1951.

Government Reports and Publications

Idaho Militia Records, Nez Perce War, 1877. Boise, Idaho, Territorial Executive File.

U.S. Army. *American Military History, 1607–1953*. Washington, D.C.: Government Printing Office, 1956. (R.O.T.C. Manual.)

————. Department of Dakota. Reports, Letters. 3531 DD 1877, 3595 DD, 3754 DD, 4070 DD, 4085 DD, 4095 DD, 4124 DD, 4263 DD, 4352 DD, 4398 DD, 1877.

U.S. Commissioner of Indian Affairs. *Annual Reports to the Department of the Interior*, 1877, 1878, 1881, 1888, 1890–1894, 1897–1899.

U.S. Congress. House. *Message from the President. . . .* Washington, D.C.: Government Printing Office, 1856. 34th Congress, 1st Session, House Executive Document No. 93.

————. *Nez Percé Indian Reservation*. Washington, D.C.: Government Printing Office, 1872. 42nd Congress, 2nd Session, House Executive Document No. 307.

————. *Treaty with Nez Percé Indians*. Washintgon, D.C.: Government Printing Office, 1872. 42nd Congress, 2nd Session, House Executive Document No. 198.

————. *Nez Percé and Bannock Indian Wars*. Washington, D.C.: Government Printing Office, 1884. 48th Congress, 1st Session, House Report No. 386.

U.S. Congress. Joint Special Committee on the Condition of the Indian Tribes. *Report*. Washington, D.C.: Government Printing Office, 1867. 39th Congress, 2nd Session, Senate Report No. 156.

U.S. Congress. Senate. *Report of the Secretary of the Interior*. Washington, D.C.: Government Printing Office, 1867. 40th Congress, Special Session, Senate Executive Document No. 4.

————. *Message from the President. . . .* Washington, D.C.: Government Printing Office, 1871. 41st Congress, 3rd Session, Senate Executive Document No. 39.

————. *Letter from the Secretary of War,* Washington, D.C.: Government Printing Office, 1879. 46th Congress, 2nd Session, Senate Executive Document No. 2.

————. *Letter from the Secretary of the Interior.* Washington, D.C.: Government Printing Office, 1889. 51st Congress, 1st Session, Senate Executive Document No. 12.

————. *Message from the President.* . . . Washington, D.C.: Government Printing Office, 1890. 51st Congress, 1st Session, Senate Executive Document No. 70.

————. *Claims of the Nez Perce Indians.* Washington, D.C.: Government Printing Office, 1900. 56th Congress, 1st Session, Senate Document No. 257.

————. *Memorial of the Nez Perces Indians.* Washington, D.C.: Government Printing Office, 1911. 62nd Congress, 1st Session, Senate Document No. 97.

U.S. Department of the Interior. *Annual Reports of the Secretary of the Interior,* 1859–1860, 1872–1878.

U.S. Department of War. *Annual Reports of the Secretary of War,* 1854–1855, 1858–1877.

————. Missouri Division. *Record of Engagements with Hostile Indians within the Military Division of the Missouri from 1868 to 1882, Lieutenant General P. H. Sheridan, Commanding.* Chicago: Headquarters Military Division of the Missouri, August 1, 1882.

————. *Message from the President.* . . . Washington, D.C.: Government Printing Office, 1878. 45th Congress, 2nd Session, Executive Document No. 14.

Newspaper Articles

Anaconda Standard, "Chief Joseph Was a Good Indian before He Died," September 25, 1904.

Anaconda Standard, "The Story of Joseph, Chief of the Nez Perce," by Donald McCrae, August 16, 1925.

Avant Courier (Bozeman, Montana), June 18, 1877, to October 10, 1877.

Benton Record, "Snake Creek Battle," by J. J. Healy, October 12, 1877.

Big Hole Breezes (Jackson and Wisdom, Montana), September 2, 1915; August 1, 1927.

Boise Capital News, June 17, 1877, to October 10, 1877. Also November 19, 1931.

Bozeman Times, August 30, 1877; September 29, 1877.

Butte Miner, August 21, 1877; August 5, 1926; November 19, 1931.

Chicago Tribune, October 25, 1877.

Daily Bee (Portland, Oregon), November 11, 1877.

Daily Oregonian, February 28, 1877.

Dillon Examiner, September 14, 1938; December 14, 1938; March 27, 1940; October 23, 1940; September 3, 1941.

Dillon Tribune, July 9, 1936.

Fallon County News, November 24, 1930.

Great Falls Tribune, June 17, 1877, to October 10, 1877. Also February 16, 1936; December 31, 1944; January 14, 25, 1945.

Helena Daily Independent, June 15, 1896.

Helena Evening Herald, "Battle of the Big Hole," August 8, 1902.

Helena Herald, June 17, 1877, to October 10, 1877.

Helena Weekly Independent, "An Account of Richard Dietrich's Death," September 6, 1877. Also August 2, 9, 23, 1877; October 4, 11, 1877.

Idaho Semi-Weekly World (Idaho City), August 7, 1877, to August 28, 1877.

Idaho Statesman (Boise), December 5, 1926; September 4, 1927; September 13, 1931; June 18, 1933.

Idaho Tri-Weekly Statesman, June 19, 1877, to October 6, 1877.

Lewiston Daily News, March 2, 12, 1948.

Lewiston Morning Tribune, March 24, 1877, to October 10, 1877. Also January 22, 1933; April 16, 1933; October 18, 1936.

Lewiston Teller, June 17, 1877, to October 10, 1877.

Miles City Daily Star, May 24, 1934.

Missoulian, "When Charlot Changed," February 1, 1925; "An Interview with Sergeant Martin Brown," June 14, 1925; "Last Survivor of Big Hole Tells Story," August 5, 1934; "The Battle of Big Hole Fought Sixty Years Ago," August 8, 1937.

Montana Free Press (Butte), December 2, 1928.

Montana Standard (Butte), March 1, 1931; August 10, 1958; November 23, 1958.

New Northwest (Deer Lodge, Montana), June 17, 1877, to October 12, 1877. Also "The Nez Perce Indian War," by Duncan McDonald, November, 1877, to April, 1878.

New York Sun, "An Account of the Death of Chief Joseph," September 25, 1904. Reprinted in Cyrus Townsend Brady, *Northwestern Fights and Fighters.*

Seattle Post-Intelligencer, "Reburial of Chief Joseph and the Potlatch Ceremonies," June 25, 1905. Also on May 15, 16, 17, 1950.

Spokesman-Review (Spokane), June 10, 1956.

Walla Walla Statesman, March 24, 1877.

Wallace Press Times (Wallace, Idaho), August 14, 21, 1921; September 4, 11, 18, 1921.

Weekly Oregonian (Portland), March 31, 1877.

Wenatchee Daily World, June 13, 1956.

Western News (Hamilton, Montana), XX, May, 1910, pp. 6–7.

Unpublished Sources

Bessette, Amede. Visit to the Big Hole Battlefield. Montana Historical Society, Helena, Montana.

Buck, Henry. The Nez Perce Indian War of 1877. Montana Historical Society, Helena, Montana.

Cappius, Samuel S. A History of the Bitter Root Valley to 1914. Unpublished Master's thesis, University of Washington, 1939.

Cave, Will. Notes concerning the Nez Perces. Montana Historical Society, Helena, Montana.

Clark, W. S. An Account of Walla Walla and Dayton, Washington, Volunteers in the Nez Perce War. Idaho State College Historical Archives, Pocatello, Idaho.

Clough, J. P. Recollections of the Nez Perce Indian War of 1877. Idaho Historical Society, Boise, Idaho.

Comba, Richard. Official Report on Company D, Seventh Infantry, during the Nez Perce Campaign. Montana Historical Society, Helena, Montana.

Cone, H. C. White Bird Battle. Idaho Historical Society, Boise, Idaho.

Cottrell, Mary. Scrapbook. Village Library, Wisdom, Montana.

Cruickshank, Alexander. The Birch Creek Massacre. Idaho State College Historical Archives, Pocatello, Idaho.

Dorrity, Mrs. James. Mrs. James Dorrity's Story concerning the Battle of the Bear Paws. Idaho State College Historical Archives, Pocatello, Idaho.

Fisher, Don C. The Nez Perce War. Unpublished Master's thesis, University of Idaho, 1931.

Gallogly, Mary. The Nez Perce War as I Knew It. Big Hole Battlefield National Monument, Montana.

Garver, Frank H. A Visit to the Big Hole Battlefield Told by Amede Bassette. Montana Historical Society, Helena, Montana.

Gibbon, John. Report of the Battle of the Big Hole, with the List of Killed and Wounded. Box 23, Document 3595, 1877, National Archives, Washington, D.C.

Goulder, W. A. Personal Recollections. Idaho State College Historical Archives, Pocatello, Idaho.

Hathaway, Ella C. Battle of the Big Hole, August 9, 1877. Yellowstone National Park Library.

Leeper, Robert D. The Soul of a Pioneer. Lecture delivered to the Sons and Daughters of the Pioneers, 1932. Idaho State College Library, Pocatello, Idaho.

Liljeblad, Sven. Indian Peoples of Idaho. Idaho State College Library, Pocatello, Idaho.

McConville, Edward. Report to Governor Brayman concerning the Record of Idaho Volunteers in the Nez Perce Campaign. Idaho Historical Society, Boise, Idaho.

McCreery, H. C. Reminiscences of the Nez Perce War in 1877 in Idaho Territory. Idaho State Historical Archives, Pocatello, Idaho.

McDonald, Angus. The Nez Perce Campaign. Montana Historical Society, Helena, Montana.

Manning, C. F., Mrs. The Nez Perce War as I Knew It. Idaho State College Historical Archives, Pocatello, Idaho.

Metlen, George R. Letter describing the route taken by the Nez Perces. Montana Historical Society, Helena, Montana.

Moelchert, William. Correspondence regarding the Cow Island affair. Montana Historical Society, Helena, Montana.

Noblett, L. A. Letter concerning the Bear Paws battle. Montana Historical Society, Helena, Montana.

Noyes, Alva J. The Battle of the Big Hole as I Saw It. Montana Historical Society, Helena, Montana.

Noyes, C. R. The Last Stand, or the Battle of the Bear Paws. Yellowstone National Park Library, Mammoth, Wyoming.

Partoll, Albert J. Commentary on Colonel Gibbon's report on the Battle of the Big Hole. Montana Historical Society, Helena, Montana.

Poe, James W. Letter to Governor Brayman concerning the Nez Perce atrocities in Washington County. Idaho Historical Society, Boise, Idaho.

Samples, John. Letter describing the battle at Cow Island. Montana Historical Society, Helena, Montana.

Shearer, George M. Letter to Major E. C. Mason concerning conduct of the Nez Perce War. Idaho Historical Society, Boise, Idaho.

Stuart, Granville. Recollections. Montana Historical Society, Helena, Montana.

Talkington, Henry L. Manuscript History of the Nez Perce Reservation. Idaho Historical Society, Boise, Idaho.

Weikert, Andrew J. Journal of a Tour through Yellowstone National Park in August and September, 1877. Document 9787, W. 421, Yellowstone National Park Library, Mammoth, Wyoming. Also in *Contributions to the Historical Society of Montana,* Vol. IV, Helena, Montana.

Wells, Donald. Governor Brayman and the Nez Perce War. Idaho Historical Society, Boise, Idaho.

Wilmot, Luther P. An Account of White Bird, Cottonwood, Misery Hill and Clear Water Battles. University of Montana, Missoula, Montana.

Wilson, Eugene. The Nez Perce Campaign. Washington State Historical Society Library, Tacoma, Washington.

Woodruff, C. A. The Battle of the Big Hole. Montana Historical Society, Helena, Montana.

Personal Correspondence and Interviews

Barry, J. Neilson. Portland, Oregon.

Brenner, Charles. Armstead, Montana.

Buck, Charles A. Stevensville, Montana.

Campbell, Calvert. Laurel, Montana.

Cary, Alvin. Cody, Wyoming.

Chaffin, Alexander. Hamilton, Montana.

Chaffin, Moses. Corvallis, Montana.

Cochran, William. Stevensville, Montana.

Cottrell, Mary N. Wisdom, Montana.

Cypher, Ralph D. Bridger, Wyoming.

Darrow, George. Billings, Montana.

Doyle, Blaine T. Dillon, Montana.

England, Roy. Baker, Idaho.

Francis, Bertha. Wisdom, Montana.

Fry, W. E. Dillon, Montana.

Gallogly, James. Sula, Montana.

Golden, Lloyd. Laurel, Montana.

Gregg, Mrs. Robert. Dillon, Montana.

Groff, Albert S. Corvallis, Montana.

Harrington, J. A. Boise, Idaho.

Henderson, Floyd A. Craters of the Moon National Monument, Idaho.

Henninger, Elvin. Dubois, Idaho.

Hirschy, Flora B. Wisdom, Montana.

Looney, Mrs. Rella. Oklahoma City, Oklahoma.

Lord, Herbert. Conner, Montana.

Luckenville, Lee. Cody, Wyoming.

McCormick, Wm. J. Stevensville, Montana.

McWhorter, Lucullus V. (Fifty letters concerning the Nez Perce war and the Battle of the Big Hole, addressed to Flora B. Hirschey and/or Merrill D. Beal.)

Mansfield, Mrs. James. Armstead, Montana.

Martin, Charles E. Billings, Montana.

Mitchell, A. C. Hamilton, Montana.

Ovitt, Mable. Bannack, Montana.

Sassman, H. H. Dillon, Montana.

Scott, Parke T. Armstead, Montana.

Sherrill, Mrs. T. E. Conner, Montana.

Stearns, Hal. Harlowtown, Montana.

Templeton, C. C. Seattle, Washington.

Wampler, Cloyed. Wisdom, Montana.

White, Thain. Lakeside, Montana.

Zimmerman, Charles. Billings, Montana.

INDEX

391